McKeachie's

# Teaching Tips

McKeachie's

# Teaching Tips

*Strategies,*

*Research, and*

*Theory for*

*College and*

*University*

*Teachers*

*Thirteenth*

*Edition*

MARILLA
SVINIVKI
AND
WILBERT J.
MCKEACHIE

WITH CHAPTERS BY

David Nicol

Barbara Hofer

Richard M. Suinn

Mary Deane Sorcinelli
and
Peter Elbow

Matthew Kaplan
and
Erping Zhu

Brian Coppola

Claire Ellen Weinstein

Jane Halonen

WADSWORTH
CENGAGE Learning

Australia • Brazil • Japan • Korea • Mexico • Singapore • Spain • United Kingdom • United States

**WADSWORTH**
CENGAGE Learning

**McKeachie's Teaching Tips: Strategies, Research, and Theory for College and University Teachers**
**Thirteenth Edition**
Marilla Svinivki
Wilbert J. McKeachie

Executive Editor: Linda Schreiber-Ganster

Assistant Editor: Caitlin Cox

Editorial Assistant: Linda Stewart

Marketing Manager: Kara Kindstrom

Marketing Assistant: Dimitri Hagnéré

Marketing Communications Manager: Martha Pffeifer

Content Project Manager: Samen Iqbal

Creative Director: Rob Hugel

Art Director: Maria Epes

Print Buyer: Rebecca Cross

Rights Acquisitions Account Manager, Text: Bob Kauser

Rights Acquisitions Account Manager, Image: Leitha Etheridge-Sims

Production Service: Lynn Lustberg, MPS Limited, A Macmillan Company

Text Designer: Norman Baugher

Copy Editor: Catherine M. Albano

Cover Designer: Norman Baugher

Cover Image: © Norman Baugher

Compositor: MPS Limited, A Macmillan Company

For product information and technology assistance, contact us at **Cengage Learning Customer & Sales Support, 1-800-354-9706**

For permission to use material from this text or product, submit all requests online at **www.cengage.com/permissions**
Further permissions questions can be e-mailed to **permissionrequest@cengage.com**

Library of Congress Control Number: 2009934814

Student Edition:

ISBN-13: 978-0-495-80929-6

ISBN-10: 0-495-80929-2

**Wadsworth**
20 Davis Drive
Belmont, CA 94002-3098
USA

Cengage Learning is a leading provider of customized learning solutions with office locations around the globe, including Singapore, the United Kingdom, Australia, Mexico, Brazil, and Japan. Locate your local office at **www.cengage.com/global**

Cengage Learning products are represented in Canada by Nelson Education, Ltd.

To learn more about Wadsworth, visit **www.cengage.com/wadsworth**

Purchase any of our products at your local college store or at our preferred online store **www.ichapters.com**

Printed in the United States of America
1 2 3 4 5 6 7 13 12 11 10 09

*We dedicate this edition to all the teachers over the years who have said that they have been introduced to more systematic, reflective ways of teaching by reading this book. We appreciate their interest and applaud their efforts.*

# CONTENTS

*Chapter* **6**   **How to Make Lectures More Effective**   **55**

*Skills for Use in Other Teaching
Situations 267*

Part **6** *Teaching for Higher-Level Goals* 291

TEACHING TIPS was originally written to answer the questions posed by new college teachers, to place them at ease in their jobs, and to get them started effectively in the classroom. It has proven useful as well to experienced instructors, to teachers in community colleges, to distance educators, adult educators, adjunct faculty, and faculty members in many other countries.

The organization of the book begins with the issues involved in getting started, then moves on to the basic skills needed by all teachers—getting student participation, lecturing, assessing learning, and assigning grades (Parts 1 and 2). Equally important are awareness of, respect for, and ability to adapt to differences among students (Part 3). Parts 4 and 5 deal with additional skills and strategies important for other aspects of teaching. In Part 6 we discuss goals of education going beyond simple memorization of facts, concepts, and theories, and in Part 7 we point toward your continued development as a teacher.

Effective teaching demands more than the acquisition of skills. To adapt to the educational needs of a particular class at a particular time, the teacher needs to understand the underlying theory of learning and teaching so that each teacher can develop his or her own methods. Thus, the "teaching tips" are supported by discussion of relevant research and theory. Skill in teaching is not something to be learned and simply repeated; what makes it exciting is that there is always room to grow. As you reflect on your classes, you will get new insights and will continue to develop both your theory of teaching and learning and your repertoire of skills and strategies.

It is because Marilla Svinicki combines great practical knowledge with a good grasp of theory that I invited her to write two chapters for the 7th edition of *Teaching Tips* and to join me as co-author of the 12th edition. With this 13th edition she becomes the senior author with my hope that she will carry it on.

*Teaching Tips* has stressed learner-centered teaching since the very 1st edition, in which I emphasized the importance of active learning. In the 2nd edition I introduced a longer section on learner-centered teaching and the role of the teacher as a facilitator of learning. It is gratifying that in the last several years authors have begun to write about the shift from teacher-centered to learner-centered education and the shift of the teacher's role from that of dispenser of information to facilitator of learning. Whether *Teaching Tips* has contributed to that shift, I do not know, but I hope that "learner-centered" does not become one of the buzz words that come and go—like the fifties' "master teachers" (who were to be televised and teach large numbers of students), or the sixties' "programmed learning" (which would teach more efficiently), or the seventies' "technological revolution." All were believed to be panaceas (and all contained worthwhile elements), but after a period of ascendancy, all faded before the next great enthusiasm. What counts in education is not so much what the teacher does as what goes on in the students' minds, and this will be true even if the term "learner-centered" falls into disuse. This does not mean, however, that "learner-centered" implies a particular method of teaching.

"Learner-centered" may appear to diminish the importance of the teacher. Not so! Your unique qualities as a person, your integrity, your commitment to your students' development—these are even more important than they were when the teacher's role was simply that of a talking textbook. Your role is now expanded to include that of mediator between your content and your students' understanding of it, on multiple, and increasingly higher, levels. *There is no one best way of teaching*. If you are to continue to develop as a teacher, you will need well-practiced skills, but you also need fresh thinking about why some things worked or didn't work in your last class. I do not offer a set of rules to follow. Rather, I suggest strategies to consider and modify as needed by the ever-changing dynamics of your classes. What is best for you may be quite different from what is best for me. By introducing research and theory relevant to the strategies suggested, I hope to encourage your reflection and continuing development as a thinking, observing, and caring teacher. Also, while providing current research is always a major goal, in this edition, you will see that "classic" references are now denoted with a diamond icon in the end-of-text references section. This has been added to point out the classic, seminal works that still offer the most reliable scholarship on their topic.

WILBERT J. MCKEACHIE

A Tribute to Wilbert McKeachie

As Bill notes above, it is now my honor to take over the bulk of the writing and editing work for *Teaching Tips*. However, Bill will always be there, in fact as well as in spirit, to help me keep what has made *Teaching Tips* one of the best selling and most widely used books on college teaching, in the United States and around the world. The nature of *Teaching Tips* is really a reflection of Bill himself, as anyone who knows him personally will tell you. He is a straight speaking, pragmatic, unpretentious individual in spite of being one of the most influential voices for college teaching for the last 50+ years. He cares deeply about teaching and learning, and has spent his life speaking out on its behalf. He has been my role model for 35 years. I cannot match his impact, but I'll try to match his voice and fulfill his goals.

And a word about our writing. Bill and I both tend to use first person because we are generally talking about our own thoughts and experiences. Sometimes the "I" in a sentence is really Bill talking, and sometimes it's me. But it doesn't really matter because we think a lot alike and probably teach a lot alike. I just thought you should know that these aren't all my ideas just because the text says "I"!

MARILLA D. SVINICKI

## NEW TO THIS EDITION

This edition includes a brand new chapter on assessment and feedback by David Nicol (Chapter 9), and we've updated existing chapters where new developments in technologies and instructional strategies have become more prominent since the last edition. For example, as you might expect, the entire chapter on using technology had to be revised to build in new tools such as audience response systems (the "clickers") you've heard so much about. We've given more space to online discussions and student-led discussions to reflect recent developments in teaching by discussion. We've greatly expanded the discussion of alternative ways to use group work in teaching due to the increasing popularity of that model. We've reordered the chapters in the section on Active Learning to stress that you should consider writing to be one of the best examples of active learning available to the instructor and to provide more of an overview at the beginning of that section. With the increasing emphasis on assessment, we've updated much of that material to help you understand the instructor's role in providing accurate assessments and embedding assessments in the everyday activities of the classroom. To make it all fit, we had to delete some of the chapters from the previous edition, but we've incorporated most of that material into other chapters instead, such as information about plagiarism or distance education. We've also tried to bring new materials and Websites on teaching to your attention where appropriate with expanded or revised Supplemental Readings sections. We hope this meets with your approval. If you find something we've taken out that you think is crucial or missed some new developments that are important to the field, please let us know. *Teaching Tips* will never stop changing with the times and we count on you, the readers, to keep us on our toes!

# ACKNOWLEDGMENTS

Our thanks to all the reviewers, who will see evidence of the impact of their comments:

Ferald J. Bryan, *Northern Illinois University*
Terri L. Flowerday, *University of New Mexico*
Gerri Hura, *Buffalo State College*
Linda Jones, *University of Arkansas*
Marilyn Lockhart, *Montana State University*
Ruslan Slutsky, *University of Toledo*
Diane Tetreault, *Bentley College*

**Marilla Svinicki** is a Professor in the Department of Educational Psychology and the former Director of the Center for Teaching Effectiveness at the University of Texas at Austin. She earned both her B.A. and M.A. at Western Michigan University and her Ph.D. at the University of Colorado. Her research interests include application of principles of learning to instruction in higher education and development of faculty and graduate students as teachers. She regularly teaches the course "College Teaching Methodology" at UT–Austin along with courses in the psychology of human learning and instructional psychology. She was the editor of *New Directions for Teaching and Learning*, an influential journal on instructional issues for faculty, for 20 years.

**Wilbert J. McKeachie** is Professor Emeritus of Psychology and former Director of the Center for Research on Learning and Teaching at the University of Michigan, where he has spent his entire professional career since taking his doctorate in 1949. His primary activities have been college teaching, research on college teaching, and training college teachers. He is past President of the American Psychological Association; the American Association of Higher Education; the American Psychological Foundation; the Division of Educational, Instructional, and School Psychology of the International Association of Applied Psychology; and the Center for Social Gerontology. He is also past Chairman of the Committee on Teaching, Research, and Publication of the American Association of University Professors, and of Division J. (Psychology) of the American Association for the Advancement of Science. He has been a member of the National Institute of Mental Health Council, the Veteran's Association Special Medical Advisory Group, and various other government advisory committees on mental health, behavioral and biological research, and graduate training. Among other honors, he has received eight honorary degrees and the American Psychological Foundation Gold Medal for Lifetime Contributions to Psychology.

# Part 1

*Getting Started*

# Chapter

## 1

# Introduction

The first few months and years of teaching are all important. Experiences during this period can either blight a promising teaching career or start one on a path of continued growth and development.

Most of us go into our first classes as teachers with a good deal of fear and trembling. We don't want to appear to be fools, and so we have prepared well, but we dread the embarrassment of not being able to answer students' questions. We want to be liked and respected by our students, and yet we know that we have to achieve liking and respect in a new role that carries expectations, such as evaluation, that make our relationship with students edgy and uneasy. We want to get through the first class with éclat, but we don't know how much material we can cover in a class period.

In most cases anxiety passes as one finds that students do respond positively, that one does have some expertise in the subject, and that class periods can be exciting. But for some teachers the first days are not happy experiences. Classes get off on the wrong foot. Sullen hostility sets in. The teacher asserts authority, and the students resist. The teacher knows that things are not going well but doesn't know what to do about it.

One likely response of the teacher is retreat—retreat to reading lectures with as little eye contact with students as possible, retreat to threats of low grades as a motivating device, retreat to research and other aspects of the professional role.

What makes the difference in these first few days?

It's probably not the subject matter. More often than not, the key to a good start is not the choice of interesting content (important as that may be) but rather the ability to manage the activities of the class effectively—simple teaching techniques get the students involved so that they can get to work and learn.

The new teacher who has techniques for breaking the ice, for encouraging class participation, and for getting the course organized is more likely to get off to a good start. Once you find that teaching can be fun, you will enjoy devoting time to it, you will think about it, and you will develop into a competent teacher.

When you are just starting, discussions of philosophy of education and theories of learning and teaching can be helpful, but they are probably not as important as learning enough techniques and simple skills to get through the first few weeks without great stress and with some satisfaction. Once some comfort has been achieved, you can think more deeply about the larger issues discussed in later chapters, and you can have more fun, too.

## THE COLLEGE OR UNIVERSITY CULTURE

A course cannot be divorced from the total college or university culture.

First of all, the institution makes certain requirements of instructors. In most institutions, you must submit grades for the students' work. You probably must give a final course examination. A classroom is assigned for the class, and the class meets in this assigned place. The class meets at certain regularly scheduled periods.

There are, in addition, areas not covered by the formal rules or routine practices of the college, in which instructors must tread lightly. For example, in most college cultures, instructors who become intimately involved with their students are overstepping the bounds of propriety. Certain limits on class discussion of religion, sex, or politics may exist. Instructors must learn not only to operate within the fences of college regulations but also to skirt the pitfalls of the college mores. And it is not just the culture of the institution that matters. Each department or discipline has its own culture with customs related to teaching methods, testing, standards, and styles of communication and instruction.

Each reader will need to adapt my suggestions to the college culture of which he or she is a part. When you begin a new teaching position, talk to other faculty members about their perceptions of the students, about how these instructors teach and perceive others as teaching. Ask for examples of syllabi, tests, and other course materials.

In many institutions, students have had experience in previous classes with instructors who, in a more or less parental way, gave information and rewarded those students who could best give it back. The sort of tests, frequency of tests, and methods of grading also have conformed closely to certain norms. As a result, instructors who attempt to revolutionize teaching with new methods or techniques may find that they are only frustrating the needs and expectations their students have developed in the culture of the college. So, if you are trying something new, be sure that students understand why the new method is likely to be valuable.

Although there are many norms and folkways that characterize an entire campus, you need to recognize that there are many subcultures. Some of them are subcultures of faculty in different disciplines, but it is important to recognize that there are student subcultures that have their own norms and expectations. And within the student cultures there are important individual differences among students. Taking account of the diversity of students is so important in teaching that "Understanding Students" is a separate part (Part 3) of this book.

## RESEARCH VERSUS TEACHING?

One critical aspect of the local culture for new teachers is the definition of the proper role of a faculty member. In many universities, for example, formal definitions of the criteria for promotion give research and teaching equal weight, but it is not uncommon to find that research is "more equal."

Studies have demonstrated that research and teaching are not necessarily in conflict. Many faculty members are excellent researchers and excellent teachers as well. Some excellent researchers are poor teachers; some excellent teachers do not publish research. Most faculty members enjoy both teaching and scholarship. Most also provide service to their institutions, and many provide service to their community and nation.

### Teaching as Scholarship

In 1990, Ernest Boyer's book *Scholarship Reconsidered* stimulated discussion throughout higher education about the nature of scholarship.

In most American universities scholarship has been evaluated in terms of published research. Boyer suggested that teachers who keep up with current developments, who devise and assess better ways to help students learn, or who do research on methods of teaching are also scholars. As a result of the debates about Boyer's proposal, there is increasing acceptance of the idea that good teaching involves much scholarly activity.

Find out what the local norms are, and if you feel a conflict, choose the balance that suits your own talents and interests with an informed awareness of the likelihood of support for that self-definition. Although time is not infinitely elastic, most faculty members find that a 50- to 60-hour work week is satisfying because they enjoy both teaching and research.

Whatever your choice, it is likely that teaching will be a part of your role. *Teaching skillfully may be less time consuming than teaching badly.* Teaching well is more fun than teaching poorly. After class or at the end of the day, think about what went well and what didn't. Make a few notes to remind you of what to do, or not do, the next time you teach. Moreover, you will be better able to focus on your research if you are not worrying about teaching. Thus, some investment of time and attention to developing skill in teaching is likely to have substantial payoff in self-satisfaction and effectiveness in your career.

One of the best aspects of teaching is that we, too, are learners. Each time we teach, we not only learn more about the subject matter, but are also learning more about teaching. Don't be afraid to share your insights with others. Every discipline has a journal dealing with teaching of that discipline, and the *Journal of Higher Education* and other journals, such as *Innovative Higher Education*, might also welcome your contributions.

## *IN CONCLUSION*

Because the suggestions I make are based on my own philosophy of teaching, you should be forewarned of seven of my biases or hypotheses.

1. What is important is learning, not teaching. Teaching effectiveness depends not just on what the teacher does, but rather on what the student does. Teaching involves listening as much as talking. It's important that both teacher and students are actively thinking, but most important is what goes on in the students' minds. Those minds are not blank slates. They hold expectations, experiences, and conceptions that will shape their interpretation of the knowledge you present. Your task is to help

them develop mental representations of your subject matter that will provide a basis for further learning, thinking, and use.

2. Teachers can occasionally be wrong. If they are wrong too often, they should not be teaching. If they are never wrong, they belong in heaven, not a college classroom.

3. Classes are unpredictable. This can be frustrating, but it also makes teaching continually fascinating. Don't be discouraged if some students don't appreciate your teaching. You can interest all of your students some of the time; you can interest some of your students all of the time; but you can't interest all of your students all of the time.

4. There are many important goals of college and university teaching. Not the least of these is that of increasing the student's motivation and ability to *continue* learning after leaving college.

5. Most student learning occurs outside the classroom. This is both humbling and reassuring for the beginning teacher. It means that the students' education will neither succeed nor fail simply because of what you do or don't do in the classroom. At the same time it reminds one to direct attention to stimulating and guiding student learning outside class even more than to preparing to give a dazzling classroom performance.

6. Students can learn more in talking to one another than listening to us if we prepare them for such interaction.

7. One key to improvement is reflection—thinking about what you want to accomplish, and what you and the students need to do to achieve these goals. What is contained in this book will not make you a Great Teacher. It may be that Great Teachers are born and not made, but anyone with ability enough to get a job as a college teacher can be a *good* teacher. This book will give you some tips for avoiding common problems and some concepts to think with, but eventually it comes down to you, your personality, and your values. My hope is that this book will help you feel enough at ease that you can reveal the best that is in you.

## Supplementary Reading

When the first edition of *Teaching Tips* was published, it was almost the only book offering guidance to college teachers. Now there are a great many, as well as journals and newsletters published in the

United States and other countries. Almost every discipline has a journal concerned with teaching that particular discipline. Check out the holdings of your institution's library. If your institution has a faculty/instructional developmental center, it will have lots of material and a helpful staff.

I am reluctant to list only a few of the many good books on college teaching because I see them all as meeting a need and complementing one another as well as *Teaching Tips*. I will limit myself to fewer than twenty.

- D. Bernstein and R. Bass, "The scholarship of teaching and learning" *Academe*, 9(4), 37–43.

- Robert Boice, *Advice for New Faculty Members: Nihil Nimus* (Boston: Allyn and Bacon, 2000).

- P. Cooper and C. Simonds, *Communication for the Classroom Teacher*, 8th edition (Boston: Pearson/Allyn and Bacon, 2007).

- B. G. Davis, *Tools for Teaching*, 2nd edition (San Francisco: Jossey-Bass, 2009).

- S. F. Davis and W. Buskist (eds.), *The Teaching of Psychology: Essays in Honor of Wilbert J. McKeachie and Charles L. Brewer* (Mahwah, NJ: Erlbaum, 2002).

- L. Dee Fink, *Creating Significant Learning Experiences* (San Francisco: Jossey-Bass, 2003).

- Deborah DeZure (ed.), *Learning from Change: Landmarks in Teaching and Learning in* Change Magazine, *1969–1999* (Sterling, VA: Stylus Publishing, 2000).

- K. Eble, *The Craft of Teaching*, 2nd edition (San Francisco: Jossey-Bass, 1988). Don't think that a 1988 book must be out of date by now. This is a good book to read when you've lost your initial anxiety and want to think about teaching as a craft and a calling.

- Linc Fisch, *The Chalk Dust Collection: Thoughts and Reflections on Teaching in Colleges and Universities* (Stillwater, OK: New Forums Press, 1996). A thoughtful, often amusing collection of essays with much good sense.

- A. Grasha, *Teaching with Style* (Pittsburgh: Alliance Publishers, 1996).

- Diane F. Halpern and Milton D. Hakel (eds.), "Applying the Science of Learning to University Teaching and Beyond," *New Directions for Teaching and Learning*, no. 89, March 2002.

▶ P. Hutchings and L. Shulman "The Scholarship of Teaching," *Change*, 31(5) 10–16.

▶ David E. Johnson has a good chapter, "Teaching, Research, and Scholarship," in S. F. Davis and W. Buskist (eds.), *The Teaching of Psychology: Essays in Honor of Wilbert J. McKeachie and Charles L. Brewer* (Mahwah, NJ: Erlbaum, 2002).

▶ L. Michaelsen, M. Sweet, and D. Parmalee (eds.), "Team-Based Learning: Small Group Learning's Next Big Step," *New Directions for Teaching and Learning*, 116, Winter, 2008.

▶ Ray Perry and John Smart (eds.), *Effective Teaching in Higher Education* (New York: Agathon Press, 1997).

▶ R. Prieto and S. A. Meyers, *The Teaching Assistant Handbook* (Stillwater, OK: New Forums Press, 2001).

▶ Parker Palmer's book, *The Courage to Teach: Exploring the Inner Landscape of a Teacher's Life* (San Francisco: Jossey-Bass, 1998). This book will inspire you.

The following five books come from authors writing from the perspective of experience in other countries. Their contents are relevant to university teachers in all countries.

▶ J. Biggs, *Teaching for Quality Learning at University* (Buckingham, UK, and Philadelphia: Society for Research into Higher Education and Open University Press, 1999).

▶ Nira Hativa, *Teaching for Effective Learning in Higher Education* (Dordrecht: Kluwer, 2000).

▶ Linda B. Nilson, *Teaching at Its Best*, 2nd edition (Bolton, MA: Anker, 2003).

▶ Daphne Pan, *Learning to Teach, Learning to Learn* (Singapore: National University of Singapore, 2001).

▶ P. Ramsden, *Learning to Teach in Higher Education* (London and New York: Routledge, 1992).

Many university faculty development centers publish newsletters for their own faculties. In addition there are two national publications on college teaching: *The National Teaching and Learning Forum* and *The Teaching Professor*. Both have helpful articles.

Websites that might be of interest:

▶ National Teaching Learning Forum—www.ntlf.com/html/lib/bib/bib.htm

▶ Professional and Organizational Development Network in Higher Education—www.podnetwork.org/resources/periodicals.htm and www.podnetwork.org/resources/facultydev.htm

▶ The Carnegie Foundation for the Advancement of Teaching—www.carnegiefoundation.org

*Chapter*

**2**

# Countdown for Course Preparation

For teachers, courses do not start on the first day of classes. Rather, a course begins well before you meet your students. I shall present a series of steps, but planning does not usually follow a perfectly orderly, linear pattern. The components of course planning are all shown in Figure 2.1. Experts typically say that you should start with your objectives, but don't get stuck on this. In all your planning, you'll do at least one thing that will remind you to modify earlier steps. So, you move back and forth as you progress. The main thing is to get started!

## TIME: THREE MONTHS BEFORE THE FIRST CLASS

### Write Objectives, Goals, or Outcomes

The first step in preparing for a course is working out course objectives, because the choice of textbook, the selection of the type and order of assignments, the choice of teaching techniques, and all

---

This chapter incorporates material from Graham Gibbs's chapter in the tenth edition, "Planning Your Students' Learning Activities."

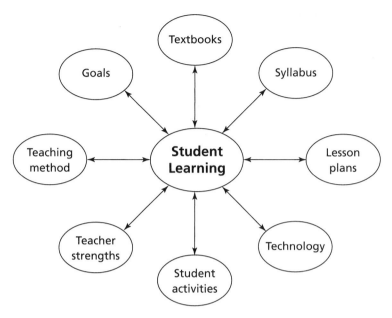

**FIGURE 2.1**

the decisions involved in course planning should derive from your objectives. What are your students like? What do they expect? What outcomes do you expect them to achieve? At this point, your list of goals or objectives should be taken only as a rough reminder to be revised as you develop other aspects of the course plan and to be further revised in interaction with students. Writing out your goals helps clarify your thinking.

Your objectives have the great advantage of pointing clearly to what you can look for as evidence that the objective has been achieved. Your students see your methods of assessing or testing achievement of the objectives as the most important operational definition of your goals; hence, goals and testing are inseparable teaching tasks. This does not mean that all of your goals should be assessed and count toward a grade. Some of your goals will involve motivational, attitudinal, and value outcomes, as discussed in the chapters "Motivation in the College Classroom," "Teaching Students How to Become More Strategic and Self-Regulated Learners," and "The Ethics of Teaching and the Teaching of Ethics." Course grades are typically based only on cognitive and skill outcomes.

## What Goals?

The answer obviously depends on the course and discipline, but it is important to note that the overall course objectives involve *educating students*; the objective of a course is not just to cover a certain set of topics, but rather *to facilitate student learning and thinking.* Ordinarily we are concerned not simply with the learning of a set of facts, but rather with learning that can be applied and used in situations outside course examinations. In fact, *in most courses we are concerned about helping our students in a lifelong learning process*; that is, *we want to develop interest in further learning and provide a base of concepts and skills that will facilitate further learning, thinking, and appreciation.* Thus, in framing your goals, think about what will be meaningful to your students. Will these goals really be relevant to them now and in the future?

Your personal values inevitably enter into your choice of goals. Although many of us were taught to be strictly objective, I have come to believe that this is impossible. Our teaching is always influenced by our values, and students have a fairer chance to evaluate our biases or to accept our model if we are explicit about them. Hiding behind the cloak of objectivity simply prevents honest discussion of vital issues.

In thinking about your goals, remember that each course contributes to other general goals of a university education that transcend specific subject matter, such as critical thinking, being willing to explore ideas contrary to one's own beliefs, knowing when information or data are relevant to an issue and how to find that information, and developing skills for learning and self-regulation. (See the chapters "Teaching Students How to Become More Strategic and Self-Regulated Learners" and "Teaching Thinking.")

In addition to this general perspective, you need to keep in mind characteristics of the setting in which you teach. What is the role of this course in the curriculum? Are other instructors depending on this course to provide specific kinds of background knowledge or skill? What are your students like? How do they differ? (See Part 3 of this book, "Understanding Students.") What are their current concerns? Self-discovery? Social action? Getting a job? How can their goals be integrated with other goals of the course? Talk to some of your colleagues.

A committee of college and university examiners developed two books, which are now classics, to assist faculty members in thinking about their objectives: *Taxonomy of Educational Objectives, Handbook I: Cognitive Domain* (Bloom, 1956) and *Handbook II: Affective Domain* (Krathwohl, Bloom, & Masia, 1964). Krathwohl and others have completed a revision (Anderson & Krathwohl, 2001). Another good framework is the SOLO (*S*tructure of the *O*bserved *L*earning *O*utcome) taxonomy (see Biggs, 1999).

A recent expansion of these taxonomies was provided by L. Dee Fink (2003), which he characterizes as significant learning experiences. The list includes most of the other previous lists along with suggestions about how to achieve them.

Having said all this about the importance of starting with clear goals, I would nonetheless not want to make you feel guilty if you started on your syllabus with only vague notions about goals. Although it seems logical to start with goals, content, teaching methods, and the nature of the students, all of these interact in dynamic ways. So if you find it easier to start by outlining the content of the course, do so. Ideally you would then tie the content to goals, but many effective teachers never state their goals very explicitly, yet their students achieve the kinds of motivational and cognitive outcomes that we all desire. College teachers are individualists. There are lots of different ways to do a good job. Goals emerge as you teach.

## Order Textbooks, Lab Supplies, or Other Resources Students May Need

**Should You Use a Textbook?\*** With paperback books, reprint series, photocopiers,\*\* and the World Wide Web, young instructors are immediately beguiled by the thought that they can do a much better job of compiling a set of required readings than any previous author or editor. "Coursepacks"—compilations of relevant articles and book chapters—may be used in place of a textbook or as supplementary reading.

There is much to be said for such a procedure. It provides flexibility, a variety of points of view, and an opportunity to maintain maximum interest. Moreover, since no single text covers every topic equally well, the use of a variety of sources enables the teacher to provide more uniformly excellent materials, ranging from theoretical papers and research reports to applications. Some publishers are even developing electronic books or sites to help customize textbooks for your course.

The disadvantages of not using a textbook are apparent. Without a textbook the task of integration may be so overwhelming that great pressure is placed on instructors to provide integration. This may limit your freedom to use the class period for problem solving, applications, or other purposes. With a well-chosen textbook, you may rely on the students to obtain the basic content and structure of the subject matter through reading and thus be freer to vary procedures in the classroom.

---

\*You can skip this section if your department has already chosen the textbook.

\*\*Check the copyright laws before making multiple copies. Many institutions have ways of smoothing the clearing of copyright permissions.

Moreover, the managerial task of determining appropriate readings and arranging to have them available for students is not to be taken lightly. If students are expected to use certain print sources in the library, consult a librarian to be sure enough copies are available or that the library has electronic availability of such materials. Access to course resources is particularly important in distance learning and upper division or specialized courses.

A final consideration is the extent to which you want to use required versus free reading, as in my use of a journal (see the chapter "How to Enhance Learning by Using High-Stakes and Low-Stakes Writing"). I use a textbook as a base to provide structure and then require students to write journal entries or online discussion-board posts on readings they choose. To assign diverse required readings and additional free reading seems to me to require too much integration even for well-prepared, bright students.

## Choose a Textbook or Other Reading Materials*

In choosing reading materials, the most important thing is that they fit your objectives. One of the most annoying and confusing practices for students is instructor disagreement with the textbook. It is doubtful that any book will satisfy you completely, but if you use a textbook, choose one that is as much in line with your view as possible.

Students prefer going through a book as it was written. If the author wrote the book in a systematic way, building one concept on another, there may be good pedagogical reasons for following the author's order. I know of no text that completely suits every teacher, however, so I can only recommend that you keep skipping around to a minimum and make sure that students understand why.

There is no substitute for detailed review of the competing texts for the course you are teaching. As textbooks multiply, it becomes increasingly tempting to throw up your hands in frustration over the time required for a conscientious review and to choose the book primarily on the basis of appearance, the personality of the sales representative, or the inclusion of your name as author of one of the studies cited. Yet research on teaching suggests that the major influence on what students learn is not the teaching method but the textbook. What should you do?

1. Winnow the possibilities down to two to five. You may be able to do some winnowing on the basis of the table of contents and preface,

---

*Some of these ideas were stimulated by Russell Dewey's article, "Finding the right introductory psychology textbook," *APS Observer*, March 1995, 32–35.

by checking with colleagues who have taught the course, or by reading reviews.

2. Read a couple of chapters. It is tempting to simply leaf through each book, reading bits here and there. But reading a couple of complete chapters will give you a better idea of the difficulty and interest level of each book. Try picking one chapter on a topic you know well and one that is not in your area of expertise.

3. Pick three or four key concepts. See how each text explains them. Will the explanations be clear to students? Interesting?

4. Beware of seductive details or pictures that were included to make the book more attractive but may distract from the basic concepts.

# TIME: TWO MONTHS BEFORE THE FIRST CLASS

## Begin Drafting a Syllabus for the Course

When we think about teaching, we usually think about what goes on in the classroom, but most student learning occurs outside the classroom. Planning assignments and out-of-class activities is even more important than planning for class meetings. A syllabus typically contains such a plan, with assignments correlated with topics to be discussed in class. If you are teaching a distance-learning course, a syllabus is indispensable. Like a contract, a syllabus should help students understand both their responsibilities and yours.

Constructing your syllabus will force you to begin thinking about the practicalities of what you must give up in order to achieve the most important objectives within the limitations of time, place, students, and resources. If you have taught the course before, what worked? What didn't?

A new wrinkle to the design of the syllabus is to create a graphic syllabus (Nilson, 2007), which is built like a flow chart or concept map of the course rather than a listing of activities. It helps the students see how things fit together more effectively and shows them how you think about the course activities as integrated into a whole system. It might do the same thing for you as well.

**How Much Student Time Does Your Course Involve?** It is easy to imagine that your course is the only one your students are taking. After all, it is the only one you see. However, your students may be taking three, four, or five other courses in parallel. Given a realistic studying week of about 40 hours, you therefore have between about 6 and 10 hours a week of your students' time available to allocate to learning on your course, including in-class time. If your students spend 3 hours a week in class with you, then you have between 3 and 6 hours a week of out-of-class learning activity to plan. You should expect to use all of this time, and you should be quite explicit with your students about what you expect them to do with it. Exactly how many hours you have and are taking up is rather important. Students experience wide variations in demands among courses because teachers often do not estimate or plan this time carefully. The most common problems are caused by, at one extreme, specifying nothing and leaving students to their own devices. At the other extreme, teachers overload students with inappropriate and unproductive activities that actually limit their learning. For example, science teachers often fill their students' time with writing up lab reports, leaving them no time to read. It can be helpful to calculate the total number of study hours available to your course and to plan what all of those hours would ideally be used for, estimating the time demands of each activity. In reality, student efforts will vary. Some will work harder or slower than others, and some will spend more of their time on some learning activities, and on some of their courses, than on others. But being explicit will help you to make realistic demands and will help students to see what is expected of them.

**What Should Be in the Syllabus?** There is no one model. Take the following as suggestions, not rules. If you have followed my recommendations up to this point, you now have a list of goals, have chosen a textbook, and have a general schedule of when you will cover each topic and maybe a flowchart showing how things fit together. The core of your syllabus will be that schedule. In introducing the schedule, explain the purpose for the organization you have chosen.

Under the topic headings, you can schedule assignments and the dates when they are due. I make a calendar of the semester showing the important dates and topics. This relieves you of the task of making assignments every few days and of repeating the assignments for students who were absent when each assignment was announced. State your expectations and policies about class attendance.

As you lay out your schedule, consider alternate ways students might achieve the goals of a particular day or week of class. You will seldom have perfect attendance at every class. Why not build in periodic alternatives to your lecture or class discussion? Be sure also to consider the diversity of your students. Alternative assignments can help. Students who have options and a sense of personal control are likely to be more highly motivated for learning.

Be clear about when and how learning will be assessed. What students do is strongly influenced by their anticipation of the ways learning will be evaluated. You may also include other items that will be helpful for student learning, such as sites on the World Wide Web, interesting readings to supplement textbook assignments, strategies for maximizing learning, and what to do when having difficulty.

Finally, you may include any special rules you want to emphasize, such as a statement to the effect that assignments for the course are to be completed by the dates indicated in the course outline.

But isn't a syllabus that is printed or on a Website a clue that the course is really instructor centered and that student needs are not going to be considered? Not necessarily so. Research by Mann and colleagues (1970) suggests that students may see a less organized approach as an indication that the teacher is not interested in their learning. The syllabus helps students discover at the outset what is expected of them and gives them the security of knowing where they are going. At the same time, your wording of assignment topics can convey excitement and stimulate curiosity. Ken Takeuchi (personal communication) of the State University of New York at Buffalo has a nice acronym for guiding syllabus construction:

S—Specific

M—Measurable

A—Agreed (clearly understood)

R—Related, with a clear structure and links between assignments

T—Time frame

## TIME: ONE MONTH BEFORE THE FIRST CLASS

### Begin Preparing Class Session Plans

If you are planning to lecture, outline the content of the first few lectures and the ways you will get student involvement. Planning several classes at a time will make them more integrated and allow you some wiggle room if you get off schedule. You can lighten up on later sessions or expand them if you're not tied to the exact class period. If you are planning to teach by discussion, cooperative learning, or other methods, don't assume that they will take less preparation. Work out your plans.

(See also the chapters "Meeting a Class for the First Time" and "Facilitating Discussion.") Think about what students need for the tests you will give. If you spend a little time on your plans each day and let them percolate in your mind, ideas will come to you while driving, jogging, or walking to your office.

## Plan for Out-of-Class Learning

It is easy for teachers to imagine that what happens in class is overwhelmingly important to students' learning and that they and their classes are at the center of students' learning universe. It is the component of student learning that teachers see—the rest is often invisible. When they do their planning, most teachers give their attention to covering content in class rather than to what happens out of class (Stark & Lattuca, 1997). However, in studies of what students believe most influenced change during the college years, and of what students believe were their most important experiences at college, ideas presented by instructors in courses, and instructors themselves, rank far behind a range of other influences (Feldman & Newcomb, 1969). In most courses students spend at least as much time studying out of class as they do in class. Thus, you need to focus as much on what you expect students to do outside class as on what goes on in class. Look at your objectives. If you want students to become better problem solvers or critical thinkers, they need to practice these skills.

Reading an assignment passively will produce poorer learning than reading with an activity in mind, such as preparing a question for class discussion, drawing a concept map, or writing examples or possible applications.

## Choose Appropriate Teaching Methods

A final point at which your preparation for a course is determined by your objectives is in the type of instruction you will use. For some goals and for some materials, an orthodox lecture presentation is as good as or better than any other. For others, discussion may be preferable. For the accomplishment of still other ends, cooperative learning or role-playing techniques described later in the book may be useful. The most successful teachers probably vary their methods to suit their objectives. Thus, you may wish one day to present some new material in a lecture. You may then follow this with a class discussion on implications of this material or with a laboratory or field exercise. Since your choice in the matter is determined as much by your own personality as by your course objectives, I shall not dwell on it here. From the description of these techniques in later sections of the book, you may be able to decide which techniques are suited to your philosophy of teaching, your abilities, the class you are teaching, and the particular goals you are emphasizing at a particular time. Recent syntheses of the research on teaching effects on learning have been provided by Pascarella and Terenzini (2005) in *How College Affects Students*. They make fascinating reading and can give you some good guidelines about what to choose.

## Select Appropriate Technology

It is quite possible to teach an effective course without technology, but advances have taken its usefulness to outside the classroom (as in class management systems) as well as inside (as in bringing things into the classroom that couldn't have been accessed before). The chapter "Technology and Teaching" gives you a good overview of some of the possibilities. When used appropriately, technology can provide opportunities for students to interact with the content and with one another. It is an important instructional resource. But just as in considering other resources, ask yourself, "Will this help my students learn more effectively?" or "Will this save me and the students time and effort by enhancing communication?"

## TIME: TWO WEEKS BEFORE THE FIRST CLASS

## Check Resources

Preparation and planning are still note done even after you've firmed up the syllabus. Now look back over the syllabus to see what resources are required. Presumably your check with a colleague (as suggested in the chapter "Introduction") has turned up any gross problems—such as assuming an unlimited budget for materials. This is a good time for another check. What are the library policies relevant to putting on reserve any books you may want? What computer resources are available? Can you assume unlimited photocopying of exams and course materials to give to students? What do you do if you want to show a film? Go on a field trip?

Visit the classroom you've been assigned. Will the seating be conducive to discussion? Can you use the technology you need? If the room is unsuitable, ask for another.

## Start a Portfolio

A teaching portfolio not only will be useful when you discuss your teaching with your department head or superior, it will also be useful in your thinking about teaching and your development. Plan on adding to it throughout the semester as you assess how well things went.

## TIME: ONE WEEK BEFORE THE FIRST CLASS

If you teach first-year students and have a class list and e-mail addresses, send an e-mail welcoming the students to your class. (It's also not a bad idea to do this with more advanced students.) Some instructors are beginning to invite students to introduce themselves online.

At this point, you're ready to prepare for the first class. For ideas about what to do and how to handle this meeting, read the next chapter.

### *Supplementary Reading*

▷ Robert Diamond's *Designing and Assessing Courses and Curricula: A Practical Guide* (San Francisco: Jossey-Bass, 1998) has a good chapter, "Developing a Learning-Centered Syllabus."

▷ Barbara Davis's book *Tools for Teaching*, 2nd ed. (San Francisco: Jossey-Bass, 1993) has a fine chapter on the syllabus (pp. 14–28).

▷ Chapter 6, "The Natural History of the Classroom," in *The College Classroom* by Richard Mann, S. M. Arnold, J. Bender, S. Cytrynbaum, B. M. Newman, B. Ringwald, J. Ringwald, and R. Rosenwein (New York: Wiley, 1970), is still the best material on the changing needs of classes over the course of a semester.

▷ *Teaching Within the Rhythms of the Semester* by Donna K. Duffy and Janet W. Jones (San Francisco: Jossey-Bass, 1995) is also a perceptive and readable guide to thinking about the flow of the course over the term.

▷ An excellent aid for preparing your syllabus is M. A. Lowther, J. S. Stark, and G. G. Martens, *Preparing Course Syllabi for Improved Communication* (Ann Arbor: NCRIPTAL, University of Michigan, 1989) or Grant Wiggins and Jay McTighe, *Understanding by Design* (Columbus, OH: Merrill Education/ASCD College Textbook Series, 2001).

▷ If you are teaching first-year students, the book *Teaching College Freshmen* by Bette Erickson and D. W. Strommer (San Francisco: Jossey-Bass, 1991) will be helpful to you.

Chapter

3

# Meeting a Class for the First Time

The first class meeting, like any other situation in which you are meeting a group of strangers who will affect your well-being, is at the same time exciting and anxiety-producing for both students and teacher. Some teachers handle their anxiety by postponing it, simply handing out the syllabus and leaving. This does not convey the idea that class time is valuable, nor does it capitalize on the fact that first-day excitement can be constructive. If you have prepared as suggested in the previous chapter, you're in good shape; the students will be pleased that the instruction is under control, and focusing on meeting the students' concerns can not only help you quell your own anxiety, but also make the first class interesting and challenging.

Other things being equal, anxiety is less disruptive in situations where stimulus events are clear and unambiguous. When the students know what to expect, they can direct their energy more productively. An important function of the first day's meeting in any class is to provide this structure; that is, to present the classroom situation clearly, so that the students will know from the date of this meeting what you are like and what you expect. They come to the first class wanting to know what the course is all about and what kind of person the teacher is. You need to know what the students expect. To these ends, the following concrete suggestions are offered.

# SETTING THE STAGE

One point to keep in mind on the first day and throughout the term is that yours is not the students' only class. They come to you from classes in chemistry, music, English, or physical education, or rushing from their dormitory beds or from parking lots. The first few minutes need to help this varied group shift their thoughts and feelings to you and your subject.

You can ease them into the course gradually, or you can grab their attention with something dramatically different, but in either case you need to think consciously about how you set the stage to facilitate achieving the course objectives. Even before the class period begins, you can communicate nonverbally with such actions as arranging the seats in a circle, posting an agenda, putting your name on the board or projecting it and the course identifier on the front screen, and chatting with early arrivals about what class they have come from or anything else that would indicate your interest in them. While students are coming in, suggest that they spend the time before class starts by getting acquainted with the students sitting near them.

# BREAKING THE ICE

You will probably want to use the first period for getting acquainted and establishing goals. You might begin by informally asking first-year students to raise their hands, then sophomores, juniors, seniors, or out-of-staters. Because I teach a class taken by students from lots of different majors, I run through the most frequent ones and have folks identify themselves according to majors. This gives me and the students some idea of the composition of the class and gets students started participating. Varied student backgrounds enrich discussions, and I try to explain how the course will help each group in their own area.

In my relatively large lecture classes I have then asked the students to take a minute or two to write down words and phrases that describe their feelings on the first day of class. I then ask them, "What have you written?" and list their responses on the board.

Next, I ask them, "How do you think your teacher feels on the first day of class?" This takes them aback, but they begin writing. We now list these responses in a second column, and they see some parallels. I comment briefly on my own feelings. (I remember with special affection the senior who came up to me after class and said, "I've been at this university almost four years, and this is the first time it ever occurred to me that professors have feelings.")

In a small class, you might then ask all class members (including yourself) to introduce themselves, tell where they're from, mention their field of concentration, and answer any questions the group has. Sometimes I ask the students to tell one thing about themselves that isn't obvious from looking at them. We find out all kinds of skills and interests that are represented in the class. Or, you can ask each student to get acquainted with the persons sitting on each side and then go around the class with each student introducing the next or each repeating the names of all those who have been introduced—a good device for developing rapport and for helping you learn the names, too. A more demanding but surprisingly effective device is to have each person introduce everyone who was introduced before, ending with the teacher repeating everyone's names. (Try it! You'll be surprised at how well you do.)

Learning names is a start, but students are probably even more interested in you than in their classmates; give them a chance to ask questions of you. Sometimes I have asked for one or two students to act as interviewers for the class, asking questions they think the other students would like to ask.

Even if you remembered all of the students' names in the "Name Game," you may not recall them later; so it is helpful to supplement the memory in your head with an external memory. I ask a former student who has a camera to take a picture of each student. At the next class meeting I ask students to write their names, phone numbers, e-mail addresses, and other information on the photos for me. The "other information" might include previous experience relevant to the course, interests, distinctive characteristics that will help me remember them, possible major field, and so on. Some institutions now provide a photo roster of the class even before the semester starts, which means you can get started learning names before class begins! I've also found that name tents that students put at the front of their desks for the first few weeks of the semester help me to call on students by their names instead of just saying "Yes?" Eventually I can learn quite a few of the names just by that simple system.

Having established some freedom of communication, you can then go on to assess students' expectations and goals, and let them know what yours are. One technique for doing this is question posting.

## QUESTION POSTING

Question posting is a method of getting students involved and active that can be used in classes of all sizes. For this first class meeting you might say:

"What sorts of concerns or issues do you think we might deal with?"

"What are your expectations for this course?"

"What goals do you have for this course?"

"What have you heard about this course?"

You might ask students to write for a minute about their question and then ask them what they have written. Your task then becomes that of recorder, listing responses on the board, overhead projector, or electronic smartboard. Lately, I've been projecting my computer in a word processing program to the front screen and just typing in what they suggest so everyone can see it. To make sure you understand, you may restate the response in your own words. If you feel that some response is ambiguous or too general, you might ask for an example, but you must be ready to accept all contributions, whether or not you feel they are important. It is crucial that the atmosphere be accepting and non-evaluative. Students should feel that you are genuinely interested in what they have to contribute.

By the end of the question posting the class normally has become better acquainted, has become used to active participation, has taken the first step toward developing an attitude of attempting to understand rather than competing with one another, has reduced the attitude that everything must come from the teacher, has learned that the teacher can listen as well as talk (and is not going to reject ideas different from his or her own), and, I hope, has begun to feel some responsibility for answering its own questions rather than waiting for them to be answered by the instructor.

## WHAT THEY REALLY WANT TO KNOW: INTRODUCING THE SYLLABUS

Your syllabus will provide some of the answers to the questions raised in the question posting. In presenting the syllabus, you give the students some notion of the kind of person you are. The syllabus is a contract between you and your students. But a contract cannot be one-sided. Thus, it is important to give students time to read and discuss it. I usually tell the students that they can bring up any questions they have at the next class meeting because I know it's hard to digest all that information in such a short time. Give them a chance to have input and to be sure that they understand what you expect. Help the students understand the reasons for the plan you have presented, but if they have good reasons for changes, accept them. The students are, of course, interested in course requirements, but they are at least as much interested in what kind of person you are. One important issue is fairness.

## Testing, Grading, and Fairness

Promoting the notion that you are objective or fair can best be handled in connection with marks and the assignment of grades. (See the chapter "Assessing, Testing, and Evaluating") A large part of the students' motivation in the classroom situation is (perhaps unfortunately) directed toward the grades they hope to get for the course. The very least that students can expect of you is that their marks will be arrived at on some impartial basis. Thus give some time to discussing this section of your syllabus. Try to help the students understand how grading and testing are tied to course goals.

The simplest way to show students that you are objective and fair is to let them know that you are willing to meet and advise them. Let them know they can tell you if they are likely to have special difficulties because of health or personal issues. Indicate your office hours. In addition, students appreciate it if you are willing (and have the time) to spend a few minutes in the classroom after each class, answering specific questions. Such queries most often concern questions of fact that can be answered briefly and would hardly warrant a trip to your office at a later time. If time permits, adjournment to a convenient snack bar or lounge may give students with special interests a chance to pursue them and get to know you better. If you teach an evening class, schedule some evening time to see students.

The first class is not the time to make sure students understand your inadequacies and limitations. Frankly admitting that you don't know something is fine after the course is under way, but apologies in advance for lack of experience or expertise simply increase student insecurity. They need to feel that you are competent and in charge even if you are shaking in your boots.

## ▶ INTRODUCING THE TEXTBOOK

To continue with the discussion of the first meeting of the class, we turn now to the presentation of the textbook. Explain the features that led you to choose it. Describe how students can learn from it most effectively. Explain what you mean by "be prepared for class" because your interpretation and theirs might be different (Svinicki, 2008).

Because disagreement between the teacher and the text is inevitable, the students have a right to know what they are supposed to do about such discrepancies on examinations. By facing the situation squarely, you can not only escape from the horns of this dilemma, but also turn it to your advantage. Explain that rival interpretations stand or fall on the basis of pertinent evidence and plan to give your reasons for disagreeing with the textbook. This procedure will accomplish two things: (1) it will give the student the notion that your opinions are based on evidence, and (2) it will frequently point out current problems in theory that often have great appeal for the serious student.

## ASSESSING PRIOR KNOWLEDGE

The most important characteristic determining student learning is prior knowledge. Thus you need to get some sense of the diversity of your class's background. You might simply ask questions such as, "How many have had more than X previous courses in this subject?" Or, you might give a short, noncredit test of relevant knowledge some time during the first few class sessions. Another strategy I've used is to list the main topics and then, using a scale of 1 to 5, I have the students indicate how familiar they are with each topic. For students who lack sufficient background, you might advise that they transfer to the needed courses, or if this isn't feasible, you can at least suggest materials for their own self-study that would help them keep up with the other students. For those with very high scores, you might suggest that they skip your course and go on to a more advanced course, or at least suggest supplementary materials that would be enriching and challenging.

In a diverse class, adult students or students from other cultures may feel at a disadvantage relative to students who have had previous courses that are relevant. Reassure them by pointing out that a diversity of experiences not directly related to the course can enrich class discussion and contribute to learning.

## QUESTIONS AND REACTIONS

Even in a large lecture it seems wise to interrupt these first descriptions of the course for student questions. Some of the questions will be designed as much to test you as to get information. Often the underlying questions are:

- "Are you rigid?"
- "Will you really try to help students?"
- "Are you easily rattled?"
- "Are you a person as well as a teacher?"
- "Can you handle criticism?"

Ask students to take two minutes at the end of class to write their reactions to the first day (anonymously). This accomplishes two things: (1) it indicates your interest in learning from them and starts building a learning climate in which they are responsible for thinking about their learning and influencing your teaching; and (2) it gives you feedback, often revealing doubts or questions students were afraid to verbalize orally.

## WHAT ABOUT SUBJECT MATTER?

Many instructors dismiss class early on the first day. As the preceding sections indicate, I think the first day is important even though the students have had no prepared assignment. I like to give at least some time to subject matter. Typically, I give at least a brief overview of the course, indicate some of the questions we'll try to answer, and perhaps introduce a few key concepts. Either on the first day or during the second class period, I ask students to fill in concepts on a concept map (a diagram of key concepts and their relationships). I like to give a couple of real-life examples that they're going to learn about during the semester so that they can see how the class relates to them.

But there is a limit to what you can do. The balance between content and other activities is one that different teachers will decide in different ways. My only admonition is to use the time. The first day is important, and by using it fully you communicate that you take class periods seriously. By the end of the class period, students should feel, "This is going to be an exciting course."

## IN CONCLUSION

By the end of the first day, students will have:

1. A sense of where they're going and how they'll get there.

2. A feeling that the other members of the class are not strangers, that you and they are forming a group in which it's safe to participate.

3. An awareness that you care about their learning and will be fair.

4. An expectation that the class will be both valuable and fun.

## *Supplementary Reading*

▶ B. G. Davis, *Tools for Teaching*, 2nd ed. (San Francisco: Jossey-Bass, 1993), Chapter 3.

▶ Baron Perlman and Lee McCann, "The First Day of Class," *American Psychological Society Observer*, 2004, *17*(1), 13–14, 23–25.

▶ D. Duffy and J. Jones, *Teaching within the Rhythms of the Semester* (San Francisco: Jossey-Bass, 1995) has some good ideas about points throughout the semester and how to enliven the classes.

Part **2**

*Basic Skills for Facilitating Student Learning*

# Reading as Active Learning

hile professors like to think that students learn from professors, it seems likely that students often learn more efficiently from reading than from listening. The chapter "Teaching Students How to Become More Strategic and Self-Regulated Learners" describes skills and strategies to improve learning and retention from reading. The journals and papers described in the chapter "Using High-Stakes and Low-Stakes Writing to Enhance Learning" illustrate two ways to get students into the library and reading primary sources. Nonetheless, textbooks are still a basic tool for teaching most courses, and you can teach students to be active readers of textbooks.

## READINGS

For decades, the demise of the textbook has been eagerly predicted by advocates of each of the new panaceas for the problems of education. First television, then teaching machines, then the computer—each was expected to revolutionize education and free students and teachers from their longtime reliance on textbooks. Now there is talk of providing an electronic textbook reader that could download the texts of some publishing companies directly to the students. With electronic access becoming more and more available for that wide variety of materials, I think that we may stop thinking about the textbook as only a real book and start thinking about the "text" as the printed materials we want the students to access.

The introduction of open-stack libraries, paperback books, inexpensive reprint series, and the photocopier has given the college teacher the opportunity to choose from sources varying in style, level, and point of view. Many teachers are substituting paperback books, reprints, and collections of journal articles for the textbook as the sources of the basic information needed by students. Nevertheless, the choices we make among those materials and the way we put them together requires a lot of preparation.

A key tenet to remember is that learning is facilitated by organization. Without organization, facts and concepts become subject to interference and are quickly forgotten and inaccessible. With input from field experience, discussion, paperbacks, reprints, the World Wide Web, and other sources, the student needs, more than ever, some frame of reference within which to assimilate the bloomin', buzzin' confusion of points of view present in a modern course. Ideally, the "textbook" can provide such a structure.

If individual differences are to be attended to, students need an opportunity to learn in laboratory settings, field experiences, discussion, lectures, or reading from diverse sources. Texts are an important part of the teacher's compendium of tools, and the newer teaching methods and aids supplement rather than supplant reading. In fact, a goodly part of higher education is education in how to read—how to read poems, how to read social science, how to read legal briefs, how to read the literature of our culture and our professions.

## HOW DO YOU GET STUDENTS TO DO THE ASSIGNED READING?

The main reason students come to class unprepared is that they don't see what difference it makes. In many courses, reading assignments and lectures are independent parts of the course, sometimes overlapping, sometimes supplementary, but often not perceived as interdependent. Thus, the first strategy for encouraging reading is frequent use of the phrase "As you read in your reading assignment for today..." or the question "What was your reaction to [the author of the reading]'s discussion of...?"

A second strategy is to have students write a one-minute paper at the beginning of occasional class periods on "The most important idea (or two or three ideas) I got from the reading assignment for today." Alternatively, you can have students write a question—either something they would like explained or something that was stimulated by the reading.

One instructor (Roser, 2008) reports good results when she has her students participate in a jigsaw information-sharing activity. Each student is assigned to two small groups: an expert group and a teaching group. Each expert group is assigned a reading and works together to prepare a handout analyzing that reading and its main ideas. These groups are then split into teaching groups, each teaching group having one representative from each of the expert groups. Each member of the teaching group then in turn uses the handout to explain their particular reading to the others. This technique has the students practicing both critical reading (in the expert group) and summarization (in the teaching group), two key strategies in improving reading comprehension.

Probably the surest strategy is to announce that there will be a brief quiz on the assignment. Let's hope that once we have formed in our students the habit of reading the assignments, they will develop enough intrinsic motivation that the quizzes become unnecessary.

The basic problem often may be found in the meaning of the word *read*. To many, "read" is simply to pass one's eyes over the words as one does in reading a story. One has completed the assignment when one has reached the end of the assigned reading.

We need to teach students how to read—how to read with understanding, how to think about the purpose of the author, about relationships to earlier learning, about how they will use what they've read.

## Research on Learning from Reading

A number of classic studies have compared printed materials with lectures, and the results—at least with difficult materials—favor print (Hartman, 1961).

Study questions intended to guide the students' reading are often helpful. Marton and Säljö (1976b) found that questions designed to produce more thoughtful, integrative study were more effective than questions of fact. For example, in the assignment description, you might ask the students to compare the assertions of the author in one reading with those in another reading. How are they similar? How are they different?

Nevertheless, study questions do not automatically guarantee better learning. Students sometimes tended to look only for answers to the questions while disregarding the other content of the chapter (Marton & Säljö, 1976a). Andre (1987) reviewed research on study questions and concluded that questions generally do aid learning and that higher-level questions, rather than low-level factual questions, increase the effectiveness of student processing of the reading. Similarly, Wilhite (1983) found that prequestions focusing on material at the top of the organizational structure (big ideas, for example) facilitated learning, especially for the less able students, who are less likely to think in those terms in general. You need questions that get students to *think* about the material. One way to encourage thoughtful reading is to ask students to write a half-page answer to a thought-provoking question and to bring multiple copies to class to share with peers in small groups. Discussion after the students have read one another's papers is usually lively.

---

### Examples of Study Questions to Encourage Thought

Your assignment for Monday is to study the next chapter, "Memory." Here are some study questions:

1. How would you apply the idea of "depth of processing" to your learning from this chapter?
2. How does the limited capacity of working memory affect your learning in lecture classes?
3. How is the approach taken by researchers in memory like, and how is it different from, that taken by other researchers?

## Teaching Students to Learn More from Reading

As you will see in the chapters on assessment, tests, and grading, students' study methods and learning are influenced by the sort of test questions they expect. Thus, many students can read thoughtfully if tests require deeper understanding and thinking. But other students faithfully read and reread regardless of the type of assignment, memorizing definitions and facts without thought of the goal of the author and the relationship of this reading assignment to their previous learning. You can help by discussing with the students why you chose the reading and how they should read it.

There is ample evidence that students benefit from specific instruction in selecting main ideas, asking themselves questions, looking for organizational cues, and attempting to summarize or explain what they have read. Particularly in introductory classes, you will help learning if you make explicit reference to your goal in assigning a particular chapter and discuss ways in which students can best achieve that goal (McKeachie et al., 1985; Weinstein & Mayer, 1986). Suggest that your students:

1. Look at topic headings before studying the chapter.

2. Write down questions they would like to answer.

3. Make marginal notes as they read.

4. Underline or highlight important concepts.

5. Carry on an active dialog with the author.

6. Comment on reading in their journals. (See the chapter "Using High-Stakes and Low-Stakes Writing to Enhance Learning.")

The above strategy is a general one that can be used for almost any kind of reading. It is also useful to show students how it might be modified to fit different types of texts. For example, Williams (2005) suggests what she calls the SQ6R, a modification of an earlier strategy expanded to fit the needs of reading the research literature. Her steps include: **S**urvey the reading first, write down some **Q**uestions that it seems to address, and then **R**ead, **R**eflect, **R**eview, **R**ehash, **R**ethink, and **R**e-evaluate. She has found that pointing out this strategy to her students opens their eyes about what it means to read carefully. My own experience as a student serves as another caveat about different strategies for different types of reading. As a psychology student, I had to take a lot of statistics courses, and I generally read the textbooks the way I would read any psychology textbook: Read the prose, skip over the problems. Bad strategy! I learned much later that the appropriate strategy was: Skip the prose and work the problems. I wish someone had told me that early on. I would have saved a lot of time and frustration.

For a fuller description of ways to help students become better learners, see the chapter "Teaching Students How to Become More Strategic and Self-Regulated Learners."

## *IN CONCLUSION*

1. Reading is an important tool for learning.

2. To facilitate learning, a teacher needs not only to choose appropriate reading materials, but also to help students learn how to read them effectively.

3. Despite the availability of photocopies, coursepacks, paperbacks, and the World Wide Web, textbooks and well-organized reading materials are still useful tools for teaching.

4. If the material students need to learn is in print, in a form conveniently accessible for them, they may learn more efficiently from reading than from listening to you.

## *Supplementary Reading*

▷ T. M. Chang, H. F. Crombag, K. D. J. M. van der Drift, and J. M. Moonen, *Distance Learning* (Boston: Kluwer-Nijhoff Publishing, 1983), Chapter 4.

▷ R. G. Crowder and R. K. Wagner, *The Psychology of Reading: An Introduction*, 2nd ed. (New York: Oxford University Press, 1992).

▷ J. Hartley, "Studying for the Future," *Journal of Further and Higher Education*, 2002, *26*, 207–227.

▷ F. Marton, D. Hounsell, and N. Entwistle (eds.), *The Experience of Learning* (Edinburgh: Scottish Academic Press, 1984).

# Facilitating Discussion: Posing Problems, Listening, Questioning

**A**ctive learning is the buzz word (or phrase) in contemporary higher education. The prototypic teaching method for active learning is discussion. Discussion methods are among the most valuable tools in the teacher's repertoire. Often teachers in large classes feel that they must lecture because they think discussion is impossible. In fact, discussion techniques can be used in classes of all sizes. Generally, smaller classes *are* more effective, but large classes should not be allowed to inhibit the teacher's ability to stimulate active learning—learning experiences in which the students are *thinking* about the subject matter.

Discussion techniques seem particularly appropriate when the instructor wants to do the following:

1. Help students learn to think in terms of the subject matter by giving them practice in thinking.

2. Help students learn to evaluate the logic of and evidence for their own and others' positions.

3. Give students opportunities to formulate applications of principles.

4. Develop motivation for further learning.

5. Help students articulate what they've learned.

6. Get prompt feedback on student understanding or misunderstanding.

Why should discussion be the method of choice for achieving such objectives? The first justification is a very simple extrapolation of the old adage "Practice makes perfect." If instructors expect students to learn how to integrate, apply, and think, it seems reasonable that students should have an opportunity to practice these skills. To help students learn and think, you need to find out what is in their heads. Discussion can help.

## A LITTLE BIT OF THEORY

Research in cognitive psychology has found that memory is affected by how deeply we process new knowledge. (See the chapter "Teaching Students How to Become More Strategic and Self-Regulated Learners.") Simply listening to or repeating something is likely to store it in such a way that we have difficulty finding it when we want to remember it. If we elaborate our learning by thinking about its relationship to other things we know or by talking about it—explaining, summarizing, or questioning—we are more likely to remember it when we need to use it later. This may help relieve your anxiety about covering the material. In lectures, teachers cover more material, but research shows that most of the material covered does not get into the students' notes or memory (Hartley & Davies, 1978). Classic studies over the last five decades have repeatedly shown that, in discussion, students pay attention and think more actively.

Because many students are accustomed to listening passively to lectures and some students equate that with learning, when you introduce discussion you probably need to explain why and how discussion will help them construct knowledge they can find and apply when needed.

## PROBLEMS IN TEACHING BY DISCUSSION

In discussion groups the instructor is faced with several problems:

1. Getting participation in the discussion.

2. Making progress (or making the student aware of the progress) toward course objectives.

3. Handling emotional reactions of students.

4. Listening to the students supportively.

This chapter should help you cope with each of these problems.

# STARTING DISCUSSION

After a class has been meeting and discussing problems successfully, there is little problem in initiating discussion, for it will develop almost spontaneously from problems encountered in reading, from experiences, or from unresolved problems from the previous meeting. But during the first meetings of new groups, you need to create an expectation that something interesting and valuable will occur.

## Starting Discussion with a Common Experience

One of the best ways of starting a discussion is to refer to a concrete, common experience through presentation of a demonstration, film, role play, short skit, or brief reading. It could be a common experience of all students or an issue on campus or in the media, or you can provide the experience. These days there is a wealth of material available on the Web to spark a discussion. For example, the thought-provoking lectures presented at the TED (Technology, Entertainment, Design) Website seem to be an endless array of short discussions of current issues from the annual conferences they sponsor (http://www.TED.com/talks). Teachers are encouraged to make use of this site to foster expanding understanding of current events. For example, in my own class, I showed a 10-minute lecture on neuroscience advances and whether mind control was possible. Following such a presentation it's easy to ask, "What are the implications of what you've just seen?"

Such an opening has a number of advantages. Because everyone in the group has seen it, everyone knows something about the topic under discussion. In addition, by focusing the discussion on the presentation, the instructor takes some of the pressure off anxious or threatened students who are afraid to reveal their own opinions or feelings.

However, you will not always be able to find the presentation you need to introduce each discussion, and you may be forced to turn to other techniques of initiating discussion. One such technique is question posting, which was discussed in the chapter "Meeting a Class for the First Time."

## Starting Discussion with a Controversy

A second technique of stimulating discussion is through disagreement. Experimental evidence is accumulating to indicate that a certain degree of surprise or uncertainty arouses curiosity, a basic motive for learning (Berlyne, 1960). Some teachers effectively play the role of devil's advocate; others are effective in pointing out differences in points of view.

I have some concerns about the devil's advocate role. I believe that it can be an effective device in getting students to think actively rather than accept passively the instructor's every sentence as "Truth." Yet it has its risks, the most important of which is that it may create lack of trust in the instructor. Of course, instructors want students to challenge their ideas, but few want their students to feel they are untrustworthy, lying about their own beliefs.

Two other dangers lurk in the devil's advocate role. One is that it will be perceived as manipulative. Students may feel (with justification) that the instructor "is just playing games with us—trying to show how smart he is and how easily he can fool us." It can also be seen as a screen to prevent students from ever successfully challenging the instructor.

Yet the devil's advocate role can be effective. Its success depends a good deal on the spirit with which it is played. Linc Fisch (2001) handles this problem by donning a T-shirt with "Devil's Advocate" on the front. My own compromise solution is to make it clear when I'm taking such a role by saying, "Suppose I take the position that ___" or "Let me play the role of devil's advocate for a bit."

In any case, the instructor should realize that disagreement is not a sign of failure but may be used constructively. When rigid dogmatism interferes with constructive problem solving following a disagreement, the instructor may ask the disagreeing students to switch sides and argue the opposing point of view. Such a technique seems to be effective in developing awareness of the strengths of other positions.

As Maier (1963) has shown in his studies of group leadership, one barrier to effective problem solving is presenting an issue in such a way that participants take sides arguing the apparent solution rather than attempting to solve the problem by considering data and devising alternative solutions. Maier suggests the following principles for group problem solving:

1. Success in problem solving requires that effort be directed toward overcoming surmountable obstacles.

2. Available facts should be used even when they are inadequate.

3. The starting point of the problem is richest in solution possibilities.

4. Problem-mindedness should be increased and solution-mindedness should be delayed.

5. The "idea-getting" process should be separated from the "idea evaluation" process because the latter inhibits the former.

## Starting Discussion with Questions

The most common discussion opener is the question, and the most common error in questioning is not allowing students time enough to think. You should not expect an immediate response to every question. If your question is intended to stimulate thinking, give the students time to think. Five seconds of silence may seem an eternity, but a pause for 5 to 30 seconds will result in better discussion. In order to alleviate that awkward feeling in my own class, I actually endorse silence by saying, "I want you to think about the following question and no one can say anything for the next 2 minutes." In some cases you may plan for such a thoughtful silence by asking the students to write down one element that might help answer the question. Such a technique increases the chance that the shyer or slower students will participate, since they now know what they want to say when the discussion begins. In fact, you may even draw one in by saying, "You were writing vigorously, Ronnie. What's your suggestion?"

**Factual Questions**    There are times when it is appropriate to check student background knowledge with a series of brief factual questions, but more frequently you want to stimulate problem solving. One common error in phrasing questions for this purpose is to ask a question in a form conveying to students the message "I know something you don't know, and you'll look stupid if you don't guess right."

**Application and Interpretation Questions**    Rather than dealing with factual questions, formulate discussions so as to get at relationships, applications, or analyses of facts and materials. Solomon, Rosenberg, and Bezdek (1964) found that teachers who used interpretation questions produced gains in student comprehension. A question of the type "How does the idea that ___ apply to ___?" is much more likely to stimulate discussion than the question "What is the definition of ___?" The secret is not to avoid questions or to lecture in statements, but rather to listen and to reflect on what is heard. Dillon (1982), a leading researcher on questioning, advises that once you have defined the issue for discussion, keep quiet unless you are perplexed or didn't hear a comment. Questions are tools for teaching, but as Dillon demonstrated, they sometimes interfere with, as well as facilitate, achievement of teaching goals. What happens depends on the question and its use.

**Problem Questions**  A question may arise from a case, or it may be a hypothetical problem. It may be a problem whose solution the instructor knows; it may be a problem that the instructor has not solved. In any case it should be a problem that is meaningful to the students, and for the sake of morale, it should be a problem they can make some progress on. And even if the teacher knows an answer or has a preferred solution, the students should have a chance to come up with new solutions. The teacher's job is not to sell students on a particular solution, but rather to listen and to teach them how to solve problems themselves. Don't be afraid to express your own curiosity, question, or "what if..." wonder about a topic. Ask the students what they think. It is better to be an open-minded, curious questioner than the fount of all knowledge.

Suppose you ask a question and no one answers, or the student simply says, "I don't know." Discouraging as this may be, it should not necessarily be the end of the interaction. Usually the student can respond if the question is rephrased. Perhaps you need to give an example of the problem first; perhaps you need to suggest some alternative answer and ask the student what evidence might or might not support it; perhaps you need to reformulate a prior question. More often than not, you can help the students discover that they are more competent than they thought by sticking with them as they struggle to answer.

**Other Types of Questions**  *Connective and causal effect questions* involve attempts to link material or concepts that otherwise might not seem related. One might, for example, cut across disciplines to link literature, music, and historical events, or one might ask, "What are the possible causes of this phenomenon?"

*Comparative questions*, as the name suggests, ask for comparisons between one theory and another, one author and another, one research study and another. Such questions help students determine important dimensions of comparison.

*Evaluative questions* ask not only for comparisons but for a judgment of the relative value of the points being compared; for example, "Which of two theories better accounts for the data? Which of two essays better contributes to an understanding of the issue?"

*Critical questions* examine the validity of an author's arguments or discussion. Television, magazines, and other media provide opportunities for using critical or evaluative questioning. For example, "An eminent authority states thus and so. Under what conditions might that not be true?" Being so critical that students feel that their reading has been a waste of time is not helpful, but presenting an alternative argument or conclusion may start students analyzing their reading more carefully, and eventually you want students to become critical readers who themselves challenge assumptions and conclusions.

## Starting Discussion with a Problem or Case

One of the biggest problems in teaching by discussion is focus. Getting the discussion headed in the right direction and keeping it there requires that both students and the instructor be focused on the same questions. One of the better methods for producing focus is to use a problem or a case study as the main topic of discussion. The chapter "Experiential Learning" discusses problem-based learning and the case method in more detail, but what follows here are some general ideas about working with problem-based discussions more efficiently.

## Breaking a Problem into Subproblems

One of Maier's (1952) important contributions to effective group problem solving, as well as to teaching, is to point out that groups are likely to be more effective if they tackle one aspect of a problem at a time rather than skipping from formulation of the problem, to solutions, to evidence, to "what-have-you," as different members of the group toss in their own ideas. In developmental discussion the group tackles one thing at a time.

One of the first tasks is likely to be a *clarification of the problem*. Often groups are ineffective because different participants have different ideas of what the problem is, and group members may feel frustrated at the end of the discussion because "the group never got to the real problem."

A second task is likely to be: *What do we know?* or *What data are relevant?*

A third task may be: *What are the characteristics of an acceptable solution?*—for example: What is needed?

A fourth step could be: *What are possible solutions?* and a fifth step may be to *evaluate these solutions* against the criteria for a solution determined in the previous step.

The developmental discussion technique can be used even in large groups, since there are a limited number of points to be made at each step regardless of the number of participants. Maier and Maier (1957) have shown that developmental discussion techniques improve the quality of decisions compared with freer, more nondirective discussion methods.

## Socratic Discussion

The "classic" (and I do mean *classic*) discussion technique is the Socratic method. In television, novels, and anecdotes about the first year of law school it is usually portrayed as a sadistic, anxiety-producing method of eliciting student stupidity, and even when I place myself in the role of the slave boy taught by Socrates in the *Meno*, I feel more like a pawn than an active learner.

Perhaps this is why I've never been very good at Socratic teaching; nonetheless, I believe that it can be used as an effective method of stimulating student thinking, and it can have the quality of an interesting game rather than of an inquisition. The leading modern student of Socratic teaching is Allen Collins, who has observed a variety of Socratic dialogues and analyzed the strategies used (1977; Collins & Stevens, 1982).

Basically, most Socratic teachers attempt to teach students to reason to general principles from specific cases. Collins (1977) gives 23 rules, such as the following:

1. Ask about a known case. For example, if I were trying to teach a group of teaching assistants about student cheating, I might say, "Can you describe a situation in which cheating occurred?"

2. Ask for any factors. "Why did the cheating occur?"

3. Ask for intermediate factors. If the student suggests a factor that is not an immediate cause, ask for intermediate steps. For example, if a teaching assistant says, "Students feel a lot of pressure to get good grades," I might say, "Why did the pressure for grades result in cheating in this situation?"

4. Ask for prior factors. If the student gives a factor that has prior factors, ask for the prior factors. For example, "Why do students feel pressure to get good grades?"

5. Form a general rule for an insufficient factor. For example, "Do all students who feel pressure cheat?"

Check out Collins's article for a good list of ways to move such a discussion forward.

In general, the rules involve formulating general principles from known cases and then applying the principles to new cases. Even if one does not use the Socratic method to its fullest, the questioning strategies described in Collins's rules may be generally useful in leading discussions.

# BARRIERS TO DISCUSSION

One of the important skills of discussion leaders is the ability to appraise the group's progress and to be aware of barriers or resistances that are blocking learning. This skill depends on attention to clues such as inattention, hostility, or diversionary questions.

---

## Why Students Don't Participate

- Student habits of passivity
- Failure to see the value of discussion
- Fear of criticism or of looking stupid
- Push toward agreement or solution before alternative points of view have been considered
- Feeling that the task is to find the answer the instructor wants rather than to explore and evaluate possibilities

A primary barrier to discussion is the students' feeling that they are not learning. Occasional summaries during the hour not only help students chart their progress but also help smooth out communication problems. A summary need not be a statement of conclusions. In many cases the most effective summary is a restatement of the problem in terms of the issues resolved and those remaining. Keeping a visible record on the chalkboard of ideas, questions, data, or points to explore helps maintain focus and give a sense of progress. Asking students to summarize progress and what now needs to be done helps them develop as learners.

Another common barrier to good discussion is the instructor's tendency to tell students the answer before the students have developed an answer or meaning for themselves. Of course, teachers can sometimes save time by tying things together or stating a generalization that is emerging. But all too often they do this before the class is ready for it.

When you oppose a student's opinions, you should be careful not to overwhelm the student with the force of the criticism. Your objective is to start discussion, not smother it. Give students an opportunity to respond to criticisms, examining the point of view that was opposed. Above all, avoid personal criticism of students.

And perhaps the most common barrier is our own discomfort. We are not dispensing knowledge and not in control. It is all too easy to slip back into our old methods of teaching.

## WHAT CAN I DO ABOUT NONPARTICIPANTS?*

In most classes some students talk too much, and others never volunteer a sentence. What can the teacher do?

Unfortunately, most students are used to being passive recipients in class. Some of your students may come from cultures whose norms discourage speaking in class. To help students become participants, I try to create an expectation of participation in the discussion section. You can start to do this in the first meeting of the course by defining the functions of various aspects of the course and explaining why discussion is valuable. In addition to this initial structuring, however, you must continually work to increase the students' awareness of the values of participation. Participation is not an end in itself. For many purposes widespread participation may be vital; for others it may be detrimental. But you want to create a climate in which an important contribution is not lost because the person with the necessary idea did not feel free to express it.

What keeps a student from talking? There are a variety of reasons—boredom, lack of knowledge, general habits of passivity, cultural norms—but most compelling is a fear of being embarrassed. When one is surrounded by strangers, when one does not know how critical these strangers may be, when one is afraid of the teacher's response, when one is not sure how sound one's idea may be, when one is afraid of stammering or forgetting one's point under the stress of speaking—the safest thing to do is keep quiet.

What can reduce this fear? Getting acquainted is one aid. Once students know that they are among friends, they can risk expressing themselves. If they know that at least one classmate supports an idea, the risk is reduced. For both these reasons the technique of subgrouping

---

*Some students who are reluctant to participate orally will participate in a computer conference or by e-mail.

helps; for example, you can ask students to discuss a question in pairs or small groups before asking for general discussion.

Asking students to take a couple of minutes to write out their initial answers to a question can help. If a student has already written an answer, the step to speaking is much less than answering when asked to respond immediately. Even the shy person will respond when asked, "What did you write?"

Rewarding infrequent contributors at least with a smile helps encourage participation even if the contribution has to be developed or corrected. Calling students by name seems to encourage freer communication. Seating is important too. Rooms with seats in a circle help tremendously.

Getting to know the nonparticipant is also helpful. For example, I have found that it is helpful to ask students to write a brief life history indicating their interests and experiences relevant to the course. These autobiographies help me to gain a better knowledge of each student as an individual, to know what problems or illustrations will be of particular interest to a number of students, and to know on whom I can call for special information. One of the best ways of getting nonparticipants into the discussion is to ask them to contribute in a problem area in which they have special knowledge.

The technique of asking for a student's special knowledge deals directly with one of the major barriers to class discussion—fear of being wrong. No one likes to look foolish, especially in a situation where mistakes may be pounced upon by a teacher or other students. One of the major reasons for the deadliness of a question in which the teacher asks a student to fill in the one right word—such as, "This is an example of what?"—is that it puts the student on the spot. There is an infinity of wrong answers, and obviously the teacher knows the one right answer; so why should the student risk making a mistake when the odds are so much against the student? And even if the answer is obvious, why look like a pawn of the teacher?

One way of putting the student in a more favorable position is to ask general questions that have no wrong answers. For example, you can ask, "How do you feel about this?" or "How does this look to you?" as a first step in analysis of a problem. Students' feelings or perceptions may not be the same as yours, but as reporters of their own feelings, they can't be challenged as being inaccurate. While such an approach by no means eliminates anxiety about participation (for an answer involves revealing oneself as a person), it will more often open up discussion that involves the student than will questions of fact. Question posting, the technique discussed in an earlier chapter as a method for establishing objectives during the first day of class, is an example of a discussion technique minimizing risk for students. It can be useful in introducing a new topic at the conclusion of a topic, or for analysis of an experiment or a literary work. An added advantage is that it can be used in large as well as small groups.

Another technique for reducing the risk of participation for students is to ask a question one class period before the discussion and ask students to write out answers involving an example from their own experience. Similarly, one can ask students to bring one question to class for discussion. This helps participation, helps students learn to formulate questions, and also provides feedback for you.

Finally, remember that out-of-class learning is often more important than that in class. E-mail, computer conferencing, and other interactive technologies can support active learning, discussion, and debate.

All of these techniques will still not make every student into an active, verbal participant. Two group techniques can help. One is buzz groups; the other is the inner-circle technique.

## Buzz Groups

One of the popular techniques for achieving student participation in groups is the buzz session. In this procedure, classes are split into small subgroups for a brief discussion of a problem. Groups can be asked to come up with one hypothesis that they see as relevant, with one application of a principle, with an example of a concept, or with a solution to a problem. In large classes I march up the aisles saying, "Odd," "Even," "Odd," "Even" for each row and ask the "odd" row to turn around to talk to the "even" row behind, forming themselves into groups of four to six. I tell them to first introduce themselves to one another and then to choose a person to report for the group. Next, they are to get from each member of the group one idea about the problem or question posed. Finally, they are to come up with one idea to report to the total class. I give the group a limited time to work, sometimes 5 minutes or less, occasionally 10 minutes or more, depending on the tasks. Peer-led discussions need not be limited to 5 or 10 minutes or even to the classroom. (See the chapter "Active Learning.")

## The Inner Circle or Fishbowl

In using the inner-circle technique I announce that at the next class meeting we are going to have a class within a class, with several of the students (6 to 15) acting as the discussion group and the others as observers. If the classroom has movable chairs, I then arrange the seating in the form of concentric circles. I am impressed that students who are normally silent will talk when they feel the increased sense of responsibility as members of the inner circle.

## THE DISCUSSION MONOPOLIZER*

If you have worked on nonparticipation effectively, the discussion monopolizer is less likely to be a problem, but there will still be classes in which one or two students talk so much that you and the other students become annoyed. As with nonparticipation, one solution is to raise with the class the question of participation in discussion—"Would the class be more effective if participation were more evenly distributed?"

A second technique is to have one or more members of the class act as observers for one or more class periods, reporting back to the class their observations. Perhaps assigning the dominant member to the observer role would help sensitivity.

A third possibility is to audiotape a discussion, and after playing back a portion, ask the class to discuss what might be done to improve the discussion.

A fourth technique is to use buzz groups with one member chosen to be reporter.

Finally, a direct approach should not be ruled out. Talking to the student individually outside class may be the simplest and most effective solution.

## HOW CAN WE HAVE A DISCUSSION IF THE STUDENTS HAVEN'T READ THE ASSIGNMENT?

It's hard to have a discussion if students haven't studied the material to be discussed. What to do?

One strategy is to give students questions at the end of one class, asking them to get information on the questions before the next class. You can ask students to evaluate the validity of different Internet sources providing relevant information. You might even give different assignments to teams of students. Another strategy is to ask students to bring one or

---

*Be sensitive to the fact that the most common monopolizer is the teacher. In our research, our observers reported that in a typical discussion class, the teacher talked 70 to 80 percent of the time. Have an observer check your percentage.

more questions on the assignment to be turned in at the beginning of the next class.

If there are extenuating circumstances, you (or a student who is prepared) can summarize the needed points. Alternatively, you can give students a few minutes to scan the material before beginning the discussion. If used often, however, such strategies may discourage out-of-class preparation.

If the problem persists, present it to the students. What do they suggest? One likely proposal is a short quiz at the beginning of class—which usually works. However, you'd like to have students motivated to study without the threat of a quiz. Usually the quiz can be phased out once students find that discussion really requires preparation and that the assignments are more interesting as they develop competence.

## HANDLING ARGUMENTS

In any good discussion conflicts will arise. If such conflicts are left ambiguous and uncertain, they, like repressed conflicts in the individual, may cause continuing trouble. You can focus these conflicts so that they may contribute to learning.

- Reference to the text or other authority may be one method of resolution, if the solution depends on certain facts.

- Using the conflict as the basis for a library assignment for the class or a delegated group is another solution.

- If there is an experimentally verified answer, this is a good opportunity to review the method by which the answer could be determined.

- If the question is one of values, your goal may be to help students become aware of the values involved.

- Sometimes students will dispute your statements or decisions. Such disagreements may often be resolved by a comparison of the evidence for both points of view, but since teachers are human, they are all too likely to become drawn into an argument in which they finally rest on their own authority. To give yourself time to think, as well as to indicate understanding and acceptance of the students' point, I suggest listing the objections on the board. (Incidentally, listing evidence or arguments is also a good technique when the conflict is between two members of the class.) Such listing tends to prevent repetition of the same arguments.

- In any case it should be clear that conflict may be an aid to learning, and the instructor need not frantically seek to smother it.

- If you're having problems with a particular student, check the chapter "Dealing with Student Problems and Problem Students."

## The Two-Column Method

Another of Maier's (1952) techniques, the two-column method, is a particularly effective use of the board in a situation in which there is a conflict or where a strong bias prevents full consideration of alternative points of view. Experimental studies (Hovland, 1957) suggest that when people hear arguments against their point of view, they become involved in attempting to refute the arguments rather than listening and understanding. Disagreement thus often tends to push the debaters into opposite corners, in which every idea is right or wrong, good or bad, black or white. The truth is often more complex and not in either extreme.

The two-column method is designed to permit consideration of complications and alternatives. As in question posting, before the issues are debated, all the arguments on each side are listed on the board. The leader heads two columns "Favorable to A" and "Favorable to B" or "For" and "Against" and then asks for the facts or arguments that group members wish to present. The instructor's task is to understand and record in brief the arguments presented. If someone wishes to debate an argument presented for the other side, the instructor simply tries to reformulate the point so that it can be listed as a positive point in the debater's own column. But even though an argument is countered or protested it should not be erased, for the rules of the game are that the two columns are to include all ideas that members consider relevant. Evaluation can come later.

When the arguments have been exhausted, discussion can turn to the next step in problem solving. At this point the group can usually identify areas of agreement and disagreement, and in many cases it is already clear that the situation is neither black nor white. Now the issue becomes one of *relative* values rather than good versus bad. When discussion is directed toward agreements, some of the personal animosity is avoided, and some underlying feelings may be brought to light. The next stages of the discussion are thus more likely to be directed toward constructive problem solving.

Challenges and disagreements may be an indication of an alert, involved class. But the instructor should also be aware of the possibility that they may be symptoms of frustration arising because the students are uncertain of what the problem is or how to go about solving it.

# TEACHING STUDENTS HOW TO LEARN THROUGH DISCUSSION

I have already implied that classes don't automatically carry on effective discussions. To a large extent students have to learn how to learn from discussions, just as they have to learn how to learn from reading. How can this occur?

First, they need to understand the importance of discussion for learning. Expressing one's understanding or ideas and getting reactions from other students and the teacher makes a big difference in learning, retention, and use of knowledge.

What skills need to be learned? One skill is clarification of what the group is trying to do—becoming sensitive to confusion about what the group is working on and asking for clarification.

A second attribute is the students' development of a willingness to talk about their own ideas openly and to listen and respond to others' ideas. It is important for students to realize that it is easy to deceive themselves about their own insights or understandings and that verbalizing an idea is one way of getting checks on and extensions of it. Teachers can encourage development of listening skills by asking one group member to repeat or paraphrase what another said before responding to it, and repeatedly pointing out the purpose and values students gain from discussion.

A third skill is planning. Discussions are sometimes frustrating because they are only getting under way when the end of the class period comes. If this results in continuation of the discussion outside the class, so much the better, but often learning is facilitated if students learn to formulate the issues and determine what out-of-class study or follow-up is necessary before the group breaks up.

A fourth skill is building on others' ideas in such a way as to increase their motivation rather than make them feel punished or forgotten. Often students see discussion as a competitive situation in which they win by tearing down other students' ideas. As Haines and McKeachie (1967) have shown, cooperative discussion methods encourage more effective work and better morale than competitive methods.

A fifth attribute is skill in evaluation. If classes are to learn how to discuss issues effectively, they need to review periodically what aspects of their discussion are proving to be worthwhile and what barriers, gaps, or difficulties have arisen. Some classes reserve the last 5 minutes of the period for a review of the discussion's effectiveness.

A sixth attribute is sensitivity to feelings of other group members. Students need to become aware of the possibility that feelings of rejection, frustration, dependence, and so on may influence group members' participation in discussion. Sometimes it is more productive to recognize the underlying feeling than to focus on the content of an individual's statement. One way of helping students develop these skills is to use student-led discussions preceded by a training meeting with the student leader.

## STUDENT-LED DISCUSSIONS

In pioneering experiments in educational psychology and general psychology, Gruber and Weitman (1962) found that students taught in small, student-led discussion groups without a teacher not only did at least as well on a final examination as students who heard the teacher lecture, but also were superior in curiosity (as measured by question-asking behavior) and in interest in educational psychology. In a later study by Phillips and Powers (1979), the amount of student interaction was a function of the discussion leader. When students were leading the discussion, the amount of student participation was almost twice as great as when the discussion was led by the instructor. Phillips and Powers said that it was impossible to tell if this was because students as leaders facilitated discussion or the absence of an expert as discussion leader led to less inhibition of discussion, but it's an interesting question to ponder. Having a student as the discussion leader could easily change how the other students perceive their role in the class. In a more recent study, Casteel and Bridges (2007) found that students did indeed report being more comfortable disagreeing with others when it was students who were leading the discussion.

As it is probably the experience of disagreeing that causes the most self-reflection by a learner, and self-reflection causes better learning, feeling freer to disagree could lead to better learning from a discussion. This phenomenon has been described by Johnson and Johnson (1995) and referred to as "creative controversy." After an extensive meta-analysis of the literature, Johnson and Johnson reported impressive effect sizes (the amount of difference made by an intervention) for studies that used formats that followed the creative controversy model. Johnson, Johnson, and Smith (2000) provided an excellent analysis of what is probably happening with that model. In this model of discussion, students are divided into groups of four and then each group is divided into pairs. One pair of the group researches the pro side of an issue and the other pair researches the con side. The pairs have to construct good arguments backed by the literature and other forms of evidence. Once this has been done and each side has made its case and refuted the other, the pairs switch sides.

They are required to come to some consensus on the best position with regard to the problem. Johnson and Johnson propose that such activity not only motivates students to dig deeply into the topic, but also causes them to experience the kind of conceptual conflict that research has shown leads to a re-examination of beliefs and attitudes. To learn more about this very interesting process, I recommend you read the Johnson, Johnson, and Smith (2000) article referenced in the Supplementary Reading list for this chapter.

## TAKING MINUTES OR NOTES, SUMMARIZING

One of the problems with discussion is students' feeling that they have learned less than in lectures where they have taken voluminous notes. Thus, I like to summarize our progress at the end of the period or ask students to contribute to a summary. Better yet, use the last 5 to 10 minutes for getting feedback. For example, ask students to write a summary of the issues discussed, the pros and cons, and their conclusions.

## ONLINE DISCUSSIONS

This is probably the most rapidly growing type of discussion in our arsenal today. As discussed in Chapter 17, "Technology and Teaching," e-mail, list servers, computer conferences, and other online experiences extend the opportunities for discussion far beyond what is possible in the classroom. Online discussions also provide practice in writing. They can facilitate cooperative learning. The impersonality of e-mail may reduce the inhibitions of those who are shy in the classroom, but research suggests that it may also reduce inhibitions against rudeness. Thus, in initiating an online discussion, remind your students that respect for others and rational support for arguments are just as important online as in the classroom. For a really thorough discussion of this topic, I recommend going to Chapter 17 or consulting some of the most recent work on the topic, which has been reviewed by one of the leaders in the field, Alfred Rovai. In a very thorough analysis (Rovai, 2007), he has recommended some key strategies. For example, he suggested providing rubrics for online discussion to help students understand the kind of thought you expect from them in the discussions. He has also emphasized the importance of creating a sense of community for students in courses that depend heavily on online discussion. He has been studying the issue of social presence in virtual classrooms, the idea that there is a real person behind the words on the screen. Although many of his recommendations apply to face-to-face discussions, it's good to remember that the ability to discuss serious issues online is a very different behavior than the social networking that many students are accustomed to, so we can't just assume that this level of thought will happen automatically.

## *IN CONCLUSION*

Teaching by discussion differs from lecturing because you never know what is going to happen. At times this is anxiety-producing, at times frustrating, but more often exhilarating. It provides constant challenges and opportunities for both you and the students to learn. When you can listen for several minutes without intervening, you will have succeeded.

## *Supplementary Reading*

C. C. Bonwell and T. E. Sutherland, "The Active Learning Continuum: Choosing Activities to Engage Students in the Classroom," in T. E. Sutherland and C. C. Bonwell (eds.), "Using Active Learning in College Classes: A Range of Options for Faculty," *New Directions for Teaching and Learning*, no. 67, October 1996, 3–16.

S. D. Brookfield and S. Preskill, *Discussion as a Way of Teaching: Tools and Techniques for Democratic Classrooms* (San Francisco: Jossey-Bass, 1999).

A. Collins, "Different Goals of Inquiry Teaching," *Questioning Exchange*, 1988, 2(1), 39–45.

J. T. Dillon, *Teaching and the Art of Questioning* (Bloomington, IN: Phi Delta Kappa Educational Foundation, 1983).

B. S. Fuhrmann and A. F. Grasha, *A Practical Handbook for College Teachers* (Boston: Little, Brown, 1983), Chapter 6.

D. Johnson, R. Johnson, and K. Smith, "Constructive Controversy: The Educative Power of Intellectual Conflict," *Change Magazine*, January/February, 28–37.

# How to Make Lectures More Effective

The lecture is probably the oldest teaching method and still the method most widely used in universities throughout the world. Through the ages a great deal of practical wisdom about techniques of lecturing has accumulated. Effective lecturers combine the talents of scholar, writer, producer, comedian, entertainer, and teacher in ways that contribute to student learning. Nevertheless, it is also true that few college professors combine these talents in optimal ways and that even the best lecturers are not always in top form. Lectures have survived despite the invention of printing, television, and computers.

Is the lecture an effective method of teaching? If it is, under what conditions is it most effective? I will tackle these questions not only in light of research on the lecture as a teaching method but also in terms of analyses of the cognitive processes used by students in lecture classes.

## RESEARCH ON THE EFFECTIVENESS OF LECTURES

A large number of studies have compared the effectiveness of lectures with other teaching methods. The results are discouraging for those who lecture. Discussion methods are superior to lectures in student retention of information after the end of a course; in transfer of knowledge to new situations; in development of problem solving, thinking, or attitude change; and in motivation for further learning (McKeachie et al., 1990).

Similarly, print offers advantages over lecture. Students can read faster than lecturers can lecture, and they can go back when they don't understand, skip material that is irrelevant, and review immediately or later. Lectures go at the lecturer's pace, and students who fall behind are out of luck. But don't despair; lectures can still be useful.

## WHAT ARE LECTURES GOOD FOR?

- Presenting up-to-date information (There is typically a gap between the latest scholarship and its appearance in a textbook.)
- Summarizing material scattered over a variety of sources
- Adapting material to the background and interests of a particular group of students at a particular time and place
- Helping students read more effectively by providing an orientation and conceptual framework
- Focusing on key concepts, principles, or ideas

Lectures also have motivational values apart from their cognitive content. By helping students become aware of a problem, of conflicting points of view, or of challenges to ideas they have previously taken for granted, the lecturer can stimulate interest in further learning in an area. Moreover, the lecturer's own attitudes and enthusiasm have an important effect on student motivation. Research on student ratings of teaching as well as on student learning indicates that the enthusiasm of the lecturer is an important factor in affecting student learning and motivation. You may feel that enthusiasm is not learnable. Clearly some people are more enthusiastic and expressive than others, but you can develop in this area just as in others. Try to put into each lecture something that you are really excited about. Notice how your voice and gestures show more energy and expressiveness. Now try carrying some of that intensity and animation over into other topics. Like other learned behaviors, this takes practice, but you can do it. Murray (1997) showed that enthusiastic teachers move around, make eye contact with students, and use more gestures and vocal variation, and that teachers could learn these behaviors. Both research and theory support the usefulness of enthusiastic behaviors in maintaining student attention.*

The lecturer also models ways of approaching problems, portraying a scholar in action in ways that are difficult for other media or methods of instruction to achieve. You can say, "Here is how I go about solving this kind of problem (analyzing this phenomenon, etc.). Now you try it." One of the advantages of live professors is the tendency of people to model themselves after other individuals whom they perceive as living, breathing human beings with characteristics that can be admired and emulated. So lectures can be effective—but sometimes more effective in stimulating our own learning and thinking than in stimulating that of the students!

## A LITTLE BIT OF THEORY

The preceding section has included a little bit of theory of learning and motivation, and more of that type of material is spread throughout this book¨, but I want to be more explicit about one aspect of the cognitive theory of learning and memory. As I noted in the preceding chapter, memory depends heavily on the learner's activity—thinking about and elaborating on new knowledge. A key difference between modern theories of memory and earlier theory is that earlier theory considered knowledge as single associations, in some ways like tucking each bit of knowledge into a pigeonhole. Now we think of knowledge as being stored in structures such as networks with linked concepts, facts, and principles. The lecture thus needs to build a bridge between what is in the students' minds and the structures in the subject matter. Metaphors, examples, and demonstrations are the elements of the bridge. Providing a meaningful organization is thus a key function of the lecture. Our research (Naveh-Benjamin, Lin, & McKeachie, 1989) showed that students begin a course with little organization but during a course develop

---

*Don't feel that you have to show high energy every minute. There will be times when calm, quiet, slow speech may be needed—times when you may need to wait and reflect before responding.

¨For a really good summary of theory and research, you can consult either Svinicki (2004), *Learning and Motivation in the Postsecondary Classroom* or Halpern and Hakel (2003), *Applying the Science of Learning to University Teaching*. Both books were written with the university faculty member in mind and contain a good grounding in basic learning and memory and their application to instruction.

conceptual structures that more and more closely resemble those of the instructor.

## ▶PLANNING LECTURES

A typical lecture strives to present a systematic, concise summary of the knowledge to be covered in the day's assignment. Chang and associates (1983, p. 21) call this approach "conclusion oriented." While there are times when this is useful, more often you need to teach students how to read and understand the assignments themselves. Your job is less knowledge dispensing than teaching students how to learn and think.

I was a conclusion-oriented lecturer for 30 years. Now more of my lectures involve analyzing materials, formulating problems, developing hypotheses, bringing evidence to bear, criticizing and evaluating alternative solutions—revealing methods of learning and thinking and involving students in the process.

One of the implications of the theoretical approach I have taken is that what is an ideal approach to lecturing early in a course is likely to be inappropriate later in the course. As noted earlier, the way students process verbal material depends on the structures that not only enable them to process bigger and bigger chunks of subject matter but also give them tacit knowledge of the methods, procedures, and conventions used in the field and by you as a lecturer. Intentionally or not, you are teaching students how to become more skilled in learning from your lectures.

Because this is so, one should in the first weeks of a course go more slowly, pause to allow students with poor backgrounds time to take notes, and give more everyday types of examples. Pausing to write a phrase or sketch a relationship on the chalkboard will not only give students a chance to catch up but also provide visual cues that can serve as points of reference later. Later in the term, students should be able to process bigger blocks of material more quickly.

Adapting to the differences in students' knowledge from the beginning to the later stages of a course is but one example of the principle that one key to good lecturing is an awareness of the audience, not only in lecturing but in preparing the lecture. In every class there is student diversity—not only in background knowledge but also in motivation, skills for learning, beliefs about what learning involves, and preferences for different ways of learning (learning styles). Shulman (2002) described the skilled instructor's ability to balance all these things as "pedagogical content knowledge," the knowledge about how students actually learn the content and how to adapt teaching to support that learning.

## PREPARING YOUR LECTURE NOTES

One of the security-inducing features of lectures is that one can prepare a lecture with some sense of control over the content and organization of the class period. In lectures the instructor is usually in control, and this sense of controlled structure helps the anxious teacher avoid pure panic.

But no matter how thoroughly you have prepared the subject matter of the lecture, you must still face the problem of how to retrieve and deliver your insights during the class period. If you have plenty of time and are compulsive, you may be tempted to write out the lecture verbatim. Don't! Or, if you must (and writing it out may be useful in clarifying your thoughts), don't take a verbatim version into the classroom. Few lecturers can read a lecture so well that students stay awake and interested.

At the same time, few teachers can deliver a lecture with no cues at all. Hence, you will ordinarily lecture from notes. Most lecturers use an outline or a sequence of cue words and phrases. Try forming your notes as a series of questions.

Day (1980) studied lecture notes used by professors at over 75 colleges and universities. She notes that extensive notes take the instructor out of eye contact with students so that students fall into a passive, nonquestioning role. Day suggests the use of graphic representations to increase teaching flexibility and spontaneity. Tree diagrams, computer flowcharts, or network models enable a teacher to have at hand a representation of the structure that permits one to answer questions without losing track of the relationship of the question to the lecture organization. Pictorial representations using arrows, faces, Venn diagrams, or drawings that symbolize important concepts may not only provide cues for the instructor but can also be placed on PowerPoint or the board to provide additional cues for students.

Color coding your notes with procedural directions to yourself also helps. Because I try to get student involvement, I have a tendency to run overtime; I put time cues in the margin to remind myself to check. I also put in directions to myself, such as

- "Put on board." (usually a key concept or relationship)
- "Check student understanding. Ask for examples."

- "Ask students for a show of hands."
- "Put students in pairs to discuss this."

Whatever your system, indicate *signposts* to tell students what is ahead, *transitions* that tell students when you are finishing one topic and moving to the next, *key points* or *concepts*, and *links* such as "consequently," "therefore," and "because."*

Allow time for questions from students, for new examples or ideas that come to mind during the lecture, and for your own mis-estimation of the time a topic will require. If perchance you finish early, let the students use the remaining time to write a summary. Finally, use your notes to prepare a handout with a structure that students can use for filling in their notes and asking questions.

## ORGANIZATION OF LECTURES

In thinking about lecture organization, most teachers think first about the structure of the subject matter, then try to organize the content in some logical fashion, such as building from specifics to generalization or deriving specific implications from general principles. Too often we get so immersed in "covering" the subject that we forget to ask, "What do I really want students to remember from this lecture next week, next year?"

Some common organizing principles used by lecturers are cause to effect; time sequence (for example, stories); parallel organization such as phenomenon to theory to evidence; problem to solution; pro versus con to resolution; familiar to unfamiliar; and concept to application.**

Leith (1977) has suggested that different subjects are basically different in the ways in which progress is made in the field. Some subjects are organized in a linear or hierarchical fashion in which one concept builds on a preceding one. The logical structure of one's subject should be one factor determining the lecture organization, but equally important is the cognitive structure in the students' minds. If we are to teach our students effectively, we need to bridge the gap between the structure in the subject matter and structures in the students' minds. As is indicated in all of the chapters in this book, you are not making impressions on a

---

*These four types of signposts are discussed in George Brown, *Lecturing and Explaining* (London: Methuen, 1978).

**Stories not only interest students, they also aid memory. If you can make your story a mystery, you'll hold attention (see Green, 2004).

blank slate. Rather, our task in teaching is to help students reorganize existing cognitive structures or to add new dimensions or new features to existing structures. Thus, the organization of the lecture needs to take account of the student's existing knowledge and expectations as well as the structure of the subject matter. Analogies linking new ideas to similar ones that students already know can help. Remember that what you are trying to do is get an organization into your students' heads that will help them fit in relevant facts and form a base for further learning and thinking.

## The Introduction

One suggestion for organization is that the *introduction* of the lecture should point to a gap in the student's existing cognitive structure or should challenge or raise a question about something in the student's existing method of organizing material in order to arouse curiosity (Berlyne, 1954a, 1954b). There is a good deal of research on the role of prequestions in directing attention to features of written texts. Prequestions in the introduction of a lecture may help students to discriminate between more and less important features of lectures. For example, before a lecture on cognitive changes in aging, I ask, "Do you get more or less intelligent as you get older?" and "What is a fair test of intelligence for older people?" Such questions may help create expectations that enable students to allocate their cognitive capacity more effectively. If students know what they are expected to learn from a lecture, they learn more of that material (sometimes at the expense of other material; Royer, 1977). In a recent study, Nevid and Mahon (2009) showed that putting these questions into a set of pre-post mastery quizzes before and after each lecture helped direct student attention to the key concepts and resulted in better unit-test performance at the end of the unit. Although there are other factors probably operating here, this is such a simple procedure, and students seem to like it.

Another approach is to begin with a demonstration, example, case, or application that captures attention. In many fields it is possible to begin some lectures with presentation of a problem or case from a current newspaper or television show, then ask students how they would think about it in the light of this course, or alternatively illustrate in the lecture how experts in this field would think about it.

## The Body of the Lecture

In organizing the *body* of the lecture, the most common error is probably that of trying to include too much. The enemy of learning is the teacher's need to cover the content at all costs. When I began lecturing, my mentor told me, "If you get across three or four points in a lecture so that students understand and remember them, you've done well." Lecturers very often overload the students' information processing capacity so that they become less able to understand the material than if fewer points had been presented. David Katz (1950), a pioneer Gestalt psychologist, called this phenomenon "mental dazzle." He suggested that, just as too much light causes our eyes to be dazzled so that we cannot see anything, so also can too many new ideas overload processing capacity so that we cannot understand anything.

Use the board, an overhead projector, or PowerPoint to give the students cues to the organization of the lecture. Progressively displaying points of an outline or key words is useful in three ways:

1. It gives a *visual* representation to supplement your oral presentation. Using a diagram or other graphic representation will help visualization.

2. Change helps retain (or regain) attention so everyone is on the same page at the same time.

3. It gives students a chance to catch up with what you have said (perchance to think!).

**Using Examples.**   Move from the concrete to the abstract. To link what is in your head with what is in the students' heads, you need to use examples that relate the subject to the students' experience and knowledge. I am not as effective a teacher today as I was decades ago because I do not know the students' culture and am thus limited in finding vivid examples of a concept in students' daily lives. Because no single example can represent a concept fully, you usually need to give more than one example. Concept formation research suggests that examples differing from one another are likely to be most effective if you point out the essential features of the concept exemplified in each example. If you can find a cartoon or funny story that illustrates your point, humor helps maintain interest. But the danger is that students may remember the humor and not the concept, so repeat the concept. And, most important, give students a chance to give examples.

**Periodic Summaries within the Lecture.**   From our knowledge of students' note-taking behavior, we know that students would be better able to learn from lectures if there were periodic summaries of preceding material. These give students a chance to catch up on material covered when they were not tuned in and also give them a check on possible misperceptions based on inadequate or misleading expectations. Repeat main points once, twice, thrice, during the lecture. Such summaries can help make clear to students transitions from one theme to another, so that they are aided in organizing the material not only in their notes but in their minds. In fact, you might try thinking of your lecture as two or more mini-lectures separated by short periods for questions, discussion, or writing.

**Checking Student Understanding.** Although it may seem irrational to cover material when students are not learning from it, one should not underestimate the compulsion one feels to get through one's lecture notes. A remedy for this compulsion is to put into the lecture notes reminders to oneself to check the students' understanding—both by looking for nonverbal cues of bewilderment or of lack of attention and by raising specific questions that will test the students' understanding.

Most lecturers recognize that they need to check student understanding periodically; so they ask, "Any questions?" and after 3 to 5 seconds without response assume that everyone understands. Not so! If you really want to know, give students a minute to write down a question, then have them compare notes with students sitting near them before asking for questions. You'll get some.

Once you have used this procedure a few times, so that students have found that questioning is not dangerous, you can simply say, "What questions do you have?"

**The Conclusion.** In the conclusion of the lecture, one has the opportunity to make up for lapses in the body of the lecture. Encouraging students to formulate questions or asking questions oneself can facilitate understanding and memory. By making the oral headings visible once again, by recapitulating major points, by proposing unanswered questions to be treated in the reading assignments or the future lectures, and by creating an anticipation of the future, the lecturer can help students learn. One good (and humbling) technique is to announce that you will ask a student to summarize the lecture at the end of the period. Another—less threatening—is to have students spend 3 minutes writing a summary of main points, a technique sometimes called a "minute paper" (Wilson, 1986), and then asking one of them to read what they wrote. I also suggest collecting those minute papers as an ongoing assessment of what students are learning. Either method helps the process of elaboration, which is critical for memory. And, of course, as I mentioned earlier, a post-mastery quiz can serve to check students' understanding as well.

Having suggested all this, I must admit that my own greatest problem as a lecturer is that I never seem to be ready for the conclusion until it is already past time to dismiss the class.

# HOW CAN LECTURES BE IMPROVED?

The message of this chapter is that one way of improving lectures is to think about how students process lectures. What are students trying to do during a lecture?

As you observe student behavior during a lecture, the most impressive thing you might notice is the passive role students have in most classrooms. Some students are having difficulty in staying awake; others are attempting to pass the time as easily as possible by reading other materials, texting their friends, counting lecturer mannerisms, or simply doodling and listening in a relatively effortless manner. Most students are taking notes. Ideally, many students are attempting to construct knowledge by linking what the lecturer says with what they already know.

## Attention

One of the factors determining students' success in information processing is their ability to pay attention to the lecture. Attention basically involves focusing one's cognitions on those things that are changing, novel, or motivating. Individuals have a limited capacity for attending to the varied features of their environment. The individual's total capacity for attention may vary with the degree of activation or motivation. At any one time, part of the capacity may be devoted to the task at hand (in this case listening to the lecturer), part may be involved in taking notes, and part may be left over to shift primary attention to distractions or daydreams when boredom occurs.

Wilson and Korn (2007) did a very good job of analyzing a lot of the research on the patterns of student attention during lectures in order to determine if students really did experience a waning of attention after about 10 minutes. As is often the case with classroom-based research, the measures used to evaluate level of attention varied from the amount of notes taken to observational data on student behavior to retention of the material. And as is often the case, they found that nothing was ever so simple as the definitive 10–15 minutes span of attention rule.

They suggested that there are many individual variables of the student, the instructor, the content, and the environment that influence students' ability to maintain their focus. Wilson and Korn did suggest that you as an instructor would learn a lot from looking at what ends up in your students' notes and that might be the best guide for estimating how well and how often your students are paying attention. If they're not getting down the main ideas, then you begin to worry about how to help them pay attention at the right moments in the class.

## What Can Be Done to Maintain Attention?

In determining how to allocate attention, students use various strategies. Any lecturer knows that one way of getting attention is to precede the statement by the phrase, "This will be on the test." In addition, students listen for particular words or phrases that indicate to them that something is worth noting and remembering. Statements that enumerate or list are likely to be on tests and thus are likely to be attended to.

Changes in the environment recruit attention. The ability of changes to capture attention can work to the advantage of the lecturer. Variation in pitch, intensity, and pace of the lecture; visual cues such as gestures, facial expression, movement to the board; the use of demonstrations or audiovisual aids—all of these recruit and maintain attention to the lecture.

Auditory attention is directed to some extent by visual attention. Distracting movements in the classroom are thus likely to cause students to fail to recall what the lecturer has said. On the positive side, students' comprehension is greater when the students can see the speaker's face and lips (Campbell, 1999). Look at your audience; eye contact helps communication.

Motivation is important in holding student attention. Linking lectures to student interests, giving examples that are vivid and intriguing, and building suspense toward resolution of a conflict— these are all techniques of gaining and holding attention.

All of these devices will help, but the best device for maintaining attention is to break up the lecture rather than trying to hold attention for an hour or more. Student activities such as question posting, the minute paper (mentioned earlier in this chapter), pairing, or small-group activities can reactivate students' attention.* If you spot signs of drowsiness or fidgeting, ask students to stand up and stretch.

---

*Brown and Atkins (1988, p. 29) list these and other student activities to get students' attention and to get them thinking during lectures.

Bligh's research summary indicated that the gain in learning after such a break more than compensates for any learning that might have occurred in the time taken for the break (Bligh, 2000).

A recent innovation that does wonders for student attention is the use of personal response systems, called "clickers," during the course of the period. These computer-input devices allow the instructor to interject activities throughout the class period and have the students respond by tapping keys on a small handheld device. These responses can then be projected in the aggregate for the entire class to see and captured to monitor individual student selections. The use of clickers is discussed in much greater detail in Chapter 17 on the use of technology, but I mention it here because it is making a big difference in getting instructors to involve the students more actively during a lecture, and that is a wonderful way of maintaining attention. Of course, you don't really need to use high tech for such opportunities for active responding; you can have students raise their hands to indicate their choice of answer to a question. I use this type of activity sheet throughout the class period to interject sample test questions or applications of the material just covered, and it has been very useful for the students and me to see if we are on the same page. The technology allows you to summarize and display the class's responses instantly, so they can inform what is happening in class immediately and retain the information for improvement purposes later. A recent study by Mayer and colleagues (2009) attempted to evaluate the educational value of using clicker-supported questioning during lectures in comparison to paper-based quizzes at the end of class and a control condition of no questions. Mayer and associates found that the class in which the clickers were used throughout the lecture had one third of a grade higher than the other two conditions, which did not differ from one another. There are some methodological issues that might be a problem in interpreting the results of this study, but in general the idea that clicker-based questioning in the course of the lecture resulted in better exam performance was supported. As it takes so little time to interject this type of questioning in class, it is certainly worth trying.

## TEACHING STUDENTS HOW TO BE BETTER LISTENERS

We assume that listening is an innate skill, but you can train your students to be better listeners. For example, you might begin by asking students to write for 1 minute on "What do I hope to get out of this lecture?" or "What was the most important point in the reading assignment for the day?" Then explain how this strategy will help them to be more effective listeners in any lecture. Both of these strategies act as a "warm-up," focusing attention and activating relevant prior knowledge.

Another useful strategy is to ask students to listen to you (for 5 to 15 minutes) without taking notes and then to write a summary. You might then ask them to compare their summaries with those of one or two classmates sitting near them.

A related strategy is to tell students that you will give them 5 minutes at the end of the lecture to summarize the main points of the lecture for someone sitting near them. At the end of the class period, ask them what effect this had on their listening to the lecture, and point out that they can use this approach to lectures even if they summarize them only in their own notes.

## HOW DO STUDENTS PROCESS THE CONTENT OF A LECTURE?

Let's assume that students are allocating attention appropriately to the lecture. This alone, however, does not ensure that the content of the lecture will be understood, remembered, and applied appropriately. Even though students are trying to meet the demands of the situation, they may differ in the ways they go about processing the words that they have heard.

Marton and Säljö (1976a, 1976b) and other researchers at the University of Göteborg have described differences in the way students go about trying to learn educational materials. Some students process the material as little as possible, simply taking as many verbatim notes as they can. This would be described by Marton as a "surface approach." Other students try to see implications of what the lecturer is saying, relate what is currently being said to other information either in the lecture or in their own experience and reading, and try to understand what the author intended. They elaborate and translate the instructor's words into their own. They may question. This more thoughtful and more active kind of listening is what Marton and Säljö refer to as "deep processing."

Experienced students can probably vary their strategies from surface to deep processing of concepts, depending on the demands of the situation. Generally, deep processing better enables students to remember and use knowledge for thinking and further learning.

Pointing out relationships, asking rhetorical questions, or asking questions to be answered by class members are ways of encouraging deeper processing. You can also ask for examples of how students apply concepts to their own experiences, thus encouraging all students to realize that it is important to try to think about how concepts relate to oneself.

## SHOULD STUDENTS TAKE NOTES?

Note taking is one of the activities by which students attempt to stay attentive, but note taking is also an aid to memory. *Working memory,* or *short-term memory,* is a term used to describe the fact that one can hold only a given amount of material in mind at one time. When the lecturer presents a succession of new concepts, students' faces begin to show signs of anguish and frustration; some write furiously in their notebooks, while others stop writing in complete discouragement. Note taking thus depends on one's ability to maintain attention, understand what is being said, and hold it in working memory long enough to write it down. A study of students' lecture notes by Baker and Lombardi (1985) showed that "most students included in their notes less that 25% of the propositions judge worth of inclusion and only 50% of the targeted main ideas" (p. 28). The students did, however, distinguish between main ideas and supporting details by recording more of the former and less of the latter in their notes. Finally, there was a relationship between the notes taken and their performance on test questions related to main ideas.

However, research does support two values of note taking. One is that the notes provide an external memory that can be reviewed later; the other is that note taking involves elaboration and transformation of ideas, which aids memory (Babb & Ross, 2009; Hartley & Davies, 1978; Peper & Mayer, 1978). But note taking has costs as well as benefits. Student note-taking strategies differ. Some students take copious notes; others take none. We know that cognitive capacity is limited; that is, people can take in, understand, and store only so much information in any brief period of time. Information will be processed more effectively if the student is actively engaged in note taking—analyzing and processing the information rather than passively soaking it up—but taking notes takes capacity that may be needed for comprehension if material is difficult. Thus, encourage students to take *fewer* notes and to listen carefully when you are introducing new, difficult material. They can then fill in their notes after class.

Students' ability to process information depends on the degree to which the information can be integrated or "chunked." No one has great ability at handling large numbers of unrelated items in active memory. Thus, when students are in an area of new concepts or when the instructor is using language that is not entirely familiar to the students, students may be processing the lecture word by word or phrase by phrase and lose the sense of a sentence or of a paragraph before the end of the thought is reached. This means that lecturers need to be aware of instances in which new words or concepts are being introduced and to build in greater redundancy, as well as pauses during which students can catch up and get appropriate notes.

Snow and Peterson (1980) point out that brighter students benefit more from taking notes than less able students. For students with less background knowledge, note taking takes capacity needed for listening and comprehending, so they simply miss much of what is being said. This is not simply a matter of intelligence; rather, a student's ability to maintain materials in memory while taking notes and even to process and think about relationships between one idea and other ideas depends on the knowledge or cognitive structures the student has available for organizing and relating the material.

Hartley's research, as well as that of Annis (1981) and Kiewra (1989), suggests that a skeletal outline is helpful to students, but that with detailed notes students relax into passivity. It is better simply to provide an overall framework, which they can fill in by selecting important points and interpreting them in their own words. Because student capacity for information processing is limited and because students stop and go over a confusing part of a lecture again, you need to build more redundancy into your lectures than into writing, and you need to build in pauses where students can catch up and think rather than simply struggle to keep up.

A question that I get asked a lot these days is whether the instructor should make lecture notes available beforehand to help students take better notes. Research on this will be ongoing forever because there are so many factors to consider in answering it. However, Babb and Ross (2009) conducted a well-designed study comparing attendance, participation, and exam performance of classes that received class notes either before or after the lecture. Contrary to popular beliefs among faculty, students who received the notes prior to the lecture actually attended class more regularly and participated more during class. The researchers speculated on why that might be the case. They suggested that having the notes alerted the students to things that would be discussed in class and allowed them to prepare more efficiently. However, there was no difference on the exam performance of the two conditions, which led the researchers to propose that there are many more variables that influence exam performance than the quality of the notes that students use to study, a reasonable conclusion. There were several more side conclusions of this research, but the main conclusion of these researchers was that giving notes before class is beneficial.

If I have to make a recommendation, based on all I know about learning, I would stick with giving outline notes prior to class and allowing students to fill in the details during class. That format seems to me to be most consistent with learning and motivation research.

One can train students to write better notes by collecting student notes, evaluating the degree to which they summarize, translate, and show relationships as opposed to simply representing more or less verbatim accounts, and reporting back to the class suggestions for improvement.

## HOW TO GET STUDENTS ACTIVELY THINKING IN A LECTURE SITUATION

As we have seen, a major problem with the lecture is that students assume a passive, nonthinking, information-receiving role. Yet, if they are to remember and use the information, they need to be actively engaged in thinking about the content presented. One easy and effective device is the "minute paper" (Wilson, 1986). The minute paper is, as its title indicates, a paper literally written in a minute (or it can be a 2-minute or 3-minute paper).* Announce at the beginning of the class period that you will interrupt your lecture midway through the period so that the students may write a 1-minute paper on a topic derived from the lecture or that you will ask them at the end of the lecture to write the most important thing they have learned. Even better, you can ask them also to write the most important thing they learned from the previous week's lecture.

In the chapter "Teaching Large Classes" I describe other activities to stimulate thinking. The chapters "Facilitating Discussion" and "Active Learning" also describe methods for getting discussion in large classes.

Because many students feel that the best way to learn is to listen to an expert, you will need here (as in other departures from lecturing) to explain why active thinking is vital for effective learning.

---

*The minute paper was invented by University of California physics professor Charles Schwartz.

## *IN CONCLUSION*

What is the role of the lecturer in higher education? To communicate the teacher's enthusiasm about the subject.

The lecture is also sometimes an effective way of communicating information, particularly in classes where variations in student background, ability, or interest make feedback to the lecturer important. We have also shown that the organization and presentation of lectures may influence their effectiveness in achieving application of knowledge or in influencing attitudes. Discussion, however, is likely to be more effective than lecturing in achieving higher-level cognitive and attitudinal objectives, and combinations of lecture and discussion may be optimal.

Becoming conscious of what is going on in the students' heads as we talk; being alert to feedback from students through their facial expressions, nonverbal behavior, and oral comments; adjusting your strategies in reference to these cues—these will help you learn and help students to learn more effectively.

Be yourself!

### *Supplementary Reading*

▶ The most comprehensive book on lecturing is Donald Bligh's *What's the Use of Lectures?* (San Francisco: Jossey-Bass, 2000).

▶ A very practical guide for lecturers is George Brown's classic paperback, *Lecturing and Explaining* (London: Methuen, 1978).

▶ Barbara Davis's *Tools for Teaching*, 2nd ed. (San Francisco: Jossey-Bass, 2009), gives practical tips on preparing, delivering, and personalizing lecture classes.

▶ Jerry Evensky's chapter "The Lecture," in L. Lambert, S. L. Tice, and P. Featherstone (eds.), *University Teaching* (Syracuse, NY: Syracuse University Press, 1996), is excellent. I like his statement, "You should not think of the lecture as the passive period to be relieved by 'Now we're going to do active learning.'"

▶ The paper by James Hartley and A. Cameron, "Some Observations on the Efficiency of Lecturing," in *Educational Review*, 1967, 20(1), 30–37, is a classic.

# Assessing, Testing, and Evaluating: Grading is Not the Most Important Function

**W**hen we think about evaluating learning, most of us think about examinations—multiple-choice tests, essay tests, oral examinations, perhaps performance tests. Currently there is much interest in other methods of assessment. In this chapter I begin with suggestions for conventional testing and then suggest other methods of assessing student learning.

Let me start with nine assertions:

1. What students learn depends as much on your tests and methods of assessment as on your teaching, maybe even more. What is measured is often what ends up being valued, so be sure your measures reflect what you want the students to learn.

2. Don't think of tests simply as a means for assigning grades. Tests should facilitate learning for you as well as for your students.

3. Use some nongraded tests and assessments that provide feedback to the students and you. The CATs (Classroom Assessment Techniques; Angelo & Cross, 1993) methods for gathering information about student learning can be a real boon to you and the students. They provide several ways of gathering information and providing feedback while learning is still in progress.

4. Check your assessment methods against your goals. Are you really assessing what you hoped to achieve: for example, higher-order thinking?

5. Some goals (values, motivation, attitudes, some skills) may not be measurable by conventional tests. Look for other evidence of their development.

6. Assessment is not synonymous with testing. You can assess students' learning with classroom and out-of-class activities, what the experts refer to as embedded assessment.

7. After the course is over, students will not be able to depend on you to assess the quality of their learning. If one of your goals is the development of lifelong learning skills, students need practice in self-assessment. Peckham and Sutherland (2000) showed that developing accurate student self-assessment requires training and practice. Peer assessment of one another's papers helps develop assessment skill and improves performance (Gibbs, 1999).

8. Don't rely on one or two tests to determine grades. Varied assessments will give you better evidence to determine an appropriate grade. This is what experts call triangulation of data, which means seeing it from multiple perspectives.

9. To summarize: assessment is *not* simply an end-of-course exercise to determine student grades. Assessments can be learning experiences for students. Assessment throughout a course communicates your goals to students so that they can learn more effectively; it will identify misunderstandings that will help you teach better; it will help you pace the development of the course; and, yes, it will also help you do a better job of assigning grades.

## PLANNING METHODS OF ASSESSMENT

The first step in assessment of learning is to list your goals and objectives for the course. Once you have specified objectives, you can determine which kind of assessment is appropriate for each objective. Later in this chapter, you'll find ideas for assessing learning other than within class tests. Be open to trying something different if you're the person who gets to choose the assessment strategies. Also consider using some variety in assessing learning. Not every student can show understanding on high-stakes tests; some students might do better on written assignments or on projects or shorter assessments.

One way of maintaining a balance is to construct a grid, listing objectives along the side of the page and content areas along the top. If you then put a tally mark in the appropriate cells of the grid as you decide on assessment types you are going to use, you can monitor the degree to which your overall assessment plan adequately samples the objectives and content desired. Some objectives will be appropriate for in-class tests, some for out-of-class assignments, some for short periods of time, some for longer time periods. If you're having a hard time balancing content coverage in your assessment, this is one way to make sure you emphasize higher-level thinking along with basic information. The grid also helps you see gaps or overlaps so you can adjust the system as you create the syllabus or assignments.

Admittedly, it is more difficult to devise measures of complex, higher-level objectives. Yet the very effort to do so will, I believe, have an influence on student motivation and learning. Moreover, consideration of these objectives may help you break out of the conventional forms of testing. For example, in my classes in introductory psychology, the desired goals include developing greater curiosity about behavior, awareness of dimensions of behavior that might ordinarily be ignored, and increased ability to describe and analyze behavior objectively. To get at this I have sometimes used a video as a stimulus, and then had them write in response to questions that have to do with their reactions to the film; or I have asked students to leave the classroom for 15 minutes and then return and report on some interesting behavior they observed. I have brought in scientific journals and asked students to find an article of interest and to write their reactions to it. I have asked for analyses of newspaper items to get at the degree to which students can read critically. These kinds of assessments embedded in the ongoing class activities are often not recognized as being "tests" and therefore do not fall prey to all the misconceptions and anxieties that students have about being tested. If you then have the students talk about what they have written, they often frame these assessments as learning activities rather than tests, which is a good way to think about them. Using materials with somewhat greater apparent relevance to course objectives than that of typical test items is more fun for the students taking the test—and more fun to grade.

## METHODS OF ASSESSING LEARNING

### Tests: In and Out of Class

Because grades in many courses are determined to a great degree by test scores, tests are among the most familiar, but often most frustrating, aspects of the course to many students and arouse a great deal of overt and covert aggression. If teachers attempt to go beyond the usual practice of asking simply for memory of information from the textbook or lectures, they are immediately deluged with the complaint, "These are the most ambiguous tests I have ever taken!" This type of assessment is covered in Chapter 8, "Testing: The Details," but just to put them in the context of assessment in general, I have included a few more general ideas here along with other assessment strategies.

Because some course examinations emphasize the recall of facts, many students demand *teaching* that emphasizes memorization of facts. One student wrote on a slip evaluating me, "The instructor is very interesting and worthwhile, but I have rated him low because he doesn't give us enough facts. The sort of job I get will depend on my grades, and I have little chance of beating other students out for an A unless I can get a couple of pages of notes each period."

Students may object at first to tests requiring them to think, but if you emphasize that the tests will measure their abilities to use their knowledge, you can greatly influence their goals in the course. This is indicated by a student comment we received: "More of the course should be like the tests. They make us apply what we've learned." Marton and Säljö (1976b) showed that questions demanding understanding rather than memory of detailed facts resulted in differing styles of studying for later tests and better retention. Foos and Fisher (1988) showed that tests requiring inferences enhanced learning more than those requiring memorized knowledge.

However, sometimes you just want to know if the students are getting the basics down before you move on to the bigger issues. For this level of assessment, in-class quizzes and tests are just the thing. They don't have to be the major mid-semester type of marathon unless you are doing summative assessment (that means assessments that demonstrate what the students have learned after they have finished learning it). The short pre-post lecture mastery quizzes and questions spread throughout a lecture can be both assessments and spurs to learning, so think beyond the standard 60 minute exam or take-home test we're all so used to and consider other ways of getting similar or related information about learning.

## Performance Assessment (Authentic Assessment)

Over two decades ago, Alverno College in Milwaukee, Wisconsin, instituted a student-centered curriculum and performance assessment plan that has become a significant model for American colleges and universities. Faculty members construct learning situations in which they can observe student performance and judge the performance on the basis of specified criteria. The faculty has defined developmental levels in each of several abilities that students are expected to achieve. Since no one situation is sufficient for assessing a complex ability, the assessment plan stresses multiple modes of assessment related to real-life contexts. In addition, faculty actively train students in methods of self-assessment, an important outcome if students are to continue learning when there are no longer teachers around to evaluate their work (see Alverno College Faculty, 1994; Mentkowski & Loacker, 1985; Mentkowski et al., 2000).

Many other college teachers are using methods of evaluating learning that are more authentically related to later uses of learning than are conventional tests. For example, in chemistry, mathematics, and engineering courses instructors now use fewer standard abstract problems that can be solved by algorithms and more problems that describe situations in which more than one approach could be used and in which alternative solutions are possible. Such "authentic" assessments are particularly appropriate for service learning situations.

Simulations (on computers or role-played), hands-on field or laboratory exercises, research projects, and juried presentations (such as are used in music, art, and architecture) are also methods related more closely to later use of learning. Paper-and-pencil tasks used to evaluate these types of learning may require similarity judgments, sorting, or successive choices or predictions following sequential presentation of information about a case, scenario, or situation based on the real problems that a professional might face.

## Graphic Representations of Concepts

An organized framework of concepts is important for further learning and thinking. Graphic representations of conceptual relationships may be useful both for teaching and for assessing learning. Our research group (Naveh-Benjamin, Lin, & McKeachie, 1991; Naveh-Benjamin et al., 1989; Naveh-Benjamin et al., 1986) developed two methods (the "ordered tree" and "fill-in-the-structure," or FITS) that we use to assess the development of conceptual relationships during college courses. In both of these methods the instructor chooses a number of concepts and arranges them in a hierarchical structure like that depicted in Figure 7.1 (which shows an example used in my Learning to Learn course). For the FITS task the instructor gives the students a copy of the basic structure with some concepts missing. The students are then asked to fill in the blanks.

Fill in the blanks from the list below. (12 points)

a. Attention
b. Chunking
c. Elaboration
d. Encoding
e. Expectancy
f. Extrinsic
g. Information processing
h. Means-end analysis
i. Memory
j. Motivation
k. Planning
l. Recognition
m. Retrieval
n. Schema
o. Self-efficacy
p. Self-regulation
q. Working backward
r. Working memory (STM)

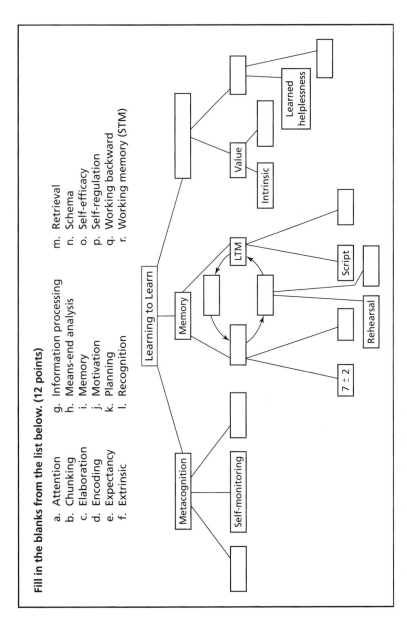

**FIGURE 7.1 Learning to Learning Chart**

## Journals, Research Papers, and Annotated Bibliographies

Journals, research papers, and reports come closer to the goals of authentic assessment than do most conventional tests. Journals are particularly useful in helping students develop critical reflection and self-awareness (MacGregor, 1993; Rhoads & Howard, 1998; Connor-Greene, 2000). The chapter "Using High-Stakes and Low-Stakes Writing to Enhance Learning" deals with such writing in detail. Annotated bibliographies can be a useful preparation for writing as well as a tool for assessment. Moreover, annotated bibliographies can be a resource for the whole class (Miller, 1998). Evaluating these products can be improved if you use the rubric method described in Chapter 10 on grading. A rubric is basically a carefully laid out analysis of the key characteristics of the assignment and how well the student met your expectations for each of them. Creating one prior to grading and using it during grading keeps you from being inconsistent in evaluating the papers and makes explaining the grades a lot easier later.

## Portfolios

Traditionally used in art and architecture classes, portfolios are becoming popular in a variety of subjects and at all levels of education. Although there are many types of portfolios, they basically are used to highlight work that individual students have accomplished over a period of time. A portfolio might include early as well as later examples in order to demonstrate progress, or a portfolio may be simply a presentation of the student's best work or, better yet, the student's own descriptions of how the work helped his or her development. In mathematics or science a portfolio might consist of problems or lab reports representing various course topics written up to show the student's understanding. Portfolios in other courses might include entries from journals describing reactions to reading, classroom experiences, or learning occurring outside the classroom; papers; notes for presentations to the class; and other materials. A portfolio helps both the students and the instructor see how students have progressed. Students report increased self-awareness, and I frequently find evidence of learning (or the lack of it) that I otherwise would have missed. Palomba and Banta (1999) provide a thorough discussion of the use and pragmatics of portfolios.

## Peer Assessment

Even if you use the best assessment and grading procedures, some students will be frustrated with their grades. You can prevent some aggression if you help students develop skills in self-assessment. As mentioned earlier, this takes practice, but a lot of instructors are beginning to incorporate peer assessment into their classes (Topping, 1998). In these instances, students learn about the criteria used for assessing their work, and they learn to apply those criteria to their work before they turn it in, a real benefit for the instructor. Some instructors have developed computer-based peer reviewing systems (called "calibrated peer review") that involve students grading other students' work online using a carefully refined rubric given by the instructor (Robinson, 2001; Davies, 2000).

On a more modest level, you can have your students evaluate one another's work in hard copy. After collecting tests or papers, redistribute them randomly with a rubric for evaluation. Encourage the students to write helpful comments as well as an evaluation. After students evaluate the papers they were given, ask them to exchange with a neighbor, evaluate the paper given to the neighbor, and then compare notes on their evaluations.

What you do next will probably depend on the size of your class. In a small class I collect the papers and evaluations and review them before returning them to the evaluators and students evaluated. If the class is larger, I ask the class to discuss the process, what problems they encountered, and what they learned.

## Assessing Group Work

As teachers use more and more team projects and cooperative learning, one of the frequently asked questions is "How can I assess group work?" First let's be clear about what we're assessing. You might be assessing student learning in the form of papers or products produced by the group or by members of the group. Or you might be assessing the way in which students worked together in the group, focusing on group process and teamwork more than on content learning.

To measure how much content each student has learned, I sometimes ask group members to write individual reports. Students are told that purely descriptive parts, such as the research design, may be the same on all papers but that parts representing thinking are to represent the students' own thinking—although students are encouraged to read and discuss each other's papers before submitting them. I sometimes include an exam question relevant to the group projects; currently, I ask each group to submit a single report, which I evaluate.

To evaluate individual contributions to the group, I also ask each student to turn in a slip of paper listing the members of his or her group and dividing 100 points in proportion to each member's contribution. Almost all groups apportion the points equally because I monitor the group's progress and try to get problems solved before the final product. In addition, students understand that the grade will be lowered for any student whose contribution is perceived to be less than that of other group members. Thus, on a 100-point project I might give only 50 points to a student whose contributions were 10 percent or less as judged by his or her teammates. In most such cases I would have been aware of the problem earlier and discussed it with the group and the student, but even then I try to talk with the student before assigning the lower grade.

Another strategy is to ask group members to simply describe the work contributed by other members without assessing its value. This allows them to be nonjudgmental, leaving the judgment calls up to me. Group members' descriptions of each member's contribution can be compared to get a more accurate picture of what each individual contributed.

Some instructors develop group rating forms that list the key group contributions that each member is expected to make. Each group member evaluates the other members according to those criteria. I've found it very useful to include the students in the process of identifying those key contributions. At the beginning of a group-oriented project, I have a class discussion about what constitutes good group work. Once we all agree on the behaviors that fit that designation, I draw up a contract that all the students agree to. The peer assessment and my assessment of each student's work are then based on those criteria. Because they have contributed to defining the criteria, the students have a pretty clear idea about what is expected of them.

## Embedded Assessment

Wilson and Sloane (2000) have provided a good description of the spirit behind embedded assessment. "By using the term *embedded* we mean that opportunities to assess student progress and performance are integrated into the instructional materials and are virtually indistinguishable from the everyday classroom activities" (p. 182). A great example of embedded assessments that has surfaced recently is the use of personal response systems in the classroom, as discussed in Chapter 17 on technology. What sets embedded assessments apart from just plain classroom activities and makes them assessment is that the instructor can gather information about individual as well as class performance, information that can be used to diagnose student problems, provide feedback, and make adjustments, but also be graded and figured into an overall grade. Another unique aspect of embedded assessment is that it can be repeated across the semester and give you an idea about student growth in understanding across time. Seeing that they are making progress serves as a good source of motivation for students, too.

You should think about what goes on in your class meetings and whether there are data that could be collected in the process of learning that would be useful. For example, in my class the students are constantly working on applying the ideas we are discussing to their future professional situations by responding to scenarios on an in-class activity sheet. The sheet forms the basis of our discussions and lets both me and the students know if they are really understanding the concepts. If the students were actually out in the field observing children's behavior, their field notes and write-ups could be used as assessments as well.

## Classroom Assessment

The primary purpose of assessment is to provide feedback to students and teacher so that learning can be facilitated. *Classroom assessment* is the term popularized by Pat Cross and Tom Angelo to describe a variety of non-graded methods of getting feedback on student learning. I described minute papers in the preceding chapter. Question posting (discussed in the chapter "Meeting a Class for the First Time") and the two-column method (in the "Facilitating Discussion" chapter) are ways of getting feedback as well as of facilitating student learning. Angelo and Cross (1993) describe a variety of classroom assessment techniques. Regular use of such formative assessment may change the way students view what should happen in class. My own students consistently report how much they valued these regular assessments.

## *IN CONCLUSION*

1. Learning is more important than grading.

2. Tests and other assessments should be learning experiences as well as evaluation devices.

3. Providing feedback is more important than assigning a grade. You can use nongraded evaluation as well as evaluation for assigning grades.

4. Try to assess the attainment of all your objectives, even if some objectives (such as increased motivation for learning) are not appropriate criteria for grades.

5. Avoid evaluation devices that increase anxiety and competition.

## *Supplementary Reading*

Paul Ramsden's chapter "Assessing for Understanding," in his book *Learning to Teach in Higher Education* (London: Routledge, 1992), presents a wise perspective on assessment and gives examples from chemistry, anatomy, materials technology, engineering, history of art, statistics, medicine, and physics.

Tom Angelo and Pat Cross's *Classroom Assessment Techniques* (1993) has become almost a bible for faculty interested in incorporating more ongoing assessment in their classes.

*500 Tips on Assessment* by Sally Brown, Phil Race, and Brenda Smith (London: Kogan Page, 1996) is a marvelous compendium of useful suggestions on all types of assessment, ranging from self-assessment through group assessment, multiple-choice tests, and assessment of performance, lab work, and dissertations.

Graham Gibbs discusses modern methods of assessing learner-centered courses in his book *Assessing Student-Centered Courses* (Oxford: Oxford Centre for Staff Development, 1995). Chapters give case studies illustrating assessment of group work, projects, journals, skills, and portfolios.

*Assessment Matters in Higher Education*, edited by Sally Brown and Angela Glasner (Buckingham, UK, and Philadelphia: Society for Research into Higher Education and Open University, 1999), describes innovative approaches to assessment and current United Kingdom practices in a variety of disciplines. There is an entire section on peer assessment and self-assessment. (I suspect that the pun in the title was intentional.)

*Assessment Essentials: Planning, Implementing and Improving Assessment in Higher Education* by Catherine Palomba and Trudy Banta (San Francisco: Jossey-Bass, 1999) is a fine resource on all manner of assessment strategies and the rules that guide their use.

# Testing: The Details

f your assessment plans call for the use of in-class testing (and they probably will), you can do a lot to make sure that the test you design serves the assessment purposes you had in mind. In this chapter, I'm going to get down to the nitty-gritty details of writing a test. Not all the details will fit every testing situation, but the planning and execution of most tests will follow this decision process.

## WHEN TO TEST

Because tests are so important in making the goals of a course concrete and influencing student methods of learning, I give an ungraded quiz during the first week and a graded test after the third or fourth week of a 14-week semester. To reduce the stress I weight early tests very little in determining the final grade. An early test gets students started—they don't delay their studying until the conventional midterm examination—and it will help you to identify problems early while they are still remediable. Thus, early tests should demand the style of learning you expect, and they need to be constructed carefully even though their purpose is more motivational and diagnostic than evaluative.

The amount and frequency of tests should depend on the background of your students and the nature of the content. In a first-year course in an area new to students, frequent short tests early in the term facilitate learning, as demonstrated in the Personalized System of Instruction (Keller, 1968). Generally, however, I want to wean students from studying for tests, so that they will become lifelong learners able to evaluate their own learning. This implies less frequent testing as learners become more experienced. It probably also implies questions requiring broader integration and more detailed analysis as learners advance.

# CONSTRUCTING THE TEST

In planning your tests you may want to use a mix of different types of questions in order to balance measurements of the varied goals of education. The following sections describe the strengths and weaknesses of each type of question, as well as offer tips on constructing items.

## Choosing the Type of Question

The instructor who is about to give an examination is in a conflict situation. The administration of an examination consists of two time-consuming procedures: (1) construction of the examination and (2) grading. Unfortunately, it appears to be generally true that the examinations that are easiest to construct are the most difficult to grade and vice versa.

Teachers often base their choice of question types solely on class size, using multiple-choice tests for large classes, short-answer questions for medium-sized classes, and essay questions for small classes. Class size is certainly an important factor, but your educational goals should take precedence. Your goals almost always will require the use of some essay questions, problems, or other items requiring analysis, integration, or application.

**Problems.** In mathematics, science, and some other disciplines, a test typically consists of problems. The value of problems depends on the degree to which they elicit the sort of problem-solving skills that are your goals. Some problems are too trite and stereotypic to have much value as indicators of whether students understand the steps they are following. In other cases the answer depends to such a large extent on tedious calculations that only a small sample of problems can be tested. In such cases you might provide calculations leading up to a certain point and ask students to complete the problem, or you might use a multiple-choice question about the proper procedure—for example, "Which of the following problems can be solved by procedure $x$?" Or you might have students set up the problem without actually calculating the final answer. Many instructors who have problem solving as their goal say that setting the problem up correctly is more than half the battle, yet students often jump right to a formulaic response. If the grade is based solely on problem setup, students will pay more attention to it. Many teachers use problems that may be solved in more than one way or that have more than one satisfactory answer. In this case special emphasis in both teaching and grading should be on justifying the solution strategy rather than on the specific answer. This has the advantage of focusing students' attention on the process rather than on the product.

**Short-Answer Items.**  Here is an example of a short-answer item: "Give one example from your own experience of the concept of elaboration." In responding, a student might describe an experience of explaining a concept to another student or of thinking about the relationship of a fact to a general principle. Such a question is restricted enough that it is not often difficult to judge whether the expected answer is there. Furthermore, such questions can be presented in a format that allows only a small amount of space for the answer. The student tendency to employ the "shotgun" approach to the examination is thus inhibited.

Short-answer questions permit coverage of assigned materials without asking for petty details. Unfortunately, many short-answer questions test only recall of specific facts. Short-answer questions, however, can do more than testing recall. If you are trying to develop skill in analysis or diagnosis, for example, you may present case material or a description of an experiment and ask what questions they would ask. You can then provide additional information that they can use in an analysis. Or a short-answer question can ask students to solve a problem or propose a hypothesis relevant to information learned earlier. An example is the following question from a course on the psychology of aging:

1. Given the *differences* in ways in which men and women experience middle age, and the fact that depression rises as a psychiatric symptom in middle age, how might the *causes* of the depression differ for men and women at this time in life?

**Essay Items.**  Although the short-answer examination is very useful in certain situations, I recommend that, if possible, you include at least one essay question on examinations in most college courses. Experiments indicate that students study more efficiently for essay-type examinations than for objective tests (d'Ydewalle, Swerts, & de Corte, 1983; McCluskey, 1934; Monaco, 1977). Thus in addition to the values of essay tests as evaluation devices, you should take into consideration their potential educational value as stimuli to students' reflection about conceptual relationships, possible applications, or aspects of thinking. One strategy is to pass out several questions the week before the test and tell students that these are the sorts of questions you will use—that, in fact, you may even use one of these very questions.

Where the tests can be returned with comments, essay examinations may give students practice in organized, creative thinking about a subject and an opportunity to check their thinking against the standards of someone with more experience and ability in the field. Johnson (1975) demonstrated that when marginal comments on earlier tests emphasized creativity, creativity on the final exam was improved.

In large classes where time is limited and in classes where the writing itself is not the point of the question, you can format the answer sheet to break a long, complex answer into its critical components, each of which has a space for an answer. For example, in my class the last problem on every exam is a case to which the students must apply whatever theory we have been studying. So at the top of the sheet, there is a short description of the scenario. Then there is a space headed "In five sentences or fewer, describe your proposed solution to this scenario based on theory X." About two inches farther down the sheet there is another instruction: "In the spaces below connect the components of your solution to three aspects of theory X that are relevant and explain their relevance." That is followed by three spaces, each headed like this:

aspect one: (space)

connection to your solution and why: (space)

This considerably speeds up my grading time because rather than searching through a long essay organized (I hope) by the student, I can at a glance see if the student has provided a reasonable solution and tied it to the theory. I'm not "giving away the answer" because the prompts are fairly broad; I'm simply imposing a little organization on the answer to make my grading easier. And maybe students learn something about structuring an answer efficiently, too.

Finally, if you read the examinations yourself (or at least some of them), you get some excellent information on what students are learning.

**True-False Items.** Although true-false examinations are rather easy to make up, I don't ordinarily advocate their use. Toppino and Brochin (1989) showed that students tend after the test to remember the false items as being true—an outcome not conducive to achieving your objectives. If you do use true-false items, ask students to explain their answers. This will encourage reflection and help you understand why there were some common misunderstandings.

**Multiple-Choice and Matching Items.** It is improbable that most teachers can adequately measure all their objectives with a test made up entirely of multiple-choice questions. Matching questions are similar to multiple-choice in that the student must discriminate between the correct answer and other choices. Nonetheless, for some purposes multiple-choice items are useful. They can measure both simple knowledge and precise discrimination. They can measure ability to apply concepts or principles; they can assess elements of problem solving. But they are not likely to assess organization of ideas, conceptual relationships, or many of the skills involved in higher-order thinking.

Good multiple-choice questions are difficult to construct. (The greater your experience in their construction, the more you realize how long it takes per item to construct a reasonably fair, accurate, and inclusive question.) Because of this difficulty, the construction of such items is probably not worthwhile unless they will be administered to several hundred students, either in a single year or in successive years. Some books that can help you write high-quality items, if you are so inclined, are referenced at the end of this chapter.

Even if you don't pretest the items on students, it is worthwhile to have someone take the test before it is in its final form. If you can persuade a skilled test taker who doesn't know the subject matter to take the test, you will probably be surprised at how many he or she gets right simply from cues that you provided in the questions.

## How Many Questions Should You Use?

Obviously, the number of questions depends on the type and difficulty of each question. I prefer to give tests without a time limit, but the constraints of class scheduling usually require that you clear the classroom so that the next class can begin. Thus, you must plan the length of the exam so that the slowest students have time to finish before the end of the period. As a rule of thumb I allow about 1 minute per item for multiple-choice or fill-in-the-blank items, 2 minutes per short-answer question

## Constructing Multiple-Choice Items

1. Teachers' manuals that accompany many textbooks contain multiple-choice items. You should not rely on a manual as the source of all your questions, because the manual probably will not contain many good questions and may cover only textbook material. You need to assess what students have learned in class as well as their understanding of what they have read.

2. A second source of multiple-choice items is the students themselves. They are not a particularly satisfactory source of test questions, because only about 10 percent of the items thus written will be usable. However, this technique is a useful pedagogical device because it gets the students to read their assignments more analytically. It also gives the instructor a good index of what the students are getting out of the various sections of their reading, and it gives you a chance to remind them of the goals of the course going beyond recall of details.

3. There are statistical methods for evaluating questions, but the best suggestions for improvement come from students themselves in their discussion of the test. It seems almost criminal to waste this experience with items; therefore I recommend a permanent file.

4. If you have a problem but no good distractor (incorrect alternative), give the item in short-answer or essay form and use the students' own responses for alternatives for a later use of the item in multiple-choice form.

5. Multiple-choice questions typically have four or five alternatives. Rather than wasting your and your students' time with extra alternatives that don't test a discrimination that is important, use only as many alternatives as make meaningful discriminations. Costin (1972) showed that three-choice items are about as effective as four-choice.

6. For measuring understanding, I like questions that require the student to predict the outcome of a situation, rather than questions that simply ask the student to label the phenomenon.

7. Multiple-choice items need not stand alone. You can use a sequence of related items to measure more complex thinking.

8. Grouping items under headings will improve student performance (Marcinkiewicz & Clariana, 1997).

requiring more than a sentence answer, 10 or 15 minutes for a limited essay question, and a half-hour to an hour for a broader question requiring more than a page or two to answer. You can get a rough estimate of time requirements by simply timing how long it takes to actually read the items without answering them. That can serve as a minimum time requirement. If you ask someone else to take the test as suggested above, time that person, too.

## TESTS FROM THE STUDENT PERSPECTIVE

It's not surprising that our students get so concerned about tests and other assessments. More is riding on their performance than just a grade in the class. All kinds of things depend on a student's grade point average, many of them with no apparent relationship to scholarly achievement. For example, in some areas, students with good grades get lower car insurance rates! Maybe the insurance companies figure that you must be home studying all the time to get such good grades, so you're not as likely to have an accident!

On a more serious note, no one is totally comfortable with being assessed, and, rightly or wrongly, students often equate grades with self-worth. We owe it to them to help them maximize their potential for good performance by dealing with some of the things that might get in the way.

## REDUCING STUDENT FRUSTRATION AND AGGRESSION

Most beginning teachers find the aggression that students direct against them after a test very disturbing. It is likely to impair the instructor's rapport with the class and may actually be a block to learning. Thus, strategies for reducing the aggression seem to be worthwhile.

The most obvious solution to the problem is to reduce students' frustration when taking tests. You can do this by emphasizing the contribution the course can make to students' long-range goals. Explaining how and why you test as you do will also help. A nongraded practice test will provide guidance. Periodic assessments of learning (not necessarily graded) to help students assess their own progress and to help you identify problems, as well as frequent explanations of why and how you test and assess learning, should reduce students' anxiety and frustration about testing.

Yet no matter how much you emphasize long-range goals, the tests will in large measure determine what students do. Do you want them to memorize details? Then give the usual memory-of-details test. But if you want more, make your objectives clear, and make sure that your tests measure the attainment of those objectives. If you used the Bloom Taxonomy of Educational Objectives or Biggs's SOLO Taxonomy as suggested in the chapter "Countdown for Course Preparation," remind the students of these levels before each test.

Test instructions should indicate whether students are to guess, what the time limit is, and any other directions that define the nature of the expected responses. For the typical classroom examination, there is no point in a correction for guessing. Emphasizing in the multiple-choice test introduction that students should choose the *best* answer may help prevent lengthy discussion with students who dream up a remote instance in which the correct alternative might be wrong.

Research I did with my colleagues (1955) and research by Smith and Rockett (1958) demonstrated that on multiple-choice tests the instruction "Feel free to write comments," with blank space by each question for the comments, results in higher scores, especially for anxious students. A problem with this strategy is that students these days have been taught to make notes to themselves on the test, so you may find yourself reading a lot of stuff not really written to you. Here is how I have solved this problem and the problem of students who want to explain every item. I allow students to explain their choices for up to three questions. They star the question that they want to elaborate on; then on the last page of the test, called the "explanations page," they write their thoughts and indicate why they answered the way they did. I only read the explanations to questions that they have missed. This process greatly reduces their anxiety and saves me grading time. It also forces them to pick their battles; they can't simply write everything they know for every question in hopes that the correct answer is in there somewhere.

## HELPING STUDENTS BECOME TEST-WISE

Particularly in the case of multiple-choice examinations, I have found that a good morale builder is spending 15 minutes or so the day before the first test telling students how to take a test of this sort and familiarizing them with the format. Some of the points that I make in such a lecture follow.

## Taking Multiple-Choice Tests

The student taking a multiple-choice examination is essentially in the same position as a poker player. The object is to get into a position where you are betting on a sure thing. If this is impossible, at least make your bet on the choice where the odds are in your favor. In poker, you are in the strongest position if you know exactly what your opponent has; in the examination situation, you are in the strongest position if you know the material. There is no substitute for study. Nevertheless, you are not likely to be absolutely certain of all the right answers, and when you are not, certain techniques may help.

What I recommend to the student is this. First go through the examination and answer all of the items you know. In addition to getting a certain amount of the examination done without spending a lot of time on single, difficult items, you probably will find that going through the complete test once in this way will suggest the answers to questions that might have been difficult had they been answered in numerical order. When you have gone through the test once in this fashion, go through it again and answer any questions whose answers are now obvious. Usually there will still be a few unanswered questions. It is in connection with these that certain tricks may be useful.

If the item is multiple choice, don't simply guess at this stage of the game. See whether it is possible to eliminate some of the choices as incorrect. In a four-choice multiple-choice item, the probability of getting the answer right by pure guesswork is one in four; if you can eliminate two of the choices, your chances improve to 50–50. So take advantage of the mathematics of the situation.

After completing the examination, go through the whole thing again to check your choices to make sure that you still regard them as correct and to make sure that you made no clerical errors when recording them. In this connection, it is worthwhile to point out to students the common misconception that when you change your answers, you usually change from right answers to wrong ones. Mueller and Wasser (1977) reviewed 18 studies demonstrating that most students gain more than they lose on changed answers.

## Taking Essay Tests

My instructions for essay exams are simpler.

1. Outline your answer before writing it. This provides a check against the common error of omitting one part of the answer.

2. If a question completely baffles you, start writing on the back of your paper anything you know that could possibly be relevant. This starts your memory functioning, and usually you'll soon find that you have some relevant ideas.

3. If you are still at a loss, admit it, write a *related* question that you can answer, and answer it. Most instructors will give you at least a few points more than if you wrote nothing.

4. Write as well as you can. Even if I intend not to grade on writing ability, my judgment is negatively influenced when I have to struggle to read poor handwriting or surmount poor grammar and sentence structure. Moreover, because I believe that every course is responsible for teaching writing, writing always enters into my grading.

## Why Teach Test Taking?

Is it wise to give students these tips? The answer to this question depends on your purposes in giving an examination. If you want to test for "test-taking" ability, you will not want to give students such hints. At any rate, this orientation seems to have the effect of conveying to students the notion that you are not trying to "outsmart" them and are instead interested in helping them get as high a grade as their learning warrants.

### Coping with Test Anxiety

Many students struggle with test anxiety because of the high-stakes testing they experienced in the past and the emphasis on grades they're experiencing now. A student may know the material but blank out during the test and be unable to show what he or she knows. If my students are having such problems, I can do several things to help:

1. I can lower the stakes of any given test. By having several assessments of learning, I can lower the overall importance of any one test and thereby lower students' anxiety about their performance on it.

2. I can offer "second chances" to students who experience difficulties while taking a test. This means allowing them after the test to earn back some of the points they missed. I describe this process later in this chapter. This is a good learning strategy, and more important for test-anxious students, it relieves some of the pressure and therefore some of the anxiety.

3. I already mentioned the strategy of allowing students to explain their answers more thoroughly on the test itself. This also removes some of the pressure that comes with uncertainty about a particular answer.

4. Prior to the test day I familiarize students with what the test will actually look like, the kinds of questions, any special procedures they'll need to follow, and how I'll grade the test. This removes a lot of the unknowns associated with the test, which are a big source of anxiety.

5. I offer ideas about studying and about getting physically ready for the test, relaxation strategies (taking deep breaths, putting down the pencil and flexing your fingers, and so on). Sometimes I even coach students to think about what they're saying to themselves that contributes to their anxiety—for example, saying, "I've *got* to get an A," instead of, "I'm going to do OK," is more likely to produce anxiety.

## ADMINISTERING THE TEST

Handing out a test should be a simple matter. Usually it is, but in large classes, simple administrative matters can become disasters. It is hard to imagine how angry and upset students can become while waiting only 10 minutes for the proctors to finish distributing the test forms. And if this doesn't move you, imagine your feelings when you find that you don't have enough tests for all of the students. (It has happened to me twice—deserving a place among my worst moments in teaching!)

How can you avoid such problems?

1. If you are having tests duplicated, ask for at least 10 percent extra—more if the test is administered in several rooms. (Some proctor always walks off with too many.) This gives you insurance against miscounting and against omitted or blank pages on some copies.

2. Unless there is some compelling reason to distribute the tests later, have your proctors pass out the tests as students come into the room. This protects students from mounting waves of panic while they wait for the tests to be distributed.

3. Minimize interruptions. Tell students before the exam that you will write announcements, instructions, or corrections on the board. Some exam periods are less a measure of achievement than a test of the students' ability to work despite the instructor's interruptions.

# ALTERNATIVE TESTING MODELS GAINING FAVOR

## Group Testing

Given the prevalence of group work in classes these days, some instructors have begun to administer group tests as well. Since the students have been encouraged and actually required to study and work in groups while learning, the logic is that asking them to perform in an individual situation on the test contradicts what they have learned about peer support. Although I may not agree with that logic, I do agree that taking a test in a group situation is a good learning experience for the same reasons that collaborative learning is a good teaching method: students learn a lot from one another and from having to explain their own answers.

The most common method for this strategy is to have the students initially take the test on their own. Then after turning their copy in, they get into a group (usually the one they've been working with all semester) and go through the test again to come up with a group response to the test. It is amazing how much energy there is during this activity! It has the advantage of giving the students immediate feedback on their test performance by comparing their responses to their groupmates', and it also corrects any misconceptions right away—something that we can't do very easily in a regular test situation. Grades are a combination of individual test performance and group test performance.

There are many concerns about this strategy, most of them having to do with grading and with difficulties posed by room configurations. There is also the possibility of one student dominating the group's responses to the test. These are the same problems that arise whenever group work is suggested, and they must be at least acknowledged. Achacoso and Svinicki's (2005) descriptions of group testing by a couple of different instructors in different settings may inform your understanding of this trend.

## Online Testing

Another new trend in testing is the use of testing online. In this model students take their tests on a computer, either their own or at a testing center. There are almost as many varieties of this strategy as there are instructors. Achacoso and Svinicki (2005) provide examples of different online testing strategies.

The advantage of online testing is that it can allow an instructor to give a customized test to each student through the miracles of technology and a large database of questions. Given what you know about computers, I'm sure you can imagine all the clever ways that the technology can modify, randomize, customize, and evaluate a student's test. For example, there is one format that calibrates the difficulty of each subsequent item based on whether the current item was answered correctly. This particular mode is being used with the large standardized placement tests, such as the GRE or LSAT. That's probably a little too fancy for a regular classroom test, but future developments in software may make it possible for individual instructors to design such systems just as we can now design online tutorials much more easily.

Another advantage of the online testing idea is that the instructor can include simulations that are interactive. Such questions would provide a much better test of student understanding than the static problems that can be included in paper-and-pencil tests.

The difficulty with such testing is maintaining testing integrity. Unless the test is administered under secure conditions—for example, in a computer lab or testing facility—the instructor may not be able to ensure that the person submitting the test is really the designated student or whether the student is making inappropriate use of support materials during the test. Many institutions are considering the feasibility of providing large computer-based testing centers, and it will be interesting to see whether such efforts are scalable to the kinds of large classes in which they might be the most useful.

## WHAT TO DO ABOUT CHEATING

It may be hard for you to believe that your students would ever cheat—"Maybe other students cheat, but not mine!" Unfortunately, studies of cheating behavior over several decades invariably find that a majority of students report that they have cheated at some time (McCabe & Trevino, 1996). A recent Google search on "cheating in college" turned up over 400,000 pages! Most students would rather not cheat, but the pressures for good grades are so intense that many students feel that they, too, must cheat if they believe that other students are cheating. In my experience the most common excuse given by a student caught cheating is that other students were cheating and the teacher didn't seem to care, at least not enough to do anything to prevent or stop cheating. Many students thus feel less stress when an examination is well managed and well proctored.

## Why Do Students Cheat?

The research on this question is alarmingly consistent. The most significant factor in a student's decision to cheat is peer influence (McCabe, Trevino, & Butterfield, 2001). McCabe and Trevino (1996) report that students don't believe they'll get caught because instructors are indifferent to their activities. Gerdeman (2000) reports students' belief that if they do get caught they won't be punished severely even if the institution has policies for dealing with such misconduct. In today's high-stakes testing environment, where there is such a strong emphasis on grades, students believe there is a large reward for success at any cost (Whitley, 1998). Certainly they see on the news successful cheaters in the real world constantly getting away without severe penalties.

## How Do Students Cheat?

1. Students pass information to a neighbor; for example, they may loan a neighbor an eraser with the answer on the eraser.

2. Students use notes written on clothing, skin, or small note cards.

3. Students store answers in calculators or cassette recorders used during the exam.

4. Students peek at a knowledgeable neighbor's exam (sometimes seated in groups around the best student in the fraternity).

5. Students use tapping, hand code, cell phones, instant messaging, or other communication.

6. Students accuse the teacher of losing an exam (that they never turned in).

7. Students pay someone else to take an exam or write a paper for them.

8. Students copy or paraphrase material for a paper without acknowledging the source.

## Preventing Cheating

"OK, so we want to prevent cheating. What can we do?"

If it's true that cheating comes from some of the causes just mentioned, then there is a lot of proactive action that you can take to prevent it or discourage it from happening. Researchers are fairly consistent in many of their recommendations. Here are a few that I've gleaned from the now extensive literature on cheating in college (Gerdeman, 2000; McMurtry, 2001; Pulvers & Diekhoff, 1999; plus Websites from teaching and learning sites at many of the major universities around the country such as the University of Illinois and the University of California at Santa Barbara). They're fairly consistent with my own practices.

An obvious first answer is to reduce the pressure. While you can't affect the general academic atmosphere that puts heavy emphasis on grades, you can influence the pressure in your own course, for example, by providing a number of opportunities for students to demonstrate achievement of course goals, rather than relying on a single examination. A second answer is to address the issue in your syllabus or have a discussion on the topic early in your course.

A third answer is to make reasonable demands and write a reasonable and interesting test. Some cheating is simply the result of frustration and desperation arising from assignments too long to be covered adequately or tests requiring memorization of trivial details. In some cases cheating is simply a way of getting back at an unreasonable, hostile teacher.

A fourth answer is to develop group norms supporting honesty. I frequently give my classes a chance to vote on whether or not we will conduct the tests on the honor system. I announce that we will not use the honor system unless the vote is unanimous, since it will not work unless everyone feels committed to it. If the vote is unanimous, I remind the students of it on the day of the exam and ask whether they still wish to have the test under the honor system. I haven't collected data on the success of this approach, but I've never had a complaint about it. Although only a minority of classes vote for the honor system, a discussion of academic dishonesty is itself useful in helping students recognize why cheating is bad. I've taken to having the students sign a pledge of academic integrity prior to each exam. I think it reminds them of my expectations and reinforces the impression that I care.

Fifth, if some students are not doing well in the course, talk to them and find out what has gone wrong and what they can do to improve. Try to reduce the stress that leads to cheating. If there are stresses originating beyond your course, suggest counseling.

What else can be done?

One principle is to preserve each student's sense that he or she is an individual with a personal relationship both with the instructor and with other students. Students are not as likely to cheat in situations in which they are known as in situations in which they are anonymous members of a crowd. Thus, if a large course has regular meetings in small discussion or laboratory sections, there is likely to be less cheating if the test is administered in these groups than if the test is administered en masse. Moreover, if the test is given in their regular classroom, they may perform better because of the cues to their original learning (Metzger et al., 1979).

Even in small groups, cheating will occur if the instructor seems unconcerned. Graduate student teaching assistants often feel that any show of active proctoring will indicate that they do not trust the students. There is certainly a danger that the teacher will appear to be so poised to spring at a miscreant that the atmosphere becomes tense, but it is possible to convey a sense of alert helpfulness while strolling down the aisles or watching for questions.

The most common form of cheating is copying from another student's paper. To reduce this I usually ask to have a large enough exam room to enable students to sit in alternate seats. I write on the board before students arrive, "Take alternate seats." Some students fail to see the sign, so in large exams you not only need two proctors at each door passing out exams but at least one more to supervise seating.

In the event that you can't get rooms large enough to permit alternate seating, you probably should use two or more alternate forms of the test. Houston (1983) found that scrambling the order of items alone did not reduce cheating. Since I prefer to have items on a test follow the same order as the order in which the material has been discussed in the course, I scramble the order of items only within topics and also scramble the order of alternatives. I typically write separate sets of essay questions for the two tests. It is difficult to make two tests equally difficult, so you probably will want to tabulate separate distributions of scores on each form of the test.

Whether you use one form or two, don't leave copies lying around your office or the typist's office. One of our students was nearly killed by a fall from a third-floor ledge outside the office where he hoped to steal the examination, and janitors have been bribed to turn over the contents of wastebaskets thought to contain discarded drafts of the test.

## Handling Cheating

Despite preventive measures, almost every instructor must at some time or another face the problem of what to do about a student who is cheating. For example, as you are administering an examination you note that a student's eyes are on his neighbor's rather than on his own paper. Typically you do nothing at this time, for you don't want to embarrass an innocent student. But when the eyes again stray, you are faced with a decision about what to do.

Most colleges have rules about the procedures to be followed in case of cheating. Yet instructors are often reluctant to begin the procedure. The reasons for instructor reluctance vary. Sometimes it is simply uncertainty about whether or not cheating really occurred. Students' eyes do wander without cheating. Answers may be similar simply because two students have studied together. "If the student denies the charge, what evidence do I have to support my accusation?"

Again, unwillingness to invoke the regulations concerning cheating may be based on distrust of the justice of the eventual disposition of the case. Cheating is common in colleges; many teachers have been guilty themselves at some stage in their academic careers. Thus, most of us are understandably reluctant to subject the unfortunate one who gets caught to the drastic possible punishments that more skillful cheaters avoid. Such conflicts as these make the problem of handling a cheater one of the most disturbing of those a new teacher faces.

Unfortunately I've never been completely satisfied that I handle the problem adequately; so my "advice" should, like the rest of the advice in this book, be regarded simply as some ideas for your consideration rather than as dicta to be accepted verbatim. However, much of what I'm going to say is backed up by most writers in this field.

First, let me support the value of following your college's procedures. Find out what they are and what legal precedents may affect what you should do. Even though it may not have been long since you were taking examinations yourself, your role as a teacher requires that you represent established authority rather than the schoolboy code that rejects "tattlers." Moreover, your memories of student days may help you recall your own feelings when you saw someone cheating and the instructor took no action.

Further, student or faculty committees dealing with cheating are not as arbitrary and impersonal as you might expect. Typically, they attempt to get at the cause of the cheating and to help students solve their underlying problems. Being apprehended for cheating may, therefore, actually be of real long-term value to the students.

Finally, following college policies protects you in the rare case in which a student initiates legal action against you for an arbitrary punishment.

There still remain cases where the evidence is weak and you're not quite sure whether or not cheating actually occurred. Even here I advise against such individual action as reducing a grade. If you're wrong, the solution is unjust. If you're right, you've failed to give the student feedback that is likely to change his behavior. In such cases I advise talking to the student and calling the head of the committee handling cheating cases or the student's counselor. It's surprising to find how often your suspicions fit in with other evidence about the student's behavior. Even when they don't, advice from someone who has additional information about the student will frequently be helpful.

Finally, let's return to the case of the straying eyes. Here you haven't time for a phone call to get advice; your decision has to be made now. Rather than arousing the whole class by snatching away the student's paper with a loud denunciation, I simply ask the student unobtrusively to move to a seat where he'll be less crowded. If he says he's not crowded, I simply whisper that I'd prefer that he move. So far no one's refused.

# AFTER THE TEST

## Grading Objective Tests

Of course the most wonderful thing about objective tests is they are easier to grade. Or are they? The important point to remember is to get the scoring key right! There's nothing more disconcerting to students than to find that the test was scored incorrectly. I strongly recommend that you check and double check the keys to be sure that the marks are correct. Then, before you give the tests back, it **really** pays to do a short analysis of overall student performance on each item. This is called an item analysis. It consists of figuring what percentage of the students missed each question and how did the performance of the top third of the class compare to the bottom third as measured by their overall score. You can short-circuit a lot of student complaints by identifying items that were troublesome and knowing why. For example, if an item is missed by more than half of the class, I always reread the item to see whether there was something unclear. Or if a large number of the students in the top group miss an item, I consider which answer they gave to see if for some reasons the question misled those who actually knew a lot, maybe too much. You still have time to make the necessary adjustments in the scoring to allow for poorly worded questions or a distractor that turns out to be correct after all. By making all these adjustments before you give the papers back, you avoid a lot of confusion about which items were right and which were wrong.

Once the students recognize that you are making a good-faith effort to identify or remediate poorly worded items, they are more likely to give you the benefit of the doubt. You also have the advantage of having at your fingertips solid data on each question so that if a student challenges a question after the test, you will know whether there is any merit to that challenge and be able to respond immediately and authoritatively.

## Grading Essay Questions

I recommend that you use some essay questions because of their powerful effect on the way students study, but there is a drawback. Instructors don't grade essay tests very reliably. One problem is that standards vary. First papers are graded differently than later papers. A paper graded immediately after several poor papers is graded differently than one graded after several good papers.

There are seven procedures you can initiate to improve your evaluation of essay examinations—but they entail work.

1. Establish a rubric or set of criteria—not just a list of facts to be included. Are you looking for integration, for analysis, for rational arguments for and against a conclusion? Be prepared to modify your criteria as you find student responses that you hadn't thought of. Learning to create a good grading rubric is worth the effort because it can help you write good questions, maintain reliable grading of answers, and, if shared with the students, help students understand how their answer was graded. Walvoord (1998) has an excellent book on how to create rubrics based on "primary trait analysis."

Creating a good rubric through primary trait analysis involves laying out the key aspects of the response that figure into the grade. For example, on a given essay question, the analysis might list four main points that must be included in the answer, plus criteria for a clean argument and criteria for good writing itself. Then each "trait" is described along a scale of acceptability. Here is an example of a scale for the trait of "solid argumentation":

Best answer (100 percent credit)—An answer at this level provides clear statements of the thesis or theses being asserted in a logical order that builds to the final conclusion. Each thesis is accompanied by sufficient reasonable evidence to support it. Each thesis also considers and counters reasonable arguments against it. The theses stand together and are internally consistent with one another.

Acceptable answer (80 percent credit)—An answer at this level provides fewer theses but still provides reasonable and primary ones in light of the conclusion. There is evidence offered for each thesis, although possibly overlooking some minor supporting assertions. Several of the more obvious counterarguments are raised and refuted. The order is logical and builds to the conclusion. Transitions between theses are present but ordinary.

Unacceptable answer (no credit)—Any two or more of the following characteristics constitute an unacceptable answer. The answer contains many errors of assertion and omission. No evidence is given or the evidence given is incorrect or unrelated to the assertion. No attempt or a weak attempt is made to introduce and refute counterarguments. The order of presentation is not logical or convincing. The conclusion is not justified by the arguments.

Creating this type of rubric helps you clarify for yourself what you want in an answer. It also increases the reliability of grading across graders and across time within a single grader's work.

2. Read exams without knowledge of the name of the writer.

3. If you're unsure of what to expect, first read briefly through a random sample of answers. Then, having identified papers of differing levels of excellence, compare them to determine what the distinguishing features are. You will find some characteristics that were not in your original criteria. Now set up the criteria you will use, but don't be rigid. Give students credit when they come up with creative answers that don't fit the rubric.

4. Write specific comments on the papers. One of the problems in using essay exams and in assigning term papers is that students feel that the grading represents some mysterious, unfathomable bias. The more helpful comments you can write on the paper, the more students will learn.

I am finding that computer technology is a big help in my grading of papers (but not essay exams unless they're also done on the computer). I use the editing software available in common word processing programs to read and mark the papers that my students submit in electronic format. I can give a lot more feedback because I'm not limited by how much I can squeeze into the margins, and I can type a lot faster than I can write by hand. In addition, the students can probably read my typing better than my handwriting. (There is more about this in the chapter "How to Enhance Learning by Using High-Stakes and Low-Stakes Writing.")

5. Develop a code for common comments. For example, you might want to use a vertical line alongside paragraphs that are particularly good or "NFD" for "needs further development." Or you can identify the most commonly occurring errors with numbers. When you grade, you can put the number next to the error on the paper and give students the numbered list of errors for reference. They may learn something from reading the whole list even if they didn't make any of those errors.

6. Don't simply give points for each concept or fact mentioned. Doing that just converts the essay into a recall test rather than a measure of higher-level goals of integration and evaluation. Developing rubrics like those described earlier can be helpful in increasing reliability of grading.

However, don't use them mechanically. Your overall impression may be as valid.

7. If possible, do your grading in teams. My teaching assistants and I gather after administering a test. We bring in draft model answers for each question. We discuss what we expect as answers for each question. We then establish two- or three-person teams for each essay question. Each team picks eight to 12 test papers, which are circulated among the team members. Each team member notes privately his or her grade for the question. Team members then compare grades and discuss discrepancies until they reach consensus. A second group of tests is then graded in the same way, with grades compared and discrepancies discussed. This procedure continues until the team is confident that it has arrived at common criteria. From this point on, each member grades independently. When a team member is not sure how to grade a paper, it is passed to another team member for an opinion.

We stay with the grading until all the papers are done, but we make a party of it to alleviate fatigue and boredom. Funny answers are read aloud. Sandwiches are brought in from a delicatessen. Teams help other teams for a change of pace or to balance the workload.

If you don't have a team, try to develop your own strategies for maintaining motivation. If you begin to be bored, irritated, or tired, take a break. Or before beginning, pull out the answers of some of your most interesting students and read those when you begin to feel dispirited. Take notes to use in discussing the papers in class. Also take separate notes for yourself on what seem to be common problems that you need to correct in your teaching in the future.

Grading papers is still time consuming but does not become the sort of aversive task that makes for procrastination and long delays in providing feedback to students.

## Helping Yourself Learn from the Test

Often we get so wrapped up in the pure mechanics of correcting and grading tests that we overlook the fact that measures of student performance not only can diagnose student weaknesses but also can reveal areas in which our teaching has failed to achieve its purposes. The item analysis process described earlier is especially helpful with this. Once you've achieved some ease with the grading process, look back at the papers to see what they reveal about problems in student understanding. There may be some things about which the entire class seems a bit shaky; in addition, there may be areas of difficulty experienced by certain subgroups of students—perhaps those with background knowledge or experience different from that of the rest of the class. In short, think about what *you* need to do as well as about what the *students* need to do.

## Returning Test Papers

Remember that tests are important tools for learning and that discussion of a test can be a worthwhile use of class time. However, it's also a pretty emotional time for some of the students, and it might pay to delay the discussion until that emotion settles down. In fact, in my own class, I give students the opportunity to challenge the answer to a question in writing before the next class period. I've found that often once the student has had a chance to look over the items and tried to justify their incorrect answers, they realize what they did wrong much more readily than if I just tell them. Sometimes they are actually able to make a good case for their choice, in which case I'll give them credit for their answer. I don't think you should discuss every question in class, but when there are common errors, try to find out why the error occurred and suggest strategies for avoiding such problems in the future. Although you should avoid spending class time quibbling over some individual items, you should make known your willingness to discuss the test individually with students who have further questions.

## Helping Students Learn from a Test

The most important function of testing is *not* to provide a basis for grading. Rather, tests are an important educational tool. They not only direct students' studying but also can provide important corrective feedback. The comments that you write on essay tests are far more important than the grade. Students do learn from their corrected papers (McCluskey, 1934). I recommend looking at the suggestions for giving feedback that are included in Chapter 9 of this book. They apply equally to essays, papers, and objectively scorable tests like multiple choice. If you have the time and the temperament, you can increase the probability that students will take that opportunity to learn if you give them a chance to redo an assignment based on your feedback, as described in the previous section.

## Dealing with an Aggrieved Student

What about the student who comes to your office in great anger or with a desperate appeal for sympathy but no educationally valid reason for changing the test grade? First of all, listen. Engaging in a debate will simply prolong the unpleasantness.

Ask the student to think aloud about what he or she was thinking when answering the questions that he or she is unhappy about. Once you have heard the student out, if you have decided not to change the grade, try to convert the discussion from one of stonewall resistance to problem solving. Try to help the student find alternative modes of study that will produce better results: "What can we do to help you do better next time?" Encourage the student to shift from blaming you toward motivation to work more effectively. Ask the student to summarize what he or she plans to do before the next test. Although these suggestions may save the instructor some bitter moments, they cannot substitute for the time (and it takes lots) devoted to the construction of good tests.

## What Do You Do About the Student Who Missed the Test?

In any large class some students are absent from the test. Their excuses range from very legitimate to very suspicious, but making that discrimination is not always easy.

Makeup tests can involve a good deal of extra work for the instructor. If you devise a new test, you may have trouble assigning a norm with which to grade the makeup comparable to grades on the original test. If you use the same test that the student missed, you cannot tell how much the student has learned about the test from students who took it at the scheduled time. I simply average marks from the tests the student did take to determine the grade, counting the missed test neither for nor against the student.

Another strategy is to drop the lowest score or missed test out of all the tests a student takes. (This, of course, presumes you have enough exams during the semester that one can be dropped.) This also lowers test anxiety because the stakes on any one test are lower. Depending on how strongly you feel about final exams, you could allow students to use the final as the test they drop if they've taken all the other exams and are satisfied with their grade. You'd be surprised what an incentive that is for working diligently during the semester.

## *IN CONCLUSION*

1. Consider using both graded and ungraded tests and moving from less frequent tests to more frequent, where each test can count less.

2. Select question types that target your educational goals.

3. Prepare your students to take the test.

4. Create a class atmosphere that values academic honesty and support and discourages cheating.

5. Develop grading strategies for essay questions so that you won't shy away from using them.

6. Be prepared to address students' complaints about test scores in a way that helps them learn.

7. Learn from the test yourself and show your students how to learn from it as well.

## *Supplementary Reading*

*Effective Grading: A Tool for Learning and Assessment* by Barbara E. Walvoord and Virginia Johnson Anderson (San Francisco: Jossey-Bass, 1998) does a good job of describing how to create grading rubrics for all manner of written assessments.

*Constructing Test Items: Multiple-Choice, Constructed-Response, Performance, and Other Formats*, 2nd ed., by Steven J. Osterlind (Boston: Kluwer Academic Publishers, 1998) is a fairly complete discussion of the process of writing different types of test items. It may be a bit long on detail, but the guidelines for item construction are solid and fairly straightforward.

The following resources are drawn from the ERIC Digest series. This is a series of short summaries of research and best practices provided online for educators in a searchable database.

- www.ericfacility.net/databases/ERIC_Digests/index.
- Childs, R. (1989). *Constructing Classroom Achievement Tests*. ERIC Digest. ERIC Clearinghouse on Tests Measurement and Evaluation. ED315426.
- Grist, S., and others (1989). *Computerized Adaptive Tests*. ERIC Digest No. 107. ERIC Clearinghouse on Tests Measurement and Evaluation. ED315425.
- Kehoe, J. (1995). *Basic Item Analysis for Multiple-Choice Tests*. ERIC/ AE Digest. ERIC Clearinghouse on Assessment and Evaluation. ED398237.

▶ Kehoe, J. (1995). *Writing Multiple Choice Test Items*. ERIC/AE Digest. ERIC Clearinghouse on Assessment and Evaluation. ED398236.

Readings about helping students:

▶ C. E. Weinstein and L. Hume, *Study Strategies for Lifelong Learning* (Washington: American Psychological Association, 1998). The American Psychological Association Division 15 has a whole series of publications on helping students improve their learning. Access them through the APA Publications site.

▶ D. Sadker and K. Zittleman, "Test Anxiety: Are Students Failing Tests—Or Are Tests Failing Students?" *Phi Delta Kappan*, 2004, *85*(10), 740.

The entire September 2004 issue of *Anxiety, Stress, and Coping* is devoted to test anxiety and research on it, including how to cope with it.
Readings about cheating:

▶ S. F. Davis, C. A. Grover, A. H. Becker, and L. N. McGregor, "Academic Dishonesty: Prevalence, Determinants, Techniques, and Punishments," *Teaching of Psychology*, 1992, *19*(1), 16–20.

▶ J. McBurney, "Cheating: Preventing and Dealing with Academic Dishonesty," *APS Observer*, January 1996, 32–35.

One might assume that it would be un-British to cheat. But Stephen Newstead, Arlyne Franklyn-Stokes, and Penny Armstrong found that British students are not much different from Americans in this respect. Their article "Individual Differences in Student Cheating," *Journal of Educational Psychology*, 1996, *88*, 229–241, is consistent with American data.

A particularly interesting set of recommendations comes from the Website "On the Cutting Edge" of the National Association of Geoscience Teachers, which provides workshops for faculty in the geological sciences (serc.carleton.edu/NAGTWorkshops/index.html).

The Center for Academic Integrity at Duke University, Durham, North Carolina (www.academicintegrity.org/cai_research.asp), can provide a lot of information and sponsors workshops and research on academic integrity. They also have a searchable database of 700-plus articles on this topic.

# Good Designs for Written Feedback for Students

**T**here is no such thing as good teaching without good feedback. The teacher, as knowledgeable expert, gives feedback to students with the intention of scaffolding their learning. By scaffolding, I mean supporting and helping students reach higher levels of learning and achievement but without doing the work for them. Students value the feedback comments that instructors write on their assignments, especially when these comments help explain gaps in understanding, are supportive in tone, and suggest ways of improving future work.

To get the best out of feedback comments, however, it is vital that students engage with them. No matter how much feedback the instructor delivers, students won't benefit unless they pay attention to it, process it and ultimately act on it. Just as students don't learn to play basketball just by listening to the coach, so they cannot learn to produce a better essay or solve problems just by reading teacher feedback. Effective feedback is a partnership; it requires actions by the student as well as the teacher. Indeed, while the quality of teacher comments is important, engagement with and use of those comments by students is equally important.

In higher education, it is usual to think about the instructor as the initiator and provider of feedback. However, this is not the whole story.

This chapter was written by David Nicol, University of Strathclyde, Scotland.

Students frequently give each other feedback when tackling the same assignment (peer feedback). They also generate their own feedback while writing an essay or report; for example, they might consult a textbook to evaluate the accuracy of an argument or to identify gaps in a theoretical explanation. Significant learning benefits can be achieved when teachers harness peer feedback and build on these informal feedback processes (Nicol and Macfarlane-Dick, 2008).

It is also important that feedback is not too narrowly conceptualized as something that happens after the student has produced some work. Feedback is not always backward looking and a consequence of action. It can also be forward-looking. In project supervision the instructor provides advice about what might be done next, while the work is in progress and not just at the end. Also feedback does not occur in isolation; it is normally provided in relation to the assignment goals. When students understand and share these goals they are more receptive to the feedback they receive.

In the following sections I first provide a set of recommendations on how to improve the quality of teacher feedback comments. Then, consistent with a broader conception of the feedback process, I discuss ways of ensuring that these comments have maximum impact on learning. This involves creating structured opportunities for students to engage in feedback conversations with their teachers and with peers and to reflect on the meaning of feedback in relation to subject knowledge. In what follows, my assumption is that feedback is being generated in relation to a written assignment, for example, an essay or report, even though most of the discussion also applies to other feedback scenarios.

# THE FORMULATION OF WRITTEN FEEDBACK COMMENTS

What are the features of good written teacher comments? The following is a set of recommendations for good practice. These are based on investigations of students' perceptions of what constitutes helpful feedback and on researchers' suggestions about how to translate these ideas into practice.

## Understandable, Selective, and Specific

Overall, the research on feedback shows that students do value written comments on their work (e.g., Weaver, 2006). However, they also express concern when these comments are illegible, ambiguous

## Research on Feedback Comments

**Written feedback should be:**

- **Understandable:** Expressed in a language that students will understand.

- **Selective:** Commenting on two or three things that the student can do something about.

- **Specific:** Pointing to examples in the student's submission where the feedback applies.

- **Timely:** Provided in time to inform the next piece of work.

- **Contextualized:** Framed with reference to the learning outcomes and/or assessment criteria.

- **Nonjudgmental:** Descriptive rather than evaluative, focused on learning goals not just performance goals.

- **Balanced:** Pointing out the positive as well as areas in need of improvement.

- **Forward Looking:** Suggesting how students might improve subsequent assignments.

- **Transferable:** Focused on processes, skills and self-regulatory abilities.

(e.g., "poor effort, could do better"), too abstract (e.g., "lack of critical thinking"), too general or vague (e.g., "you've got the important stuff") and too cryptic (e.g., "why?"). Sometimes this is a question of language, at other times of detail. Much feedback uses a disciplinary discourse that is difficult for students, especially beginning students, to decode. The teacher can remedy this by trying to write comments in plain language and by providing an explanation where disciplinary or technical terms are used. It is also important to provide enough detail so that students understand what the guidance means. This has led to the suggestion that comments should be formulated as small lessons, and that these should be limited to two or three well-developed points for extended written assignments (Lunsford, 1997). It can help students if teachers also point to examples in the submission where the feedback applies rather than provide comments with no referent. For instance, highlight a positive feature, explain its merit, and suggest that the student do more of that (e.g., a good example of logical transitions or of a disciplinary argument).

## Timely

Numerous studies show that students receive feedback too late to be helpful, due to their receiving it after the next assignment. Students are also quite vocal about this problem. At one level, dealing with this issue is straightforward and might simply involve specifying turnaround times for grading and feedback on assignments; some institutions make a commitment to a three-week turnaround. However, the timeliness dimension is also related to opportunities to use feedback and the requirement that students get feedback when they experience difficulty rather than wait too long.

Multistage assignments can address some of these problems. If the assignment allows drafting with feedback provided on the draft, students are more likely to see the feedback as timely and make good use of it. Alternatively, teachers might provide feedback on aspects of the work in progress (e.g., essay plans, introductions, a sample of the argument and supporting evidence) with the task sequenced with each stage building to a more complex final assignment. Providing feedback on drafts need not necessarily increase teacher time; teachers can limit the feedback that they provide when they grade the completed assignment or students might give each other feedback at intermediate stages. A further concern is that on a graded assignment it is important that the student actually does the work and that the teacher does not rewrite the assignment as part of the feedback. This requires careful consideration of the kinds of feedback comments teachers provide.

## Nonjudgmental and Balanced

Teachers need to consider the motivational as well as the cognitive aspects of feedback. Feedback comments can be discouraging, lead to defensiveness, or reduce confidence (e.g., "no, that's all wrong, you really have not understood the literature"). Kluger and DeNisi (1996) found that 30 percent of comments were of this type. Much motivational research has focused on whether feedback comments direct students' attention towards learning or performance goals, that is, towards the mindset that mistakes are part of learning and that effort can enhance achievement or to the mindset that achievement depends on ability, which is more fixed (Dweck, 1999; Dweck, 2006).

Research in this area also suggests that teachers should try to ensure that students perceive comments as descriptive rather than evaluative or authoritarian. One approach is for the teacher to reflect back to the students the effects of the writing, in other words, how the teacher has interpreted what is written (e.g., "here's what I see as your main point …"). This helps students see the difference between their intention and the effects that are produced. Some experts argue that faculty should start and end commenting on positive aspects of what the student has done, with a middle section focusing on those aspects in need of improvement. However, a word of caution is needed here; if the student perceives that praise is gratuitous or that it does not align with the grade awarded, then this can be confusing or have a negative effect on motivation.

Feedback could also emphasize learning goals by acknowledging the role that mistakes and effort play in learning and by avoiding normative comparisons with other students. Some teachers have addressed such issues by providing encouragement in their comments (e.g., "analyzing a case is complex and can be very demanding but all students who put in the time and effort get there eventually"). This emphasizes success and lets students know that they have the capacity to succeed. Acknowledging the role that mistakes play in learning when giving feedback is another useful tactic (e.g., "this is a common misconception; when you identify the reason for this misconception you will have a good grasp of this topic").

## Contextualized

Research suggests that feedback is more effective when it is related to the instructional context, that is, to the learning outcomes and the assessment criteria. Sadler (1989) defines feedback as information about the gap between what the student did (actual performance) and what was expected (the assignment outcomes), information that is intended to help the student close that gap. Hence, alignment of feedback to the instructional context is essential for learning. It also increases the likelihood that students will actually understand the feedback. Many teachers use feedback forms with assessment rubrics wherein feedback is written under or alongside the stated objectives or assessment criteria.

A related recommendation deriving from Sadler's definition is that students spend time at the beginning of an assignment actively unpacking what is required; for example, by translating criteria into their own words or by comparing samples of good and poor assignments submitted by classmates in earlier years so as to identify which is better and why. By enhancing their understanding of the requirements and criteria students are more likely to understand and use the feedback advice they receive. Glaser and Chi (1988) have also shown that the time experts spend constructing the initial representations of complex tasks partly accounts for their better performance when compared to novices.

## Forward-looking and Transferable

The most consistent request from students is that the feedback tells them about their strengths and weaknesses and specifically about what they need to do to make improvements in subsequent assignments. Knight (2006) calls the latter "feedforward" rather than feedback. Examples might include suggesting goals to focus on in future assignments or specific strategies that might apply. Some feedback sheets include an "action-point" box where the instructor can outline the specific actions that would lead to greatest improvement in the next assignment. Walker (2006) sees the focus as being on skills development rather than on specific content; developing the skills to solve problems or write essays in the discipline is more effective in the long run than solving a single problem or writing a specific essay. Another perspective is that comments should focus not on gaps in knowledge and understanding but on the students' representations of the knowledge in their discipline. Comments should help students find alternative ways of looking at the problem rather than simply highlight misunderstandings. The intention here is to promote new ways of thinking about concepts, their relationships, and their applications.

Hattie and Timperley (2007) identified four orientations to the provision of feedback comments; teachers could provide comments on the task, stating where the assignment is correct or incorrect or requires more input; they might be about the writing process (e.g., "this assignment could be better if you planned out the structure and sequence of arguments"); they might focus comments on the student's ability to self-regulate, for example, feedback on students' own assessments of their work would fall into this category (see below); or the comments might be personal (e.g., "that's a sophisticated response; well done"). Hattie and Timperley maintain that focusing comments on the process and on self-regulatory activities is most effective, if the goal is to help students transfer learning to new contexts.

I have discussed encouraging students to use feedback earlier in relation to multistage assignments. However, here is an additional example, based on a variation of a strategy used by a colleague. Students are required to write an essay, let's say on ethics. The instructor provides written feedback, usually a few paragraphs, on the subject content, the ideas, arguments, and evidence. Specifically, the feedback points to new ways of looking at the issues and refers briefly to other theorists. The students are then allowed to produce a second assignment in the same content area but using a different format (e.g., a report to the government on this ethics issue). Those who choose this option are told that to get a good grade on the second assignment they must go well beyond the ideas in the first assignment and demonstrate good use of the feedback. This is intended to encourage students to use the feedback, read more widely and to interrelate and apply ideas from other sources in the report. Why is this design of interest? First, the students have a strong incentive to act on the feedback. Secondly, both the student and the teacher see the direct benefits of feedback in future action. Importantly, students do not repeat the same assignment, so they will not perceive this as duplication, nor will their teachers. This is a good example of the forward use of written comments.

## FOSTERING FEEDBACK DIALOGUES

The advice on the formulation of comments above is a useful starting point in thinking about feedback. However, it does not really go far enough. Feedback is not a monologue. The meaning of feedback comments is not transmitted from the teacher to the student; rather, meaning comes into being through interaction and dialogue. So how might we enrich feedback and make it more meaningful to students?

First, teachers must, as far as possible, tailor their feedback comments to students' needs. Students differ in their understanding and in their reactions to feedback, so this is a challenge, especially with large classes. However, progress is possible by designing teacher-student interactions in ways that promote responsive and contingent feedback conversations. Second, teacher feedback must be supplemented by feedback from other sources. Students must be exposed to and interact with a greater variety of feedback responses. Multiple sources of feedback help students see their work from many perspectives, and this enhances understanding and capability. The most readily available source of supplementary feedback derives from peers enrolled in the same course.

Third, feedback must be geared to strengthening the students' ability to judge the quality of their own work. The long-term purpose of feedback is that students become independent of their teachers. Students already engage in inner dialogue and generate their own feedback when they produce an assignment. A systematic focus on strengthening these processes will not only make teacher and peer feedback more effective but it will also help develop your students' ability to monitor and evaluate their own learning. Last, we must try to create the conditions that will motivate students actively to seek and use feedback. This, however, is more likely to happen if we strive to meet the other three conditions. The following sections develop these ideas and suggest strategies for implementation.

## MAKING TEACHER FEEDBACK CONTINGENT ON LEARNERS' NEEDS

Wood, Wood, and Middleton (1978), in their work on contingent tutoring, demonstrated that there is no ideal level of feedback from a teacher. What is optimal is continual dynamic adjustment of the level of teacher input depending on the degree of learner understanding. More iteration is not necessarily better, neither is more specificity or detail; the point is to match the feedback to each student's needs. Unfortunately this can be difficult to achieve when student numbers are large.

One way of making teacher feedback more sensitive to individual needs is to have students express a preference for the kinds of feedback they would like when they hand in an assignment. Teachers, for instance, might ask students to request feedback, to attach questions with their submission identifying areas with which they would like help; while some might be about the writing process, others might concern concept understanding and use. The teacher would then focus the comments on these areas. Bloxham and Campbell (2008) tested this approach with first-year university students and found benefits, although they found that some students had difficulty formulating high-level conceptual questions. However, teachers can address this issue through better initial support for question formulation and/or by beginning with a collaborative essay task where groups of students work together to form questions. This procedure shifts the balance of responsibility for feedback towards the student. Requesting feedback based on their own concerns empowers students more than just receiving feedback based on the teacher's interpretation of weaknesses. However, this procedure need not stop teachers using feedback to highlight additional issues not identified by students.

Elbow and Sorcinelli provide a structured version of the requested feedback approach (Chapter 14 in this book); they ask students to write an informal cover letter to hand in with an essay, but they provide the framework using specific questions: what was your main point?; what were your sub-points?; which parts of the submitted essay feel strong and weak?; what questions do you have for me as reader? The cover letter ensures that the students' comments form the beginning of a dialogue that is continued by the teacher through the feedback. They note that dialogue can extend further by having students respond to the teacher's feedback; for example, they might write a short note that tells what they heard in the comments and how they will use them. Importantly, when feedback comments are contingent on what the student does, it is more likely that they will actually meet the criteria for good commenting I discussed earlier, that is, be understandable, selective, specific, and even forward-looking.

Contingent dialogues could also start with teachers formulating their feedback as questions on students' work that are then followed through in face-to-face discussions, individually or in small group tutorials. A recent innovation is audio feedback. The teacher reads the student script and attaches audio files. Early reports suggest that students respond more positively to audio feedback, seeing it as closer to a dialogue. Teachers can produce reactions to the writing as they read, can ask questions, and suggest improvements. Variations in tone and the naturalness of the approach seem to give students more of a sense that teachers are interested in what students have written. Teachers or students could also build on the dialogues prompted through audio feedback in class. Early research shows, however, that it can take time for some teachers to get used to this feedback format.

## SUPPLEMENTING TEACHER FEEDBACK WITH PEER FEEDBACK

It is natural to think about feedback as if only teachers are able to provide it. Yet, many learning benefits derive from peer feedback; it is not just about saving time (Boud, Cohen, and Sampson, 2001). It can be difficult for teachers to address all areas of weakness in students' work or to provide comments in an accessible language. Peers, however, who are tackling the same assignment, might be able to provide feedback in a student-centered discourse. Also, some students might actually be more receptive to teacher feedback if the comments they receive from peers agree with those from the teacher.

While consistency is important in marking and grading, this is less important in feedback. Indeed, there are significant benefits to be gained from variation. Having different readers respond to and comment on an assignment provides multiple perspectives, and this invokes multiple opportunities for scaffolding. Seeing examples of the work of others and commenting on them also helps students become more objective and critical about their own work. When students respond to others' work and receive comments on their own work, this enhances their understanding of what quality looks like and how to produce it. They learn that quality does not come in a pre-defined form; rather, there is a spectrum of possibilities.

## Collaborative Assignment Production

There are many ways of implementing peer dialogue in relation to written assignments. Informally, it can be provided during the execution of a task by getting students to work together collaboratively to produce an assignment. This is the approach that one teacher adopted in a first-year psychology course with an enrollment of 560 students. He required his students, in groups of six or seven, to collaborate and write six short essays online over two semesters (Nicol, 2009). All the group discussions and the final submission were recorded within WebCT (now Blackboard), the institution's learning-management system. Students remained in the same closed discussion group throughout the year with members of each group giving each other feedback while writing the essays and while negotiating about and agreeing upon the final submission.

The teacher provided online guidance that emphasized the value of peer feedback for learning and that instructed students in good practice in peer feedback. The teacher supplemented this with feedback through essay exemplars and with general feedback to the whole class through an open discussion forum. The exemplars were selected from the students' submissions and posted online after all groups had submitted their assignment. The students were encouraged to compare their submissions against the range of exemplars. This approach proved highly motivational and a majority of the students (64 percent) agreed that the peer dialogue increased their understanding of the topics studied. There was a significant improvement in essay performance in the final exams compared to previous years. One notable feature of this design was that the instructor organized rich and motivational feedback for 560 students without the over-burdening himself with the provision of individual feedback to every student.

## Peer Commenting on Assignments

A formal approach to peer feedback is to organize classroom sessions (or online opportunities) where can students critique each other's work. For example, students might write a short 500-word essay (e.g., 500 words) and bring three copies to a tutorial. The instructor distributes these across the tutorial group with the result that each student provides and receives three sets of peer feedback comments. Instructions might be to identify two weaknesses in the text and make recommendations for improvement or to identify whether the evidence sufficiently supports the argument. In some scenarios the instructor might provide the assessment criteria or rubric for the comments, whereas in others the students might derive the criteria during the act of assessing the work for peers. There are advantages in using both approaches.

Some students lack confidence in the ability or knowledge of peers. Hence they can show resistance to peer critiquing. This can be addressed through training and by linking peer to instructor feedback; for example, after peers have provided structured comments the instructor could provide her own comments not on the assignment but on the comments provided by peers. Software has been developed to support peer commenting, which also makes it easy to implement this with large classes.

## Learning through Peer Collaboration and Review

Although the findings from research suggest that students improve their writing in the disciplines through practice and feedback, most teachers are overwhelmed by the workload associated with providing this feedback. Hence a different approach is required. The approach I advocate here is that students learn writing through reviewing (see also chapter on writing). In collaborative authorship and in peer commenting, students analyze each other's writing, detect problems in understanding and in the writing process, and make suggestions for improvement. This is beneficial to all students but especially for those who might fail to detect their own misunderstandings or flaws in their writing as well as for those who might overestimate their own understandings and capabilities. This approach can also give students more practice in writing without significantly increasing instructor workload.

Importantly, peer feedback builds on teacher feedback. It further optimizes the adaptation of comments to individual student needs, and it links comments directly to the production of a specific output. In effect, peer feedback helps ensure that comments meet the criteria presented earlier, that they are timely, forward-looking, and actionable.

Finally, when students engage in peer-feedback activities, they are also put in the role of the assessor. This helps develop their ability to evaluate their own work.

# ACTIVATING AND STRENGTHENING INNER FEEDBACK

When students engage in learning activities there is always a feedback dimension, even when there is no external source of feedback advice. For example, when writing an essay students usually generate a great deal of inner dialogue and feedback during the act of production (e.g., "Have I expressed this clearly?" "What if I tried it this way?"). This inner dialogue leads to tracking maneuvers (re-workings of the text) that ensure a match between the student's goals and the finished essay. These inner or reflective dialogues are a natural consequence of engaging in any purposeful action.

Making these reflective dialogues more conscious and public offers many benefits. For instance, asking students to assess their own assignment either during its production or at the end before handing it in helps develop evaluative skills. These skills are important if students are to become less dependent on their teachers and more independent and autonomous. Also, if the products of these self-assessments are made public, teachers gain insight into how students think about their own work, which in turn enables them to better target their feedback.

It is also important to note that self-assessment is already embedded in students' use of teacher feedback (Black and Wiliam, 1998). When students receive teacher feedback, they must be able to use this information as a reference point to evaluate their own work; unless they do this, they will not be able to make subsequent improvements. However, through this evaluative process, students are in fact already engaging in acts of assessment not dissimilar to those carried out by their teachers when they produce feedback. So, as well as improving teacher feedback, it might be more productive in the long term to focus some of our effort on developing the student's own evaluative capabilities.

## Harnessing Inner Feedback: More Frequent Tasks

To help students develop their self-assessment skills it is important to provide them with many opportunities to reflect on their work; this is relatively easy to do, for example by replacing one large assignment at the end of a course with regular small assignments during the course. This gives students repeated occasions to benefit from feedback from their own evaluative activities; they will find out which concepts and ideas are difficult to express and where they have problems in writing. For some students this will be enough to trigger further study to clear up misunderstandings or even to seek out feedback from other students, which is also beneficial. And all this occurs without teacher feedback.

Support for the idea of regular and distributed assignments comes from the robust research finding about "time on task." This shows that the more time students spend studying in and out of class, the more they learn (Chickering and Gamson, 1987). This is not a consequence of practice alone; rather it is the result of the feedback students generate through that practice. The main drawback with numerous assignments is that teachers might feel they have to grade and provide feedback on them all. However, a small proportion of marks might be awarded for effort, for actually producing the assignment. And teacher feedback can be limited by using a simple rubric and/or by giving general feedback on a sample of these assignments to the whole class. Alternatively, peer feedback of the kind I described earlier might be appropriate.

## Having Students Reflect on Teacher-Provided Comments

Students might also reflect on and evaluate the relevance of the comments that teachers provide. When a teacher provides comments, each student normally receives them in relation to their assignment. However, many students report that such comments do not meet their needs; for example, they might not address areas where they suspect they are weak. From the teachers' perspective, providing individual comments to students is a high workload activity that has low-benefit if the student does not find the comments helpful. The instructor could, however, multiply the benefits of comments if he collated all the comments for the same assignment and used them in new ways. A master list would suffice, although some software now enables comments to be stored in and accessed from a databank. For example, students might be asked to select from the collated list the comments that they consider most relevant to their assignment and to say how they might act on them. This would encourage inner reflection both on the comments and on their own work. Importantly, the students rather than the teacher would be the protagonist in identifying the relevance of comments. Engaging with the comments that other students receive for the same assignment alerts students to pitfalls they may not have noticed, puts individual feedback comments in a wider context, engages students actively, and helps them develop a better understanding of the assignment requirements.

Comments might be shared in many ways. The teacher might produce a printed summary ideally using an online environment, as this will give more flexibility for sharing. Importantly, this approach need not take more faculty time as the feedback comments produced in one year could be reused with new students in subsequent years, if the teacher set the same assignment. Taking this idea further, students could be encouraged to set up their own study groups where they meet and discuss their work and feedback comments. Some students are probably already doing this.

## Strengthening Self-assessment

It is also possible to structure assignments in ways that encourage formal self-assessments. Indeed, instructors can integrate such self-assessments into any course or assignment. Students might be required to make an evaluative judgment when they hand in an assignment (e.g., "What did you do well? Give examples," "Where do you think the assignment is weak?"). In a pharmacy course in my own university, an assignment cover sheet was developed for essay self-assessment. The students were required to rephrase the essay question in their own words, make a judgment about whether they had met some stated criteria, estimate the grade they expected, and provide a justification for this. Teachers then commented on these self-assessments. This approach not only encouraged students to stand back and evaluate their own essay but also provided the teacher with insights into how students' perceive and judge their own competence.

Self-assessment is even more powerful if the teacher asks students not only to judge their own work but also to formulate the criteria and standards that should apply. This often happens in later years in project classes, but it could be brought forward to earlier years. Students might, for example, be invited to generate the criteria by which to assess an unfamiliar assignment (e.g., a blog, a wiki) and then to carry out their own self-assessment of progress. The rationale is to move students away from dependence on the judgment of others to a greater reliance on their own judgment. This will better prepare students for professional practice and for future learning.

## IN CONCLUSION

This chapter has provided many ideas and practical approaches to improving the power of written feedback. Some of these have been about the quality of the written feedback message, while many have been about improving students' interaction with and use of those messages. In this conclusion the essence of this advice is distilled into three overarching guidelines. These are that instructors should ensure that feedback:

1. *Is expressed in learner actions.* Make sure that feedback actually feeds-forward into action rather than backwards. This is the most consistent recommendation from the research on written comments, both from the point of view of students and of faculty. Perhaps the ideal feedback scenario in higher education is project supervision, where the student has frequent meetings with the teacher to discuss and rework a developing assignment. If we could make large class feedback more like project supervision, feedback would have maximum impact.

2. *Is contingent on and responsive to student needs.* There is no right level of specificity or detail in feedback; it all depends on students' needs and your purpose in giving feedback. Contingency requires that students should have relevant and responsive feedback conversations not only with the teacher but equally with peers; this is necessary because the right level of specificity or detail cannot really be predicted in advance. It also means involving students actively in reflection on feedback and on their own work so that they are required to locate the contingency relationship, not just the teacher.

3. *Is perceived by students as nonjudgmental.* Feedback is about helping students succeed, not about exercising power over them. This means setting high expectations that challenge students while always assuring them that they have the capacity to succeed. Most of what has been suggested, if appropriately implemented, would lead to positive engagement with feedback; that is, reader-response commenting (Lunsford, 1997), contingent feedback, self-assessment which gives students a sense of control over their learning, and peer feedback, which also fosters a sense of community.

The final word is about grading. Grading is often a concern given that many students focus more on their grades than on feedback comments. In this volume there is a chapter on grading (Chapter 10) and on motivation (Chapter 11). However, the essential advice here is to ensure that grading does not have a negative impact on feedback processes. Simple approaches might work, for example, asking students to respond to comments before giving the grade or asking them to come to class to discuss the feedback before distributing their grades. However, this all boils down to motivation; if the recommendations in this chapter are followed, then students will come to appreciate the value of feedback and how it helps them succeed in their learning.

## *Supplementary Reading*

Nicol, D. J. and Macfarlane-Dick, D. 2006. Formative assessment and self-regulated learning: A model and seven principles of good feedback practice, *Studies in Higher Education*, 31(2), 199–218.

Nicol, D. (2009). Transforming assessment and feedback: Enhancing integration and empowerment in the first year, Published by the Quality Assurance Agency for Higher Education, available at: http://www.enhancementthemes.ac.uk/documents/firstyear/First_Year_Transforming_Assess.pdf. Taking the perspective that the purpose of assessment and feedback is to help develop in students the ability to monitor, evaluate, and regulate their own learning, these two publications reinterpret and distill the research on feedback into a set of principles that can be used to guide practice. Seven principles of good feedback practice are suggested in Nicol and Macfarlane-Dick (2006), and numerous practical applications are suggested. These feedback principles provide another way of interpreting and implementing the ideas presented in this chapter. Nicol (2009) is a further development of the feedback principles but with a focus on first-year teaching. This publication includes a literature review, short definitions of each principle, a range of examples of their implementation, and strategic guidelines for senior managers. All this material and more can be found on the REAP (Re-engineering Assessment Practices) Website (www.reap.ac.uk). REAP was a project funded by the Scottish government (£1m). Its goal was to show how technology might be used to enhance assessment and feedback practices in large enrolment classes.

Black, P. & Wiliam, D. (1998) Assessment and classroom learning, *Assessment in Education*, 5(1), 7–74. Paul Black and Dylan Wiliam provide the most comprehensive review of formative assessment and feedback available. They analyze the results of over 250 selected studies across all levels of education. This is the starting point for those with a passionate and deep interest in this topic.

Bryan, C and Clegg, K. (2006). *Innovative Assessment in Higher Education*, London: Routledge. This book provides an up-to-date overview of thinking and research on formative assessment. It is grounded in the idea that assessment is *for* learning and that students should be active partners in assessment. The first part of the book provides frameworks for thinking about assessment and feedback while the second provides examples of innovative practice.

Grant Wiggins (1991) *Educative Assessment*. This is the best example of U.S. practice in this area. Although the book has a school perspective its title "Educative Assessment" highlights the idea of assessment *for* learning rather than just assessment *of* learning. The focus is on designing assessments to inform and improve student performance.

# The ABCs of Assigning Grades

**G**rading is almost always in the news. Grade inflation, grading leniency, contract grading, mastery grading—all of these stimulate heated discussion and cries of dismay. My own ideas about grading have become somewhat clearer as I have talked to my teaching assistants about grading policies. That may explain why I am not overly emotional about each of these issues.

First let's agree that grades are fundamentally a method of communication. The question then becomes, What does the professor intend to communicate to whom? When we put grading into this context, four things become apparent:

1. Evaluation is a great deal more than giving a grade. As we have seen in the preceding chapters, the major part of evaluation should be in the form of comments on papers, responses to student statements, conversations, and other means of helping students understand where they are and how to do better. A professor giving a course grade is communicating to several groups—individual students, professors teaching advanced courses, graduate or professional school admissions committees, prospective employers, and so on.

2. What professors communicate by a grade depends on the meaning of the grade to the person reading it—the effect that it has on that person.

3. Professors cannot change the meaning of grades unilaterally. The students' interpretations will be colored by their previous experiences with grades, and they are likely to be disturbed, or to feel that they are being misled, when a professor uses grades in new ways. This explains the strong emotional reaction to so-called grade inflation and to practices deviating from traditional meanings.

4. The meaning of A's, B's, and C's has changed over the last 50 years. In the mid-1900s, C was the average grade. Today, B is more typical. This is not a problem as long as those who assign and interpret grades understand the current meaning. Whether they do is open to debate.

What are grades used for? I suggest that the person reading a grade typically wants information with respect to some decision involving a judgment about the student's *future* performance. Mastery systems of grading, pass-fail grading, and other alternative systems are resisted because they may not be efficient conveyors of information useful for predicting future performance. The accompanying box describes how three groups—students, professors, and employers—use grades.

## DO GRADES PROVIDE INFORMATION USEFUL FOR DECISION MAKING?

One of the arguments against conventional grading is that grades do not provide useful information for the major purposes for which they are usually used. Teachers assume that grades have some informational and motivational value for students. Critics, however, argue that the threat of low grades is often a crutch used by poor teachers. Moreover, a heavy emphasis on grades is likely to reduce motivation for further learning and may even result in poorer achievement by the students who are most motivated by grades. In fact, those who achieve the most tend to have moderate grade motivation and high intrinsic motivation (Lin et al., 2003).

What about information for employers? Probably most human-resources psychologists would agree that the best predictor of success on a job is successful performance on a similar job. For a young person entering the job market, the only previous employment has been in low-level part-time jobs. The employer's decision must then depend largely on other information, such as interviews, letters of recommendation, biographical data, family background, and test scores. Each source is only partially adequate. Insofar as the new job requires some expenditure for training, it seems likely that

## What Do Students, Professors, and Employers Want from Grades?

### Students

Students want to be able to use grades to assist them in making decisions such as the following:

1. Will I do well if I take additional courses in this field?
2. Should I major in this field? Does it represent a potential career in which I'm likely to be successful?
3. Do I have the skills and ability necessary to work independently in this field—learning more, solving problems, ability to evaluate my own work?

### Professors

Professors advising a student or making admissions decisions expect grades to tell them:

1. Does this student have the motivation, skills, knowledge, and ability needed to do well in advanced courses (insofar as the type of problems dealt with in the earlier course are relevant to the demands of the advanced courses or program)?
2. What kind of person is this? What does the pattern of grades tell us about this student's ability and work habits?

### Employers

Prospective employers want to use grades to assist in decisions about whether a student is likely to do well on the job.

1. How well will the student be able to solve on-the-job problems related to the area of his or her coursework?
2. Does the overall pattern of grades indicate that this individual is the sort of person who will do well in our organization?

From this analysis it seems evident that grades are used not only as a historical record of what has happened but also as information about what a student can do in situations outside the class for which the grade was awarded. For employers and graduate admissions committees, the grade is not so much historical as potentially predictive.

grades—representing the result of skills applied in study, learning, and problem solving—will add some useful albeit incomplete information. Grades might also be used by others as a surrogate measure of a strong work ethic, persistence, and flexibility in adapting to a wide range of situations. (I'm not saying that is an accurate interpretation of grades, however.)

Because grades are commonly used in combination with other variables, no one should expect grades always to correlate with success for the students who are selected. It is a simple mathematical truism that when we use several selection criteria—each of them having some validity—we should expect low positive, zero, or even negative correlations between any one selection variable and the ultimate criterion of performance. This outcome occurs because we balance criteria against one another. We select some people who are low in some important attributes because they have high grades, and we select others despite low grades because they are high in other important attributes. The common criticism that grades don't predict later performance is largely invalid because most of the studies cited were carried out in situations where grades and other predictors had already been used in selection.

## CAN WE TRUST GRADES?

The information value of the grades we assign is heavily influenced by the methods used to evaluate learning. In Chapter 7, "Assessing, Testing, and Evaluating," I described several ways of measuring student learning, from the typical in-class tests to out-of-class papers and authentic assessments. For grades to be truly useful, they need to be based on what the measurement field refers to as valid and reliable methods.

Assessments that are *valid* measure what they say they measure. For example, the best way to measure students' ability to structure a persuasive argument is to have students create their own unique argument on a topic and deliver it in either written or oral form. Answering multiple-choice questions about the parts of an argument isn't measuring the same thing. Even critiquing someone else's argument measures a different skill. When we grade argumentation skills with real argument-development activities, we have the most valid measurement and probably the best predictor of future argumentation success. The farther away from that situation we get, the less valid the measurement becomes.

One thing we should look for when determining how valid the measures to generate grades were is what went into the grade calculation. Lots of instructors give or take away points for student actions that have little or nothing to do with measures of student learning. For example, they make deductions for late papers or failures to follow instructions. Although these are possibly valid surrogates for qualities such as personal responsibility, maturity, or professional behavior, they are not valid measures of what a student has learned. Including them in an assignment grade lowers the overall validity of that grade. I'd be tempted to have a totally separate grade category called something like "demonstrated responsibility" or "diligence" that would be used to measure things such as tardiness, late assignments, or inattention to class policies. These would be separate from the quality of the work itself yet still part of the overall evaluation of a student. I suspect that in many cases that type of measure would be as good a predictor of future success—perhaps even a better one.

Another important quality of an assessment is its reliability. An assessment that is *reliable* produces fairly consistent results either across time or across multiple graders. Multiple-choice tests, for example, are very reliable because no subjective judgment influences grading; the answer is either right or wrong. Essay tests and papers are less reliable unless you consistently use a rubric to grade them. If you have a reliable measure, everyone's grade indicates a very specific performance, and all individuals whose performance is the same get the same grade.

What does all this mean for you as the person giving the grades? It means that in order to communicate accurately with all the consumers of those grades, you need to be sure that the bases for your grading are both valid and reliable. If you can do that, then they can believe you when you provide them with evidence of student performance.

|            | Pro                                                                             | Con                                       |
| ---------- | ------------------------------------------------------------------------------- | ----------------------------------------- |
| Contract   | Commitment to contract motivates students.<br><br>May be individualized.        | May reward quantity rather than quality.  |
| Competency | Ties grade to course goals. Encourages teacher and student to think about goals. | May be difficult to operationalize.       |
| Both       | Reduce student anxiety about competition and grades.<br><br>Encourage student cooperation. |                                           |

**TABLE 10.1 Contract Versus Competency Grading**

Of course, in reality, there are no grade police out there trying to make us all conform to the same exact standards. As a profession, we have to police ourselves. It's up to us to uphold our standards, not to keep grades from becoming inflated but rather to give honest grades that truly communicate what a student has achieved.

## ASSIGNING GRADES: ON A "CURVE" OR AGAINST A STANDARD?

One of the persistent controversies in college teaching is whether to grade "on the curve" (norm-referenced grading) or against an absolute standard (criterion-referenced grading). These two positions are probably not as far apart as the argument would indicate. Even teachers who grade on the curve are influenced in setting their cutoff points between grades by their feelings about whether the class was a good or a poor one. Similarly, teachers who do not grade on the curve set their standards in line with what previous experience leads them to regard as reasonable accomplishment in the course. Personally, I believe that grading on the curve is educationally dysfunctional. If possible, your grades should, both in the students' eyes and in actuality, be more nearly based on absolute standards than on relative standing in a particular class.

The use of an absolute standard becomes easier if you formulated your major and minor objectives and tested their achievement. Travers (1950b) proposed one set of absolute standards:

- A: All major and minor goals achieved.
- B: All major goals achieved; some minor ones not.
- C: All major goals achieved; many minor ones not.
- D: A few major goals achieved, but student is not prepared for advanced work.
- E or F: None of the major goals achieved.

Ideally, I should be able to list my goals for the course and at the end of the course assess each goal in such a way that I could use such a criterion-based system. In fact, however, my tests, papers, journals, research studies, and other elements of the assessment of learning are seldom pure measures of a single goal. For example, my tests assess knowledge and understanding of the major concepts and facts as well as ability to apply and think with these concepts. To separate each component would be almost impossible. Consequently, I assign points to each test, paper, and other assignment, and I give grades on the basis of the total percentage of points earned by the student over the term. This strategy at least avoids the detrimental effects of grading students' performances relative to one another and probably approximates the outcomes described by Travers.

There is a larger, more philosophical issue lurking behind the great norm-referenced versus criterion-referenced grading debate. The issue is the one we discussed earlier: What do grades mean? Is the purpose of the grade to identify the "best" students in a group (norm referencing), or is it to indicate what each student has achieved (criterion referencing)? Both are legitimate positions and can be and are argued for vociferously. There are no pat answers to the choice. For example, there are many times when we have to allocate limited resources or awards to only the best of a group. In those instances it makes sense to use intra-group comparisons. But what if everyone in the group does poorly or does really well? Do we pick "the best of a bad lot" or abandon good people who in another group would be the top performers? What if the skills needed for the next class or on the job are so critical that failure to achieve an absolute level of competence could have dire consequences? Should we pass only those who meet the standard? (Thinking of getting a shot from a nurse or doctor who was the top student in a class of klutzes, I'd much prefer that all medical personnel meet a set standard for shot giving, thank you!)

I don't have a pat answer for this dilemma. The choice rests on factors such as these:

1. How valid is the instrument on which the grade is based? How reliable is it? It may not be appropriate to use criterion referencing if the measures are not accurate or fair.

2. How select is the group being evaluated? If the group is very homogeneous, norm referencing is inappropriate because there's not really a distribution of skills across the group.

3. How critical is the content being evaluated? If it's critical, I favor criterion referencing every time.

4. Does future work depend on this content? If it does, then criterion referencing will at least be sure that everyone who passes has the prerequisites for that future work.

There are many more things to consider, but the important point is to consider them rather than choosing blindly.

# REDUCING STUDENT ANXIETY ABOUT GRADES

Because to many students grades represent a fearsome, mysterious dragon, their anxiety can sometimes be reduced by encouraging the students to participate in planning the methods by which grades will be assigned. Students usually can recognize the instructor's need to conform to college policy in grade distribution, and the dragon seems less threatening if they have helped determine the system by which they are devoured (or rewarded).

Some instructors go so far as to let students determine their own grades or to have groups of students grade one another. I like the idea that students should develop the capacity for self-evaluation, but I recognize that many students resist this procedure, either through modesty or through fear that they will underrate themselves. If you use it, I suggest having a thorough discussion of the plan with students and an agreed-upon, well-defined set of criteria that all students should use.

Whether or not students participate, you need to be clear about your criteria. Examples of previously graded work may be helpful. Asking students to hand in their own estimates of their grades may help you to motivate them better and may also develop their abilities for self-evaluation.

In general, motivation is not helped simply by high grades; nor is it helped by tough standards. Students are most motivated when they feel that they can achieve success with a reasonable effort (Harter, 1978).

By keeping students informed during the course about where they stand, you help them control much of the anxiety they feel when the grading system is indefinite and unstructured. Sometimes it may seem easier to fight off grade-conscious students by being very indefinite about grades, but student morale is better when the students know the situation with which they must cope.

Whatever your grading strategy, being more generous in assigning grades to tests and papers than in the final distribution of grades guarantees visits from aggrieved students. One way in which you get yourself into this position is by providing opportunities for students to omit questions on an exam or to submit extra work for a higher grade. On the other hand there is much to be said in favor of adopting procedures that take the sting out of the occasional failure by allowing a re-do or throwing out the lowest grade. It will be a constant balancing act between measurement consistency and concern for student mental health. Any procedures you choose can have some educational justification, but you need to be able to convince administrators or colleagues that the pattern of grades you assign is appropriate for the achievement of your students.

## WHAT ABOUT THE STUDENT WHO WANTS A GRADE CHANGED?

If you keep students informed about their grades on tests, papers, and other graded work during the term, you will avoid most complaints. But there still may be some. My basic strategy is the same as that used in returning tests or papers (see Chapter 8): listen first and then go over the criteria used. Try to understand the student's reasoning. This may be a learning experience for both of you.

If students are worried about their grades in connection with their admission to a specialized school or because they are on probation, I may offer to write a letter to their advisor or other authorities describing their work in detail and pointing out any extenuating circumstances that may have influenced the grade. This may serve to cushion a refusal to change the grade.

In addition, of course, you may try to explain to the students the rationale of grades. Usually this doesn't seem to do much good. Both students and faculty sometimes confuse two possible criteria on which grades may be based. One is the relative amount of *progress* the student has made in achieving the goals of the course; the other is *achievement of the goals of the course* at the end of the term. In most classes, research has demonstrated a relatively low correlation between these two criteria. If you were to mark solely on progress, students who came into the course with the least background might still be the poorest students in the class at the end of the course yet get an A for their progress. Most employers, registrars, and professors interpret a grade in terms of the achievement of course goals; hence professors who grade solely on students' progress may send students into advanced courses or jobs for which they lack the requisite skills and knowledge.

Progress, however, is relevant to prediction. A student who has made a great deal of progress despite a poor background may do as well in an advanced course or job as someone with somewhat better performance at the end of the course who made relatively little progress. My own solution is to assign grades primarily for achievement of course goals (total performance), but when a student's total points or overall performance is close to the boundary between grades, I assign the higher grade if there has been much progress.

No matter how you grade, some student will be unhappy. Be sympathetic, but beware! If you begin changing grades, the jungle drums of the campus will soon spread the word. Be sure that you understand your institution's regulations with respect to grade changes. Check, too, on procedures that students may use to appeal capricious grading.

Don't finish reading this chapter with your own anxiety aroused by the dangers of grading. It is proper that good teachers should be humble as they see how great is the power they have over the happiness of their students by printing a simple A, B, C, or D. Nevertheless, one of the real satisfactions of teaching is giving a good grade to an ordinarily average student who has come to life in your course.

## GRADES VS. LEARNING: SOME RELATED RESEARCH

A lot has been written about goal orientation and its effects on learning. Carol Dweck (1986), among others, has discussed the finding that many learners seem to be pursuing goals that are focused on *appearing* competent rather than on actually learning anything. This is the phenomenon of goal orientation. Some students are pursuing mastery goals (they really want to learn and are what we might call non-grade-conscious); others are working primarily for a grade (called in this literature "performance oriented"). You will find a more complete explanation of this theory in Chapter 11 on motivation, but here is how the theory is relevant to grades.

Although originally these orientations were thought to be related to some personality traits, more recent literature relates these orientations to the conditions of learning, to what rewards and punishments are in place for success. The researchers even assert that a single person can have both types of goals in the same situation but for different aspects of the task. All of us have had students whose only interest seemed to be in their grades. The research on this topic has shown that these students are usually very literal-minded, not willing to try anything new, and likely to stick to the familiar so they know they can succeed. Sometimes you run across a student who wants to learn no matter what it takes. The research literature shows that students like this are willing to risk mistakes, to interpret failures as something to learn from rather than avoid or hide. Obviously we'd all like to have the latter students rather than the former. The great thing is that we can influence which type of goals students will work toward in our classes: learning or grades. Ames (1992) and Maehr and Midgley (1991), all researchers in the area of motivation, have given some very good guidelines about how to turn students into learning-oriented learners. Their recommendations* include the following:

1. Focus on meaningful activities that students can see are related to their own future. This helps them focus on becoming skillful rather than on simply earning a grade.

2. Make the learning interesting through the use of variety and novelty. The goal is to distract the students from focusing on grades by making the learning worthwhile in and of itself.

3. Make the learning challenging but doable. Challenge is a big source of motivation for students, but only if there is hope of success.

4. Give learners some choice in what they are going to do. When you are able to choose, you are more likely to work toward something in which you have a vested interest.

5. Focus on individual improvement rather than on comparisons with others. This is probably the most important but most difficult thing to control. Students have a long history of comparing themselves to others with their grades.

6. Make evaluation private rather than public. This actually supports item 5. Private evaluations make it harder for students to focus on how they compare to others.

7. Recognize effort and progress. Try to get students' minds off getting the right answer as the only goal.

8. Help students see mistakes as opportunities for learning. This is best done through the way you react when a student makes a mistake. Do you criticize, or do you try to help students work through their thought processes? These two behaviors result in very different reactions by students.

9. Encourage collaborative learning. Students who are working together toward a common goal are less likely to be comparing themselves to others.

---

*These recommendations are adapted from a set created by Pintrich and Schunk (2002, pp. 238–239), who combined the findings of all these researchers into a coherent set.

The research on student goal orientation indicates that if you can structure your class along these lines, students will be more comfortable in putting grades aside and focusing on learning because they can trust you to help them accomplish as much as they can. Perhaps that will help take the sting out of grades and as a result decrease their importance overall.

## IN CONCLUSION

1. Grades are not just a communication between teacher and student; they are a decision-making tool for future professors, employers, admissions committees, and others.

2. Useful assessments are both valid and reliable.

3. Involving students in the planning of assessment methods can reduce grade anxiety.

4. Grading on the curve can have detrimental effects. Tread carefully.

5. Try to focus students on learning rather than on grades.

### Supplementary Reading

What grades mean to faculty, parents, personnel directors, and students is described in O. Milton, H. R. Pollio, and J. Eison, *Making Sense of College Grades* (San Francisco: Jossey-Bass, 1986).

A fine vignette about the problem of assigning grades is Linc Fisch's "Students on the Line," in *The Chalk Dust Collection: Thoughts and Reflections on Teaching in Colleges and Universities* (Stillwater, OK: New Forums Press, 1996), pp. 132–134.

Barbara Davis describes a number of systems for determining grades and gives sensible advice in her chapter "Grading Practices," in *Tools for Teaching*, 2nd ed. (San Francisco: Jossey-Bass, 2008).

Another good resource is B. E. Walvoord and V. J. Anderson, *Effective Grading: A Tool for Learning and Assessment* (San Francisco: Jossey-Bass, 1998).

Read more about goal orientation and its relationship to grading practices in P. R. Pintrich and D. H. Schunk's *Motivation in Education: Theory, Research and Applications*, 2nd ed. (Upper Saddle River, NJ: Merrill/Prentice Hall, 2002).

With the change in instructional methods comes the need for a change in grading practices. Rebecca S. Anderson and Bruce W. Speck's "Changing the Way We Grade Student Performance: Classroom Assessment and the New Learning Paradigm," *New Directions for Teaching and Learning,* no. 74, July 1998, gives some good suggestions about new ways to grade student work.

*Grading Students* by Lawrence H. Cross (ERIC Digest, 10/1995). The ERIC Digests were very good summaries of research and practice provided by the ERIC Clearinghouses on different issues. The service has been discontinued, but some of the materials are still available. A site that provides access to the material is www.ericdigests.org.

Part **3**

*Understanding*
*Students*

# Motivation in the College Classroom

**F**ew topics concern teachers at all levels as much as the motivation of students. We worry over the students who appear disengaged or who attend sporadically, and we often disparage those who appear to care only about grades. We delight in the students who share our passion for the subject matter, who are eager to ask intelligent questions, who view grades as informational feedback, and who not only prepare for class but seek us out to learn more. We marvel when we compare notes with a colleague and learn that these contrasting motivational profiles sometimes describe the same student—but in different courses, suggesting that motivation is something other than an abiding characteristic of an individual.

We all want students who are motivated to learn. These are the students who choose to attend class regularly, participate constructively, persist when learning is difficult, make the effort to prepare for class and to study effectively, who solicit help when they need it, and who translate all this into academic success. Knowing more about how students are motivated and what you can do to structure a class that positively affects student motivation can make a significant difference in student engagement and learning. A classroom of motivated learners affects *our* motivation as well and can make teaching a more satisfying experience for the instructor.

---

This chapter was written by Barbara Hofer, Middlebury College.

# MOTIVATIONAL THEORIES: AN OVERVIEW

Researchers typically consider three indices of motivation: choice, effort, and persistence; achievement is an outcome of these variables. Accordingly, students who are motivated to learn choose tasks that enhance their learning, work hard at those tasks, and persist in the face of difficulty in order to attain their goals. So it should be no surprise that motivation is important to consider if we want to enhance student learning. Why students vary in their motivation is a compelling question, and several theoretical frameworks help provide answers.

Some students may be driven by a high *need for achievement* (McClelland et al., 1953). Need for achievement may be characterized as an individual trait or disposition, and it is likely to be the outcome of early environments in which parents set high standards and valued achievement. In general, students differ from one another in the degree to which achievement for its own sake is meaningful to them, but this difference explains only one aspect of motivation, which is also considered to be contextual and malleable. A particular student may exhibit a striving for achievement on the soccer field but not in your class, or perhaps appears more motivated to achieve in some parts of your course than in others; and we have all known students who did not appear motivated at the start of a course but became deeply engaged. Most importantly, classroom environment and instructional practices can foster certain types of motivation over others, as can the overall climate of an educational institution.

## Autonomy and Self-determination

Many psychologists posit that human beings have a fundamental need for autonomy and self-determination (Deci & Ryan, 2000). In general, individuals want to be in charge of their own behavior, and they value a sense of control over their environment. We can enhance students' sense of control by offering meaningful opportunities for choice and by supporting their autonomy, which in turn enhances motivation. Quite often these opportunities for choice can be relatively simple things such as a choice of paper topics, test questions, due dates, or reading assignments, yet they go a long way toward acknowledging a student perspective. For example, I typically list on my syllabus three due dates for papers and tell students that they can choose which of these dates work best for them. The actual assignments are similar at each of these points, but draw on material from that section of the course, and I list four or five topics from which students can choose. Too much choice, however, is not helpful, as

Barry Schwartz (2004) has shown in *The Paradox of Choice*, so students typically don't benefit as much from highly open ended assignments such as being allowed to "write about anything" they choose. Providing some parameters and guidance, and some choice within that framework, seems most effective (and simplifies your assessment).

## Intrinsic and Extrinsic Motivation

Most educational researchers acknowledge that what matters is not only whether a student is motivated but also what type of motivation the student has. Instructors at the college level often complain of student preoccupation with grades, typified by the perpetual classroom question "Will that be on the test?" *Extrinsically* motivated students are likely to engage in the course for reasons of external rewards, such as grades, recognition, or the approval of others (notably instructors and parents). Individuals who are *intrinsically* motivated engage in an activity for the value of the activity itself, rather than for an external reward. These students learn for the pleasure of learning and who have a sense of self-determination about their educational path. Intrinsic motivation has been shown to foster conceptual understanding, creativity, involvement, and a preference for challenge. Research on college-student learning indicates that students with an intrinsic orientation are more likely to use cognitive strategies such as elaboration and organization, resulting in deeper processing of the material (Pintrich & Garcia, 1991).

Although the image of a classroom of intrinsically motivated learners might sound ideal, students are also driven by the desire for grades, approval, praise, and other rewards, and understandably so. Intrinsic motivation and extrinsic motivation exist not on a single continuum but on two separate ones, and students may often have multiple goals for the same course. A student enrolled in a required course, for example, may be deeply interested in the material but may also see it as a step in her professional development and may desire to earn an A so that she will be likely to gain admission to graduate or professional school. Even students who initially appear only extrinsically motivated to take a course, perhaps viewing it merely as a requirement toward graduation, can become more intrinsically motivated if the instructor arouses their curiosity, provides appropriate levels of challenge, and offers them choices that enhance their control (Lepper & Hodell, 1989). Faculty members are also excellent models for intrinsic motivation, and talking about your own enthusiasm and passion for the field can be contagious.

Although studies have indicated that external rewards may diminish intrinsic motivation by undermining self-determination (Ryan & Deci, 2000), recent research seems to support the judicious use of external rewards as a complement to other motivational approaches. Extrinsic rewards may be particularly useful when intrinsic motivation is lacking—and it is reasonable to assume that students are not always going to be intrinsically motivated to learn everything they are expected to learn during the college years. Students may also find extrinsic rewards to be productive during the early stages of learning in a new subject before they feel they can begin to master it and when the necessary nature of the tasks (such as memorizing vocabulary in a foreign language or learning a large number of terms in the sciences) may not be intrinsically interesting. There is also evidence from a study of intrinsic motivation in college undergraduates that the pursuit of grades may not be all bad (Covington, 1999), in that the attainment of grade goals can foster an increase in interest, at least among those whose goals are not driven by the desire to avoid failure.

Extrinsic rewards are most beneficial when they *contain informative feedback* and enable students to focus on improvement. Thus grades alone are less helpful than grades accompanied by narrative feedback that addresses specific directions for change. It is also possible to defer awarding grades and provide comments for improvement only. In the required Research Methods course that I teach I give feedback but no grades on the first draft of research proposals, conveying how students might improve their work in the next version.

Taking the time to provide students with constructive feedback on papers as well as using class time when returning tests as an opportunity for further teaching can facilitate student engagement and motivation. Students appreciate knowing that their learning matters to you, and that you can help guide them toward success. I typically do a frequency count of missed items on a test, for example, and I use a few minutes of class to review any questions that more than a few students missed so that I can address misconceptions. If more than half of the class misses an item, I don't count it and try to determine if it was simply a poorly written question or if I need to spend more time re-teaching the material.

## Expectancy-Value Theory

Students typically direct their behavior toward activities that they value and in which they have some expectancy of success (Wigfield & Eccles, 2000). From this social cognitive perspective, motivation is viewed as the outcome of multiplying these two forces; if either one is absent, the resulting product is zero. Instructors can benefit by knowing that they need to foster both. Students need to feel that there is a reasonable possibility of success and that the work is of value. Thus even students who believe they can do well in an introductory course might not continue with the subject if they do not see that learning the material is worthwhile; likewise, even those who entered with professional ambitions dependent on the course may not persist in the field if they think that they cannot expect success. You may assume that students know the value of your field or of your particular course, but often this is not the case, and it may be worth the time to explain the relevance of what you are teaching. Fostering expectancy for success is equally important. Students benefit when instructors have high expectations for success and also provide the conditions for achieving it. Informative feedback is also critical here, as is availability in office hours or providing access to tutors, whether graduate student assistants or undergraduate peers.

## Mastery and Performance Goals

Motivated behavior is directed toward goals, and goals related to learning tend to reflect two broad types of purposes: mastery goals and performance goals (Ames, 1992). Students who adopt *mastery goals* are those whose primary desire is to understand and master the material. By contrast, students with *performance goals* are more likely to focus on their achievement relative to the performance of others. The classrooms we create may implicitly foster either type of goals, depending on grading practices, classroom climate, and other such factors, and here the faculty member can be particularly influential in affecting productive motivational beliefs.

In a class that is focused on mastery, instructors generally use criterion-referenced grading rather than normative (grading on a curve), foster a supportive climate where students can take intellectual risks, and provide opportunities for students to demonstrate improvement. A mastery orientation may be visible in classroom discussions when students ask genuine questions to which they do not already know the answers, driven by a desire to better understand the material, rather than to impress their peers and the instructor. Mistakes are viewed as an opportunity for learning, rather than as a measure of worth, subject to the judgment of others.

In a class that is focused on performance, instructors often use normative grading practices, which imply that only a specified percentage of students are likely to succeed no matter how hard the entire class works, and provide no opportunities for revising and improving written work. Student questions may be formulated to present the inquirer in the best light and to gain recognition and reward. In contrast to students with mastery goals, students who are ego-involved with their performance may compare grades with one another and take academic shortcuts, such as avoiding more effort than is necessary to acquire the desired grade or, as recent research indicates, engaging in academic dishonesty (Jordan, 2001).

Overall, mastery goals lead to more adaptive outcomes, for such students are likely to focus on learning, use effective cognitive strategies, and experience less performance-impeding anxiety (Pintrich, 2003). Students in highly competitive college classrooms, however—which are performance oriented by design—may find it adaptive to pursue a performance orientation (Harackiewicz, Barron, & Elliott, 1998). Faculty members thus may have considerable power in shaping goal approaches within their classrooms. Fostering a particular goal orientation begins with course design and syllabus construction, when we make choices about evaluation and grading practices and how we plan to communicate them to students. Take time the first day of class to explain your grading practices and, if you are using a criterion-referenced grading system, to make it clear that students are not competing with one another for grades. This also makes it evident that it is advantageous to form study groups and support one another's learning. Students in required courses that are essential for their progression toward professional goals (medical school, business school, etc.) can benefit from an environment that teaches them that their success does not come at the expense of others. Goal orientation is also reflected in an array of teaching practices. Mastery orientation thrives in a classroom climate of warmth and acceptance where instructors support and value intellectual risk-taking and avoid comparisons among students.

## Attribution Theory

When individuals need to seek an explanation for unexpected outcomes, they make attributions about the probable causes, and these attributions have motivational consequences (Weiner, 2001). In the academic sphere, this often arises when students fail to perform well on a test or get a grade that differs from what they had expected. Typical attributions are effort ("I didn't study hard enough"), ability ("I'm just not good at this subject"), or luck ("The test emphasized the material I actually studied!"). Attributions can be categorized along three dimensions: locus, stability, and responsibility, which refer respectively to whether the cause is internal or external, stable or unstable, and whether the cause is controllable or not. Students who explain their disappointments with internal, controllable attributions ("I know I didn't prepare adequately for the test") are likely to do better next time, because they believe they can affect the outcome. Students who attribute failure to stable, uncontrollable causes ("I will never understand statistics") are less likely to be motivated for improvement and understandably pessimistic about future outcomes.

Instructors can assist students in making adaptive attributions, particularly by helping them attribute failure to effort rather than ability, as well as by communicating their own positive attributions about students' capabilities to learn. When meeting with students to confer about low performance or an unexpected poor grade, you can help them reframe their thinking about the cause of their difficulties and help them gain a sense of control over future outcomes by helping them think diagnostically and rationally. Ask them to describe how they studied (or went about writing the paper), review the types of questions they missed or the most significant flaws in a paper, and help them know how to prepare or write more effectively in the future. In addition, referring students to a study skills center on your campus in order to improve their learning strategies can communicate that the problem is remediable and that they can take charge in addressing it.

## The Motivational Power of Beliefs about Intelligence

Fostering students' beliefs about the power of effort and hard work also reinforces the notion that intelligence is incremental and can be developed, a powerful motivational belief, according to Carol Dweck, author of *Mindset* (2006). Students with this "growth mindset" are likely to take on challenging work, learn from mistakes, and approach new learning with enthusiasm, as these are opportunities for improvement. By contrast, individuals who believe in an entity view of intelligence, or what she calls a fixed mindset, are dedicated to preserving their own and others' impressions of their ability. Such students fear that having to work hard for accomplishment simply displays a lack of ability and talent, so even if they do exert effort they may try to hide it. Those with a growth mindset are more likely to appreciate how they have developed in the process of applying themselves well.

Dweck's research, supported by a large number of experimental studies, shows that the feedback of teachers (and parents and coaches and employers) has dramatic effects on how students perceive their own intelligence and what mindset they adopt. A student who does well on a paper and is told "You're really very smart at this" will do what it takes to protect that image, perhaps not speaking in class unless they are confident of the answer, choosing less demanding assignments, and avoiding novel tasks. A student who is told "You did well at this and must have worked hard to reach such a level of understanding" is likely to feel acknowledged for the effort and want to continue to seek challenges.

## Social Goals and Social Motivation

Students are obviously motivated by more than academic achievement. For example, they also have social goals that are operative in the classroom: they want to be socially responsible and to form social relationships with peers (Patrick, Hicks, & Ryan, 1997; Wentzel & Wigfield, 1998). Although most studies of the relation between social goals and academic motivation and achievement have been conducted with younger adolescents, certainly no college instructor would doubt that social goals are operative in the college classroom. Enabling students to make new acquaintances in your classroom in conjunction with meeting academic goals may enhance student motivation to attend class and to participate in academic work. For example, a brief moment to discuss a question with a partner works well from a cognitive perspective because it fosters elaboration and retention and provides opportunities for clarification, but it also gives students an opportunity to get to know one another. Helping students form study groups prior to exams fosters preparation and also addresses social needs. Group projects, as long as they are well structured and include individual accountability, can also be ways for students to meet new people and make friends with common interests.

## ▶ PUTTING MOTIVATION THEORY INTO PRACTICE

These principles can be used in many ways to structure classes that foster student motivation to learn. Here are a few suggestions:

1. When planning assignments, consider issues of choice and control. If you would like students to write two papers during the term, provide assignments during three time periods and let them choose which two to complete. This enables students to take charge of planning their work in the context of requirements from other courses and allows them to select issues of greatest interest. (This also has the advantage of spreading out the grading that you will need to do, an added bonus.) Similarly, provide a choice of topics for each assignment and consider a range of options that engage interest. Foster initiative by allowing students to propose alternative topics that meet the intent of the assignment.

2. Project your own motivation—for the subject matter and for the students. Take opportunities to describe your own intrinsic motivation for both research and teaching and your mastery orientation to learning. Too much of the literature on faculty "rewards" has focused on the extrinsic reinforcement for teaching, neglecting our own intrinsic motivation for academic work (as well as the intrinsic satisfaction of teaching). You are a powerful role model for your students as they develop their own passion and motivation for learning as well as for their future professions. Get to know your students as individuals with lives beyond your classroom.

3. Foster students' intrinsic motivation to attend class by being well pre-pared, making lectures and discussions interesting, varying the instruc-tional format, inducing cognitive dissonance and stimulating thought, and adding interactive elements where appropriate. Students are more motivated to come to class when the learning experience clearly exceeds what can be copied from another's notes.

4. Foster mastery by encouraging students to revise their writing. Although it might not be reasonable for you to read drafts of every paper, you might do this for the first written assignment and then create peer review groups for additional papers. Or you can vary this process by responding to outlines for one paper and then reading drafts of opening paragraphs for the second. You can further foster mastery by uncoupling feedback and grading, so that early drafts receive written comments but no grades.

5. Adopt a criterion-referenced approach to grading rather than a nor-mative one. Outline course requirements so that the point value for each assignment is clear from the beginning and students know what they need to do to succeed—and know that they can succeed without wor-rying about their standing relative to others in the course. This fosters a sense of control, creates a cooperative rather than a competitive climate, and appeals to both intrinsically and extrinsically motivated students.

6. Test frequently enough that students become accustomed to the for-mat and have opportunities to learn from their mistakes; at the very least consider a similar format for the midterm and final. Allow students to justify and elaborate on their multiple-choice answers, which enhances control, and give partial or full credit for acceptable and reasonable jus-tifications of alternative answers. Provide choices of essay questions to answer (e.g., "Answer five of the following six questions"). Consider pro-viding one of the essay questions in advance, particularly one that might require more thoughtfulness and preparation.

7. When grading tests, consider dropping questions missed by a large number of students—and then reteach the material when you return the tests. This sense of shared responsibility for the learning process heightens student awareness that you are committed more to their mastery of the material than to penalizing them for what they do not yet know.

8. Provide feedback that is constructive, noncontrolling (e.g., avoid words like "should"), and informative, thus enhancing student desire to improve and to continue to learn. View problems as something that can be addressed, not statements about an individual's worth.

9. In your supervision of teaching assistants, make the motivational implications of your instructional decisions explicit. I am indebted to Paul Pintrich, Bill McKeachie, and Scott Paris, who were extraordinary role models in their design of graduate seminars that fostered student motivation, but who also provided me with opportunities as a TA to understand the motivational structure of their undergraduate courses, which I have happily put into practice in my own teaching.

## *IN CONCLUSION*

1. Recognize students' needs for self-determination and autonomy, and provide opportunities for choice and control.

2. Foster intrinsic motivation by arousing curiosity, providing challenge, and offering choices, and provide extrinsic rewards that contain informative feedback and focus on improvement.

3. Make the value of your courses explicit, and take time to help students understand why what they are learning matters. Teach with a sense of purpose.

4. Create high expectations as well as the conditions that enable students to expect to succeed.

5. Create a classroom environment that promotes a mastery orientation, focused on the development of understanding and mastery of material and skills, rather than on relative performance to others.

6. Foster adaptive attributions: help students value the application of effort and learning strategies, and communicate your belief in their capability.

7. Foster a growth mindset that encourages students to see their own ability as malleable. Avoid praising students for ability or talent.

8. Provide opportunities for students to meet social goals in ways that are compatible with academic goals—such as through constructive uses of group work and interactive lectures.

## Supplementary Reading

Although some of the following works are directed more toward the motivational issues of K–12 schooling, the theories and many of the suggestions are useful to those who are interested in the issue of motivation in the college classroom.

▶ J. Brophy, *Motivating Students to Learn* (Mahwah, NJ: Erlbaum, 2004).

▶ C. Dweck, *Mindset, The New Psychology of Success* (New York: Ballantine, 2006).

▶ D. H. Schunk, P. R. Pintrich, and J. Meece, *Motivation in Education: Theory, Research, and Applications*, 3rd ed. (Upper Saddle River, NJ: Merrill/Prentice Hall, 2007).

▶ M. D. Svinicki, *Learning and Motivation in the Postsecondary Classroom* (San Francisco: Jossey Bass, 2004).

# Teaching Culturally Diverse Students

**R**esponding to the individual student may be the most important way to improve your instruction. Appreciating the unique needs and characteristics of your students sets an educational environment that will better enhance learning by each student.

Many dedicated teachers seek feedback in the classroom either by observing students' reactions or by directly soliciting comments: "How am I doing?" "Am I being clear?" "Is this too basic—do you want me to speed up?" For the most part, such feedback will enable you to accurately gauge the pace of student progress as well as the effectiveness of your approach to teaching. However, with a culturally diverse class, some basic differences in the students' and the teacher's backgrounds may cause feedback communications to fail. This chapter suggests some common cultural characteristics of some students coming from ethnic-minority heritages. It highlights some illustrations of how a faculty person of a white, European American background—which I will refer to here as a "Western" background—may stumble in working with a student from a different cultural background.

Cultural advice can provide useful general guidelines, but those guidelines are not necessarily appropriate for all ethnic students. Keep in mind that just as "All Asians are not alike," all students within *any*

This chapter written by Richard M. Suinn, Colorado State University.

ethnic group are not going to be alike—for two reasons. First, there are different nationalities and cultures even within an ethnic category. Among Asians, for instance, are over 60 different cultural groups, among them Chinese, Japanese, Hmong, Korean, Vietnamese, and others (Kim, McLeod, & Shantzis, 1992; Maki & Kitano, 1989; Vea, 2008). Second, within each subgroup there may be individual differences. Varying levels of acculturation, or the fact of being raised in a nontraditional ethnic family, might invalidate the cultural premises in this chapter (Suinn, in press). For instance, to apply these suggestions to a highly acculturated, westernized ethnic student would be equivalent to employing a stereotype (Stuart, 2004).

Having offered this caution, I would like to offer some insights from a nonwhite cultural perspective. At a minimum I hope that instructors will gain a perspective that avoids the *deficit model*, the view that inadequate performance from an ethnic person automatically means the student is academically deficient, unmotivated, uninterested, or poorly prepared. Instead I will highlight new ways of understanding the communications of culturally diverse students, and I will suggest ways in which your own behavior can be adapted to enhance the students' learning environment.

# CULTURE AND COMMUNICATION

## Nonverbal Communication

**Eye Contact.** You are giving a complicated lecture. One student in the audience looks at you and nods and smiles occasionally. Another student never looks at you. Instead, he continually looks down. He is not even taking notes. Which of these students is interested in the lecture? Which is listening attentively? Which is daydreaming?

The bread and butter of teaching is the act of communication as a two-way interactional process. You as the instructor usually communicate verbally. Students also communicate, not only when you ask them a question, but also nonverbally when they are listening. Nonverbal cues provide important feedback that influences your further communication.

What we observe, we interpret. And our interpretations influence our actions. Our meaning comes from our culture as Westerners. But to be culturally sensitive teachers, we must keep in mind that behaviors from different cultures have different meanings. The interpretation from a Western perspective of a student not making eye contact is that the student is inattentive, distracted, uninterested, or daydreaming. What is the consequence in your behavior? You might spend more lecture time going over the same point to arouse interest, or even talk louder (maybe the student will hear you the second time!). You might glare at the student or call him in for a conference. You might even dismiss this student as a lost cause.

Are you aware that for some ethnic groups, such as Asian Americans, African Americans, and Native Americans, looking away may be indicative of *careful attention* rather than inattention (Baruth & Manning, 1991; Garwick & Auger, 2000; Gudykunst, 2004)? It is estimated that white Americans make eye contact 80 percent of the time when listening and look away 50 percent of the time when speaking, and that African Americans make more eye contact when speaking and less when listening (Sue & Sue, 2003). In addition, among Asian cultures, staring at a person of higher status is considered rude (Sue & Sue, 2003) and mutual gaze among Mexican American parents and youngsters is also uncommon (Schofield et al., 2008). So eye contact or the lack thereof is not an automatic sign of attentiveness or inattention.

**Nonparticipation.**  In the middle of your lecture, you want to know not only if the students are listening, but whether they are also understanding and grasping the topic. So you ask, "Have I been clear? Anyone have any questions…any questions at all?" And what happens is…nothing. No one offers a question. No one even raises a hand.

From a Western perspective, because no one speaks up and no hands are raised, you might be congratulating yourself: "All right! My presentation is clear. I must be a great teacher!" Consequently, you rapidly complete your discussion and move speedily on to the next topic. But silence among ethnic minorities can have various meanings (Schrader-Kniffki, 2007). Are you aware that in some cultures it is very important to show great respect for elders or for persons with wisdom greater than one's own, and it may be considered disrespectful and insulting to raise a question? Doing so may imply that the elder (or instructor) is at fault for being unclear. Thus an ethnic student who fails to understand a teacher might blame himself or herself for being poorly prepared.

Questioning the speaker can also imply that the student is challenging the teacher. And such a challenge may be a taboo either because a challenge shows arrogance or because it disrupts harmony. Native Americans and Asian Americans value nonconfrontational interpersonal styles as a way to protect harmony in the interpersonal system. It would be unseemly to act otherwise (Lee, 1991; Swinomish Tribal Mental Health Project, 1991).

Other culturally based reasons for nonparticipation include the following:

- *A culturally ingrained value of humility.* Some cultures value modesty, not standing out in a crowd. A Japanese saying observes that "The nail that sticks out is hammered down." Another saying proclaims that Westerners place a premium "not only on knowing but on saying what you know," while the Asian "values knowledge but discourages verbalizing knowledge" (Nishida, 1996). Such a background might lead to what I call the "spotlight" effect. Like a deer that freezes in the glare of headlights, the ethnic student may freeze when the teacher focuses attention by directing a question to that student.

- *A history of distrusting the motives or intentions of others.* Students coming from experiences of racism, of being put down, and of experiencing the deficit model may feel especially vulnerable (Vontress & Epp, 1997). Out of caution, an African American student might be reluctant to volunteer or might be close-mouthed when asked a question. "Am I being picked on to make me look dumb in front of the class?" a student might wonder. "Are you setting me up so you can criticize my answer and say I'm wrong again?"

**What You Can Do.** A better understanding of the actual meaning of student behaviors will put you in a better position to respond to nonverbal feedback. Your first step is to avoid the false assumption that lack of eye contact and nonparticipation mean lack of attention, disinterest, or boredom. Also avoid the false assumption that a lack of questions means that your presentation has been well understood. Consider the possible cultural meanings of nonverbal behaviors and silence in communications.

Finding out what is going on will require gaining verbal participation from students at some point, if the nonverbal cues are not reliable indicators. This leads us to the topic of cultural aspects of oral communication.

## Verbal Communication

**Reluctant Speech.** You stop your lecture to obtain feedback. You directly ask a student to tell you whether your lecture has been clear; or you ask whether the student has any questions; or you even ask the student to explain in his or her own words what you covered. The student gets up slowly, looks sheepish, shifts from foot to foot, keeps her head down as though she is carrying the weight of the world, and quietly offers a very brief reply … that leaves you wanting more. You are still in the dark about how much the student has understood your presentation.

If you were not feeling so sympathetic toward the tongue-tied student, you might feel mystified about what's going on and speculate that she is being evasive and uncooperative. But as you saw in the earlier examples, there are possible cultural explanations for the student's reluctance to verbalize much. Perhaps the student is being careful to remain respectful by not challenging or insulting the higher-status expert—you, the teacher (McGregor, 2006). Or perhaps the student feels the need to get away from the focus of the spotlight as quickly as possible through a brief answer. Or perhaps underlying distrust about your intentions prompts her cautiousness.

**What You Can Do.** How might an instructor overcome an ethnic student's reluctance to respond more extensively even to a direct prompt? There are various strategies an instructor could try yet still be sensitive to various cultural concerns.

- *Concern about insulting the teacher.* How you word your prompt can make a difference. "Is my explanation clear?" is a very difficult question for a respectful student. Instead restructure the situation so that the student's reply is collaborative rather than critical. For example, "By the way, you know I've covered this topic with so many classes that sometimes I forget how familiar this topic is to me, and I leave out some important details, so you can help me…"

- *Concern about being in the spotlight.* Despite many years of experience as a lecturer and classroom teacher, at times I feel this discomfort, such as when I'm taking part in a discussion with a group of people I've just met. It is a feeling of embarrassment, of suddenly being aware that everyone is quiet, that all eyes and ears are focused not on the discussion leader but on me! All of my cultural sensitivities become stirred: avoid standing out, do not embarrass yourself, be modest and defer to others to take the lead, you can be seen but certainly not heard, avoid arrogance.

One solution to discomfort from being in the spotlight is to shorten the exposure. Turn the spotlight off or away. Let the students know that you are going to ask a question but you want them to limit themselves to a brief reply because you want to quickly move to other students' replies to obtain a group viewpoint. This strategy shines the spotlight on any individual for only a brief moment. You might also add that students need not stand up when called on. Addressing your question to other students first can give the reluctant student time to be ready.

■ *Concerns related to trust.* It takes time to build distrust and to establish trust. Individuals with difficult life experiences sometimes learn to be very observant and to attribute meaning to the tone associated with statements, to the implied meaning of terms, to the signals of posture, or to other nonverbal behaviors. Often these serve as guides for survival, particularly in an unfamiliar environment. So how a teacher words a question, what tone or posture accompanies the query, and what an instructor says after the student replies—all offer information influencing trust/mistrust.

When you ask a student to answer, could it seem as though you are issuing a challenge, or is it clear that you honestly want to know what the student has to say—no strings attached? To improve trust, carefully consider the wording of your questions, perhaps taking a bit more time to explain *why* you are asking ("So I know how to think up more examples that help make sense out of this messy topic"). Avoid abruptness not only in wording a question but in your comments following a response. Consider what you say after the student replies. Is your follow-up comment supportive, or is it a correction that implies that the student was wrong or that you didn't like the reply? A little bit of encouragement and a positive attitude will go a long way to building bridges.

**Circularity vs. Linearity.** At your initial class meeting you decide to establish rapport by asking for a simple personal opinion: "Did you enjoy your vacation?"

You receive a fairly extensive response: "Well, like, you know, spent first day at home.... My neighbor is getting another job soon. Some of us watched *Star Wars* on TV.... Got back yesterday...back with my roommate...was an interesting visit."

This roundabout, rambling reply might feel confusing rather than satisfying. The generic "interesting" conveys everything and nothing. But this response might represent an ethnic "circular" style of oral communication rather than a more "linear" Western one (Gudykunst, 2004; Park & Kim, 2008). Western thought and language tend to proceed in a linear fashion. You ask a question; you expect a direct answer. "What did you have for breakfast?" "Bacon and eggs." "Where and when shall we have lunch?" "There's an excellent menu today in the student center. Let's meet there at 11:30." "How was the movie?" "Excellent! I liked the part about..." A linear reply to the question "Did you enjoy your vacation?" would ultimately communicate a yes or a no. Many details might be offered, but the basic question to be answered is "Did you or didn't you?"

A teacher with a Western background who hears a student's roundabout reply may think, "The student is being evasive and is avoiding my straightforward question. Is there a reason? Maybe I'm not trusted, or maybe the student had a bad experience during vacation and doesn't want to talk about it. Maybe the student did something that was shameful, maybe even criminal… . This student rebuffs my overtures to be sociable. He is rejecting my attempts to reach out. Maybe the student just has low social skills." The teacher may be unaware of a number of cultural issues giving rise to circular communication (Gudykunst, Ting-Toomey, & Nishida, 1996; Huang, 1994; Okun, Fried, & Okun, 1999; Ting-Toomey & Chung, 2005; White & Parham, 1990):

- The student's reply may reflect a cultural tradition deriving from a preliterate period in which knowledge was passed on orally, storytelling was the medium for education, and lengthy tales or proverbs were used to convey information. The student begins in an indirect fashion well suited for imbedding a moral, a message, or the main answer. In this student's culture, grasping the overall theme of the "story" is more important than the meaning to be found in specific words, and general conversation may precede any serious interaction. Such seemingly superficial chatting or small talk develops a comfort level and establishes rapport (Ruiz & Padilla, 1977).

- A circular response might be another way of maintaining a respectful attitude toward the teacher-authority-expert. Carefully phrased replies avoid the impression that a student is so presumptuous as to offer advice, instruct the instructor, or even tell the teacher something the teacher does not know.

- A level of defensiveness may prompt the circular reply, as it keeps the student from being personally evaluated. Circularity may enable the student to avoid committing to a firm statement or being pinned down, but not because the student has anything to hide.

**What You Can Do.** Here again you can take the initiative in setting the stage for improved responsiveness from the student. Keep in mind that some of the behaviors of a culturally diverse student come from a long tradition or repeated socialization. His or her way of behaving is thus neither conscious nor intentional but rather habitual or even traditional. Thus, it may require a dedicated teacher to get the best from the student.

Patience, of course, is essential. Control your own need for a quick, precise, linear response. Permit the serpentine narrative to unwind at its own speed. Listen carefully for the overtones and the hidden theme.

Beware of phrasing questions that can put the student on the spot. Develop your own version of nonlinearity (Block, 1981; Sanchez & Atkinson, 1983). Instead of "Tell me how *you* would solve this problem?" consider asking "What might be at least one approach to dealing with this problem?" or "Suppose someone you know is facing this problem, how do you think that person would start attacking it?" or "What have you seen others do?"

# MOTIVATION AND STRESS

"Why don't these students perform like they should?" "They just don't respond to encouragement like other students. Obviously, they don't care!" "I can't seem to get through to them. I know they can do better—after all, they made it this far."

Such concerns about inadequate student performance might be explained by two contributing cultural factors: differences in motivation across cultures and cultural stressors. Increasing a student's performance toward his or her potential might be enhanced through culturally appropriate incentives or through reduction of interference from certain stressors.

## Cultural Differences in Motivation

There is a fundamental difference between Western and certain ethnic motivational orientations. The former emphasizes an individualistic orientation, the latter a collectivistic orientation.

Westerners tend to be spurred by goals such as individuation, independence, self-development, self-reliance—"being the best *you* can be," experiencing the satisfaction of personal achievement. Other cultures tend toward collectivism, perhaps tracing back to the era of tribes but now focused on the family unit. Within ethnic cultures goals are group goals, achievement honors the family, and personal failure is agonizing because it reflects negatively on the family (Avila & Avila, 1995; Fuligni et al., 1999; Garrett & Garrett, 1994; Gudykunst & Matsumoto, 1996; Lee, 2008). Thus, appeals based on individual recognition and accomplishment might fail to motivate an ethnic student, but putting the focus on family values might be more successful.

**"Family" Defined.** For various ethnic cultures, *family* means more than the nuclear family or even blood relatives. For some Hispanics, there are terms for a type of family member, *compadrazo* or *compadre/commadre*, referring to godparents who function as family (Arredondo, 1991; Ruiz, 1995). For African Americans, family roles may be assumed not only by grandparents but even by individuals outside the household, ranging from neighbors to ministers (McAdoo, 1999).

**Collectivism and Family Goals.** Calling upon family ties can be an effective approach to use with a student who requires motivational inspiration (Trusty & Harris, 1999). One underachieving Hispanic undergraduate improved his study habits when faced with the question "If you drop out, what do you think your younger brother will do with his life?" This was a more telling argument than the entreaty "You are throwing away your life unless you shape up!"—an individualistic appeal.

With family support, an ethnic student achieves great strength and feels a powerful desire to work toward goals (McGregor, 2006; Vasquez, 1982). Once when discussing weekend plans, I tentatively asked a Latina graduate student if her new boyfriend's visit might distract her from attending to her assignments for the week. Her immediate and no-nonsense reply was "No way! My parents and I agreed: I have only one reason for being here…my studies come first. Dropping out is not an option. My boyfriend understands that!"

Family-based values can also influence what defines success (Sage, 1991). For some older-generation parents, success by their adult offspring might be finding a secure job with a steady income. Thus, the value of an education is measured in those terms.

For a Native American, the collectivistic orientation may involve tribal members, who not only influence values but also offer support. Solving problems "the Indian Way" refers to seeking the wisdom of tribal members, often by returning to the reservation (Attneave, 1982; J. McDonald, personal communication, 2004; P. Thurman, personal communication, 2004).

## Cultural Stressors

Keep in mind that underachievement might be caused by impaired performance due to the stressors that the culturally diverse student faces. There are several possible unique stressor conditions: the imposter syndrome, the first-generation condition, and acculturation anxiety.

**The Imposter Syndrome.** This is the stress caused by self-doubt as the ethnic student is aware of his or her minority status. Surrounded by majority white students who are from different sociocultural backgrounds and whose English may seem more fluent or without accent, culturally diverse students cannot help but feel different. In fact, they are at least outwardly different in physical appearance.

The imposter syndrome raises questions such as "Do I really belong?" and "Perhaps it is a mistake for me to be here" (Ewing, Richardson, Jame-Myers, & Russell, 1996; McDavis, Parker, & Parker, 1995). Despite all facts to the contrary, it is often difficult to avoid such a feeling. During my own career, I was successful in being elected to several important committees and boards of the American Psychological Association. Though basically confident about my abilities, I still felt discomfort at my first meeting—the vague, gnawing sense that everyone else was familiar with one another and I was the only outsider. I finally ended my unease by reminding myself that the election procedure meant that three new people were always reporting in, so there had to be two others who were in the same situation as I. Further, instead of acting as though I didn't belong, I immediately introduced myself to the others and took my place at the table as they did.

On occasion the imposter issue is worsened by accusations from others. I recall a disgruntled, unsuccessful white applicant claiming that an ethnic student took "his" place only because of affirmative action. I also remember the experience of an African American who tested at the gifted level on standardized tests normed on white children, entered a school for the gifted, and continuously confronted other students' belief that she couldn't possibly have qualified on her own.

**The First-Generation Condition.** "First-generation students" are the first in their families to attend school at a level higher than the level their parents attained, such as being the first admitted to college. As such, they sometimes experience stress caused by lack of familiarity with the new environment—that is, university life. Entering college may be like entering a foreign country as the student faces decisions about what courses to take, misses home and family, struggles to engage with a world consisting mainly of the white majority, and tries to make sense of unfamiliar customs (Latus, 2007). The student's normal familial support system might be unable to help. Because no family members ever experienced the demands of that level of schooling, they might not understand the new pressures and strains the student is experiencing and may offer no sympathy (Fallon, 1997; Komada, 2002; Shields, 2002).

For students from an ethnic minority cultural environment, certain concepts or procedures may be difficult to grasp. Here are some that are associated with college enrollment:

- *Being on time.* Some Native Americans believe that taking the time to do things well is more important than doing things quickly but poorly. Thus, the requirement to complete an assignment "on time" might initially seem to be a troublesome demand because the student is inclined to focus more on doing a complete, high-quality job (Herring, 1997; LaFromboise, Berman, & Sohi, 1994; Sutton & Broken Nose, 1996).

- *Having grades based on class participation.* The requirement to speak out in class can come into conflict with the issues I cited earlier regarding reluctance to participate.

- *Being graded on the curve.* For ethnic groups that value cooperation and collectivism (working for the common good), the idea behind being graded on a curve may be hard to comprehend, because it involves an individual competing against everyone else for an individual goal.

- *Seeking help from strangers.* Well-meaning friends might warn an ethnic student, "You're going to be at a disadvantage. Remember, no one there will want to help you succeed. So you must be tough, be prepared to deal with things yourself" (Thompson, Bazile, & Akbar, 2004). Under these conditions, especially if the student feels any shyness with strangers for other reasons, it takes a strong student to ask for help from a teacher, to locate a tutor, or to identify a mentor.

**Acculturation Anxiety.** I remember a Native American student whose tribal elders were hesitant about her leaving the reservation. There was fear that she would find life more attractive elsewhere and that her core identity would be diminished through acculturation into the mainstream society.

Each of the four American ethnic minority groups has a term for group members who lose their ethnic identity through exposure to the Western culture. These are persons who have exchanged their cultural roots for an identification with the white culture. They are variously called "apples" (red on the outside, white on the inside), "bananas" (yellow on the outside, white on the inside), "coconuts" (brown on the outside, white on the inside), or "Oreos" (black on the outside, white on the inside) (LaFromboise, Coleman, & Gerton, 1998; Lone-Knapp, 2000; Maruyama, 1982; Tatum, 1993; Willie, 1975). What does this imply? It represents another source of stress for the ethnic person, who now is not only coping with academic tasks and possibly adapting to a new environment, but also facing the risk of denigration from his or her own cultural group.

Educational experiences often aim at enhancing personal growth and development of new knowledge, conducting inquiry, and opening new vistas into the world at large. As personal knowledge and skill levels expand, so does the sense of self. One's identity may be solidified, expanded, or even dramatically challenged. If changes in identity were without social consequences, the transformation would be easy. However, for an ethnic student with strong traditional ties, serious discomfort can be an outcome instead (Winrow, 2002). "Have I betrayed my own group?" "What am I? I am neither fish nor fowl now! And is the person I've become better or worse that what I was before?" "Am I now such a hybrid that I am an outcast from both the majority and the minority cultures?" It is easy to imagine how such a significant conflict can disrupt attention to academic studies and even raise thoughts of dropping out.

A teacher can enhance an ethnic student's learning and performance in a number of ways. The most important first step is to continue to be aware that low achievement may be due not to low ability but to motivational issues or interference from stressors. If motivation or stress is involved, then the following approaches might be useful.

## Increasing Motivation

**What You Can Do.** Remember that individualistic goals may not be as meaningful as collectivistic, family-oriented goals. In discussing goal setting with an ethnic student, find out how he or she came to be in school to begin with, and gain a sense of the familial values and expectations. Identify the strength of these familial ties, and determine if there are special family or community members whose opinions carry more weight (Fryberg & Markus, 2007). Try to differentiate between personal goals and familial goals, and be prepared to deal with conflicts between familial goals and expectations and newly developing personal desires— the student whose family expects to have "my son, the doctor" or "my daughter, the lawyer" while the student is now dreaming about being a philosophy major.

Consider inviting significant family or community persons to work with the underachieving student. This could even include problem solving.

James, an African American student, lived at home while entering his freshman year of college. As the oldest child, and now the first to attend college, James was looked up to by his family and friends. Six siblings of all ages also lived in the apartment, and the environment was lovingly described as "organized chaos." A grandmother also shared a room and helped in daily cleaning, cooking, and baby-sitting the youngest children while James's mother worked. Although James had been able to keep up with high school work, he soon discovered that in college the extra reading assignments and pressure from deadlines added new demands. Because the college campus was two hours away by public transportation, studying at home after school was the only option. However, the lack of privacy, the constant flow of activity, and the noise level were problems.

A teacher thinking along majority-culture lines would inquire about a move to a dormitory, which would provide quiet hours, have student tutors, enable being integrated into "college life," and promote individuation. However, that solution would overlook certain cultural values, beyond the issue of expenses. James would be forced to leave his major support system, his responsibility as the "man in the family," and a cultural environment that is an integral part of his current psychological development. His presence in the community and church is an inspiration to the neighborhood, a role that embarrasses him but that he recognizes as coming with the turf.

As a culturally sensitive alternative, one of James's professors, who saw the need for James to have study time, paid a visit to James's home for a conference with the entire family present. It quickly became apparent that everyone understood the problem and wanted James to be successful in his schooling. The family discussed options such as studying at a neighbor's place, but this would have been an imposition on others so it was temporarily tabled. Eventually, one solution was suggested by the grandmother. In a firm voice, she declared that henceforth all children would participate in a nightly "Help James Time." One room would be vacated and would be "James's college room" for two hours. During this period, James's grandmother, with the help of James's next oldest sibling, would arrange for each of the children activities such as story time, TV time, and outside play-time to ensure quiet. The children would rotate through the activities. A chart was posted on which James would note his study progress after each evening's session. As James completed assignments and received grades, he would share these with the family before the next "Help James Time." With this solution, James and his family eventually were able to celebrate his bachelor's degree.

## Dealing with Stressors

**What You Can Do.** Understanding the source of a student's stress may assist you in offering appropriate help. Familiarize yourself with studies that offer the ethnic students' personal views of the academic environment (Garcia-Sheets, 2008; Wimms & Maton, 2008; Winrow, 2002).

The imposter syndrome may have its roots in a history of racism, or it may be an issue of simply entering a new and unfamiliar setting, including new social/interpersonal settings. A mentor who believes in the student, who knows how to teach the student to use his or her strengths, and who recognizes the value of taking one step at a time can be a major positive influence.

The specter of presumption of special privilege through affirmative action may contribute to the imposter syndrome. There is no one action that would erase such feelings. However, the following argument might be valuable: If detractors interpret affirmative action as special privilege, it is equally important for them to recognize that "white privilege" also exists but goes unexamined. Because of white privilege a white person in the majority community never needs to be aware of how she or he is viewed by others when entering a store, restaurant, or class, or when boarding a bus, waving down a taxi, or standing up to express an opinion (Lawrence, 1998; Sue, 2003; Sue, 2004). Being accepted as belonging, never standing out, never worrying about below-the-surface evaluations, and not having your comfort level displaced in interactions are privileges. An ethnic person is continuously faced with looking different or sounding different and is unable to alter those facts. This person will adapt, of course, but will never fully acquire white privilege.

It is entirely legitimate for schools, businesses, and industries to set criteria for selection of personnel based on goals. Athletes are recruited; Merit Scholars are enticed into undergraduate programs; students with special life experiences, those who show evidence of high motivation and excellent work habits, or even those representing geographic diversity are offered admission to limited graduate programs. These represent opportunities, not guarantees of eventual success. To those of your students who might be vulnerable to the imposter syndrome I would quickly point out, "The door has been opened for you to enter. Whether you deserve to remain will be up to you to prove."

The first-generation condition is not unique to ethnic students, although a history of poverty, poorer educational preparation, or recent immigration might lead to more ethnic students being the first generation in college. Because these students lack information about the school environment that is likely to be a key factor in their success, any steps your school can take to increase their familiarity will help.

One useful solution is precollege visitation days, at which incoming students and their families can become familiar with the campus and procedures. Putting together a survival guide for culturally diverse students or distributing a section from an existing guidebook might provide an excellent resource. (APA has one for graduate students; see El-Ghoroury et al., 1999). Informative roundtable discussions sponsored by ethnic student services offices can be important, as well as a way of matching upper-division ethnic student mentors with new students.

Many students experience homesickness when they leave their homes to attend school elsewhere. The homesickness compounds the difficulty of sudden geographic displacement, separation from a support system of family and friends, being confronted with the unfamiliar college culture, and the stress of the immediate need to adapt to numerous new challenges.

Most students manage their initial homesickness, develop a new sense of freedom and self-confidence, and become comfortable with their new identities. As I mentioned previously, the ethnic student may also adapt quickly and discover the new "self" that emerges, but may also be confronted with the identity conflict this brings. For some white students, brief visits home or even phone calls to family serve as a connection that smoothes the transition. Similarly, for a culturally diverse student, making this connection can provide a refreshing energy to move forward. For some Native Americans, a powerful spiritual renewal comes from even a brief return to the reservation or tribal environment.

## TAILORING YOUR TEACHING METHODS

In addition to being sensitive to cultural differences among students, you can make your classroom more welcoming and effective for ethnic minority students by your choice of teaching approaches.

### Match Learning Styles

Try this exercise: Close your eyes. Using your imagination, develop a clear image in your mind of a very large plane flying over you. You are looking up at it. It's very close as it passes over you. Now stop and describe this airplane to a friend in as much detail as you can.

How did the airplane appear in your imagination? As you described it, what details were salient? Visual ("The plane had a long body with windows")? Auditory ("It roared past me")? Tactile ("I felt the wind rush by")? Have some friends repeat this exercise, and compare the results.

Notice the individual differences in the way a particular sense dominates in each person.

The exercise shows you that different people experience imagery in different ways. Likewise, different students—both majority and minority—may have different learning styles (Roig, 2008). Some learn best through audio input, the typical lecture format. Some learn best through visual input, seeing the material in writing. Others learn best when they themselves write down the material or when they verbalize the material aloud in their own words. It is as if their internal wiring is different, like a VCR that has video input but also audio input. Entering an audio signal into the video input will fail and vice versa. Using the correct input produces clear results. By matching your teaching method to a student's learning style, you enhance that student's ability to grasp the information and to remember the material.

## Be Concrete

Being concrete is another generic principle of teaching, but there are different ways of achieving this. You can use a demonstration/exercise, use metaphors, or use examples from students' personal life experiences. Understanding the cultural experiences of an ethnic student can help bring academic material to life in concrete ways. It is also useful to discuss the practical applications of classroom topics to satisfy the pragmatic interests of ethnic students (Reyes, Scribner, & Scribner, 1999).

## Enhance Performance Measurement

Earlier, I described some differences between Western and ethnic groups' concepts of time. Native Americans, we saw, value doing a task well rather than doing it quickly. Therefore, timed tests might be a poor indicator of their actual knowledge. Also the commonly used timed multiple-choice examinations rely extensively on memory skills. Useful alternatives would be take-home examinations that can measure analytic skills, creativity, and comprehension without the side issue of time.

One interesting approach is testing based on the triarchic theory of intelligence, which postulates three elements: analytic, creative, and practical. Sternberg (2003; Sternberg & Grigorenko, 2008) found that measures of analytic/creative/practical knowledge predict college grade point averages more accurately than the traditional SAT verbal/math test scores, and that students taught with attention to these educational priorities perform better on traditional course examinations.

## Choose Appropriate Nonverbal Behaviors

Just as the way a student speaks, listens, and stands creates an impression on you, the impact you have on your students results not only from your explicit verbal communications, but also from certain nonverbal behaviors:

- *Conversational pauses.* Typically, a Westerner pauses one second before continuing to speak; therefore, any longer pause signals that the speaker has finished. Native Americans pause a bit longer, four to five seconds, before completing a sentence or thought (Baruth & Manning, 1991). Failing to understand the meaning of this longer pause, a Westerner may begin to talk, thereby interrupting the conversation and communicating rudeness, disinterest or disrespect, or a dominating attitude.

- *Personal space.* Different cultural groups interact normally at different distances (Hall, 1966). The space each group prefers is known as personal space. If one person steps into another's personal space, this is experienced as an intrusion. Similarly, if too much distance is maintained during an interaction, this may be interpreted as aloofness. African Americans and Hispanics tend to stand closer to someone they are conversing with than do white Americans, and Asians tend to prefer greater distances (Jensen, 1985; Mindess, 1999). An understanding of personal-space norms is important for maintaining good interpersonal communications.

For some cultures, touching is not acceptable. Hence, a teacher reaching to offer support or encouragement and just lightly touching a student can have the opposite effect.

An interesting teaching exercise will point out the rigid but unconscious American rules about space. Read the following questions about elevator behaviors and see if you are aware of these rules:

1. What are the rules for standing in the elevator? Where do people stand when there are only two or three people (strangers to one another)? What happens when a fourth person enters the elevator?

2. How would you feel if there were two people on the elevator and a third stranger entered and stood right next to you?

3. What happens when the elevator becomes more crowded and there are four or more people?

4. How close will people stand? What are you allowed to "touch"?

5. What do people look at in a crowded elevator?

6. When is it permissible to talk to the other people?

Compare your answers against the rules in the Appendix, which are rules typically followed in the United States.

## Be Accessible

Cultures can be viewed as either horizontal or vertical in their interpersonal structure. A vertical, hierarchical culture establishes high- to low-status roles associated with titles of address (Feldman & Rosenthal, 1990; Gudykunst, 2004; Lee, 1999). The structure of Western cultures tends to be horizontal—everyone is on the same level. A student raised in a vertical culture may prefer to address you by your title and may be puzzled by your insistence on a more familiar mode of address (Yamauchi & Tharp, 1995). For students from a horizontal culture, the invitation to "Just call me Bill" or the remark "I'm Janet" confirms the desired message of equality. You can use a title to allow ethnic minority students to be comfortable, while still conveying by other actions your openness and accessibility.

A recent research study found that the dropout rate among Hispanic high school students was nearly three times higher than that of white students and two times higher than that of African American students (Fry, 2003). A study of factors associated with persistence in school identified teachers as the second most influential factor for Hispanics (Fuentes, Kiyana, & Rosario, 2003). Most interesting is how these teachers were described. They were seen as encouraging their students to succeed, having high expectations, and believing that their students could meet these expectations. Rather than being viewed as aloof or regimented, the teachers were described as "playful." In essence, they were seen as approachable, interested in their students, and inclined to find potential rather than deficits in the young people they teach.

It is important for you to take the initiative to be accessible and to convey genuine interest and to be welcoming in words and in behaviors (Suinn, 2007). A simple greeting helps, in the classroom, in the hallways, and outside of school.

- Take time to chat. At first you may need to take the lead, avoiding the spotlight effect.

- Have consistent office hours, but encourage drop-in visits.

- Be encouraging and positive, supportive and solution oriented, and by all means listen.

- Work on problems and engage in positive reappraisal: "Persistence will work." "A step at a time is progress." "You can make it."
- Help students identify their strengths, find ways to cope and succeed, and leverage those strengths.

## IN CONCLUSION

Pay attention to your students in order to learn about them and truly understand them. Be a caring person, a welcoming person, an interested person. Identify and build on strengths, and encourage them!

### Supplementary Reading

C. Bennett, *Comprehensive Multicultural Education*: *Theory and Practice*, 5th ed. (Boston: Allyn and Bacon, 2003).

J. Clayton, *One Classroom, Many Worlds*: *Teaching and Learning in the Cross-Cultural Classroom* (Portsmouth, NH: Heinemann, 2003).

P. Gorski, *Multicultural Education and the Internet*: *Intersections and Integration*, 2nd ed. (New York: McGraw-Hill, 2004).

W. Gudykunst, *Bridging Differences*: *Effective Intergroup Communication*, 4th ed. (Thousand Oaks, CA: Sage, 2004).

S. Lassiter, *Cultures of Color in America*: *A Guide to Family, Religions and Health* (Westport, CT: Greenwood Press, 1998).

D. W. Sue, and D. Sue, *Counseling the Culturally Diverse*: *Theory and Practice*, 5th ed. (New York: Wiley, 2007).

R. Terrell, and R. Lindsey, *Culturally Proficient Leadership*: *The Personal Journey Begins Within* (Thousand Oaks, CA: Sage, 2008).

S. Ting-Toomey, and L. Chung, *Understanding Intercultural Communication*. (Los Angeles, CA: Roxbury, 2005).

## APPENDIX

According to Judie Haynes, the following are the typical behaviors governing personal space in elevators by Americans (www.everythingesl. net/inservices/proxemics_elevator.php):

1. If there are only two or three people on an elevator, each person usually leans against the walls. If a fourth person boards the elevator, the four corners are normally occupied.

2. Being in a crowded elevator would be a breach of our personal "space." We would feel very uncomfortable and move or get off the elevator at the next stop.

3. When more than four people are on an elevator, the occupants begin to follow a complex set of rules for behavior. Everyone turns to face the door. Hands, purses, and briefcases hang down in front of the body. People usually scrunch up, rounding their shoulders, so that they take up as little space as possible.

4. People don't touch each other in any way unless the elevator becomes very crowded, and then they only touch at the shoulders or upper arms. If you see an overcrowded elevator, you will probably choose to wait for the next one.

5. Everyone usually looks at the floor indicator located above the door.

6. It is unusual for people (who are strangers) to speak to each other in an elevator unless they are sharing some kind of similar experience (such as a conference). People who do know each other will usually speak softly. When a group of people enter the elevator and do not follow these rules, other occupants usually feel very uncomfortable.

# Dealing with Student Problems and Problem Students (There's Almost Always at Least One!)

**T**here isn't a teacher in the world who hasn't had to deal with student problems and problem students. Somehow it is reassuring to know that you are not alone in having a particular problem and that the problem is probably not due solely to your own inadequacy as a teacher. This chapter discusses some common problems that teachers at all levels face, and it suggests some strategies to try. I organized the chapter into three categories of problems, ranging from those directly related to the academic side of teaching, to those stemming from the fact that we are working with humans engaged in the process of learning.

First, a word of general advice: It is human nature to perceive the problem as the student; but before focusing on changing the student's behavior, take a few moments to look at what you are doing that might be related to the student's behavior. Interpersonal problems involve at least two people.

## ▶ INTELLECTUAL/ACADEMIC PROBLEMS

The problems examined in this section arise from things that affect how people learn and what happens when they have difficulties doing it.

## Aggressive, Challenging Students

There are many reasons why one or more students might be inclined to be aggressive and always challenging what is said in class. The most desirable reason might be that they are interested in the topic and have a lot of prior experience or knowledge to contribute, even if that prior knowledge is actually wrong. Or they might be challenging you because there is genuine disagreement about a particular topic and they're flexing their academic mental muscles against someone (you) who is very knowledgeable in the area. You usually can tell the difference between these students and those who convey, both verbally and nonverbally, hostility toward you and the whole enterprise. Sometimes the attitude is not so much hostility as a challenge to your authority.

Faced with the first of these two alternatives, you should be pleased! Consider this a "teachable moment." By disagreeing or always adding their two cents, these students are giving you an opportunity to accomplish two very important teaching tasks. The first is to delve more deeply into the logic behind the facts and principles that sometimes pass for content in students' minds. Rather than blindly accepting everything you say, students should try to reconcile new information with their preconceptions. They should be asking for greater depth, more examples, more explanation. These challenging students are out in the forefront of that student push. The second teaching task that these students are allowing you to do is to model what it means to be a critical thinker in the face of challenges to your ideas. In what passes for political dissent these days, students seldom have the opportunity to see two individuals actually discuss together rather than talk past one another about a controversial point. When students challenge you, you can demonstrate scholarly debate, including careful listening, thoughtful reflection, respectful disagreement, and reasonable compromise where appropriate.

Later in this chapter, in the section on emotional problems, I discuss students who are hostile or angry about everything.

## Students Who Want the Truth and Students Who Believe that Everything is Relative

You just gave a superb lecture comparing two competing theories. A student comes up after class and says, "That was a great lecture, but which theory is right?"

All too many students feel that the teacher's task is to tell them the facts and larger truths and the student's task is to listen to the truth, learn it, and be able to give it back on exams. This conception seemed to William Perry of Harvard University to be particularly common among first-year students.

Perry (1981) suggested that individual differences in student responses to teaching may be conceptualized in terms of stages of cognitive development. Students at the earliest stages have a dualistic view of knowledge. They think that things are either true or false, right or wrong. They believe that the teacher knows the truth, and that the student's job is to learn the truth. Students in the middle stages have learned that authorities differ. They accept the idea that there seems to be no settled truth, and that everyone has a right to his or her own opinions. This stage is succeeded by the recognition that some opinions and generalizations are better supported than others, and that the student's task is to learn the criteria needed for evaluating the validity of assertions in different subject matter fields. Students in the final stages are ready to commit to values, beliefs, and goals, and to make decisions and act on their values, despite their lack of complete certainty.

Sixteen years after Perry's article was published, Barbara Hofer (1997) found that dualists were rare at the University of Michigan, where she conducted her research. Rather, college students were more likely to believe that multiple perspectives are equally valid. Students like those studied by Hofer might be the very students who challenge everything that you or any other authority says. How should you respond to the challenge?

Unfortunately, we sometimes play into the hands of these students with the kinds of teaching and testing we do. If all we ever do is deliver information in a clean and neat format, if all we ever use are tests where there really is only one right answer, why should the students believe differently? Or, if we don't critique ideas or give them feedback when their points are less than coherent or correct, why should they bother to think more deeply? Here is one instance where we have to shoulder some of the blame for the problem.

Researchers like Perry and Hofer would agree that teachers need to help students understand how knowledge is arrived at in their own disciplines, what counts as evidence, and how to read critically and evaluate knowledge claims. For development in such epistemological beliefs, students need to debate and discuss issues in which competing ideas are challenged and defended; they need to write journals and papers that are responded to by the teacher or by peers. Most important of all, they need good models of how to think about the quandaries that are a constant in higher-level thinking and learning. As I said in the previous section, they need to see how you deal with contradictions and inconsistencies, how you solve problems when you don't have enough information, how you cope with the frustration of never being sure of the "right" answer.

## Students Who are Underprepared for the Course or Struggling

Sometimes students come into our classes without the appropriate background. Perhaps they didn't have the right prerequisites, or they didn't apply themselves diligently in their previous courses. It really doesn't do you or them any good to rail against their previous efforts or castigate them for imagined or real previous failures. That was then; this is now. What are you going to do with them now?

If the gaps in students' background can be remedied by pointing students toward supplemental or remedial resources, that's a good first step. It puts the students back in charge of their own learning, which is a good source of motivation, especially for those who are behind through no fault of their own. These days a lot of remediation can be made available electronically. Resources available on the Internet might be helpful for basic skill development, such as math skills or writing skills. Alternatively, you can prepare tutorials on the most commonly occurring deficits that you've seen in students in prior semesters. Your department may even want to create a common Website that helps students with key skills needed in all courses in the discipline or that provides definitions, examples, and activities to practice the basics of the discipline. You also can put materials or alternative textbooks on reserve in the library or online for those students who may not have had the appropriate content in prerequisite courses. Include sample questions or old exams to help them decide whether they understand well enough to go on.

You know the value of working with someone else when you're having problems. So, if you can, encourage students to form study groups to work together throughout the semester, not just when there's a test coming. The hardest part of this for students is finding a time to get together. A colleague of mine who teaches a mega-course (500 students) set up an electronic matchmaker that allows students to indicate when they're free to study and in which part of town they live. Such a system helps struggling students find others who are not struggling and are willing to help them as a way of earning extra credit (all instructor certified, of course). Another way of providing help is to set up a class discussion board where students can post questions and get responses from other students or from the instructor. If enough students ask the same question, you might create a FAQs page with the best solution to the problem and make it available to everyone, including future classes.

Some students are having trouble that requires additional help. I give quizzes and tests early in the term to help students identify and diagnose their difficulties. I invite those who do not do as well as they hoped to come in to see me. When they do, I ask them for their own assessment of the cause of their difficulty and try to offer helpful suggestions. Usually, I also ask some specific questions:

"Have you missed any classes?"

"Do you study the assignments before class?"

"How do you study?" (This may lead to a discussion of learning strategies; see Chapter 20 "Teaching Students How to Become More Strategic and Self-Regulated Learners.")

"What kind of notes do you take?" (I usually ask to see them.)

"Do you discuss the class with classmates—asking questions, explaining, summarizing?"

Sometimes I refer students to other resources on campus, such as a student learning support center. I keep learning-center handouts in my office to provide to students who might need a nudge. If they see how helpful such folks can be, they might be more inclined to go and see them. I check with students later to see whether they tried any of my suggestions, and I watch later performance to see if further help is needed.

## Individualized Teaching and Mentoring

Here I want to discuss interactions dealing with larger issues of students' educational and personal development. The potentially most fruitful and most appropriate interpretation of educational counseling is the one least often defined explicitly and most neglected. Even in classes of 40 to 60 students, it is difficult for the learning process to include the meeting of a maturing and a mature intellect. Too frequently, students must be content to listen to lectures and pursue readings aimed at some abstract notion of "the student."

In out-of-class interactions with students or as a student's academic advisor, you can supplement course-related learning with personalized learning that facilitates individuals' adjustment to college. This is particularly necessary for first-year students, to whom new intellectual spheres are being opened, usually at a time when they have taken a big step away from their families and communities. This is likely to be a time when a great many new assumptions and new ways of dealing with important ideas need to be digested. Educational counselors, because they have no commitment to covering a specific subject matter, can provide students with an opportunity to digest and integrate the intellectual experiences they have been having. Far from being a chore to be assigned to the least successful faculty member, such a demanding responsibility is best undertaken by persons of broad intellectual interests and foundations who, at the same time, have strong pedagogical commitments. Pascarella and Terenzini (2005) cite faculty student interactions as one of the key variables that has an impact on college student development.

This time, when students are making big strides toward greater independence from family and are trying to seek out models who can represent innovations of the adult role to which they aspire, is a time when there should be opportunities for close relationships with faculty members. The very characteristics of the large university throw obstacles in the way of such an experience. Educational counseling is one of the important means for achieving it. It seems probable that the most effective pattern for doing this would be for counselors to plan small-group meetings with the students assigned to them for counseling to provide an opportunity for the groups of new students coming from different parts of the state and country to exchange with each other and with a person of some intellectual maturity the impacts of their initial university experiences. A number of colleges and universities group first-year students into interest groups or seminars that meet regularly during the first term to help establish both academic and social support systems. We often think first of mentoring graduate students, but mentoring is a role you will have for students at all levels.

The problems of the older student entering college are in some ways similar to those of young first-year students despite the obvious differences in life experience. Both young and older students often feel some anxiety about their ability to carry out academic work successfully. The older students, however, may have even greater concerns about their ability to adapt to the college environment and to form helpful relationships with peers (most of whom are much younger and experience quite different social and recreational lives).

## CLASS MANAGEMENT PROBLEMS

Sometimes the problems we have with students are really issues of policy or rule keeping. It's amazing how much effort some students will put into trying to get around the rules. The best way to save yourself time and effort in this area is to have fair policies that you state clearly in a readily available source (such as the syllabus or the class Website) and that you enforce consistently (but not inflexibly). Let's consider some specifics.

## Attention Seekers and Students Who Dominate Discussions

In *The College Classroom*, Dick Mann (1970) and his graduate students describe eight clusters of students, one of which is "attention seekers." Attention seekers talk whether or not they have anything to say; they joke, show off, compliment the teacher or other students—they continually try to be noticed (Mann et al., 1970).

At the beginning of the term, when I am trying to get discussions started, I am grateful for the attention seekers. They help keep the discussion going. But as the class develops, both the other students and I tend to be disturbed by the students who talk too much and interfere with other students' chances to talk. What do I do then?

Usually I start by suggesting that I want to get everyone's ideas—that each student has a unique perspective and that it is important that we bring as many perspectives and ideas as possible to bear on the subject under discussion. If hands are raised to participate, I call first on those who haven't talked recently.

If the problem persists, I may suggest to the class that some people seem to participate much more than others and ask the whole class for suggestions about what might be done to give all students a chance to participate. Alternatively, I might ask two or three students to act as "process observers" for a day, to report at the end of the class or at the beginning of the next class on their observations of how the discussion went, what problems they noticed, and what suggestions they have. (I might even ask an attention seeker to be a process observer.) Another possibility is to audiotape or videotape a class and play back one or more portions at the next class period for student reactions.

If all else fails, I ask an attention seeker to see me outside class, and I mention that I'm concerned about the class discussions, and that although I appreciate the student's involvement, it would be helpful if he or she would hold back some of his or her comments until everyone else has been heard. Sometimes I phrase it like this: "The other students are starting to depend on you to do all the work, so let's make them speak up more." Put this way, the comment makes the two of us accomplices in furthering the education of the rest of the class!

Some dominant students are knowledgeable, fluent, and eager to contribute relevant information, contribute real insights, and solve problems. We prize such students; yet we must recognize the potential danger that other students will withdraw, feeling no need to participate because the dominant student is so brilliant or articulate that their own ideas and questions will seem weak and inadequate. Here, subgrouping may help, with the stipulation that each student must present his or her question, idea, or reaction to the task of the group before beginning a general discussion.

In his newsletter *The University Teacher*, Harry Stanton (1992), consultant on higher education at the University of Tasmania, suggests that each student be given three matches or markers at the beginning of a class. Each time students speak, they must put down one of their markers, and when their markers are gone, their contributions are over for the day. Perhaps subgroups could pool their markers or one group could borrow or bargain for an extra marker for a really good idea that needs to be presented.

## Inattentive Students

Periodically, I have a class in which two or three students in the back of the room carry on their own conversations. This is annoying not only to me but to students sitting near them. What to do?

First consider whether the problem is with the material rather than with the students. Is the lecture material too difficult? Too easy? Does the topic of discussion arouse anxiety? If the answer to these questions is "no" and the behavior persists despite changes in topic or level of difficulty, what next?

My first attempt is typically to break the class into buzz groups assigned to work on some problem or to come up with a hypothesis, and to move around the room to see how the groups are progressing, making sure that I get to the group including the disruptive students to see that they are working on the group task. Usually this works, and sometimes this gets the students re-engaged in the class for the rest of the class period.

But suppose that in the next class period the same problem recurs? This time I might have the class write minute papers and call on one of the inattentive students to report what he or she has written, or alternatively I might call on someone seated near the inattentive group, centering activity toward that part of the classroom.

Another possibility is to announce that, because research evidence indicates that students who sit in front get better grades (you can explain why seeing an instructor's face and mouth improves attention and understanding), you have a policy of rotating seats periodically and next week you will expect those sitting in the back row to move to the front row and all other students to move back one row.

If all else fails, I might have a general class feedback discussion on what factors facilitated and what factors might have interfered with learning in the class thus far in the term. Alternatively, I might ask one or more of the students to see me outside of class to ask them about their feelings about the class and to express my concern about not being able to teach in a way that captures their attention.

## Students Who Come to Class Unprepared

There are often good reasons why students come to class unprepared, but some students are chronically unprepared for no apparent reason. What can we do? Here, I'll elaborate on the suggestions made in the chapters "Facilitating Discussion" and "How to Make Lectures More Effective."

In my introductory course I try to communicate from the beginning that I expect students to read the assignments before class. I announce that on the second day of class I will give a brief quiz based on the first lecture or discussion and the assignment for the second day of class. I give the quiz and then ask students to correct their own papers, indicating that this quiz had two purposes: to start the habit of reading the assignment before class, and to give them an idea of whether or not they were getting the main points of the assignment. I give a second quiz a week later and a longer one three weeks later. By this point I hope that my students have established a routine for keeping up with their assignments.

Such a procedure assumes that students know what is expected of them. One of the most common causes of underpreparation is that students don't really know what is expected. Often instructors say something like "You might want to look at the next chapter of the book before the next class," or they state that the next lecture will be on topic X but don't indicate that this is also the topic of the next reading. Giving students some questions to think about as they study the next assignment can help, as will announcement of an activity in the next class that depends on the assignment. One of the advantages of a well-written syllabus is that it communicates your expectations. You also need to communicate expectations by frequent use of phrases such as "As your assignment for today demonstrated" or questions such as "What does X (the textbook author) say about...?" or "What evidence from the assigned readings would support (or not support) your position?" I wrote a piece for the National Teaching Learning Forum entitled "The Scout's Motto: Be Prepared" (Svinicki, 2008) to offer a range of suggestions about this very problem. It really helped me to clarify for myself what I meant by being prepared for my class and sharing that with the students. You might find that even the definition of "read" varies from student to student and class to class.

## The Flatterer, Disciple, Con Man (or Woman)

If you are new or somewhat insecure, it is tempting to respond positively to anyone who tells you that you are the best teacher he or she has ever had, or who is impressed with the depth of your knowledge and wants to learn more about your special research interests. Actually, you do not need to be new or insecure; we all relish compliments and interest in our work. Often such interest is genuine and can be genuinely enriching for both you and the student, but there are students for whom such an approach is a conscious strategy for winning better grades or getting exceptions from deadlines for papers or other requirements.

The real danger presented by such students is that you will begin to mistrust all students and lose compassion for students who really need an extension of time or some other indication of flexibility. I would rather be conned a couple of times than to turn off by cold rigidity a student who is in real need. Thus, my advice is to start with an assumption of honesty; nonetheless, in general, don't change the rules of the game unless you are willing to change them for everyone or unless you are convinced that there are reasonable grounds for a special exception.

## Students with Excuses

I believe that it is better to be taken in by a fraudulent excuse than to be seen as unfair in response to a legitimate excuse. Nonetheless, no one wants to be seen as so gullible that students come to rely on excuses rather than doing their assignments. Caron and colleagues (1992) studied excuse making and in their sample found that about two-thirds of their students admitted having made at least one false excuse while in college. From these students' reports it appears that fraudulent excuses were about as frequent as legitimate ones. In most cases, the excuse was used to gain more time for an assignment.

The Caron group's data do not give many clues about what one can do to prevent or detect false excuses. If the problem is one of time, you might build in checks on the progress of a paper or other assignment to reduce the tendency to put off work until the last minute. You could, for example, have students turn in an outline or bibliography sometime before a paper is due.

Sometimes I announce in the syllabus that there will be a graded series of penalties depending on how late a paper is, indicating that this tactic is to make up for the advantage that late students gain from having extra time to look up more sources, get comments and feedback from other students, and so forth. An alternative that I have not used, which might be more advantageous psychologically, is to offer a bonus for papers turned in early. It might also be wise to say in your syllabus that you want to be flexible about deadlines, you recognize that unforeseen events may prevent students from being able to meet a deadline, but in making exceptions you will require evidence supporting the request for an extension.

I think the best defense against excuses is a good offense—that is, a well-designed course that takes into consideration the fact that lives don't always run as planned. For example, in the chapter "The ABCs of Assigning Grades" I talked about the wisdom of allowing students to drop the lowest grade on a test, no questions asked. This avoids having to judge the truthfulness of student excuses for missed exams. Students rarely are willing to make excuses for continued absences without a good way to back up their claims. The message is therefore to think about ways to provide legitimate opportunities in case students mess up. If they don't, all the better for them. If they do, you've avoided having to act as judge and jury.

# EMOTIONAL PROBLEMS

Now we come to the type of problems that are the most difficult for every teacher to face: those that involve emotional issues rather than the cold academic or managerial issues I've been describing up to this point.

## Angry Students

Earlier I described students who are aggressive in challenging ideas. Some students, however, are actually angry at you or your authority and express their anger verbally or nonverbally in or out of class. What should you do with them?

Probably the most common strategy is to try to ignore them. This strategy often succeeds in avoiding a public confrontation and disruption of the class. But it may not result in better motivation and learning for the student, and sometimes it's hard to keep from reacting hostilely in return. Hostility would be a mistake because it doesn't provide a good model of how to deal with emotional situations, either for that student or for the rest of the class.

I try to forestall situations like this by becoming better acquainted with the student. If I have had students turn in minute papers or journals, I read the angry student's writings especially carefully to try to understand what the problem is. I may ask the student to come in to see me and discuss the paper. During this meeting I ask how the student feels about the course, what things he enjoys, what topics might be interesting to him. (I use the masculine pronoun deliberately because these students are most likely to be males, although I have also encountered hostile female students.) Sometimes you will feel in such a conversation that you have to drag each word from the student, yet the student will accept your invitation to come in for another discussion. Sometimes you may need to invite a small group of students to meet with you (including the hostile student) in order to make the situation less threatening for the hostile student who hides fear with aggressiveness. Whatever your strategy, it seems to me important to let the student know that you recognize him as an individual, that you are committed to his learning, and that you are willing to listen and respond as constructively as possible.

What about overt hostility—the student who attacks your point of view during a lecture or class discussion, or the student who feels that your poor teaching or unfair grading caused his or her poor performance on a test? First of all, *listen* carefully and respectfully. Remember that nothing is more frustrating than to be interrupted before your argument or complaint has been heard. Next, acknowledge that there is a possibility that the student may be right or at least that there is some logic or evidence on his or her side. Recognize the student's feelings. Then you have at least three alternatives:

1. State your position as calmly and rationally as you can, recognizing that not everyone will agree. If the issue is one of substance, ask the class what evidence might be obtained to resolve or clarify the issue. Don't rely on your own authority or power to put the student down or to make it a win-lose situation. If the issue is one of judgment about grading, explain why you asked the question, what sort of thinking you were hoping to assess, and how students who did well went about answering the question. Acknowledge that your judgment may not be perfect, but point out that you have the responsibility to make the best judgment you can, and you have done so.

2. Present the issue to the class: "How do the rest of you feel about this?" This tactic has the obvious danger that either you or the aggressor may find no support and feel alienated from the class, but more often than not it will bring the issues and arguments for both sides into the open and be a useful experience in thinking for everyone. This might be a place to use the two-column method described in the chapter "Facilitating Discussion," listing on the board, without comments, the arguments on both sides.

3. Admit that you may have been wrong, and say that you will take time to reconsider and report back at the next class session. If the student

really does have a good point, this will gain you respect and a reputation for fairness. If the student's argument was groundless, you may gain the reputation of being easy to influence and have an increasing crowd of students asking for changes in their grades.

What about the student who comes into your office all charged up to attack your grading of what was clearly a "very good exam paper"? Again, the first step is to listen. Get the student to state his or her rationale. As suggested in the chapter "Assessing, Testing, and Evaluating," you may gain some time to think if you previously announced that students who have questions or complaints about grading of their tests should bring a written explanation to your office of their point of view and the rationale for their request for a higher grade.

But, once again, don't be so defensive about your grading that you fail to make an adjustment if the student has a valid point. I have on rare occasions offered to ask another faculty member to read the paper or examination to get an independent judgment.

If you don't feel that the student has a valid point and your explanation is not convincing, you may simply have to say that, although the student may be right, you have to assign the grades in terms of what seem to you the appropriate criteria. If you have been clear about the rubric you use in grading, both before giving the assignment or test and when you returned the papers, grievances should be rare.

## Discouraged, Ready-to-Give-Up Students

Often after the first few weeks you will spot some students who seem depressed and discouraged. Sometimes they come to class late or miss class; often their papers are constricted and lack any sense of enthusiasm or creativity. In my introductory classes, some students begin with great enthusiasm and energy and a few weeks later seem to have lost their energy. Interestingly, we spot the same phenomenon in our pro-seminar for beginning Ph.D. students. In both cases the transition to a new level of education brings demands greater than those students have experienced in the past. Often their familiar supports from family and friends are no longer available; they begin to doubt their own ability to achieve their goals.

There is a magic elixir for this problem that research has demonstrated to be surprisingly effective. This is to bring in students from the previous year who describe their experiences of frustration and self-doubt during their first year and report that they surmounted them and survived. The theory explaining why this works basically states that the task is to convince the discouraged students that their problems need not be attributed to a lack of ability that cannot be changed but rather is a temporary problem. By developing more effective strategies, investing more effort, or simply becoming less worried, students are likely to achieve better results (Van Overwalle, Segebarth, & Goldchstein, 1989; Wilson & Linville, 1982).

## Students with Emotional Reactions to Sensitive Topics

In almost every discipline there are some topics that will arouse strong feelings in some of your students. In a psychology class the sensitive topic might be "group differences in intelligence"; in biology it might be "evolution" or "animal experimentation"; in sociology it might be "the role of birth control and abortion in population policy." Often we are hesitant to open such topics up to discussion. But if the topic is relevant and important, it is probably wise to acknowledge the sensitivity of the topic, admit that it may be hard for some members of the class to feel free to contribute their ideas, and explain why the topic is relevant to the goals of the course. Comparing alternative approaches, perhaps by using the two-column method described in the chapter "Facilitating Discussion," may help students see the complexity of the issue.

When you are conducting the discussion of a sensitive topic, it is important to stress that each student should listen to other students with respect and try to understand their positions. You might ask a student to put into his or her own words what other students have said. If feelings are running high, you might cool things off by asking students to write for a couple of minutes on one thing they have learned or one point that needs to be considered. Having students write a short essay advocating a position opposed to their own is an effective way to open their minds.

Be sure to allocate enough time for adequate discussion. Students may be reluctant to participate until they feel that it is safe to speak honestly. Such fear of rejection also suggests that you schedule controversial topics late enough in the term to ensure that students have developed trust in you and in their classmates.

## Dealing with Psychological Problems

At some point you will suspect that a student needs psychological counseling. Some of the signs are belligerence, moodiness, excessive worry, suspiciousness, helplessness, emotional outbursts, or depression.

Sometimes you will spot symptoms of drug or alcohol abuse. How do you get the student to the help needed?

The first step may be to get the student to talk to you. Usually you can do so by asking the student to come in, perhaps to discuss a paper or test. Typically the student is aware that things aren't going well, and you can simply ask, "How are things going?" or "What do you think is the reason for your problems?" Listen rather than intervening. After listening and expressing concern, you might then say, "What do you think you can do?" One alternative, probably the best, is to seek professional help. (Take the time to find out what is available before you need it.) If the student agrees that professional assistance might be a good idea, I've found that it helps to pick up the phone and say, "I'll call to see when they can see you." In fact, most counseling agencies will at least carry out an initial interview with any student who walks in. But the sense of commitment involved when a faculty member has called seems to make students more likely to follow through than if they simply agree that they'll go in. Even if the student does not immediately get professional help, your concern and support will be helpful, and awareness of the availability of professional help may be valuable later.

## Potential Suicides

The increasing concern with suicide risk among college students prompts a few words on the early recognition of the kinds of depressed states that accompany such risks. If you were to notice a sudden falling off of a particular student's faithfulness in attending class, you might want to inquire further, especially if you noted signs of neglect of personal grooming and hygiene, lethargy, and any marked weight changes, or a facial expression atypically gloomy or distressed. Your interest in the student should include concern with any other changes he or she has been experiencing, including major separations or losses and mood states. You should listen for talk of death or references to suicide or to getting one's personal and legal affairs in order.

Your major concern should not be to reach an accurate assessment of suicide risk. In fact, it is definitely not within your purview to become the student's counselor; that would be inappropriate, even unethical. But you are one of those in a position to recognize a change in the student. A student manifesting any of these characteristics is surely troubled and should be urged to seek whatever professional counseling is available. A good source for advice on college student mental health is the National Academic Advising Association (www.nacada.ksu.edu/Clearinghouse/Advisingissues/Mental-Health.htm). Their Website has materials for you to consult, overviews of common problems faced by college students, and bibliographies dealing with various issues. Getting the student to a source of help should be your primary objective. On one occasion, I walked with a student to the clinic to be sure that he got there. On a couple of occasions when a student seemed unlikely to seek help, I asked the university health service to call the student in. Sometimes the idea that someone really cares is enough to get the student through the down times.

## IN CONCLUSION

1. Don't duck controversy. Use it as an opportunity to model good problem-solving skills and critical thinking.

2. *Listen*, and get students to listen to one another.

3. Keep your cool. You don't have to respond immediately.

4. Paraphrase, question, and summarize, but delay suggesting alternatives until you are confident that you understand.

5. Talk to colleagues. Ask what they would do.

6. Remember that your problem students are human beings who have problems and need your sympathy and help—no matter how much you would like to strangle them.

### Supplementary Reading

An excellent review of the attributional retraining research dealing with motivation of discouraged students is R. P. Perry, F. J. Hechter, V. H. Menec, and L. Weinberg, *A Review of Attributional Motivation and Performance in College Students from an Attributional Retraining Perspective*, Occasional Papers in Higher Education, Centre for Higher Education Research and Development, University of Manitoba, Winnipeg, Manitoba, Canada R3T 2N2.

Two interesting compilations of research and thinking on problems in classrooms are Steven M. Richardson's "Promoting Civility: A Teaching Challenge," no. 77, March 1999, and John Braxton and Alan Bayer's "Faculty and Student Classroom Improprieties: Creating a Civil Environment on Campus," no. 100, 2005, in the *New Directions for Teaching and Learning* series.

In A. W. Chickering, *The New American College* (San Francisco: Jossey-Bass, 1988), the chapter by Jane Shipton and Elizabeth Steltenpohl provides a useful perspective on the broad issues faced by academic advisors. The typical schedule of 15 minutes per advisee is clearly insufficient for planning an academic program in relation to lifelong goals.

In *Tools for Teaching* (San Francisco: Jossey-Bass, 2009), Barbara Davis offers good practical advice in Chapter 44, "Holding Office Hours," and Chapter 45, "Academic Advising and Monitoring Undergraduates."

Also see Alice G. Reinarz and Eric R. White (eds.), "Teaching Through Academic Advising: A Faculty Perspective," *New Directions for Teaching and Learning*, no. 62, 1995.

Chapter 7, "One-on-One Interactions with Students," in Anne Curzan and Lisa Damour's book *First Day to Final Grade* (Ann Arbor: University of Michigan Press, 2000), provides good advice on counseling students who have a variety of problems.

A helpful source is Mary Deane Sorcinelli's chapter "Dealing with Troublesome Behaviors in the Classroom," in K. W. Prichard and R. M. Sawyer (eds.), *Handbook of College Teaching: Theory and Applications* (Westport, CT: Greenwood, 1994).

Barbara Hofer and Paul Pintrich review the various theories about epistemological beliefs and learning in "The Development of Epistemological Theories: Beliefs About Knowledge and Knowing and Their Relation to Learning," *Review of Educational Research*, 1997, *67*, 88–140.

One particularly relevant reading is R. Harper and M. Peterson, "Mental Health Issues and College Students," *NACADA Clearinghouse of Academic Advising Resources*, 2005. Retrieved May 27, 2009 from www.nacada.ksu.edu/Clearinghouse/AdvisingIssues/Mental-Health.htm. This article particularly targets what advisors can do to recognize and help troubled students.

**Part 4**

*Adding to Your Repertoire of Skills and Strategies for Facilitating Active Learning*

*Chapter*

# 14

# Active Learning: Group-Based Learning*

## ▶ THE VALUE OF ACTIVE LEARNING ITSELF

**B**efore we start talking about how to get students active in their learning by using groups, I thought it might be worthwhile to talk about *why* to get them actively learning in the first place. Throughout this book I've tried to include ideas from the research literature on learning, and if there is one thing that the literature agrees on universally, it is the value of involving the learner in the active processing of incoming information. There is a big difference between hearing and learning. In fact, there's a difference between hearing and listening mindfully. Despite the fact that some instructors believe that telling is teaching, a learner really hasn't stored new information in long term memory until he or she does something with that information. It might be that the learner makes a connection between what he's hearing and what he already knows. Or it might be that she creates an example or image to represent the new information and its structure. Whatever the processing act is, even if it's taking lecture notes that are summaries of what's said instead of verbatim, the learner makes that information unique to his or her understanding. So some form of active learning is necessary.

Another value of active learning is that it helps eliminate the "illusion of understanding." This is that wonderful experience we've all had

---

*I use the term *group learning* to include "collaborative" and "cooperative" learning. Some authors distinguish collaborative from cooperative learning, but both involve peer learning in which there is interdependence of students working toward a common goal. Similarities in and differences between collaborative and cooperative learning are discussed in Cooper, Robinson, and Ball (2003).

of listening to an expert describe a process and thinking we understand it only to find out that we can't replicate it when we try to do it ourselves. You've heard your students say, "I understood it when you talked about it in class, but when I tried to do the homework, I couldn't!" That's an instance of this phenomenon. We feel like we understand something just because we've seen it or heard it or read it before. It takes the attempt to apply the information to prove to us that we don't understand it yet. Active learning during class breaks that cycle rather than waiting until the exam to show the students that they didn't really understand.

Finally, active learning opens up the opportunity for motivation. Doing something is generally more motivating and interesting than just taking notes. And when we do something and get it right, that's a real motivator! The inclusion of questions, non-graded quizzes, and opportunities to apply ideas can all be done very quickly and without the need for the instructor to grade or even review each student's work. A perfect example of active learning that is becoming more popular is the use of personal response systems (clickers) in lecture classes. (See Chapter 17 on technology for a more detailed description of this equipment.) This technology allows the instructor to periodically ask everyone in the class to answer a question by clicking their answer choice; the results are then immediately displayed to the class and used as feedback. If you've ever used one of these systems or seen someone else use it, you know how interested the students are to see if they got the right answer and what a great teaching moment it is when they didn't.

Although the feedback system just described is great for active learning, not all active learning requires feedback from the instructor. Sometimes it's enough to just get the students to stop and write briefly about what they are thinking at that moment. Writing is an excellent opportunity for individual active learning. (See Chapter 16 for more ideas on writing as learning.) I've already referred to the "minute paper" strategy of having the students spend 5 minutes at the end of class writing a summary of their current understanding of the topic for the day. Usually they hand these in for the instructor to read, but the writing doesn't have to be graded. It can just be read and digested to form the basis of a further conversation between the instructor and the class.

## THE VALUE OF ACTIVE LEARNING IN GROUPS

The bottleneck in educational efficiency is that learning to think requires thinking and communicating one's thinking through talking, writing, or doing, so that others can react to it. Unfortunately, a professor can read only one paper at a time, can listen to only one student's comments at a time, and can respond with only one voice.

The problem is not one of communicating knowledge from professors to students more efficiently. Printed materials have done this very well for years, and for most educational purposes are still superior to any of the modern alternatives. The problem is rather one of interaction between the learner and teacher. Fortunately, interactions that facilitate learning need not be limited to those with teachers. Often, those with peers are more productive.

## WHY DOES PEER LEARNING WORK?

The best answer to the question "What is the most effective method of teaching?" is that it depends on the goal, the student, the content, and the teacher. The next best answer may be "students teaching other students." There is a wealth of evidence that peer learning and teaching is extremely effective for a wide range of goals, content, and students of different levels and personalities (Johnson et al., 1981). Moreover, skill in working cooperatively is essential for most vocations. Miller and Groccia (1997) found that cooperative learning produced positive results in ability to work with others as well as better cognitive outcomes. Marbac-Ad and Sokolove (2000) found that cooperative learning in biology courses resulted in higher-level student questioning.

A very thoughtful review of the processes underlying group learning was written by Angela O'Donnell (2006). She describes the social/motivational as well as the cognitive basis for the advantages of group learning. For example, motivationally, peer learning has the advantages of interaction with a peer—an opportunity for mutual support and stimulation. One piece of evidence for the motivational value of peer learning (Schomberg, 1986) is that it reduces absenteeism. Knowing that your teammates are depending on you increases the likelihood of your doing your work. Cognitively it provides an opportunity for elaboration—putting material into one's own words—as well as a chance to begin using the language of the discipline. It communicates that the locus of learning is in the students' heads. An effective partner can act as a model of useful strategies as well as a teacher.

Several of the effective peer learning techniques involve alternating between listening and summarizing or explaining. Structures of peer learning such as the learning cell that reduce the chance that one participant is simply a passive recipient seem likely to be better for both motivation and learning.

The task of the successful student in peer learning is to question, explain, express opinions, admit confusion, and reveal misconceptions; but at the same time the student must listen to peers, respond to their questions, question their opinions, and share information or concepts that will clear up their confusion. Accomplishing these tasks requires interpersonal as well as cognitive skills—being able to give feedback in nonthreatening, supportive ways, maintaining a focus on group goals, developing orderly task-oriented procedures, and developing and sustaining mutual tasks. It is little wonder that peer learning sometimes fails; the wonder is that it so frequently works. And it does.

Students are more likely to talk in small groups than in large ones; students who are confused are more likely to ask other students questions about their difficulties or failure to understand than to reveal these problems with a faculty member present. Students who are not confused must actively organize and reorganize their own learning in order to explain it. Thus, both the confused and the unconfused benefit.

## GROUP LEARNING: VARIATIONS ON THE THEME

### Peer Tutoring

"Pay to be a tutor, not to be tutored" is the message from studies of peer tutoring. For example, Annis (1983a) compared learning of students who read a passage and were taught by a peer and students who read the passage and taught it to another student.

The results demonstrated that teaching resulted in better learning than being taught. A similar study by Bargh and Schul (1980) also found positive results, with the largest part of the gain in retention being attributable to deeper studying of material when preparing to teach. These results fit well with contemporary theories of learning and memory. Preparing to teach and teaching involve active thought about the material, analysis and selection of main ideas, and processing the concepts into one's own thoughts and words. However, this does not mean that those being tutored fail to learn. Peer tutoring also helps those being tutored (Cohen, Kulik, & Kulik, 1982; Lidren, Meier, & Brigham, 1991). Hartman (1990) provides useful suggestions for training tutors. Peer tutoring need not be one on one. Group tutoring is also effective.

## The Learning Pair: From Learning Cells to Think-Pair-Share

We don't often think of pairs of students as constituting a "group," but as an easy way to start using more active learning, they are simple to implement and don't take much time. One of the best-developed systems for helping pairs of students learn more effectively is the "learning cell" developed by Marcel Goldschmid of the Swiss Federal Institute of Technology in Lausanne (Goldschmid, 1971). The learning cell, or student dyad, refers to a cooperative form of learning in pairs, in which students alternate asking and answering questions on commonly read materials.

1. To prepare for the learning cell, students read an assignment and write questions dealing with the major points raised in the reading or other related materials.

2. At the beginning of each class meeting, students are randomly assigned to pairs, and one partner, A, begins by asking the first question.

3. After having answered and perhaps having been corrected or given additional information, the second student, B, puts a question to A, and so on.

4. During this time, the instructor goes from dyad to dyad, giving feedback and asking and answering questions.*

A variation of this procedure has each student read (or prepare) different materials. In this case, A "teaches" B the essentials of his or her readings; then asks B prepared questions, whereupon they switch roles. Research by Goldschmid and his colleagues demonstrated that the learning cell is effective in a variety of disciplines (Goldschmid, 1975; Goldschmid & Shore, 1974). Training students to generate thought-provoking questions enhances learning (King, 1990; Pressley et al., 1992).

The simplest form of pair work is called the "Think-Pair-Share" strategy. The actual origins of this strategy are hard to pin down, but it has been listed by virtually every author who writes about group learning in the classroom. The basic idea is to ask the class a question and have each person "think" about it for a little bit. The class forms "pairs," and each pair member "shares" with one another what they thought about; then that gets shared with the class as a whole. To recapture student attention and

---

*Students can also use the learning-cell technique outside of class. My students use it in preparing for tests. A similarly structured method is "Ask to Think—Tell Why" (King, 1997).

stimulate deeper processing, I often ask students to think about a problem for a minute, write for a minute, and then share their thoughts with a neighbor. Students then feel more free to participate in a general discussion of the problem. Pairing can also be effectively used for interviews, discussion of an issue or questions, analyzing a case or problem, summarizing a lecture or assigned reading, or even just checking if they understood what the instructor just said!

Another type of pair sharing is the use of creative controversies (Johnson and Johnson, 1995) which I discussed in Chapter 5 as a technique for discussion. In this format each student of the pair is given one side of an argument to research and develop. Then the pair compares their arguments and tries to come up with a compromise that will satisfy both sides.

## Team Learning: Syndicate and Jigsaw

The term *syndicate* has a faintly evil connotation in the United States, but in Great Britain and other countries, *syndicate* is used to describe a team-based system of learning that has proved to be effective. In syndicate-based peer learning, the class is divided into teams (or syndicates) of four to eight students. Each syndicate is given assignments (perhaps three or four questions). References are suggested, and members of the syndicate may divide the readings. The findings are then discussed by the various syndicates as they meet in small groups during the regular class period. The syndicate may then make a written or oral report to the class as a whole.

I have found that I get more interesting reports when I remind students that they have probably sometimes been bored by student reports. Hence, they need to plan not only the content of the report but also how to make it interesting. I'm impressed by student creativity; my students have developed graphic and audio aids, skits, class participation, and other devices for motivating their classmates.

The *jigsaw* method, first developed by Elliot Aronson, begins like the syndicate by dividing a class into groups that are given assignments. Members of each group report back to their group, which agrees on what and how to present to the rest of the class. However, instead of a presentation to the entire class, each member of the group next meets in a new task group with one member from each of the other groups. In this new task group each student is responsible for teaching the students from the other groups what his group has learned. Because every student is thus in a group in which every group is represented, all students have the opportunity to learn the essence of all the assignments.

Students often form groups to study difficult material together or
to prepare for an exam. Yan and Kember (2004) interviewed students
from a variety of disciplines and found that some groups collaborated to
minimize the work for the individual group members. Others, however,
collaborated to gain a better understanding of an issue or concept.

## Online Groups: Synchronous and Asynchronous

The advent of technology has made it possible to have students work
together even when they can't get together in the same place at the
same time. Many of the same strategies that I have described for in-class
group work could be replicated online, but in general the online group
work tends to be asynchronous, meaning that it doesn't have to happen
at the same time. (This use of technology to support student-to-student
and student-to-instructor learning is discussed much more completely
in Chapter 17 on teaching with technology.) Uses include discussion
boards, e-mail, wikis, and probably many more by the time this book
is published. It's hard to keep up with the changes in technology.
The technology actually allows me to bypass the common complaint
that students have about group work that is supposed to happen outside
of class. Because class-management software allows me to form group
spaces that are unique to each group in my class, it's easy for them to
"meet" whenever they can or to share their ideas at the time and place
most convenient for them. In addition, for some students, especially
international students whose English may not be as good as their peers,
this asynchronous group work allows them the time they need in order
to interpret what their peers are saying and to craft a response and edit
it before making it public.

A particularly interesting use of synchronous online groups came
in very handy this past year when I had two deaf students in my class.
Because small group work is so important in my classes, I set up chat
rooms for any group that one of these students was in. All the students in
that group would log in to the chat and everyone was able to make their
contributions without having to go through an interpreter. It was very
satisfying for me and for *all* my students, and resulted in a much great
inclusion of the deaf students in the class conversation.

A colleague of mine uses synchronous chatting in her class in order
to get a permanent record of the discussion for later analysis by her and
the students. This characteristic of online groups highlights an interesting
phenomenon in the literature. Because technology allows researchers to
capture a permanent record of the discussions they are studying, there is a
huge literature building up around computer-mediated communication,

and we know more about it than most other teaching methods. A review of the literature by Romiszowski and Mason (2004) provides all kinds of perspectives on how to use online discussions. As for my colleague, she uses it because she is interested in studying how students come to understand ideas. Her students use it to review the discussions and write papers drawing on what was said. On a more mundane level, it does give her a permanent record of who participated and what the quality of their contribution was.

## Team-Based Learning

This type of group learning is a very well-developed and structured strategy for getting students to learn from one another rather than exclusively from the instructor. It was developed by Larry Michaelsen in large management classes at the University of Oklahoma in the late 1970s, and has since spread far and wide. There are two good references about this technique listed in the supplementary readings section of this chapter, but here's a brief overview. Students are formed into groups of seven to nine students who work together through the entire semester. Before coming to class the students read the text assigned for the day. Upon arrival at class, each student independently answers a "readiness" quiz about the reading and turns it in. Then the group gets together and retakes the quiz as a group. The discussion runs hot and heavy when students disagree about the correct answer, and therein lies one of its strengths: You have to be able to convince the others that you are right, which means you'd better be sure of your answer so you don't lead the group astray. Being able to articulate your reasoning is an extremely valuable learning method and it is the core of this method. Eventually each student's grade for that quiz is a combination of his or her own performance and the performance of the group.

## Learning Communities

There is currently a big movement in postsecondary education to use all of these advantages of group learning in what are called "learning communities." Gabelnick and colleagues (1990) reported on the growth of learning communities in higher education early in their development. There are several ways to think about learning communities, but the one most relevant for our purposes is the "classroom community." The idea behind such a system is to harness all the benefits of group learning in the context of a class. Students and instructor would work together to achieve learning goals rather than the instructor assigning a task and the students carrying it out. The class makes group decisions about how to proceed and supports one another in the process. Each student would feel like a member of that community, learning from and helping others learn from the class. A critical component of this whole process is the active learning that takes place within the class. Classroom communities provide a safe place for the tough business of learning new things.

## ISSUES IN DESIGNING GROUP WORK

Here are some tips that may be helpful in initiating a variety of types of cooperative learning methods:

1. You should be the one to form the groups rather than letting students form their own. You are more likely to create diverse groups and less likely to have friends (especially couples) in a group (which can lead to some difficult group dynamics). I find that my students actually prefer to be in a group that is not the same as their social group. And they are more likely to stay on task. I suggest forming groups that are based on characteristics and skills that students bring to the group. For example, in one of my graduate classes, I have students coming from a range of fields and the goal of the class is to understand how the theories apply across fields. So in that class, I try to create groups that have one representative of each of the fields present in the class. When they work on a theory, each person is representing his or her field to the representatives of the other fields. However, in an undergraduate class made up of future teachers who are going to be teaching at a wide range of grade levels and the goal is to be able to apply the theories to designing instruction for your future students, I form the groups by grade levels: all the pre-K teachers in one group, all the first grade teachers in another, and so on. That way they will get the maximum benefit out of working on the applications. There might be some similar groupings in your class. Some instructors form groups on the basis of personality inventories. I don't recommend this for a lot of reasons, but mostly because most instructors are not trained in the use of such inventories and put too much faith in their validity and reliability. Better to ask your students straight out how they like to work in a group and put students with similar preferences together.

2. Once the groups are formed, have students discuss what contributes to effective group functioning. (See the box on group behavior for ideas to raise with the class.) Explain why working together is important and valuable even for students who don't like to work in groups. When they come to an agreement on what good group behavior is, have them sign a

contract that they will abide by those rules or suffer the consequences of being booted out of their group. If that happens, they either have to find another group that will accept them or do the work themselves. Some instructors adopt the philosophy that students have to learn to work with others they don't get along with and refuse to rearrange the groups. That might be a good idea, but the instructor should also probably facilitate a discussion about how the group can get back on track. One strategy that seems to be fairly successful if groups are going to work together for the entire semester is to have a midsemester feedback survey that provides each group member an assessment of what he or she contributes to the group and what changes the other group members might suggest. I have a colleague who has an elaborate online system that allows this to happen anonymously and privately and it seems to work fairly well at bringing errant members into line.

3. Make sure students know what their task is; for example, if it involves out-of-class work, give teams a few minutes before the end of the class period to make plans. At this time they should also report to you what they plan to do and when and where they will meet.

4. For in-class group work, move around and listen in to be sure students are not lost and confused. Use this time to get and keep them

---

### Suggestions for Students: How to Be an Effective Group

1. Be sure everyone contributes to discussion and to tasks.
2. Don't jump to conclusions too quickly. Be sure that minority ideas are considered.
3. Don't assume consensus because no one has opposed an idea or offered an alternative. Check agreement with each group member verbally, not just by a vote.
4. Set goals—immediate, intermediate, and long-term—but don't be afraid to change them as you progress.
5. Allocate tasks to be done. Be sure that each person knows what he or she is to do and what the deadline is. Check this before adjourning.
6. Be sure there is agreement on the time and place of the next meeting and on what you hope to accomplish.
7. Before ending a meeting, evaluate your group process. What might you try to do differently next time?

on the right track but don't let them suck you into doing their thinking for them.

5. The trickiest part of group work is grading it. Johnson and Johnson, the most widely published proponents of collaborative learning, recommend that you have both individual measures of accountability for learning and productivity as well as group measures. Each student's grade then is a combination of the two. I have found it helpful to ask the group members to describe in writing what each of their peers has contributed to the group across the life of the project. I do this in lieu of having them actually assign a grade. I then use those descriptions to look for strengths and weaknesses and consensus about each student's contributions.

## *IN CONCLUSION*

1. Students often learn more from interacting with other students than from listening to us. One of the best methods of gaining clearer, long-lasting understanding is explaining the topic to someone else.

2. This does not mean that we can be eliminated or have time to loaf. More of our time will be spent in helping students work together effectively, less time in preparing lectures.

3. Cooperative peer learning is one of our most valuable tools for effective teaching.

### *Supplementary Reading*

One of the pre-eminent scholars of cooperative learning in higher education is Jim Cooper, who in 1991 initiated the newsletter *Cooperative Learning and College Teaching*, an excellent source of ideas for different ways of using cooperative learning. You can subscribe by writing:

Network for Cooperative Learning in Higher Education

Dr. James L. Cooper

HFA-B-316

CSU Dominguez Hills

1000 E. Victoria St.

Carson, CA 90747

*Small Group Instruction in Higher Education*, edited by J. L. Cooper, P. Robinson, and D. Ball (Stillwater, OK: New Forums Press, 2003) is a fine resource.

Another good resource is Philip Abrami's book *Classroom Connections: Understanding and Using Cooperative Learning* (Toronto: Harcourt Brace, 1995).

Two comprehensive books on cooperative learning are D. W. Johnson, R. T. Johnson, and K. A. Smith, *Active Learning*: *Cooperation in the College Classroom* (Edina, MN: Interactive Book Co., 1991), and B. Millis and P. Cottell, *Cooperative Learning for Higher Education Faculty* (Phoenix: ACE & Oryx Press, 1998).

Cooperative learning does not imply absence of controversy. D. W. Johnson, R. T. Johnson, and K. A. Smith describe the use and value of controversy in their book *Academic Controversy: Enriching College Instruction Through Intellectual Conflict* (Washington, DC: ASHE/ERIC, 1997).

Team-based learning can be explored further in L. K. Michaelsen, A. B. Knight, and L. D. Fink, *Team-Based Learning*: *A Transformative Use of Small Groups* (Westport, CT: Praeger, 2002) and in L.K. Michaelsen, M. Sweet, and D. X. Parmalee, *Team-Based Learning: Small Group Learning's Next Big Step, New Directions for Teaching and Learning Series*, no. 116 (San Francisco: Wiley Periodicals, 2008) online.

For online group work the review by Romiszowski and Mason, "Computer-Mediated Communication" in D. Jonassen (ed.) *Handbook of Research on Educational Communications and Technology* (Mahwah, NJ: Lawrence Erlbaum, 2004) can answer a lot of questions with conclusions based on the research literature (although it does get kind of technical at times).

# Experiential Learning: Case-based, Problem-based, and Reality-based

## ▶ THE ARGUMENT FOR EXPERIENTIAL LEARNING

**O**ne of the biggest criticisms of education in general is that things that are learned in school are never used in real life. And even if they could be used in real life, students don't seem to be able to transfer what they learned from school to use in the real world. Sometimes blame is placed on schools for being too far removed from the needs of everyday experience. Sometimes blame is placed on the students for not being able to generalize what they've learned, as if it were a deficit in their character or intellect or motivation. It may be a little bit of both. But psychologists have begun to describe this phenomenon of transfer failure as "situated learning" (Lave and Wegner, 1991). This isn't an easy thing to describe, but in essence it means that knowing something is closely tied into a context, and when we learn, we learn not only the facts and skills but that context. When we try to remove the knowledge or skill from its context, we no longer have the same situation and therefore we no longer have the same response. (This is somewhat similar to what we all do when we try to remember where we put our car keys. We try to think back to the last time we remember using them, and low and behold, that triggers our memory of where we were and where they probably still are. We are taking advantage of the fact that our memories are tied to a specific place and time.) The failure of transfer can then be ascribed to the lack of the situation cues that were part of the original learning. The learned skill is "situated" in the original learning context and can't be separated from it easily, if at all. Think of it this way. Have you ever bought a new computer that used software slightly different from your old computer and found that all the skills you had learned within that old software environment were now not only useless, but sometimes interfered with using the new computer? Your computer skills were "situated" in the environment of the old computer. It then takes a lot of mindful effort to figure out which skills transfer and which don't. If your new computer was identical to your old computer, you'd transfer immediately. The less like the old computer they are, the harder it is to use the new computer. That's sort of the point of experiential learning. If you want students to be able to transfer what they learn to the real world, it helps if the learning takes place under conditions that approximate that real world.

The second part of the argument for experiential learning is that the learning in that real-world environment should reflect the real skills and activities that the students will need to use someday. The more the students are involved in real problem solving, the greater the probability that they'll be able to use what they learn after they graduate.

The final argument for experiential learning is not as obvious until you really think about it. Learning from a real environment is difficult work and requires a lot of mental effort. To be able to transfer what is learned, it helps to be "mindful" about what is learned. That means that the learners' attention should be brought to the fact that they *are* learning and what they are learning, so they're not just going through the motions. Therefore a key part of experiential learning is reflecting on the experience.

## THE ESSENCE OF EXPERIENTIAL LEARNING

In light of the above discussion, the following components are incorporated into almost all experiential learning methods:

1. The learning uses real-world situations, problems, equipment, or actions to the extent possible.

2. The situations involve complex, ill-defined problems that don't have a simple answer and may even have more than one possible answer.

3. The situations involve the learners in solving a problem that reflects the kinds of problems they would encounter in the real world using the real tools of the discipline.

4. The instructor is a resource, but not the leader of the problem-solving task.

5. When the learners have come to a solution, they spend an equal amount of time reflecting on how they reached their solution and getting feedback about the quality of their proposed solution.

For example, if I were teaching a psychology class about early childhood development and wanted the students to understand the kinds of learning activities that are appropriate at different ages, I might assign them to design a playground for a real daycare center that would fit the needs of all the students and teachers at that center. It's a real problem situation (using what they know about development to select appropriate playground equipment) that is ill-structured (there is no one right design) and involves a set of skills that they might be called upon to use some day. (I teach mostly teachers, by the way.) Teams of students would be assigned to study the center and create a proposal for the playground development based on what they learned about the children there and what they learned about children in general in the class. They'd be given a budget within which to work and the real-world children and teachers' likes and dislikes to consider. I'd have each group present its proposal to the center director and staff for selection of the top two designs. We might even go so far as to bring the designs to the attention of the center's governing board and ask for the top playground design to be implemented. Once the designs have been judged, the class would spend time individually as well as in a group reflecting on the outcome of their design choices. What did they learn? What did they omit? How effective was their process? And most important of all, what did they learn about children's needs as a result of doing this project?

Of course, not all experiential learning can be this elaborate, so a whole range of levels of complexity can be substituted for the full blown situation I just described. The following alternatives have all been used in real classes in one form or another for many years, but they all boil down to asking students to come up with solutions to real-world problems and to learn something in the process.

## TYPES OF EXPERIENTIAL LEARNING REPRESENTING LEVELS OF REALITY

### The Case Method

The case method has been widely used in business and law courses for many years and is now being used in a variety of disciplines.

Generally, case method discussions produce good student involvement. Case methods are intended to develop student ability to solve problems using knowledge, concepts, and skills relevant to a course. Cases provide contextualized learning, as contrasted with learning disassociated from meaningful contexts.

Cases are often paper descriptions of actual problem situations in the field in which the case is being used; sometimes they are syntheses constructed to represent a particular principle or type of problem. For example, in medicine a case may describe a patient and the patient's symptoms; in psychology a case might describe a group facing a decision; in biology a case might describe an environmental problem. So while cases are not done in the actual environment in question, they represent the best possible portrayal of that environment that can be made without actually being there. Whatever the case, it typically involves the possibility of several alternative approaches or actions and some evaluation of values and costs of different solutions to the problem posed. Usually cases require that the students not only apply course content but also consult other resources.

**Finding the Right Cases.**  You can write your own cases, but you may be able to find cases already written that are appropriate for your purposes and are motivating for your students. For example, Silverman and colleagues (1994) have published cases for teacher education. Other cases can be found on the Internet.

Typically, the case method involves a series of cases, but in some case method courses the cases are not well chosen to represent properly sequenced levels of difficulty. Often, in order to make cases realistic, so many details are included that beginning students lose the principles or points the case was intended to demonstrate. Teachers attempting to help students learn complex discriminations and principles in problem solving need to choose initial cases in which the differences are clear and extreme before moving to more subtle, complex cases. Typically, one of the goals of the case method is to teach students to select important factors from a tangle of less important ones, which may nevertheless form a context to be considered. One does not learn such skills by being in perpetual confusion, but rather by success in solving more and more difficult problems.

The major problem in teaching by cases involves going from the students' fascination with the particular case to the general principle or conceptual structure. In choosing a case to discuss, the teacher needs to think, "What is this case a case *of*?"

**Tips for Teaching with Cases.**  Usually, cases are presented in writing, but you can use a videotape or you can role play a problem situation. (Role playing is like a drama in which each participant is assigned a character to portray, but no lines are learned. The individuals portraying specific roles improvise their responses in a situation—a situation that presents a problem or conflict.)

Whatever method you use to present the problem, you should allow class time for students to ask questions about the process they are to use and to clarify the nature of the problem presented.

You should clarify ways of going about the case study, such as:

1. What is the problem?

2. Develop hypotheses about what causes the problem.

3. What evidence can be gathered to support or discount any of the hypotheses?

4. What conclusions can be drawn? What recommendations? Make it clear that there is no one right answer.

Very likely you will want to form teams (as described in the preceding chapter "Active Learning") and take time during class for the teams to agree on when to meet and to determine what they will do before their meeting. Some problems may involve work extending over several meetings in class and out of class.

When the teams report, your role is primarily to facilitate discussion—listening, questioning, clarifying, challenging, encouraging analysis and problem solving, and testing the validity of generalizations. You may want to use a chalkboard, overhead visuals, or a computer to keep a running summary of points established, additional information needed, and possible ethical or value considerations. Don't forget to include the evidence supporting alternative approaches.

If the case is one that actually occurred, students will want to find out what actually was done and how it worked out. You can have a productive discussion about how the actual process, variables considered, or strategies used differed from those in the class. Sometimes you might bring in someone working in the field so that the students can see how an expert analyzes the case, and also ask questions about what really happens in practice.

## Problem-based Learning

*Problem-based learning* is (along with active learning, group-based learning, and technology) one of the most important developments in contemporary higher education. The ideas embodied in problem-based learning have a long history, ranging back at least to the use of cases in Harvard Medical School in the 19th century and extending through

John Dewey's philosophy, Jerry Bruner's discovery learning, and the development of simulations in the 1960s. The current surge of interest stems from McMaster University, where in 1969 the medical school replaced the traditional lectures in first-year basic science courses with courses that started with problems presented by patients' cases. A chemical engineering professor at McMaster, Don Peters, developed a problem-based approach for his courses, and another engineering professor, Charles Wales of West Virginia University, had a little earlier developed a problem-based method called "guided design." In a few years, courses and curricula in various disciplines in universities all over the world were using similar problem-based methods. The biggest difference between problem-based learning and case-based learning is in the presentation. In most instances, case-based learning situations provide the learners with all the details of the case, sometimes even the outcome, at the very start, and the students are more involved in critiquing what was actually done and suggesting alternatives. In most problem-based situations, the students are given just the "nugget" of the situation, the problem and some introductory material and have to figure out how they'll solve the problem rather than critiquing how someone else did it.

Problem-based education is based on the assumptions that human beings evolved as individuals who are motivated to solve problems, and that problem solvers will seek and learn whatever knowledge is needed for successful problem solving. Even in cultures where students do not expect to participate actively in classes, problem-based learning (PBL) can be successfully implemented; Marjorie McKinnon (1999) describes the introduction of problem-based learning at the University of Hong Kong in her article "PBL in Hong Kong." If a realistic, relevant problem is presented before study, students will identify needed information and be motivated to learn it. However, as in introducing any other method, you need to explain to students your purposes.

The steps involved in one recommended form of PBL, called "guided design," described in the box "Steps in Problem-Based Learning," are representative of those likely to be involved in many variations of problem-based learning. Note the emphasis on assessment of constraints, costs, benefits, and evaluation of the final solution. Helping students develop skills of self-assessment is an important goal of education.

Problem-based learning does not mean that you can sit back and relax once you have presented the problem. You have to check on each group's progress regularly. If you have set a time when groups must report, you may have to help a group clear up a misconception or get out of a blind alley. It's frustrating to start a problem and not have a chance to finish.

## Steps in Problem-based Learning (Guided Design)

1. State the problem and establish a goal that will be pursued in resolving it.
2. Gather information relevant to defining the problem and understanding the elements associated with it.
3. Generate possible solutions.
4. List possible constraints on what can be accomplished as well as factors that may facilitate getting a solution accepted.
5. Choose an initial or possible solution using criteria that an acceptable solution must meet. The criteria can include tangible and monetary costs and benefits, the likely acceptance of the solution by others, and discipline or other standard criteria normally applied to such problems.
6. Analyze the important factors that must be considered in the development of a detailed solution. What has to be done, who does it, when it should happen, and where the solution would be used are possible factors to explore.
7. Create a detailed solution.
8. Evaluate the final solution against the relevant criteria used earlier, to ensure that it meets at least those requirements and others that now appear to be necessary.
9. Recommend a course of action and, if appropriate, suggest ways to monitor and evaluate the solution when it is adopted.

(Wales & Nardi, 1982. Used by permission of the authors.)

In the McMaster model of problem-based learning, students meet in small groups with a tutor who acts as a facilitator. Although the facilitator is typically a faculty member, teaching assistants or peers can also be successful if trained. Typically, after the students have presented their recommendations, classroom discussion summarizes the learning that has occurred and integrates it with students' prior skills and knowledge.

## Games, Simulations, and Role Playing

An educational game involves students in some sort of competition or achievement in relationship to a goal; it is a game that both teaches and is fun. Many games are simulations; for example, they attempt to model some real-life problem situation. Thus, there are business games, international relations games, and many others. Whatever the topic, the planner of the game needs to specify the teaching objectives to be served by the game, and then plan the game to highlight features that contribute to those objectives.

Early educational games often involved large-scale simulations in which participants played the roles of individuals or groups in some interpersonal, political, or social situation. Now many more simulations are available on computers. Research and laboratory simulations are available for courses in the sciences, and interactive social simulations can be used to teach foreign languages and the behavioral sciences. Computer simulations are often more effective in teaching research methods than are traditional "wet labs." Simulated worlds, such as "Second Life," have reached levels of sophistication that had not been possible before. While this level of simulation seems very desirable, it's also fairly complex and requires skills that most instructors don't have. However, progress is being made on software that could allow even novices to design simulated environments for problem-based learning.

As with other teaching methods, the effectiveness of simulations depends to some extent on the degree of instructional support or structure. Research on traditional as well as nontraditional teaching has shown that students with low prior knowledge tend to benefit from a higher degree of structure than students with greater knowledge or intelligence (Cronbach & Snow, 1977). Veenstra and Elshout's research (1995) on computer simulations in heat theory, electricity, and statistics found even more complex relationships. Structuredness made little difference for high-intelligence students; more structure-enhanced learning for students with low intelligence and low meta-cognitive strategies (poor analysis, planning, evaluation, and work methods).

The chief advantage of games and simulations is that students are active participants rather than passive observers. Students must make decisions, solve problems, and react to the results of their decisions. Lepper and Malone (1985) have studied the motivational elements in computer games. They found that key features are challenge, self-competence, curiosity, personal control, and fantasy.

There are now a number of well-designed games that have been used in enough situations to have the kinks worked out. Some use computers to implement the complex interaction of various decisions. One classic example is SIMSOC (Gamson, 1966), a sociology game in which students are citizens of a society in which they have economic and social roles;

for example, some are members of political parties, and some have police powers. Games like this are useful in getting students to consider varied points of view relevant to the issues addressed in the game. Like the case method, an educational game may be either too simple or complex to achieve the kind of generalization of concepts or principles that the teacher desires. The biggest barrier to the use of games is logistic. Often it is hard to find a game that fits the time and facilities limitations of typical classes. Devising one's own game can be fun but also time consuming. Nonetheless, games are potentially useful tools for effective teaching.

## Field Experience

All the previously mentioned instructional strategies involve some degree of artificiality because they don't take place in the real world. To get the full benefit of experiential learning, you would want the students to experience that world firsthand. In most cases this is done in some kind of field experience, such as research studies or internships. However, those experiences are often reserved for more advanced students and have as their goal an academic outcome primarily. The idea of experiential learning has been manifested in the various forms of "service learning" an instructional situation in which students take the skills they are learning and put them to use in real service projects in real community projects (Canada and Speck, 2001; Eyler, Giles, & Astin, 1999). The key to distinguishing service learning from community service is the emphasis on the learning component (Furco, 1996). The activity has learning goals as well as service goals, and the interests of the learners and the community are equally represented.

## *IN CONCLUSION*

Whether one uses cases, PBL, games, simulations, or service learning, experiential learning is a valuable part of one's armamentarium of teaching strategies. In fact, even if you don't use experiential learning in its traditional forms, the general principle that students like to solve problems that offer a challenge but are still solvable is important. And motivation isn't the only reason to use problems. If students are to learn how to think more effectively, they need to practice thinking. Moreover, cognitive theory provides good support for the idea that knowledge learned and used in a realistic, problem-solving context is more likely to be remembered and used appropriately when needed later.

## Supplementary Reading

Guided design is fully described in C. E. Wales and R. A. Stager, *Guided Design* (Morgantown: West Virginia University, 1977).

Kenneth France has a nice article on using PBL in service learning: "Problem-Based Service Learning: Rewards and Challenges with Undergraduates," in Catherine Wahlburg and Sandra Chadwick-Blossey (eds.), *To Improve the Academy*, 2004, 22, 239–250.

Donald Woods has published three useful books on problem-based learning: *Problem-Based Learning: How to Gain the Most from PBL* (written for students), *Helping Your Students Gain the Most from PBL* (written for teachers), and *Resources to Gain the Most from PBL*. All three are published by Donald R. Woods, Department of Chemical Engineering, McMaster University, Hamilton, ON L85 4LT, Canada.

For comprehensive help in using PBL, see Dave S. Knowlton and David C. Sharp (eds.), "Problem-Based Learning in the Information Age," *New Directions for Teaching and Learning*, no. 95, September 2003. Also see Maggi Savin-Baden, *Facilitating Problem-Based Learning* (Maidenhead, UK: Open University Press, 2003).

The Harvard Law and Business Schools were pioneers in using the case method. The following reference provides a good description of the methods they developed: C. R. Christensen and A. J. Hansen, *Teaching and the Case Method* (Boston: Harvard Business School, 1987).

A sophisticated description of the use of the case method in medical education as well as two experiments on activating and restructuring prior knowledge in case discussions may be found in H. G. Schmidt, *Activatie van Voorkennis, Intrinsieke Motivatie en de Verwerking van Tekst* (Apeldoorn, The Netherlands: Van Walraven bv, 1982). (Don't worry. Despite the Dutch title, the text is in English.)

The use of active learning in geography is described in M. Healy and J. Roberts (eds.), *Engaging Students in Active Learning: Case Studies in Geography* (Chettenham, UK: University of Worcestershire, 2003).

Linc Fisch's article "Triggering Discussions on Ethics and Values: Cases and Innovative Case Variations," *Innovative Higher Education*, 1997, 22, 117–134, has lots of practical tips.

Hank Schmidt and Joseph Moust describe four types of problems used in PBL—explanation problems, fact-finding problems, strategy problems, and moral dilemma problems—in "Towards a Taxonomy of Problems Used in Problem-Based Learning Curricula," *Journal of Excellence in College Teaching*, 2000, 11(2), 57–72.

Information about the implementation of service learning is offered in Mark Canada and Bruce Speck, *Developing and Implementing Service Learning Programs*. New Directions for Higher Education, no. 114 (San Francisco: Jossey-Bass Publishers, 2001).

To read about experiential learning in general, a good resource is Jennifer Moon's book, *A Handbook of Reflective and Experiential Learning: Theory and Practice (New York: RoutledgeFalmer, 2004).*

*Chapter*

# 16

# Using High-Stakes and Low-Stakes Writing to Enhance Learning

## ▶ A LITTLE THEORY: HIGH STAKES AND LOW STAKES

**B**ecause writing is usually learned in school (where it is nearly always graded or evaluated), and because writing tends to be used for more serious occasions than speaking ("Are you prepared to put that in writing?"), most people feel that writing is a high-stakes activity. But it is not *inherently* high-stakes. Indeed, writing is better than speaking for *low-stakes* language use—for exploring and experimenting—because writing can so easily be kept private or revised entirely before being shared with any reader. Of course, we need to set high-stakes writing assignments in our college courses, but that writing will result in more learning for students and go better for us if we also exploit the resources of low-stakes writing.

Why high-stakes assignments? If we ask students to articulate in clear writing what they are studying, we help ensure that they will in fact learn it. And without these carefully written essays and essay exams, we can't give trustworthy final course grades—grades that reflect whether students actually understand what we want them to understand.

This chapter was written by Peter Elbow and Mary Deane Sorcinelli, University of Massachusetts Amherst.

For if students take only short-answer tests or machine-graded exams, they may often *appear* to have learned what we are teaching but they don't really understand. Besides, writing is a central skill for higher education, and students will not get good at it if they write only for English or writing teachers.

And low-stakes writing? The goal here is not so much to produce excellent pieces of writing as to increase how much students think about, understand, and learn what we are teaching. Low-stakes writing is usually more informal and tends to be ungraded or graded informally. You could describe the goal this way: We can throw away the low-stakes writing itself, yet keep the neural changes it produced—the new insights and understandings.

## LOW-STAKES WRITING

### Kinds

The most obvious approach is to ask for comfortable, casual, exploratory writing about a question or topic, and urge students not to struggle too much to try to get the thoughts exactly right or the writing good. Make it clear that the writing is for exploring and processing course material—and will not be graded. Low-stakes writing also increases fluency and confidence in writing and helps with creativity and risk taking. These benefits are maximized if you sometimes ask for low-stakes writing in the mode of *freewriting*—asking students to write without stopping, putting down whatever comes to mind even if it doesn't make sense.

### Occasions

**In Class.** Many teachers ask for 5 or 10 minutes of low-stakes writing at the start of class—to help students bring to mind the homework reading they did or to explore their thoughts about the topic for today. Or in the middle of class, to ponder a particular question—especially if discussion goes dead. Or at the end of class, to summarize and reflect on what was discussed. Students will have more to say in discussion, and be less afraid to speak up, if you start with a few minutes of freewriting. After you ask a question, two minutes of quick freewriting will make all the difference in the world.

**Out of Class.** Many teachers ask students to keep a journal of informal reflections on the readings and classes. The goal is to get students to process what they are studying and connect it with the rest of their experiences, thoughts, and feelings. Because students sometimes experience journal writing as an artificial exercise and resist it as useless "busy work" (especially if no one else reads it), many teachers have found it helpful to ask for weekly *letters* that students write to a classmate or friend—letters in which they reflect on the course material (see Young, 1997). Many teachers now ask students to post letters or journal entries on a class Website—or even simply have students send e-mail entries to everyone using a group e-mail address.

## Benefits of Low-Stakes Writing

Some faculty members are nervous about inviting students to write loosely and informally. Therefore, we feel it's important to spell out a number of the benefits:

- Low-stakes writing helps students involve themselves actively in the ideas or subject matter of a course. More minds are usually at work on the course material during low-stakes writing than during a lecture or discussion.

- Low-stakes writing helps students find their own language for the issues of the course; they stumble into their own analogies and metaphors for academic concepts. Theorists like to say that learning a discipline means learning its "discourse," but students don't really know a field unless they can write and talk about the concepts in their *own* informal and personal language. Successful parroting of the textbook language can mask a lack of understanding.

- Frequent low-stakes writing improves high-stakes writing. Students will already be warmed up and fluent before they write something we have to respond to. And when they turn in an impenetrable high-stakes essay (and who hasn't tangled up one's prose through extensive revising?), we don't have to panic. We can just say, "Come on. You can revise this some more into the clear lively voice I've already seen you using."

- Low-stakes writing helps us understand how student minds are working: how students are understanding the course material, feeling about it, and reacting to our teaching.

- There's a special application of low-stakes writing to math and science courses—and to problem solving in general: Ask students to write the story of the paths their minds followed as they tried to solve a problem. These paths are interestingly idiosyncratic but instructive, and it's useful to have students share these metacognitive stories.

■ Regular low-stakes assignments make students keep up with the assigned reading every week. This means that they contribute more and get more from discussions and lectures. Quizzes can do this job, but they invite an adversarial climate and don't bring the other benefits described here—including pleasure.

■ And don't forget: Low-stakes writing takes little of our time and expertise. We can require it but not grade it. We can read it but not comment on it. In many cases we don't even need to read it. Yet we can get students to read each other's informal pieces—and (if we want) discuss them.

## Handling Low-Stakes Writing

There are still plenty of students who are not used to low-stakes writing—or who don't expect it in a "hard-nosed disciplinary course." They assume that all writing must, by definition, be read and graded by the teacher. So it's important to explain frankly to them why you are requiring it but not grading it. You can point out that much writing in the world gets no response at all. If it helps, you can say, "This is graded. You get 100 if you do it; 0 if you don't."

Most teachers set up a combination of different audience relationships for low-stakes writing: some is private and some is shared; some of the shared writing goes to the teacher and some only to fellow students. Sometimes students are invited to *discuss* the information and thinking they've heard in each other's low-stakes writing—but not give feedback on the quality of the writing. If you have time to give a nongraded response to some of their low-stakes writing, that can be useful, but most of us need to save most or all of our responding time for their high-stakes writing (but see the section later in the chapter on "middle-stakes writing").

Some teachers read journals; others treat them as private and just check that students have written. Some teachers ask students to trade journals weekly with a peer—perhaps for a response, perhaps not. Letters are natural for sharing, and lots of learning comes from this sharing.

When we start a new class with students who don't trust us and who might resist writing anything we don't see, it can be useful to collect the low-stakes pieces for a few sessions. We stress that we won't grade it or comment on it—just check quickly to make sure they explored the topic. They learn that non-graded or even private writing is not wasted busy work but, in fact, leads to new insights and better enjoyment of writing.

Many students have never had the experience of writing with their *full attention* on their thoughts. Their writing has always been for a teacher and a grade, and therefore much of their attention has leaked away in worries about mistakes in language, spelling, or wording. After a few sessions, we can stop collecting it and let these pieces be entirely private—or just for sharing with classmates.

When students are asked to do low-stakes writing in class, it's important for the *teacher* to write too. This helps students see it as a process that adult professionals and academics use for developing their thinking.

Some teachers fear that low-stakes writing will promote carelessness in writing. This is a problem only if teachers fail to emphasize the sharp distinction between low-stakes and high-stakes writing—and fail to insist on high standards for the latter.

## HIGH-STAKES WRITING

We cannot give fair course grades unless we get a valid sense of how much students have learned and understood. For this, we need high-stakes writing. The stakes are high because the writing needs to be good and bears directly on the course grade. Most readers of this book are not trained as teachers of writing and understandably feel some apprehension about high-stakes writing—especially about devising topics, writing comments, and figuring out grades. The stakes are high for teachers as well as students.

If your campus has a writing center, it can be enormously helpful with high-stakes writing. Tutors there can help students at *all stages* of the writing process: understanding the assignment; brainstorming ideas; and giving feedback on either early or late drafts. A writing center is specifically not a "copy editing service," but tutors can *help* students learn to copy edit better.

### Topics and Assignments

When devising assignments, it's worth trying to choose topics that will lead to writing that interests the writer—and also the reader. Thus, try to avoid assignments that ask for mere regurgitation of material from textbooks or lectures.

Should students learn to write in the academic forms used by professionals in your field? In a graduate course, this will certainly be a goal; perhaps also for majors. But a huge proportion of students in undergraduate courses in, say, physics or sociology or literature will never have to write like professional or academic physicists, sociologists, or literary critics. Perhaps you feel nevertheless that they should have *experience* with those forms and genres, even though they won't actually need to use them later. You get to decide. For ourselves, we lean away from using academic genres and styles for non-majors.

Our goal, instead, is what is sometimes called "essayist literacy": the ability to organize an essay around a main point, to support that point with clear reasoning, and to illustrate it with apt examples. In truth, a fully academic genre with all the rituals of academic style can sometimes *get in the way of* clear exposition and argument. We think students often learn more from explaining course concepts or making an argument to readers *outside the field*. Note how much publication there is of high-quality science writing for general readers.

Most of us are best acquainted with two common academic genres: arguing a position and analyzing complex data or a text. But there are other genres that can be very useful to assign—especially because some students fall into stale, uninvested, formulaic writing when they write in genres they are tired of. Here are some examples of alternative genres: papers written as a dialogue between two figures you are studying—or other interested parties; personal papers that start from a disagreement that came up in class discussion and analyze the issue or take a side; papers that describe an event or person or era from inside the mind of a participant or bystander. (Students sometimes understand better how an enzyme or molecule functions if they write about what it does "in its own voice" as though it had consciousness.) Collaborative papers can lead to lots of pooling of knowledge. Letters to the editor constitute a high-stakes assignment that is *short* but still takes careful thought; papers in the form of a collage are much easier to write but still ask for good thinking and writing (see Elbow, 2000a, 2000b).

## Criteria for Evaluation

"Professor, what are you actually looking for in this paper?" Students can annoy us when they ask this question, but it's a valid one and deserves an answer—ideally on the handout stating the assignment. (Teachers often regret it when they don't put assignments on a handout.) We cannot fairly comment or grade if we're not conscious of criteria our judgments derive from. How much will we care about factors like these: correct understanding of course concepts, application of concepts to new instances, creative original insights, organization, good examples, clarity of sentences and good word choice, spelling and grammar? Certain assignments will suggest other criteria (documentation, correct format for lab reports, voice). There are no right answers here—good professionals differ in their priorities—but we don't think it's fair to keep your priorities hidden.

## Multiple Papers and Multiple Drafts

There are two powerful ways to improve student writing and student learning: multiple papers and multiple drafts.

We can assign several short papers rather than just one large term paper (which is usually "terminal" in more than one sense). Students tend to delay writing term papers, they tend to pad them, and they seldom learn from our comments because the course is over before they pick up their papers (*if* they pick them up). On short papers, we can give briefer responses.

It is enormously useful to require students to write drafts of high-stakes papers, get feedback, and then revise. But does this require you to spend twice as long responding? No. Our time is limited, so we need to think strategically: How can we use our scarce response time to do the most good? (Consider the guiding principle for our better-paid medical colleagues: "At least do no harm.") If we devote most of our available time to feedback on a *draft*, we have a better chance of getting students to improve their writing *and* their understanding of course concepts. By responding to drafts, we are coaching improvement. If we respond only to final drafts (autopsy-like), students have a hard time using our feedback to improve future papers (especially if there are no other papers in the course—or if the next paper is quite different). But if we spend our limited time commenting on a draft, then we need to *save* time on final versions: We can do this by reading through them once and grading them with a grid. Here's a simple generic grid:

|  | Unsatisfactory | OK | Excellent |
|---|---|---|---|
| Content, thinking, mastery of ideas | ☐ | ☐ | ☐ |
| Organization, structure, guidance for readers | ☐ | ☐ | ☐ |
| Language: sentences, wording, voice | ☐ | ☐ | ☐ |
| Mechanics (spelling, etc.) and correct citations | ☐ | ☐ | ☐ |
| Overall | ☐ | ☐ | ☐ |

With a grid of this sort, teachers who have too many students can limit themselves to reading each paper once and merely checking the boxes. The use of multiple criteria provides feedback about strengths and weaknesses—feedback notably lacking in conventional, one-dimensional grades. Because there are only three levels for each criterion, you don't have to stop and "compute a grade" for each criterion. You need only read the paper and then hold each criterion briefly in mind to see if the paper seems *notably strong* or *notably weak* in that dimension. If neither, then the verdict on that criterion is "OK." (See the discussion later in the chapter on three-level grades and twelve-level final course grades.)

Grid criteria can be chosen to fit different genres, your priorities, or a particular writing skill you want to emphasize (e.g., research, considering both sides of an issue, skill in revising, audience awareness). It helps to try to state your criteria in plain, everyday language. (See the chapter "Assessing, Testing, and Evaluating" for more on grids.)

One of the most useful criteria to set for final drafts is *substantive revising*. For when we ask students to revise, they often settle for small corrections in wording, spelling, and grammar. It helps if we emphasize: "The main job here is *revising*, not editing; postpone *editing* till your very last 'cleaning up' stage." When you ask for revising, you can usefully startle students by saying, "Don't worry at all about spelling and grammar at this stage: your job now is to make substantive revisions to create the very best essay you can." (And surface features often improve when they work on the substance.) Many students need help understanding the difference between revising and editing. Revising is a *substantive* matter: Improve the ideas, reasoning, and organization of a paper and clarify badly tangled sentences. Editing is a *surface* matter: Fix mistakes in spelling and grammar and make small improvements in wording. There's no point in editing the surface till the substance has reached its final form. If your teaching conditions permit it, you can help students enormously by building a separation between revising and editing: set one due date for the revision and a slightly later date for the final edited or copy-edited version. (Just hold on to the revision and wait for the final edited version for giving your response.)

## Worst-Case Scenario

Teachers who have large classes or heavy teaching loads (and who have no training in the teaching of writing) will feel, understandably, that they have no time for the "luxury" of multiple papers and multiple drafts. The situation is not so hopeless, however, if we look more closely at some undeniable facts: When we assign writing and get students to write, we can trust that we are helping them learn more and probably write better, but when we comment on their writing and grade it, we can't be so confident of good results. Research points out some disturbing facts. Comments by faculty members are often unclear. After all, we write most comments in great quantity—working slowly down through thick stacks of papers; it is often late at night, and we're usually in a hurry and perhaps even discouraged or downright grumpy. Almost inevitably, we write quickly and fail to read over and revise what we've written.

Even when our comments are clear, they are not always so trustworthy. When we write typical comments (like "You should omit this paragraph or put it later" or "This hypothesis has been discredited"), respected colleagues might well disagree with us. Grades on papers are notoriously unreliable (as students sometimes prove by turning in the same paper to different teachers). It's not surprising that many bright students are cynical about teacher response. And even when we manage to write comments that are clear, valid, and helpful, students often misunderstand them because they read through a distorting lens of discouragement, resistance, cynicism—or downright denial. And dare we acknowledge all those students who don't even read our comments— looking only at "what matters," namely the grade? (See Hodges [1994] for some research on how often our comments misfire when read by students.)

So even though teachers caught in a worst-case scenario have very little "time per student," their strategic *assigning* of writing yields the biggest payoff from their scarce time. They can increase learning even more by assigning *two* or more shorter papers and save responding time by using a grid instead of writing comments. Remember that grids give feedback about different strengths and weaknesses in the writing, whereas conventional grades give nothing but a number on a yea/boo meter.

To increase learning by getting students to draft and revise, teachers in a worst-case scenario can resort to an interesting worst-case strategy that is fairly effective. Tell students openly that you don't have time to give them feedback on their drafts but that you can help them write their papers with a more productive process. Set a due date for a required *draft* of each high-stakes paper—perhaps one week before the final version is due. Collect the drafts and subtract points severely for drafts not turned in, but just glance at each one to see that it seems to be a draft on the chosen topic. Then a week later, collect final versions and respond with the grid. It's only fair to admit that of course this doesn't *force* them to revise. But most students will find ideas for a better paper coming to mind during the week after they turn in their draft. Even more students will revise if you devote some class time for students to read their drafts out loud to each other in pairs or trios. (See below for more about sharing or peer feedback.)

## Responding to High-Stakes Papers

Here are some specific suggestions.

**Response as Dialogue.** Commenting is easier and more productive if we ask students to write a brief and informal *cover letter* or *writer's log* to hand in with the draft or final version. It should answer questions like these:

> What was your main point and what were your major subpoints? How did the writing go? Which parts feel strong and weak to you? Most important of all: What questions do you have for me as reader? And when it's a revision: What changes did you make—and why?

With this cover letter, our comment is not the *start* of a conversation about the writing, but rather the *continuation* of a conversation begun by the student. Cover letters help us decide what to address with our comment. Often we can agree with much of what the student has said—and sometimes even be more encouraging about the essay than the student was. (Students write better cover letters if, on the first couple of due dates, we take 10 minutes for writing cover letters in class and hearing a couple of examples—so we can kibitz a bit.)

On a couple of occasions when we *return* papers to students, we can continue the dialogue by taking 5 minutes for students to write us a short note telling what they heard us saying in our comment and how they are reacting to it. These short notes tell us when our comments are unclear or when students misinterpret us.

**Read through the Whole Piece *Before* Making Any Comments.** Students can seldom benefit from criticism of more than two or three problems. We can't decide *which* problems to focus on till we read the whole paper through. When we write marginal comments while reading, we often get into trouble: wasting our time on something that turns out to be a minor issue; making a brief comment that the student misunderstands; saying something that's actually wrong ("you don't understand X" although later on it's clear that the student does understand X); or getting caught up in a little spasm of unhelpful irritation. If we settle for making straight and wavy pencil lines during our first reading (for passages that are notably strong or weak), these will serve as reminders after we have read it all and we are trying to decide what few issues to address. Even when we want to give "movies of the mind"—that is, to tell the story of our reactions as we were in the process of reading—we can usually do this more clearly and helpfully by waiting until we've read the whole piece.

**Write Comments on a Separate Sheet Rather Than in the Margins.** This helps us comment *as readers* about what works and doesn't and how the writing affects us—rather than falling into the trap of trying to be *editors who fix the text*. Sometimes, of course, we can say something more briefly if we put the comment in the margin, but most of us save time by writing comments on a computer—which means using a separate sheet.

**Use Everyday Language.** Comments about the writing are usually more effective when we use plain everyday language instead of technical terms from English or rhetoric or grammar. How much better to say "Your writing sounds distant and pompous to me in this passage" than to say "Too many passive verbs here." How would you talk about a writing weakness to a colleague in your field?

**About Criticizing and Encouraging.** There's an essential learning principle that is too often neglected: Students can make more improvement in a weak area if we tell them to do *more of something* they've already done well—even if there's not much of it—than if we tell them to do something they've not done here and perhaps never done. An example:

> I often got lost. I think your paper has big problems with organization. But I've indicated several places where you showed that you *can* organize. I've put straight lines along several paragraphs that hang together just fine; and also put a few lines *between* several paragraphs where you linked them well and your transition works fine. Give us more of that! You've shown you can do it.

Another useful kind of response is often overlooked because it seems too simple: *Describe the paper* as you see it. For example, "Here's what I see as your main point:…. Here's what I see as your subsidiary points:…. Here's what I see as your structure:…." This helps students learn to *see* their own writing from the outside (a difficult skill), and it tells them what got through and what didn't.

## MIDDLE-STAKES ASSIGNMENTS: THINK PIECES

These are not essays and don't have to be organized around a single point, but they are more than mere freewriting. They are short exploratory pieces that ask students to think through a topic. The task in a think piece is to *work at thinking—and also* clean up what is handed in enough so it is not unpleasant to read. We can describe them as thoughtful letters to an interested friend. A good think piece, like a good letter, might pursue one line of thinking, then discover a problem, and finish by rethinking the matter in a different frame of reference.

If your teaching conditions permit it, consider requiring a think piece every week or two (say one to three pages). You can respond to each one with just a check, check-plus, or check-minus—with or without a few words from you (not about the writing but about the ideas). No think piece would be due on weeks when a high-stakes draft or revision is due. Think pieces can also function as exploratory drafts for high-stakes essays.

Think pieces help students get more out of readings, class discussions, and lectures. Topics can be completely open (e.g., "Write about something that interests you in this week's reading"). But topics can focus on particular concepts that are slippery, or can help students practice particular intellectual tasks. Examples: "Compare these two concepts from the reading." "Use this concept from the reading or lecture (e.g., the second law of thermodynamics? internalized racism?) to describe and analyze something you have encountered in your life." "Write a true or fictional story that uses the technique of flashback or unreliable narrator." "Write about this historical event from inside the head of one of the participants." Students can take intellectual and rhetorical chances because they know their grade will be fine if they throw themselves into the task. Learning is vastly enhanced if you take 5 or 8 minutes on due dates for students to read think pieces out loud to each other in pairs or in small groups.

## PEER RESPONSE

If you are teaching a writing course, it's crucial to use peer response and take the considerable time necessary to teach students how to give it and receive it well. But most readers of this essay will not be teaching a writing course, so our advice is to emphasize peer *sharing* more than peer response. By reading their drafts and final versions aloud to classmates, students experience how each sentence fits in the mouth and sounds in the ear, and they can usually tell which sentences work and which ones are a problem. And not just sentences: Reading an essay aloud gives students an almost visceral feel for the organization and train of thinking—and when that train goes off the rails. Best of all, mere sharing—reading aloud—takes very little class time. Sharing is not just about the writing: When three students hear each other's drafts (and lots of low-stakes writing too), they are hearing different understandings of the *course content*.

Teachers and students who have not used sharing in this way will be surprised at its power—not just to help with writing and learning course material but also in building community. But many students need encouragement and even cajoling to make them read slowly and loudly enough that peers will understand. And both reader and writer can feel awkward about the silence of no response at the end of a reading. There's a simple ritual that deals with this problem: Listeners simply say "thank you" and then move on to the next reader.

The sharing of writing can be a good occasion for discussing the content ("I don't see it the way you do. In my view …"). And if you want to encourage minimal peer response, here are two simple and quick responses—(1) "pointing": "Here are the passages and ideas that seem strong or interesting and stick in mind"; (2) "say back" or summarizing: "Here's what I hear as your main point; and you also seem to be saying …" (For those who want to make a bigger commitment to peer response, see Elbow and Belanoff [2003]).

# ABOUT CORRECTNESS: SPELLING AND GRAMMAR

It's not possible or appropriate for us to try to teach grammar and spelling in a college course. But that doesn't mean we can't demand it. (We often demand typing or word processing.) The main thing students need to learn about correct spelling and grammar is schizophrenic: Correctness is *not* important for rough exploratory writing, but it's *crucial* for final drafts.

For high-stakes essays, we think it makes good sense to require not only clear, well-organized writing but also good copy editing. Here is a useful formulation: "Your final drafts must be virtually free of mistakes." Many students can't manage this without the help of friends (or paid typists), so it's not realistic to demand that they reach this standard entirely on their own. But we can demand that they learn to get whatever help they need for good copyediting. *This* is the skill and the habit they need when they write on most other occasions they'll encounter. (Most of *us* ask for help in copyediting our own writing, and we get professional help when we publish.)

It doesn't make sense to penalize students for surface mistakes on in-class writing since they have no time to revise with fresh eyes and have no access to help. For exploratory think pieces written out of class, we can require what's appropriate for an informal letter to the teacher: Clean it up enough so it's not annoying or hard to read because of mistakes or messiness.

# TECHNOLOGY AND WRITING

In the last handful of decades, technology has given writers an incredible array of tools: word processing, e-mail, hypertext, blogging, discussion sites, and various other remarkable capabilities. From early on, enthusiasts for technology have tried to gather research to show that students write better papers when they use computers—but the data come up short (see Moran, 2003). Tools are a huge benefit, but they don't, in themselves, improve writing. What they give us are potentialities—with upsides and downsides. (See Chapter 17 in this book for an extended treatment of technology and teaching. Here we will only point briefly to some matters that specifically bear on writing.)

## The Process of Writing

Since the onset of computers, e-mail, text messaging, blogging, and social sites, students have become much less afraid of the blank page than before—less hesitant to put their thoughts and feelings into visible language at a moment's notice. Heretofore, it seemed to most people like a "big deal" to sit down to write something—physically and psychologically. Before e-mail, most writing by young people was done for teachers in a school context where the writer got at least a bit of evaluative feedback. But now most students write much more out of school than in. Writers no longer feel that written words are "set in black and white." Words are just pixels on a screen—easily changed.

Students have always been able to talk to friends and classmates about their topic, but now they can explore their topic by actually using written language in the form of e-mail, threaded discussion, and chat. The stumbling block for many students in the writing of papers for school has been the transition from thinking or talking to writing, but now many students have already passed that stumbling block before they "really start." On top of all this, the technology has led a huge proportion of students to become fast, comfortable typists; this used to be rare.

Nevertheless, these tools don't always result in good writing. This newfound comfort with writing can tempt some students to use casual prose that's not carefully thought through for their *final* drafts and not just for their exploratory writing. Also, we forget about how messy papers used to be when they were typed or handwritten; now they are pristine. But lovely surface appearance can tempt students into thinking that papers are more "done" than they are. And they can be tempted to think that spell checking removes all misspellings.

## Revising

Where revising used to mean retyping or rewriting everything, computers have made it easy. Students can easily scroll among files and screens containing all their notes and passages and various drafts—and notes from others. It's a cinch to cut and paste. Deleting turns out to be the hard part. While data can't show computer written papers are on average better—it seems to show that they are on average longer. One of the big problems here is the temptation to do all revising on screen, where it's hard to see the larger structure and movement of thought—where we see only the trees and not the forest.

## The Dialogic, Collaborative Dimension of Writing

It's now much easier for students to share their drafts and get responses online—from peers and also from teachers. A responder can digitally write corrections next to the text itself—even into the text. Collaborative writing is now far less awkward and complicated: Drafts and responses can shoot easily back and forth between co-authors—and more than one person can have access to the same paper at the same site. Students' frequent use of public sites like Facebook and MySpace has tended also to make them less nervous about audience in general—about letting strangers see their words and respond to their words, even when those readers might wildly disagree.

## The Teacher's Role

When we started teaching with technology, we focused on one or two tools that supported our goals for student writing. Even if you teach at a school without computer-supported classrooms or writing software packages, you and your students can use simple word-processing features like "comment" and "track changes" when responding to or re-vising drafts. And students can easily trade those drafts—or send them to you—using e-mail. You can also set up your own Web-based discussion page fairly easily, allowing students to post and receive messages. Start where you feel comfortable and add technologies where they make sense for your teaching goals.

Many campuses now support Web-based course management software such as WebCT/Blackboard. These let teachers post syllabi, assignments, and online readings and create a communication site for various kinds of class discussion—threaded, blogs, journals, and chat. You can ask students to post comments, perhaps once or twice weekly, about the reading, lectures, or discussion. These sites are ideal for posting the low- and middle-stakes assignments mentioned earlier. Fellow students can easily read the various kinds of posted writing and respond in real time or at any time; discussion can continue outside of class. All this tends to improve both learning and writing.

It's easy and common for teachers to ask students to submit their high stakes papers digitally. Especially with course Websites, teachers can organize submissions by topic, set deadlines, and comment or grade directly in the tool while reading responses. The danger here is that some teachers get sucked into commenting as though they are editors—pointing out all weaknesses and sometimes even fixing errors. Here's a case where we as teachers need to resist one of the technological temptations and remember that we don't have time to be line editors. We must learn the old skill of writing a comment from a more global perspective so we can focus on just a couple of the weaknesses that are most fruitful to work on and on the strengths that need to be generalized more widely.

Remember, too, that there are times you may just want to turn the computers off and teach *sans* any technology. There can be tactile pleasure in handwriting in a notebook or journal—even with devil-may-care cursive. Teachers can promote "old school" social networking by having students read their writing to each other, face-to-face. And class discussion just might be more focused and engaging with e-mailing, text-messaging, posting, and Net-surfing turned off. Technology is a powerful tool, but only when it helps you to become a better teacher and your students to become better writers.

## ABOUT GRADING

There's a whole chapter in this book devoted to grading. (See the chapter "The ABCs of Assigning Grades.") We'll just briefly mention a few practices that are particularly useful because it's so difficult to give a fair grade to a piece of writing. One of the main things that makes fairness so elusive is this: A conventional grade like B– is an attempt to represent with just *one dimension* the quality of a *multidimensional* performance. (A spelling test, in contrast, asks for a fairly one-dimensional performance.) Extensive research has shown that teachers often give different grades to the same paper. (Kirschenbaum and colleagues [1971] summarize extensive research. See also Tchudi [1997] and Diederich's classic study [1974]). One obvious source of discrepancies is that different teachers understandably disagree about which dimensions should count most (e.g., accuracy of course content, validity of thinking, originality, structure, sentence/word clarity, mechanics).

Grading grids mitigate this problem because they spell out individual judgments for individual dimensions. Grids don't get rid of the inherent subjectivity in grading (How *bad* is "unsatisfactory content"? How *good* is "excellent clarity"?), but at least they reduce it. For final course grades, most of us are obliged to settle for a one-dimensional grade, but we can still use a grid to communicate the meaning of that grade to students. Here our criteria can encompass a wide array of dimensions, and we can communicate whether we have counted for dimensions such as effort, improvement, or attendance.

Our sample grid (earlier in this chapter) shows only three levels of quality (Unsatisfactory, OK, Excellent). This may seem crude; people seem to hunger for fine distinctions. But the more levels of quality we use, the more work we give ourselves, the more chances we have to be wrong (that is, to differ from how other respected readers would judge), and the more chances we have to make students disagree with us and resist our teaching. Of course, most of us have to give a course grade with something like twelve levels of quality (counting pluses and minuses), But there are many relatively simple ways to add or average multiple crude three-level grades to yield a twelve-level final grade.

## Portfolios

If we grade on the basis of a portfolio (using either a grid or a single grade), we are drawing on a more trustworthy picture of the student's ability or learning (thus "validity" is enhanced). And portfolios have other advantages. The grade seems fairer because students can choose a *selection* of their best writing and they are not so penalized for having started out the semester unskilled. Most of all, portfolios greatly enhance student learning because they function as an occasion for retrospective meta-thinking. For the final piece in a portfolio is typically a reflective analysis in which the student looks back at everything included and tries to articulate what he or she has learned. For the sake of this reflection, it's helpful for students to include some low-stakes writing and at least one example of an "instructive failure."

## Contract Grading

Contracts are mentioned in the chapter "The ABCs of Assigning Grades," but we want to mention a little-known hybrid or mixed kind of contract that can be very productive in certain courses. Students are given a list of *all* the course activities that the teacher thinks are important sources of learning, and students are guaranteed a course grade of B if they simply *perform* them all with good faith or decent effort. Typically, this list involves things like attendance, meeting deadlines, genuinely revising drafts, giving feedback to other students, satisfactory copy editing, and any other activities that are important for learning—such as labs or special projects. The teacher gives normal feedback on all these activities where it's appropriate—feedback about quality—but for the grade of B, these judgments of quality are irrelevant. This system gives students a large foundation of safety, yet it tends to get more of them to do more work. And it reduces the degree of adversarialness in grading. For grades higher than a B, however, judgments of quality come into play.

## PREVENTING—AND HANDLING—PLAGIARISM

We can't catch all plagiarism—and if we try, we'll turn ourselves from teachers into suspicious cops. It's hard to track down the sources in Internet cheating. "Using Internet search engines, DVD-based reference works, online journals, Web-based news sources, article databases, and other electronic courses, students can find information about nearly any topic and paste the data directly into their papers. Or students can take credit for documents they find or buy online, or that they get as e-mail attachments from friends living down the hall or a thousand miles away" (Sterngold, 2004, p. 16). But many schools and teachers use Internet tools to *detect* plagiarism—tools such as google.com or turnitin.com.

The issue of plagiarism gets more complicated as a growing number of students from other countries and cultures "enter the [current U.S.] college classroom believing that truth, wisdom, and cultural artifacts such as art and literature are cultural community property, the result of years of accumulated wisdom transmitted by venerated leaders and by oral traditions, many of them religious" (Swearingen, 1999; see also McLeod, 1992). Thus it's far easier to *prevent* plagiarism than to handle it after the fact. See the section "What to Do About Cheating" in Chapter 8 for a fuller treatment of cheating. Here we treat only plagiarism in writing.

Despite our best efforts to prevent plagiarism, it can happen. But when we get work that looks plagiarized, we must withhold judgment in the absence of trustworthy evidence. In particular, it's no fair saying, "This work is better than you can do," for in fact most students are capable of work that's astonishingly better than what they often turn in.

Some teachers who suspect plagiarism meet with the student right away and present their account of the situation. They try to bring samples of the student's earlier writing. If the student cited sources, they ask that he or she bring the source materials to the meeting. If the student pleads guilty, they may conclude, nevertheless, that it was not intentional plagiarism. Such cases can be resolved informally—for example, by allowing the student to rewrite the assignment rather than lowering the grade for the assignment or course.

Many campuses have a policy on academic dishonesty that forbids imposing any penalty at all without reporting the case to the official committee and allowing the student to appeal. This may seem bureaucratic at first glance, but there are two good justifications. Many students have been falsely accused and penalized; and not a few students have been found working out informal arrangements with teachers over and over again—convincing each teacher that they've never been involved in anything like this before. It's important to check out the procedures at your institution.

## Ways to Prevent Plagiarism

- Clarify in your syllabus what constitutes plagiarism in your course. Tell students what documentation is required for essays, including use of the Internet. Tell students what is acceptable and unacceptable collaboration with other students.

- Encourage students to come to you or e-mail you if they are in doubt about citations. Try to persuade them that admitting that they don't know something is much better than making a mistake that could constitute plagiarism.

- Ask students to check their syllabi in advance to see if there are some weeks in which they have too many writing assignments due at once. Allow students to hand in an assignment early so as to balance their workload—or possibly negotiate a deadline delay.

- Collect lots of low-stakes informal writing so students know that you know their style and voice.

- On high-stakes essays, where students might be more tempted to cheat, assign specific, idiosyncratic topics so they can't lift things from books, the Internet, or other courses. Examples: "Apply this theory to that set of data"; "Describe your reactions to X and then go on to ..."; "Give a sympathetic summary and then a critical summary of what X writes on page 134, and then write an essay of your own reflections about it"; "Write a short story that explains and illustrates the principles we've studied this week."

- Require drafts and revisions and cover letters that explain the revisions. Require students to hand in all previous versions and notes with every final draft.

- Write fresh topics each year so students aren't tempted to recycle papers from previous years.

- In large courses with different section leaders, have each leader make up different assignments for think pieces and essays—so students aren't tempted to copy work between sections. Circulate copies of new (and old) topics to all instructors.

- Students are less tempted to plagiarize from the Internet if you project that you are savvy and familiar with what is out there. One of our colleagues deters problems with this note in his syllabus: "Last year, we suspended paper-writing in favor of hour tests while we studied Internet plagiarism and how to detect it. Now we're ready."

## IN CONCLUSION

Teachers can enhance student learning if they use a combination of high-stakes and low-stakes writing. (Most people experience writing as a high-stakes use of language—in contrast to speaking as a low-stakes use. But writing, because it is so easily kept private, is ideal for low-stakes use.) We need high-stakes writing in order to test whether students have learned what we are teaching. If we use only short-answer exams, we don't get a trustworthy picture of whether students have a genuine understanding of course concepts and how to apply them.

Low-stakes writing is for exploration and learning: There is no concern about quality or correctness. It helps students explore and figure out new ideas, connect personally with them using their own language, become more active learners, and become fluent and comfortable in writing before they have to write the high-stakes essays that determine their course grade. (And low-stakes writing takes little teacher time or skill.)

Students learn and improve more if they are assigned two or three essays, not just one, and if they have to turn in a draft of each essay for feedback before revising it.

Teachers can handle the increased demands implied by the previous point by (a) keeping the essays short; (b) giving their main response time to drafts—when these responses can actually help students improve; and (c) spending little time responding to final drafts by using a multi-criterion grid and just checking boxes—rather than writing a comment. The multiple criteria make the final grade more valid and reliable. (We provide many specific suggestions for the process of responding and grading.)

It's far more feasible to *prevent* plagiarism than to catch and prosecute it. Methods for preventing plagiarism include making essay assignments particular and idiosyncratic so that students cannot find anything written by someone else that fits the assignment; insisting on drafts of essays and then revision on the basis of feedback to those drafts (along with a process note about how they revised); and seeing lots of students' low-stakes, informal, in-class writing so we know their writing voice and they know we know it.

## Supplementary Reading

▷ P. Diederich, *Measuring Growth in English* (Urbana: NCTE, 1974).

▷ P. Elbow, "Using the Collage for Collaborative Writing," in *Everyone Can Write: Essays Toward a Hopeful Theory of Writing and Teaching Writing* (New York: Oxford University Press, 2000), 372–378.

▷ P. Elbow, "Your Cheatin' Art: A Collage," in *Everyone Can Write: Essays Toward a Hopeful Theory of Writing and Teaching Writing*, 300–313.

▷ P. Elbow and P. Belanoff, *Sharing and Responding* (New York: McGraw-Hill, 2003).

▷ E. Hodges, "Some Realities of Revision: What Students Don't or Won't Understand," *English in Texas*, Summer 1994, 25(4), 13–16.

▷ H. Kirschenbaum, S. Simon, and R. Napier, *Wad-Ja-Get? The Grading Game in American Education* (New York: Hart Publishing, 1971).

▷ Susan H. McLeod, "Responding to Plagiarism: The Role of the WPA," *WPA: Writing Program Administration*, 1992, 15(3), 7–16.

M. D. Sorcinelli and P. Elbow (eds.), "Writing to Learn: Strategies for Assigning and Responding to Writing Across the Disciplines," *New Directions in Teaching and Learning*, no. 69, February 1997.

A. Sterngold, "Confronting Plagiarism: How Conventional Teaching Invites Cyber-Cheating," *Change*, May/June 2004, *36*(3), 16–21.

C. Jan Swearingen, "Originality, Authenticity, Imitation, and Plagiarism: Augustine's Chinese Cousins," in Lise Buranen and Alice M. Roy (eds.), *Perspectives on Plagiarism and Intellectual Property in a Postmodern World* (Albany: State University of New York Press, 1999), 5–18.

Stephen Tchudi (ed.), *Alternatives to Grading Student Writing* (Urbana: NCTE, 1997).

A. Young, "Mentoring, Modeling, Monitoring, Motivating: Response to Students' Ungraded Writing as Academic Conversation," in M. D. Sorcinelli and P. Elbow (eds.), "Writing to Learn: Strategies for Assigning and Responding to Writing Across the Disciplines."

# Technology and Teaching

**A**s network computing and tools for learning, teaching, and administration gain more power and accessibility, integrating technology into the educational process is becoming a major thrust for most colleges and universities. Some instructors are embracing technology whole-heartedly, while others feel skeptical or left behind. Based on our work with instructors, we believe that the essential questions of technology integration are threefold: 1) How will technology enhance teaching and learning? 2) What considerations go into teaching with technology? 3) What is the impact of technology on teaching and learning? In this chapter, we will address each of these issues.

## ► HOW WILL TECHNOLOGY ENHANCE TEACHING AND LEARNING?

When instructors ground their choice of technology tools in individual course goals, personal teaching philosophy, and disciplinary values, technology tools are capable of enhancing teaching and learning. As a tool, instructional technology can serve a number of very useful functions in college and university classrooms, including the following:

---

This chapter written by Erping Zhu and Matthew Kaplan, University of Michigan.

*Providing new opportunities for enhancing student learning that would otherwise be impossible or very difficult.* Course or learning management systems allow you to post reading/study questions, guides, notes, and other resources that might be prohibitively time consuming or costly to create and share, especially for larger classes. The inherent flexibility, openness, and ubiquity of the Web and Web-based applications have made them useful tools for creating learning activities that foster critical thinking, problem solving, written communication, and collaboration, core skills of a liberal education (e.g., see Uchida, Cetron, & McKenzie, 1996). Online and distance learning allow instructors and students in multiple geographical locations to work together in real time in ways that are simply impossible without technology.

*Addressing specific learning goals more effectively.* For example, in order to promote critical thinking, instructors in many disciplines can create multimedia case studies that contain video clips, images, and text information, along with questions asking students to identify problems, discuss possible solutions, and develop recommendations. By integrating games, simulations, and virtual worlds into teaching, you can help students practice and reach a level of accuracy and facility required in performance before engaging in real-world lab tests or activities. Similarly, by using e-mail lists, chats, blogs, or other communication tools, you can extend discussions in any discipline beyond the classroom, so that students are engaged in comparing and contrasting opinions and critical analysis of readings, and there is a written record of the conversation that they can return to and review.

*Taking advantage of the rich information now available online.* From searchable databases, government documents, and reports to technical information and primary sources, a wealth of information is now at students' fingertips. Instructors can take advantage of these resources to incorporate real-world applications into their courses, a strategy that promotes learning and long-term retention (Halpern & Hakel, 2003). For example, access to the online resource Papyri offers students rare opportunities to study ancient texts written in Greek and Latin (http://www.lib.umich.edu/pap/). Data and mapping "mashup" technology opens possibilities for deep understandings of events in specific contexts and geographical locations. Instructors can use such tools to involve students in research, requiring them to manipulate archival data and think critically about patterns and relationships (The EDUCAUSE Learning Initiative, 2006).

*Preparing students to succeed in the 21st century.* While many students now come to higher education having used technology, joined various online social networks, and interacted with peers who may not live in the same neighborhood, city, state, or even country, they may not have developed skills to collaborate effectively with people from different backgrounds and cultures. Students may also have extensive experience in surfing the Web and searching multiple databases, yet be unable to navigate and sift through excess information efficiently or critically evaluate the information they find. Such skills are taking on increasing significance in the workplace and beyond, and students will benefit from exposure to a variety of technologies and thoughtful consideration of sources of information and their validity. For example, instructors can create learning activities in which students use technology to think creatively, take risks, and discover new solutions for real-world problems. Instructors can also engage students in meaningful online activities, such as discussions of issues of privacy and copyright, proper behavior in online public and private spaces, and preparation for digital citizenship.

There is, of course, no guarantee that instructional technology will accomplish these ends effectively. Just as with any tool, technology can be used poorly or inappropriately. Successful incorporation of technology tools will depend upon the extent to which they are connected to course goals, combined with effective pedagogies, and designed to improve student learning, rather than being used for their own sake.

## TEACHING WITH TECHNOLOGY

The phrase "teaching with technology" may conjure up a variety of different images depending on our own experiences as instructors, students, or even conference attendees. For some it might mean using PowerPoint or student classroom response systems in lectures; others may think of podcasting lectures; and still others may think of specific disciplinary applications, such as designing Web-based interactive exercises and simulations to teach skills and concepts. While it is natural to think of the tool itself as a starting point, the use of instructional technology is more likely to be effective and appropriate (i.e., facilitate student learning and increase your own productivity) if it is integrated into a careful planning process that takes into account the various factors involved in teaching and learning.

From a systems approach, teaching with technology involves four major components: the students, the instructor, course content, and technology tools. (See Figure 17.1.) We need to attend to each component in order to make technology integration as successful as possible. **Content** can be examined in terms of learning outcomes and the discipline being taught and how technology may promote specific types of learning. As **instructors**, we can think of our own experience with technology, the

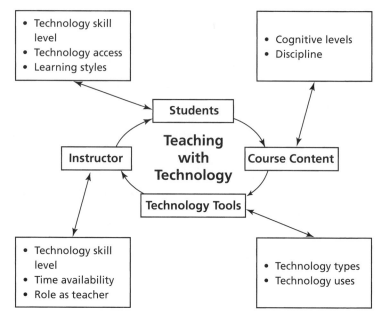

**FIGURE 17.1  Teaching with Technology**

amount of time we have for planning and teaching, and our view of our role in the teaching and learning process. We also need to think carefully about our **students**, their exposure and access to technology as well as their preferred learning styles. Finally, we can turn to the **technology** itself and analyze it according to its functions and relevance to our teaching. This approach to teaching and learning with technology assumes that the four component parts are interrelated and that effective changes in one part will require reconsideration of the other three as well.

## Content

In order to use technology effectively in teaching, we must examine our course goals as we do when we plan a new course. What do you expect students to learn from the course? What skills and knowledge do you want them to acquire by the end of the term? What teaching strategies (lecture, discussion, group work, case studies, etc.) will best help students achieve these goals? (See the chapter "Countdown for Course Preparation.") Once you have answers to these questions, you can choose the appropriate technologies to support your goals and design learning activities to help students reach the learning goals, and even employ technology to assess student learning.

To help make the connection between goals and technology tools, we can turn to the taxonomy of educational objectives developed by Benjamin Bloom (1956). Objectives at the lower levels of Bloom's taxonomy involve acquisition of factual knowledge or development of basic comprehension. Higher-level learning involves skills such as analysis, synthesis, and evaluation. Figure 17.2 briefly illustrates the basis for selecting technology in accordance with this taxonomy of objectives. For example, if you want students to record and remember materials effectively, you could use software programs such as *Microsoft PowerPoint* to ensure clear, readable outlines and post them online so that students have easy access for review and correction of their own notes. However, if you also wish to promote critical thinking through active learning during lectures, software programs alone may not be the best choice. Presentation software can lead to a teacher-centered mode of instruction in which students are relatively passive spectators (Creed, 1997).

To avoid placing students in a passive learning mode, you will need to incorporate activities that engage students in performing tasks, actively thinking, and reflecting on their own actions. In this case, you supplement PowerPoint slides with the use of a classroom response system ("clickers") to actively involve students in lecture and reinforce their understanding. You could also extend the discussion of difficult concepts or problems beyond the class to an online space such as a discussion board or a blog space.

The discipline you teach, as well as the goals you set for student learning, will affect your decisions about which technologies are most appropriate for a given course. In some disciplines, technology is a standard part of professional work in the field, and decisions about technology integration need to take these realities into account.

## The Instructor

Once you have a clear view of the course goals and learning objectives and how technology can support students' achievement of the goals, you will need to ask some questions about your own skills and confidence: 1) How skilled and experienced are you in using technology? 2) How much time do you have for course planning and selecting teaching strategies suited to your choices of technology? 3) What is your role as an instructor?

If you have little or no experience using technology, it might make sense to start slowly with tools that are established and easy to use so

*Level of Thinking*

| Comprehension | Application | Analysis | Synthesis |
|---|---|---|---|
| **Presentation & Distribution**<br>■ Taking notes on slides<br>■ Watching recorded lectures<br>■ Accessing readings electronically | **Drill, Practice, & Integration**<br>■ Using clickers for well-defined problems<br>■ Completing online grammar exercises<br>■ Completing and submitting problem sets online | **Communication & Interaction**<br>■ Editing and providing feedback to peers online<br>■ Participating in a threaded discussion<br>■ Posting responses to course readings in an online journal | **Communication, Creation, & Manipulation**<br>■ Creating course-related Websites<br>■ Creating and posting podcasts on a course topic<br>■ Researching and writing Wikipedia entries |
| Receiving | Responding | Exchanging | Creating |

*Use of Technology*

*Nature of Student Engagement*

**FIGURE 17.2 Technology and Learning Objectives**

that you build your confidence and support your students' learning. You can learn from colleagues in your department or attend a technology workshop to get started with software programs commonly used at your institution.

The time you have available for course planning and skill development should also influence the extent to which you undertake the integration of technology into your courses. (See Table 17.1.) The more complex and unfamiliar a particular tool is, the more time you will need to dedicate to course planning, development of materials and learning activities, and your own skill development. Start-up time for such activities may be greater than you expect or wish to spend on teaching. You need to be aware of this and be ready for such a time commitment when you make the decision to integrate technology into your courses. Using technology to teach without adequate preparation or time commitment could negatively impact on your teaching and student learning.

Integrating technology into teaching without considering appropriate teaching strategies can be less effective and rewarding for you and your students and may even generate unsatisfactory feedback from students. Many campuses now have teaching centers and offices of instructional technology staffed by consultants who can work with you and help you explore teaching strategies best suited to selected

| Easy (little time) (Commonly available and easy-to-learn tools) | Moderate (some time) (More complex learning curve) | Complex (more time) (Specialized software and special training may be necessary |
| --- | --- | --- |
| Examples:<br>■ E-mail, listserv,<br>■ Text-based presentation software<br>■ *Course Management Systems*<br>■ Chat, blog, and bulletin board | Examples:<br>■ Multimedia presentation<br>■ Audio or video clips<br>■ Websites<br>■ Web-conferencing<br>■ Podcast<br>■ Wiki<br>■ Social networks<br>■ Collaboration tools | Examples:<br>■ Complex animation<br>■ Simulation/game<br>■ Interactive database<br>■ Virtual world or learning environment |

**TABLE 17.1 Common Technology Tools and Their Uses**

technology tools. In addition, you may solicit ideas and feedback from graduate and undergraduate students who have experience with technology and who usually know what tools helped or didn't help them learn.

One final issue we need to consider in this category is how the instructor views his or her role in the teaching process and how technology integration can support or conflict with that view. If you see your main role in teaching as that of an expert, an authority in a given field whose main task in teaching is to convey information, you may find it disconcerting to discover that the incorporation of technology situates you to guide or facilitate. In some cases you may discover that your students know more about and are more comfortable with technology than you are. It is best to think carefully about your own view of teaching and learning, how your use of technology might challenge your teaching philosophy and change the dynamics in your class, and whether you are willing to make that shift.

## Students

As you adopt technology tools into your courses, you will need to consider students' previous experience with technology, their access to technology, and the variety of learning styles they bring to your course.

Many instructors report that student comfort and experience with technology seems to increase each year. Data from national studies confirm that, overall, Americans are gaining greater access to technology. In 2007, about 75 percent of U.S. households were connected to the Internet, and broadband connections have increased in the Internet generation. Access to computers in the public schools had already increased greatly to 99 percent by fall 2002 (http://nces.ed.gov/surveys/frss/publications/2004011/2.asp#one). The generation that grew up with the personal computer is now on campus and relies on the Internet in every dimension of college life. For this generation, computer technology has become as much a part of the learning environment as the overhead projector and blackboard were for the previous generation.

Despite these encouraging statistics, there are still segments of the population that may be far less familiar with technology. While the digital divide has narrowed over the past several years as Internet connectivity and home ownership of computers have increased, there are still disparities in who has Internet and broadband access and the use of specific technologies. For example, recent reports indicate that racial minorities, those who live in rural areas, and those in low-income families are less connected and use the Internet less frequently than other groups

(Trend Data, 2009; Kennedy et al., 2008; Fox, & Vitak, 2008; Prieger, & Hu, 2008).

Thus, it is important not to assume that all students have had the same exposure and access to the technology you plan to use in class. Instead, you can conduct a brief survey at the beginning of the semester to find out where your students stand. Even students who come from households where technology was present might not have spent much time with them and might not be familiar with the applications you expect them to use. For example, a large number of students on college campuses know how to use iTunes and have MP3 players or iPods, but they may not necessarily know how to create a podcast. When you ask students to do a podcast project, a brief orientation to the technology, as well as some tasks that would allow them to learn the technology, will help all students succeed in completing the project and accomplishing course-specific goals. When engaging students in technology projects, it is also important for you to tell them about the resources available and where students can go for help with technology questions. Finally, you can seek out the office on your campus that supports students with disabilities to learn more about services they offer so that you can be proactive (in your syllabus and in introducing the technology) about discussing accommodations for disabled students.

Aside from issues of exposure and access to technology, you will want to consider that students will come to your class with a range of learning styles and preferences. For example, today's students are much more accustomed to multimedia presentations of information, multiprocessing, and multi-tasking (Brown, 2000). For many students, presenting information in both verbal and visual modes improves information retention and transfer (Mayer, 2001). For more information on differences among students, see Chapter 12, "Teaching Culturally Diverse Students."

Beyond addressing differences among students, you will need to consider how technology alters the roles students need to take on in your classes. When you use technology in teaching, students may be required to assume new responsibilities, such as monitoring their own learning goals, setting priorities, and controlling the pace of learning. Some students may not be ready or willing to take on these responsibilities. Students can even be resentful of new expectations and challenges because they are used to learning in a passive and responsive way, rather than being active and taking the initiative. If you take a more student-centered approach, some students might see it as an abdication of responsibility, rather than a positive development. As you move toward greater student involvement and autonomy, you will need to explain why you are taking this approach and build in enough structure so that students do not feel lost. The following suggestions should help:

- Be clear about your expectations for using technology for any projects and assignments.

- Build in multiple milestones for independent or group projects so that you can check student progress.

- Provide opportunities for feedback about the class so that you can make minor adjustments when problems arise.

- Discuss options for support should students encounter difficulties.

## Technology Tools

Now that we have carefully considered the context of teaching and learning, we can turn to an examination of the technology itself. One of the challenges we all confront is the need to understand the possible uses and functions of an ever-expanding array of technologies. You need to consider which applications are appropriate for your students, course content, and teaching style. Not all tools are the same. Some are better at promoting learning in specific content areas while others are useful for a wide range of disciplines. Some technology tools are built for specific instructional goals, while others are more generally applicable.

In order to explore appropriate uses of technology, we can categorize various technology tools into groups according to function. For example, a large group of tools can be used to help students communicate and interact with each other or with the instructor. Software programs such as PowerPoint and Keynote assist users in organizing and displaying information in text and/or graphic format. Course management systems make it easy for instructors to distribute to students course materials such as a syllabus and assignments, give quizzes, and even manage students' grades. There is also a variety of discipline-specific technology tools and programs such as MetLab (numerical computing environment and programming language) and Finale (music composing and notation software). Our discussion will focus on general technology tools rather than tools that are designed for specific content and learning needs. In Table 17.2, we divide the general technology tools into four major groups: communication, presentation, information searching and resource management, and course management systems.

**Communication** technology can facilitate communication between the instructor and students or among students themselves, both within the classroom and beyond it. Tools that enable communication can be divided into two main types: those that allow for exchanges between the instructor and a single student or a group of students, either in class or online, and others that enable a more multivocal conversation among students and the instructor, usually via the Web.

| Types | Examples | Instructional Uses |
|---|---|---|
| ■ Bi-directional | E-mail, text message, audience response and polling system, Internet Relay Chat (IRC), bulletin board, listserv | Distributing/delivering information, providing instant feedback |
| ■ Multi-directional | Audio/video conference, Web conference, blog, wiki | Interacting with others, and collaborating on tasks |

**TABLE 17.2 Communication Technology: Type, Example, and Instructional Use**

*Bi-directional instructor-student(s) communication* via electronic mail or Short Message Service (SMS or "texting") is probably most familiar to instructors. E-mail in particular can be used for a variety of tasks, from communicating with individual students about logistics (e.g., office-hour appointments), handling questions, or submitting student work. E-mail and listservs can also be used to communicate with the whole class or subsets of students for announcements, clarifications, etc. The downside of e-mail is its ubiquity, which causes some students to have unrealistic expectations for rapid responses from instructors, and others to abandon it in favor of texting or social networking sites such as Facebook or MySpace as their primary means of keeping in touch. Table 17.3 provides some tips for using e-mail effectively in teaching.

■ Set up rules for class e-mail, for example:
  ○ Establish conventions for subject lines and subheadings (e.g., ECON 101 – Assignment and ECON 101 – Requesting for Appointment).
  ○ Clarify wait time for the instructor's response (e.g., a student who sends an e-mail at 3 a.m. can't expect an immediate response from the instructor).
  ○ Ask students to use consistent attachment formats (e.g., saving documents in MS Word or Text format)
■ Don't assume that your students will keep all the messages you send; keep a copy of important correspondence.

**TABLE 17.3 Tips for Using E-mail**

Instructors can also take advantage of technology to communicate with students in class by using student response systems (commonly called "clickers"). These polling devices enable a large number of students to send their individual responses to an instructor's computer. The instructor is then quickly able to assess students' prior knowledge of a subject or check their understanding of new concepts during lecture. Clickers have been shown to be particularly effective when used to gauge students' conceptual understanding and when combined with strategies for active learning, such as peer instruction (Mazur, 1997; Smith et al., 2009). Clickers seem to be less effective when used strictly for classroom management. In surveys at the University of Michigan (U-M), students responded negatively to clickers when the instructor used them primarily to check students' lecture attendance (Zhu, 2007). See Table 17.4 for tips on using clickers effectively. The book *Teaching with Classroom Response Systems* provides additional ideas for creating active learning environments with clickers (Bruff, 2009).

While clickers require specialized devices both for students to transmit answers and instructors to receive them, services provided by "Poll Everywhere" (http://www.polleverywhere.com/) now make it possible for students to use their cell phones to respond to instructor questions. Researchers and instructors are now experimenting with a variety of ways to use personal communication technology like cell phones as tools for interactive teaching and learning and for bringing student culture into the classroom (Kolb, 2008).

In addition, students and instructors sometimes also use texting via cell phone to communicate, learn, and even improve social presence in online courses. Although texting may be a very convenient tool for sending students updates and reminders and for scheduling appointments, its use as an interactive device within lectures is relatively new and the implications for teaching and impact on student learning, especially reading and writing, are unclear.

*Multi-directional communication tools* via threaded electronic discussions[1], blogs, and wikis, allow students to share information, discuss issues, and collaborate on learning tasks. Asynchronous online discussion tools make it possible for students to start a discussion before class starts and continue it after class ends (Table 17.5). For example, a music professor at the University of Michigan asks students to listen to musical excerpts and discuss their reactions with each other in a "threaded" discussion in the

---

[1] A threaded discussion is an online dialogue or conversation in which the original message and all of its replies are linked together. The "thread" is analogous to a conversational thread. One online forum or conference usually contains many threads covering different subjects.

- Examine your own teaching style and establish clear goals for using clickers in class.

- Explain to students why clickers are being used in the course.

- Clearly articulate your expectations of students and also establish rules and student responsibilities (e.g., it is the students' responsibility to bring clickers to lecture every time).

- Develop a pool of thoughtful and effective clicker questions for each lecture. Questions that ask for conceptual thinking in technical courses or critical thinking in any class are particularly effective.

- Use clickers in conjunction with teaching strategies such as "Peer Instruction" or "Think-Pair-Share" to improve students' conceptual understanding of the content, as well as their critical thinking, problem-solving, and decision-making skills.

- When using clickers for the first time, consider the first couple of class sessions experimental so that both faculty and students will have a chance to practice. It is not a good idea to give students tests using clickers on the first day of the class.

- Be sure not to allocate too many points to a single test that is given to students during lecture using clicker technology, since it may create anxiety and also increase the temptation to cheat.

- If clicker technology is used to track attendance, be sure to use the system for other purposes as well, such as assessing student understanding, generating ideas for class discussion, or engaging students in thinking critically about course content.

- When using clickers in a lecture class, be sure to use them regularly and consistently.

- When using clickers to diagnose students' understanding, be sure to comment on or explain students' responses, give students another question on the same topic if needed, or adjust lecture pace and sequence if necessary to clarify confusion or misconceptions.

**TABLE 17.4 Tips for Using Clickers**

course management system. He could then start the face-to-face discussion with topics that interested or perplexed the students. "The online discussion quickly became a core component of the course and its organization. The threaded discussion complemented the classroom experience, encouraging a richer, more open, more respectful and thoughtful dialogue." These tools also allow students to reach experts beyond campus walls and collaborate on learning tasks with peers in other countries.

**Preparation**

- Define clear goals and objectives for the online discussion.
- Design a clear organizing structure for the online discussion.
- Create an outline of different types of discussion activities.
- Make the online discussion an integral part of the course. (Do not separate what is happening in the conference from what is happening in the face-to-face class meetings.)
- Establish a clear starting and ending time for each discussion topic.
- Provide detailed instructions for students, including student roles and responsibilities.
- Establish rules for appropriate and inappropriate behaviors before starting a discussion.
- Assign points or grade percentage to students' participation in the discussion.
- Establish clear expectations and standards for assessing students' performance in the online discussion.
- Direct students to technology training classes, online tutorials, and any other assistance when necessary.

**Facilitation**

- Create a comfortable atmosphere for the online discussion, for example:
  - Be an active participant.
  - Bring your own experiences to the discussion.
  - Use personal anecdotes when appropriate.
  - Do not dominate a discussion or let a few students dominate it.
  - Challenge students without silencing them.
- Ask questions at different levels (e.g., knowledge, comprehension, application, analysis, synthesis, and evaluation).
- Paraphrase a message if it is not clear.
- Encourage active student participation.
- Energize the online discussion if needed (e.g., using role plays, simulations, and pros and cons).
- Bring closure to an online discussion (e.g., summarizing learning points).

**TABLE 17.5 Tips for Using Asynchronous Online Discussion**

Blogs have become another popular tool for sharing information, comments, and media-based resources. They are sometimes used in ways similar to a discussion space, where students can discuss and comment on questions, share insights and information about course materials, projects, or relevant events on campus. Students can also post pictures, video clips, and any digital media to blogs in ways that are not possible with a threaded discussion. The Educated Nation is one such a blog space (http://www.educatednation.com/). Blogs also have the potential to encourage students to write and to engage them in sharing and commenting on one another's writings.

Like blogs, wikis are a great tool for collaborative learning, including group projects, writing, editing, and presentations (Table 17.6). The best-known is Wikipedia, an online, free encyclopedia that anyone can edit. While skepticism about the quality of entries on Wikipedia abound (along with consternation about student willingness to start and end their research with this particular source), some instructors are actually using this site for creative assignments. For example, an instructor at the University of Michigan organized student groups to evaluate chemistry entries in Wikipedia. They would then select chemistry topics to research and update (or create) for a general audience.

Many instructors are finding that wikis are a useful teaching tool because they enable collaboration and public knowledge creation. One instructor at the University of Michigan engaged students in co-creating

- Set clear goals and objectives for class blogs and wikis (e.g., gather, apply and synthesize new ideas).
- Connect the blogs or wikis to other learning activities in the course.
- Establish clear expectations and specific standards for assessing students' learning.
- Clearly define your and students' roles and responsibilities for the class blogs or wikis.
- Collectively create ground rules for behavior for the class blogs and wikis.
- Direct students to technology training, online tutorials, and any other assistance if necessary.

**TABLE 17.6  Tips for Using Blogs and Wikis**

an online textbook in a wiki. Other instructors create wikis as resources for coordinating teaching in large classes. The wiki provides access for a large number of Teaching Assistants (TAs) to resources such as lesson plans for weekly discussions, instructions for interactive activities, and responses to frequently asked questions. In addition, there is a space where TAs can share questions and concerns that have arisen in their own sections, or they can comment on the effectiveness of particular activities and readings.

Wikis can even serve as a very flexible course management environment. A professor at U-M taught an entire business information technology course using a wiki to house all elements of the course: syllabus, assignments, lecture slides, class notes, project presentations, blogs, feedback comments, and other class interactions. This wiki-based course changed the dynamics of the classroom, with the professor and students teaching and learning from each other throughout the semester. The class time was devoted to project-based work and interaction, rather than the delivery of information, which was moved to the wiki in the form of notes, lecture videos, etc. For example, one student was responsible for posting notes after each class, and others could correct and add to them. In the process, students were able to take control of their own learning as they gathered, analyzed, and evaluated information. They then wrote up and published their findings on the Internet, with the professor providing guidance on the side throughout the process. Wikis have enormous potential to engage students in learning and creating knowledge both inside and outside of the classroom.

For distance learning courses, in particular, communication tools are essential for attending "lectures," meeting the instructor and other students in class, interacting with the instructors and peers, performing learning tasks, and forming online learning communities that connect learners at diverse locations. Students can hold group meetings, discuss course assignments and projects, or provide feedback on one another's work using asynchronous tools (such as threaded discussions, blogs, and wikis) or synchronous tools (such as chat). Similarly, instructors can use synchronous and asynchronous tools for online office hours and for on-line discussions in both distance learning and on-campus courses. For example, through asynchronous chat or other question tools, professors at the University of Michigan encourage students to send questions electronically during large lectures. Students' questions are read and discussed immediately during the class or in the follow-up discussion sections. This back-channel communication helps students overcome the intimidation of raising their hands in large classes and ensures broader participation from students.

Table 17.7 outlines the various types of presentation and organization technology and how they can be used.

**Presentation** technology allows instructors to organize and display information in text, graphic, animation, or multimedia formats. It is easy to prepare lecture notes/outlines in text and graphic format with software programs such as Microsoft Word or Microsoft PowerPoint. As they develop fluency with these tools, instructors should be careful not to overload students with slides in lectures, which can quickly overwhelm students' note-taking capacities and attention spans. While instructors hold differing opinions of whether to make lecture slides available in advance of lectures, research on note taking suggests that students learn more when they have skeletal outlines to structure their notes (DeZure, Kaplan, & Deerman, 2001). See Table 17.8 for additional tips on using PowerPoint.

The learning curve for making a PowerPoint presentation with graphics and images is not steep, and the time you need to learn the skills should be manageable. However, integrating digital media into your presentations may require specific skills, especially if you need to convert the media format. On most campuses, instructional technology labs or centers help faculty with various media conversion projects such as digitizing film clips and creating multimedia presentations. Sometimes, instructors may be able to find useful video clips from Internet Websites such as YouTube (http://www.youtube.com). Like a picture, a video may be useful and effective for illustrating abstract concepts or points, and hierarchical relationships, as well as for motivating students, sustaining their interest, or starting class discussions. (See Table 17.9.) A psychology professor at the University of Michigan uses video clips in two ways: In large lecture courses, he shows short, humorous clips (not necessarily on topic) embedded in PowerPoint to break up the lecture and help students "reset" their attention span; in small seminars, he uses iMovie to create videos of patients suffering from disorders covered in the class.

| Types | Examples | Instructional Uses |
|---|---|---|
| ■ Text<br>■ Text/Graphic<br>■ Text/Graphic/<br>   Sound/Animation | Presentation software<br>(e.g., PowerPoint and Keynote)<br>Webpage editor<br>Animation and video software<br>(e.g., Flash and iMovie)<br>Lecture capture tools | Organizing, presenting<br>information<br>Creating learning<br>modules |

**TABLE 17.7 Organization and Presentation Technology: Types, Examples, and Instructional Uses**

- Use fonts 24 points or larger for the text.
- Ensure that your slides are legible (e.g., watch your color choices for type and background).
- Avoid USING ALL CAPS. The normal use of upper- and lowercase characters is easier to read.
- Use italics or color rather than underlining to emphasize a point. Underlining makes some characters difficult to read.
- Limit seven words per line and eight lines per slide.
- Use the slide as a guide for presentation.
- Face the audience when showing the slide.
- Distribute a copy of the slides to students ahead of time if possible.
- Keep the room lights on and avoid showing slides in a dark room for more than 15 minutes.
- Avoid putting students in a passive mode of receiving information by combining the slide presentation with chalkboard/whiteboard use or other learning activities.
- Have a backup plan in case of a power outage or equipment failure.

**TABLE 17.8 Tips for Using PowerPoint**

By assigning students to create videos, instructors can engage students in learning course content. A number of studies have shown that presenting novel and difficult concepts to learners in both auditory and visual symbolic modes results in more learning than information

- Have a clear goal for using a video clip or clips (e.g., ask yourself why you are using the clip and what you want to students to learn from it).
- Provide proper context for your clip(s) (e.g., explain that a clip comes from a sequence or part of a story or conversation).
- View the entire clip before showing it in class and assess any activity designed to accompany the video.
- Limit the length of video clips. No matter how interesting they may be or how motivated students are, video clips longer than 10 minutes may fail to hold students' attention.

**TABLE 17.9 Tips for Using Video Clips in Presentation**

presented in either mode (Halpern & Hakel, 2003; Mayer, 1997; Mousavi, Low, & Sweller, 1995).

Video is also very useful as a means of archiving course lectures, demonstrations, etc. Lecture capture technology has simplified the process of recording and posting lectures for either traditional or online courses. Programs such as Camtasia and iShowU allow faculty to synchronize their lectures with a slide show or other multimedia presentation. Students can then watch the full lecture as often as they need, with time to review segments that were unclear. The ease of use of lecture capture and its potential to make course materials accessible to wider audiences has drawn the attention of many instructors and students on college campuses across the country. Institutions including Duke (http://itunes.duke.edu/), Stanford (http://itunes.stanford.edu/), UC Berkeley (http://itunes.berkeley.edu/), University of Wisconsin-Madison (http://www.uwebi.org/news/uw-online-learning.pdf), and University of Michigan are experimenting with providing lecture podcasts as supplementary learning material to students, including those who registered for distance-learning courses. Students can have access to lecture archives for reviewing material, revisiting demonstrations of difficult concepts, or seeing talks given by guest lecturers. In addition, recording and posting lectures in advance opens the possibility of freeing up in-class time for practical, hands-on work (problem sets, discussions, and team work). A number of faculty members at the University of Michigan are already capturing lectures and creating podcasts and/or screencasts as additional learning resources for on-campus students.[2]

Although lecture capture offers many potential benefits (Coghlan et al., 2007), it also presents a set of challenges for instructors, including mastery of the technology (for students as well as instructors), recording and replay quality, and intellectual property issues. See Table 17.10 for suggestions about how to get the most from this technology tool.

**Information searching and resource management** technology helps users find and manage information. The Internet offers a wealth of information and data may be used for teaching and learning. College instructors across the curriculum identify the skills associated with searching for, managing, and evaluating information on the Internet as important student learning objectives and survival skills for the 21st century. You can start helping students gain skills in Internet-search and Website evaluation by reviewing the basics of Internet search engines

---

[2] Examples of U-M faculty using lecture-capture technology are available at http://www.crlt.umich.edu.

- Before you start, make sure of the following:
  - ○ You have clear goals for podcasting lectures and the time to prepare them consistently throughout the entire semester.
  - ○ Your students are receptive to and prepared for lecture podcasts. Don't assume that all students have the same level of access to or comfort with using podcasts.
  - ○ You know the copyright policies regarding podcasts (e.g., copyright clearance of materials and release forms from students if their questions and answers will be recorded).
  - ○ You have adequate and continuing technology support and podcast hosting if you don't teach in a room with automated lecture capture system/service.
- Once you decide to podcast, make time to experiment with recording quality. Choose a reasonable podcast quality since poor sound quality may not encourage students to use the recorded lectures.
- Make podcasts available as soon as possible after a lecture, since most students download podcasts within a few days, as well as right before an exam.
- Devote additional classroom time for interactive discussion or demonstrations if podcasts can replace lectures.
- Podcasts should not replace more traditional methods of providing supplemental material to students, such as putting materials in the course management system, before you know for sure that all your students have access to devices to download and play back podcasts.
- Make reference to podcasts during lectures or when responding to students' questions, if appropriate, so that students will be more likely to take advantage of the available resource.
- Make accessing and using podcasts easy and fast by providing detailed instructions for downloading, and ensure that the file format is compatible with common media-playing devices (e.g., MP3 players, iPods, and computers).
- Provide students with a clear explanation of instructional goals and technical requirements if podcasts are used for student projects or assignments.
- Be aware of any potential implications of your lecture podcasts for other courses in a program or in the curriculum.

**TABLE 17.10 Tips for Using Lecture Capture**

| Type | Examples | Instructional Uses |
|------|----------|--------------------|
| ■ Information searching and managing | The Internet, electronic databases<br><br>Procite, EndNotes, Refworks<br><br>Excel and other data management tools | Searching, manipulating, analyzing information/data<br><br>Evaluating and researching |

**TABLE 17.11** Information Search and Research Management Technology: Type, Example and Instructional Use

(see Table 17.12) and offering information or guidelines for evaluating Websites. Most university and college libraries have these kinds of resources available for students. For example, the Undergraduate Library at the University of Michigan provides "Criteria for Web Site Evaluation" at http://guides.lib.umich.edu/content.php?pid=30524, and the University of California at Berkeley has useful information on Internet search engines and Website evaluation at http://www.lib.berkeley.edu/TeachingLib/Guides/Internet/Evaluate.html.

When asking students to use Internet resources for writing projects, the instructor should distinguish between common knowledge and plagiarism and teach students good practices for evaluating and using online resources and for recognizing and avoiding plagiarism. Resources for instructors and students on academic integrity are available at most institutions. For example, the University of Michigan has a Website with extensive resources on academic integrity at http://www.lib.umich.edu/acadintegrity/. Penn State University's information technology services gather useful resources on plagiarism at http://tlt.its.psu.edu/copyright-plagiarism including examples of acceptable and unacceptable paraphrases.

**Course management systems** were developed over a decade ago. They provide a virtual course space for distributing resources, communicating with students, giving quizzes and tests, and managing students' grades without requiring high-level programming or Web-design skills. These systems have evolved to include features beyond course administration and management. Tools for collaboration and reflection such as wikis, blogs, eportfolios, and streaming media (e.g., podcasts) are common in the current generation of course management systems.

Even course management systems that contain only administrative features have the potential to guide instructors through a course-planning process anchored in effective pedagogy and adapted to diverse

**TABLE 17.12 Internet Search Engine Types**

| Types | Example | | |
|---|---|---|---|
| **Website Search**<br>*Search Websites*<br>*(full text and media)*<br>*in a single database.* | **Directory Search**<br>*Search Websites*<br>*in directories*<br>*organized in subjects*<br>*by people* | **Meta Search**<br>*Search multiple*<br>*databases using multiple*<br>*search engines and return*<br>*search results with text*<br>*or visual display* | |
| **Google**<br>http://www.google.com | **Yahoo**<br>http://dir.yahoo.com | **Vivisimo**<br>http://www.vivisimo.com | |
| **Exalead**<br>http://www.exalead.com/search | **Librarians' Index**<br>http://www.lii.org | **Metacrawler**<br>http://metacrawler.com | |
| **Altavista**<br>http://www.altavista.com | **Academic Info**<br>http://www.academicinfo.net | **Dogpile**<br>http://www.dogpile.com | |
| **Blinkx (video search engine)**<br>http://www.blinkx.com | | **Kartoo (visual meta search)**<br>htt://www.kartoo.com | |

| Types | Examples | Instructional Uses |
|---|---|---|
| ■ Open source<br>■ Proprietary | Sakai CLE (collaborative learning environment), Moodle, CTools[3] Blackboard, Angel Learning, eCollege | Providing a space/environment for students to engage in a wide range of learning tasks |

**TABLE 17.13 Course Management Systems: Types, Examples and Instructional Uses**

student needs. As instructors use course management systems to store and distribute information and engage students in online discussion, small changes in teaching may later become the impetus for more ambitious changes. For example, a language instructor at the University of Michigan started using a course management system to post a syllabus and make class announcements, but subsequently learned how to use online reference tools, as well as peer writing, critiquing, and online editing. It is comparatively easy to use a course management system to post a syllabus, lecture notes, assignments, and resources, but more complex features may require training. (See Table 17.14.)

- Identify the features in a course management system you will use and why you will use them.
- Start with a few features if you are a novice user of the course management system.
- Provide specific instructions to students if you use online discussion or other interactive features.
- Set clear deadlines and enforce them if you use assignments, quizzing, and testing features.
- Allocate appropriate time for preparation if you decide to create online learning modules.
- Prepare students for the use of the course management system and arrange student training if necessary.

**TABLE 17.14 Tips for Using Course Management Systems**

---

[3] CTools is an advanced Web-based environment that combines course management features with project and research collaboration features.

Course management systems are particularly useful for distance learning. They provide "one-stop-shopping" for the various tasks and resources that could otherwise become difficult to juggle without the face-to-face interaction with instructor and peers.

Many instructors also create their own Websites for teaching. Instructors may take advantage of many other Internet tools to engage students in creative thinking, reflective blogs, and collaborative wiki projects; involve them in the development of content; or experiment with new ways of teaching and learning. For example, the Valley of the Shadow project (http://valley.vcdh.virginia.edu), which appeared on the Web in the early 1990s, introduced a new way of learning and studying history. The technology skills required to start a simple course Website are similar to those needed to create a multimedia presentation. Current HTML editors like Dreamweaver are straightforward and easy to learn. To publish your pages on the Web, you will need to find out how to access designated spaces on the Web server of your department or institution. (See Table 17.15.)

- Allow plenty of lead time for planning the course and designing course Web pages.
- Be sure that the course Web pages are functional and contents are accessible to students with disabilities.
- If you have interactive activities on the course Website, be sure that security and privacy issues are discussed and well understood by students.
- Have a back-up plan for lectures (e.g., save the Web pages on your thumb or local drive).
- Be well prepared for lecture when using your own course Website, for example:
  - Verify links, especially the external links.
  - Check the room lighting to see if it is suitable for both viewing the projected screen and taking notes.
  - Check the set up (e.g., browser and software for audio/video and animation).
  - Arrange for technical support staff to be in your classroom at the start of class to help with the setup if necessary.
  - Always know whom to call for help if technical problems occur.
- Emphasize the need for filtering, interpreting, and evaluating information found on the Web when encouraging students to use online resources.
- Remind students that only a small fraction of the whole archive of knowledge is available on the Web.

**TABLE 17.15 Tips for Creating Course Websites**

- Define specific goals for student Web pages or other technology projects.
- Provide detailed guidelines for student projects.
- Establish clear expectations and standards for assessing student projects.
- Make student Web pages or other technology projects an integral part of student learning experiences in the course.
- Encourage students to share and review one another's projects.
- Set periodic check-in points for a semester-long technology project.
- Arrange technology training for students if necessary.

**TABLE 17.16  Tips for Assigning Student Technology Project**

You can also build Website creation into student projects. Creating their own Websites and making their work available to a larger audience may motivate students to learn and raise their expectations about the quality of their work and the time they are willing to invest in a class. At the same time, such projects present challenges for both students and instructors. While students may be new to using this kind of medium for class projects, the instructor also might not have much experience designing or assessing this type of project. (See Table 17.16.)

For example, a professor of English at the University of Michigan encourages students in his Eighteenth-Century English Literature course to write and design their own Web pages in small groups, exploring various aspects of 18th-century life in England. This assignment serves as the final project for the course. The students find the experience enhances their intellectual and technical skills. One student noted, "Not only was this project useful in increasing my confidence with technology, but I felt that it helped me to better understand some of the novels we read, as well as the historical context in which these novels were written."[4]

# TEACHING ONLINE OR AT A DISTANCE

Teaching at a distance may include all the technology tools listed above. In addition, distance learning courses can be delivered via videoconference systems (one- or two-way audio and video) as well as Internet-based audio- and videoconference software programs. Effective teaching

---

[4] http://www.umich.edu/%7Eece/about.html#comments; this site contains useful directions for setting up a similar project.

strategies and good teaching practices work in all instructional situations. Instructors, whether teaching on campus, online or at a distance, will face similar challenges and issues. However, instructors teaching online or at a distance may encounter several additional challenges due to the lack of in-person contact with students, heavy reliance on technology for delivering instruction, and differences in student population. For example, online and distance teaching may require faculty's special attention to course planning, facilitation, and assessment of student learning.

A good start for an online or distance learning course is to develop a thoughtful plan that includes not only course goals and learning objectives, but also methods of teaching and assessing student learning outcomes. The following is a list of areas you may want to consider when planning an online or distance learning course. (See also Chapter 2, "Countdown for Course Preparation.")

- Course design
  - Clearly defined course goals and measurable learning objectives
  - Meaningful activities (assignments) that help students reach learning objectives
  - Level of student participation and involvement in the teaching/learning process
- Delivery of instruction
  - Methods of teaching that match well with course goals (e.g., pre-recorded or interactive lectures via Web conference, case studies)
  - Technology tools that support teaching and learning activities (e.g., course management systems, blogs, wikis, threaded discussion forums, and synchronous chat rooms)
- Communication and interaction
  - Effective means of communication and interaction between instructor and students and among students themselves
  - Frequent feedback from and to students on teaching and learning
  - Supportive learning community for students to share and exchange (avoid leaving students in isolation)
- Assessment of student learning
  - Clear expectations and standards for assessment (aligned with learning objectives)
  - Variety of assessment methods that address different learning styles
  - Flexible assessment methods, but rigorous standards

Ideally, the online teaching/learning environment will provide ample opportunities not only for the dissemination of information, but also for the interaction that is so important for helping students to develop higher level thinking skills (e.g., through discussion, reflection, collaborative learning, interactive real-world case studies, etc.). Incorporating such strategies may challenge some teaching practices that you may have been using for years. This learning and teaching environment may also prompt you to take on a new role, that of a guide or facilitator, leading students through the process of information gathering, evaluation, and knowledge construction (Berge, 2000).

In addition, while a medium to high level of technological competency in using online tools (such as discussion forum, blogs, wikis, and tools for online grading and progress tracking) is optional for face-to-face teaching, it is now required for teaching online and at a distance. Thus, learning adequate skills and tactics for communicating with students, interacting with them, giving feedback, and responding to their needs are now essential for teaching effectively online or at a distance.

Most higher education institutions offer workshops and seminars on using course management tools and other software programs for administering and facilitating online communication and discussion for either face-to-face or online and distance teaching. Research indicates that some part of faculty online or distance teaching training be conducted online (Ko & Rossen, 2001) in order to give faculty the experience of being online learners.

While preparing for online and distance teaching, learning technology tools and communication and facilitation skills, it is important to think about your students and what activities you may create to enable them to study and learn effectively online or at a distance. Student backgrounds and preparation are always important factors in planning for teaching online or at a distance, as they are when you plan to integrate technology into teaching on campus.

## HANDLING THE TECHNOLOGY BOOM

Finally, we need to mention Web 2.0 technology, especially social networking sites and mobile software such as Facebook, Flickr, and Google Apps. These tools have already made their way into on-campus, online, and distance teaching and learning in higher education. The whole suite of Web 2.0 technology, and even newer and emerging technology tools that may appear tomorrow, may confuse us and leave us wondering about what to use or integrate into teaching. One of the effective ways to deal with this challenge is to apply the basic principle of integrating technology into teaching and learning we introduced at the start of this chapter. Technology decisions are essentially teaching and learning decisions. Therefore, when contemplating use of a new tool, you certainly need to understand the technology and its potential implications for teaching and learning; however, you also need to think carefully about your course goals and learning objectives and the abilities and backgrounds of your students and how the technology will enhance your course and your students' learning.

## WHAT IS THE IMPACT OF TECHNOLOGY ON TEACHING AND LEARNING?

Assumptions about technology and its impact on teaching and learning vary among technology users. Some proponents of technology believe that both instructors and students can take advantage of technology to teach and learn well if they get the right hardware and software in the classroom. Others believe that hardware and software used in the class are irrelevant to student learning. These two opposing positions actually reflect the debate of medium and message in the field of educational technology (Clark, 1994a & 1994b; Kozma, 1994). The research studies collected in *No Significant Difference Phenomenon* by Tom Russell (1999) indicate that the vehicle, that is, the technology used for providing information, does not significantly affect student learning outcomes. However, other researchers, such as Kozma (1994), argue that we have not sufficiently used and examined the attributes and specific functions of individual technologies or explored and compared their effectiveness in instruction. We cannot, therefore, expect to find that technologies make a difference until we can exploit the unique capabilities of the medium.

Recently, Kulik conducted a meta-analysis that reviewed more than 100 controlled studies on the use of instructional technology in college courses during the 1980s and early 1990s. This meta-analysis showed that computer-based instruction made small but significant contributions to academic achievement and also produced positive, but again small, effects on student attitudes (Kulik, 2003). The general impact of technology on teaching and learning has also been studied for decades, but again opinions about the impact of technology are divided. Clearly, the integration of technology into teaching is associated with changes in practice, but the nature of this association is complex and multifaceted.

For practical and useful research on the impact of technology on teaching and learning, we should examine students' learning outcomes in cognitive and affective domains and their learning behaviors and strategies, as well as instructors' changed pedagogy and teaching strategies. Questions could be directed toward exploring what the best teaching and learning strategies are and how technologies best support those strategies (Ehrmann, 1995; Kozma, 1994). Some examples of faculty pursuing these types of questions can be found on the Website for the Visible Knowledge Project (http://crossroads.georgetown.edu/vkp/), which focuses in part on applying methods from the scholarship of teaching and learning to technology. The Website contains short descriptions of individual faculty projects that focus on a specific technology and its impact on student learning and attitudes. For example, faculty are "examining under what classroom conditions one is more likely to create intellectual communities that mirror and cultivate disciplinary thinking" (Elmendorf & Ottenhoff, 2009).

Similar examples of faculty investigating student learning and the impact of technology can be found at the University of Michigan. One engineering professor is studying the impact of posting recordings of lectures along with homework and quiz solutions, on student learning, studying, and problem solving. A large-scale study focused on examining the use of a student response system (Qwizdom) in large lecture courses. With thousands of responses to the survey over several semesters, the study results helped generate a set of pedagogical guidelines for using clickers effectively in teaching (Zhu, 2007).

Faculty are also researching new ways of teaching with technology and investigating the impact of new teaching structures on student learning. One faculty member, for instance, is experimenting with wikis and tracking their impact on student learning, especially on learning scientific and creative ways of thinking, which new technology supports and fosters well.

As you think about conducting research on the impact of technology on your teaching and your students' learning, it is important that you consider the full range of changes technology may bring to the entire process of teaching and learning. The following questions are designed to help you start thinking about how you might evaluate the impact of technology on teaching and student learning in a course, curriculum, or a program.

■ How did the use of technology help students achieve learning goals? Examples could include:

○ Demonstration of changes in student knowledge, skills, and attitudes (e.g., pre- and post-test results and comparison of student attitudes and learning outcomes before and after technology was integrated)

- How did the use of technology help change students' engagement in learning inside and outside of class?
  - Documentation of students' engagement during lecture (e.g., questions and answers) and outside of class (e.g., discussion or blog postings, quality of student postings and projects, tracking which subsets of students accessed lecture recordings most frequently)
  - Feedback or self-report of engagement in and outside of class

- How did the use of technology change teaching behaviors and practices? Examples of changes could include:
  - Amount of interaction between the instructor and students and among students themselves
  - Ways of addressing diverse learning styles
  - Lecture style (interactive or non-interactive)
  - Nature of student learning activities and assignments
  - Linkage of course content to real world
  - Amount and frequency of feedback to and from students

- How did the technology improve teaching effectiveness and efficiency? Examples could include:
  - Use of class time
  - Instructor's time on course preparation and management
  - Students' time on learning tasks
  - Access to course materials
  - Synchronous attendance and participation in class from off-site

## IN CONCLUSION

The successful integration of technology entails careful consideration of course content, the capabilities of various technology tools, student access to and comfort with technology, and the instructor's view of his or her role in the teaching and learning process. The use of technology may change teaching methods and approaches to learning as well as attitudes, motivation, and interest in the subject. With careful thought and planning, faculty can take advantage of developments in instructional technology to enhance their courses, re-examine their own ideas about teaching, and promote greater student academic achievement.

## *Supplementary Readings*

## PowerPoint

▷ B. Brown, "PowerPoint-Induced Sleep," *Syllabus*, 2001, *14*(6), 17.

▷ T. Creed, *PowerPoint, No! Cyberspace, Yes*, 1999, available at http://www.ntlf.com/html/pi/9705/creed_1.htm.

▷ T. Rocklin, *PowerPoint Is Not Evil*, 1999, available at http://www.ntlf.com/html/sf/notevil.htm.

▷ E. R. Tufte, *The Cognitive Style of PowerPoint* (Cheshire, CT: Graphics Press, 2003).

▷ D. D. DuFrene & C. M. Lehman, "Concept, Content, Construction, and Contingencies: Getting the Horse Before the PowerPoint Cart," *Business Communication Quarterly*, 2004, *67*(1), 84–88.

▷ Y. Gabriel, "Against the Tyranny of Powerpoint: Technology-in-Use and Technology Abuse," *Organization Studies*, 2008, *29*(2), 255–276.

## E-mail and Online Discussion

▷ T. Bender, *Discussion-Based Online Teaching to Enhance Student Learning: Theory, Practice, and Assessment* (Sterling, VA: Stylus, 2003).

▷ C. J. Bonk and K. S. King (eds.), *Electronic Collaborators: Learner-Centered Technologies for Literacy, Apprenticeship, and Discourse* (Mahwah, NJ: Erlbaum, 1998).

▷ D. Hanna, M. Glowacki-Dudka, and S. Conceicao-Runlee, *147 Practical Tips for Teaching Online Groups: Essentials of Web-Based Education* (Madison, WI: Atwood Publishing, 2000).

▷ S. Kleinman, "Strategies for Encouraging Active Learning, Interaction, and Academic Integrity in Online Courses," *Communication Teacher*, 2005, *19*(1), 13–18.

▷ C. MacKnight, "Teaching Critical Thinking through Online Discussions," available at http://net.educause.edu/ir/library/pdf/EQM0048.pdf.

▷ A. P. Rovai, "Strategies for Grading Online Discussions: Effects on Discussions and Classroom Community in Internet-Based University Courses," *Journal of Computing in Higher Education*, 2003, *15*(1), 89–107.

▷ G. Salmon, *E-Tivities: The Key to Active Online Learning* (London: Kogan Page, 2002).

## Teaching with the Web

▶ S. Horton, *Web Teaching Guide*: *A Practical Approach to Creating Course Web Sites* (New Haven, CT: Yale University Press, 2000).

▶ B. H. Khan (ed.), *Web-Based Instruction* (Englewood Cliffs, NJ: Educational Technology Publications, 1997).

▶ G. R. Morrison, S. M. Ross, and J. E. Kemp, *Designing Effective Instruction* (New York: Wiley, 2001).

▶ EDUCAUSE Learning Initiative. 7 Things You Should Know About, 2005–2009. Available at http://www.educause.edu/ELI/ELI Resources/7ThingsYouShouldKnowAbout/7495?bhcp=1.

# Part 5

*Skills for Use in Other Teaching Situations*

# Teaching Large Classes (You Can Still Get Active Learning!)

I n the middle of the 20th century, most first-and second-year courses were taught by lecture in large classrooms or auditoriums. Over the next decades, research demonstrated that better learning occurred if students had an opportunity to discuss the material. Thus, many large courses now supplement lectures with 1 or 2 hours of small-group discussion. However, with decreasing government support and increasing enrollments, more and more universities all over the world feel pressure to revert to large classes without support from small discussion groups or tutorials.

Most of this chapter deals with skills and strategies useful in large groups, whether or not they are supplemented by discussion groups. Before concluding, I discuss aspects of the teacher's role involved in supervising teaching assistants who lead discussion or laboratory groups. Teaching assistants facilitate the smooth functioning of a large course. As they are the next generation of faculty, they should be included in this learning experience.

If you are assigned to teach a large course, you are likely to assume that you must lecture and use multiple-choice or other easily scorable tests, but large classes need not constrain you. You don't need to lecture—at least not all the time.

# FACILITATING ACTIVE LEARNING

The most commonly used method of stimulating active learning is questioning and encouraging student questioning, as discussed in Chapter 5 "Facilitating Discussion" and Chapter 6 "How to Make Lectures More Effective." But many other tools in your active learning kit are usable in large classes. In the Chapter 14 "Active Learning: Group-Based Learning," I reported the research showing that students learn more in student-led discussions, or in learning cells, than they learn in traditional lectures. Thus, you can get the advantages of a multisection course by organizing students to meet in class or out of class for discussion. Active learning does not need to be restricted to in-class activity. You can organize study groups. You can use e-mail or online discussion boards. The chapter "Technology and Teaching" describes ways in which technology can facilitate learning both in and out of class.

Techniques such as think-pair-share, question posting, and the two-column method of large-group discussions were also described earlier. Small groups (described in the chapter "Facilitating Discussion") can be formed and asked to discuss how the material might be used or applied. Simply pausing occasionally to give students a couple of minutes to compare their notes can activate thinking (Ruhl, Hughes, & Schloss, 1987).

It is still possible, even using these techniques, for students to hold back in large classes, but technology may be coming to your rescue. Recent advances in wireless technology make it possible to have every student in the class actively respond to questions and problems using the personal response systems discussed in the chapter on technology. In the generic system each student has a remote control handset with a keypad. The instructor projects a multiple-choice question on a screen at the front of the room. Each student selects one of the alternatives and enters that response on his or her keypad. The choice is then transmitted to a computer, all the responses are compiled, and the results are displayed to the whole class in graphic format, showing how many folks chose each alternative. The instructor gets immediate feedback on how well the students were understanding the lecture content, and the students get immediate feedback on whether or not they understood. Some systems make it possible for the instructor to identify—for grading purposes later—which students are making which responses. Even if the instructor doesn't know which students made which responses, he or she can invite students to defend a given option (if they chose it) or to challenge another one. Because the students can see how many other students in the class agreed with them, they will feel more or less inclined to speak up when their option is challenged. This procedure can also be done in groups, with each group's response rather than an individual's response entered on the keypad. The system can be used to take roll or simply to give the students an active learning opportunity. Of course, you can go low tech and just have students raise their hands to vote for an option, but it's not nearly as effective and there's no permanent record or visual summary available. But in a pinch, it still gets students responding.

## Encouraging Student Writing in Large Classes

One of the most important drawbacks of large classes is the lack of student writing. Because grading essays is so time consuming, most faculty members reduce or eliminate writing assignments in a large class. Take heart! You can get some of the educational advantages of writing, and at the same time improve attention to the lecture, without being submerged by papers to grade.

The minute paper, described earlier, is one valuable tool.* At an appropriate point in the lecture, announce the paper and the topic or question you want students to address; for example, you might ask the students to summarize the major point or points made so far in the lecture. Or you might give the students a choice of formats, such as writing a summary, a question, an application, or an example. When the minute is up, you may either collect the papers or break the class into pairs or subgroups to review and discuss one another's papers.

If you wish, you can evaluate and comment on the papers as you would any other student papers. If the class is exceptionally large, you may announce that you'll read and return only a sample of the papers. Students can be motivated to think and write without the threat of grades, and this technique not only gets students thinking actively during the lecture, but also gives you feedback about what students are learning from the lecture.

The problem with evaluating these papers in a large class is the huge amount of work that it causes for the instructor. However, I find that after reading a sample of answers, I can give generic feedback to the whole class in the form of general comments put up on the class Website or brought up at the next class period. Students can then compare their efforts to these general comments. Another alternative is the calibrated peer review system, first discussed by Robinson (2001)

---

*The minute paper need not be 1 minute; it can be 2, 3, or as many minutes as needed for a particular topic.

as a way to increase writing in large biology classes. In this computer-based system, students review one another's papers online in a grand randomized sequencing scheme. Each student is assigned to review three other students' written work, and receives three reviews of his or her own work in return. Each student's review of other students is weighted according to a calibration system and his or her contribution to peers' papers is figured accordingly. One advantage to this system is that the act of reviewing someone else's work can help the reviewer learn about his or her own writing.

Similar to the minute paper is the "half-sheet response" (Weaver & Cotrell, 1985). In this technique students tear out a half-sheet of notebook paper to respond to a question or instruction such as:

"What do you think about this concept?"

"Give an example of this concept or principle."

"Explain this concept in your own words."

"How does this idea relate to your own experience?"

"What are some of your feelings as you listen to these ideas?"

"How could you use this idea in your own life?"

Both the minute paper and the half-sheet response can help initiate a large-group discussion.

## Other Ways to Maintain Student Involvement

There are a variety of techniques that can help break the deadly routine of lectures day after day: debates, fishbowl, and interviews.

In addition to the large-group discussion and subgrouping techniques discussed in the chapter 5 "Facilitating Discussion: Posing Problems, Listening, Questioning" and Chapter 14 "Active Learning: Group-Based Learning," you can enliven your class with debates either between faculty members or between student teams. If you use student debaters, you need to provide a clear structure, probably using a handout describing the issue, the length of talks, opportunity for rebuttal, and the goal of the debate as a learning device. If the topic is one on which students are likely to have strong biases, you can open minds by assigning groups to argue the side opposite their initial position. You can follow the debate by dividing the class into buzz groups whose task is to find a solution or resolution that takes into account the evidence and values of both sides.

The "fishbowl" can be used in small, as well as large, classes. Tell the students that at the next class meeting you will choose six students (or any convenient number) to be "in the fishbowl." You will then conduct a discussion (based on the work to date) with the students in the fishbowl. The rest of the students are to act as observers and recorders, noting both the process and the content of the discussion. Before the end of the class period, observers will write a brief summary of the discussion and raise questions that remain or answer the question, "What would you have said that wasn't said?"

Another break in lectures can be provided by an interview—perhaps of a colleague with special expertise, someone from outside the university, or one of the students with special experience. A variant might be a dialogue on a topic in which you and a colleague have somewhat different views.

Student presentations can enhance the learning and motivation of students who have special interests or expertise and can also be valuable for the other students if presentations are well done. But don't assume that this will be a chance to reduce your own preparation time. If the student simply reads a paper, the audience will be bored. So work with the student on ways of enhancing interest and attention. For some shy students, you may want to conduct the presentation as an interview.

If you plan to have a number of presentations, consider the possibility of a poster session—a method now common in scholarly conventions. Groups of students are assigned to design a poster around a controversial topic requiring extensive research. All the posters are displayed in a large room and students are allowed to circulate in shifts while others stay to represent the posters. An additional incentive is to have guest judges who evaluate the posters and award prizes. One of the instructors at my university teaches classes of up to 1,000, and she uses this technique to teach the processes involved in evaluating the commercial potential of a business in a fictional small town. Each poster is a sales pitch for that business based on extensive investigative work into whether or not it might be profitable given the conditions of the town. She invites local city government officials and business leaders to come as the judges. It's quite a production, but the students learn a lot about the practical side of the course content.

If you use these methods, some students will be frustrated. They came to hear you tell them the *truth*, which they can then memorize for tests. To handle this frustration, two things may help:

1. Explain how active participation contributes to better understanding and memory.

2. Make sure that your students realize that your tests will require thinking, not just rote memory.

# STUDENT ANONYMITY

A major problem of teaching a large class is that students not only feel anonymous, they usually *are* anonymous. And as social psychological research has shown, people who are anonymous feel less personal responsibility—a consequence not only damaging to morale and order but also unlikely to facilitate learning. Moreover, the sense of distance from the instructor, the loss of interpersonal bonds with the instructor and with other students—these diminish motivation for learning.

The larger the group, the less likely that a given student will feel free to volunteer a contribution or question. Yet the students who prefer anonymity may be the very ones who most need to find that others respect their ideas.

What can we do? The fact that with increasing class size it becomes less and less possible to know students as individuals is likely to make us feel that it is not worth trying to do anything. I think this is a mistake. In my experience, the students appreciate whatever efforts you make even if they do not take advantage of them. The "Reducing Students' Feelings of Anonymity" box shows some things I've tried.

If you don't want to or can't reduce student anonymity during the class period itself, you might consider encouraging students to form study groups outside of class. At least they will have a small number of classmates who they know and who know them. Some large-class instructors try to help students with this group formation by using technology to create a sort of mass calendar. Students who want to study at a particular time can consult the calendar and sign up to be available for studying at that time. Others who consult the calendar can see who is available when or where and get together with those other students at a time that fits their schedule.

# ORGANIZATION IS THE KEY

The biggest challenges of teaching a large class are related to being organized. With a large class you can't do things very spontaneously; things have to be planned or they will flounder. What follows are some of the areas in which organization can make or break a class.

## Giving Tests in Large Classes

In classes of 200 or more, unwary instructors are likely to run into problems they would never dream of in teaching classes with an enrollment

## Reducing Students' Feelings of Anonymity

1. Announce that you'll meet any students who are free for coffee after class. (You won't be swamped.)

2. Pass out invitations to several students to join you for coffee and to get acquainted after class.

3. Pass out brief student observation forms to several students at the beginning of class and ask them to meet with you to discuss their observations.

4. Circulate among early-arriving students to get acquainted before class starts.

5. Use a seating chart so that you can call students by name when they participate. If the room is set up with continuous desktop seating rather than tablet style seats, give each student a name tent and have them put it in front of them each class period. I make these tents do double duty by printing suggestions for active learning on the side facing the student. Of course, you have to be able to see and read the tents for this to work.

6. During your lecture, move out into the aisles to solicit comments.

7. If you can't use regularly scheduled discussion sections, set up an occasional afternoon or evening session for more informal discussion of an interesting question or for review before an examination.

8. Have students fill out an autobiographical sketch with name, hometown, year in college, and what they hope to get out of the course (Benjamin, 1991).

9. Create a set of flash cards with students' names on one side and their pictures on the other. Study them during odd moments, like when standing in lines or when on hold on the phone. Many institutions have started providing a photo roster of the class for the instructor. This saves a lot of time, but there is one caveat. You'd be surprised how often the live student looks nothing like his or her photo!

10. When students are working in groups regularly, you can learn the names of all the students in the group as a set. Then remembering any one student's name may trigger recall of all of them. I create group cards with the students' pictures on one side and their names on the other.

of 20 to 30. Most of these problems are administrative. For example, course planning almost inevitably becomes more rigid in a large class because almost anything involving the participation of the students requires more preparation time.

Perhaps you're used to making up your tests the day before you administer them. With a large class this is almost impossible. Essay and short-answer tests that take relatively little time to construct take a long time to score for 200 students; so you may spend long hours trying to devise thought-provoking objective questions for a part of the test. But once you've made up the questions your troubles are not over, for office staff or your teaching assistant (TA) may require a good deal of time to make several hundred copies of a test. Thus, spur-of-the-moment tests are almost an impossibility, and by virtue of the necessity of planning ahead for tests, other aspects of the course also become more rigid.

As I indicated in the chapter "Assessing, Testing, and Evaluating," essay examinations are superior to typical objective examinations in their effect on student study and learning. Thus, you are likely to regret the loss of the opportunity to give essay tests in a large group. But this loss is not inevitable. To some extent it can be compensated for by greater care in the construction of objective test items. But it is also possible to use essay items without increasing your load beyond reason. In a 500-student lecture course, I regularly included an essay item on the final examination with the stipulation that I would read it only if it would affect the student's letter grade for the course. Since the majority of the students were fairly clearly established as A, B, C, or D students on the basis of other work and the objective part of the final examination, the number of essays I needed to read was not excessive. My subjective impression was that knowledge of the inclusion of an essay item did affect the students' preparation for the exam.

## Making Outside Reading Assignments

The testing problem is just one of several factors structuring the conduct of large classes. Another is the assignment of readings beyond the textbook. With a small group you can assign library work with little difficulty, only making sure that the materials needed are available and, if necessary, reserved for the class. With a class of several hundred students, a library assignment without previous planning can be disastrous. The library's single copy of a book or journal is obviously inadequate. Thus, a library assignment must be conceived far enough in advance (usually several months) that enough copies of the readings can be obtained, and the librarian can prepare for the fray.

Once again, technology can come to the rescue. Some institutions have been able to establish "electronic reserve" systems as a replacement for the library reserves we're all so familiar with. In these systems, the instructor can put an electronic copy of the reading material on the library's computer. Students who are enrolled in the course for which that material is assigned can access it electronically either in the library itself or from any computer with Internet access. Because only students in the class have access to the material, some level of security is preserved and copyright is protected. My students have been particularly enthusiastic about this new system because it allows them to avoid having to make several trips to the library in hopes of being able to get the paper copy. They also can store a copy on which they take notes and save it without using extra printing. Some course management software can provide the same functionality of allowing you to post text materials on the course Website and have them password-protected. As a side benefit, you can monitor how frequently the materials are being accessed as a measure of class compliance.

## Communicating with Large Classes

Of course, the most important aspect of teaching a large class is being able to maintain up-to-date communication with such a lot of people. Being certain that every student has the latest word on class or assignment changes, deadlines, and exams can be challenging. I can't stress enough the value of having a class Website for a large class. Operating as information and communication central for the class, the Website is available to students 24/7, so you don't have to be. In addition, most course management software systems have group e-mail functions that allow you to send out a single notice to the entire class in a single e-mail without it getting blocked by spam-blocking programs. Course Websites will always have the latest word on course organization and the latest versions of any course handouts, so you will not need to constantly re-announce changes during class time. As students start asking questions via e-mail or on a class discussion board, you can gather all the similar questions together and post answers to them on the Website, where students can be encouraged to look first for answers to their questions before coming to you. My own university made it a policy that e-mail and class Websites are now considered official communication formats of the university.

Technology also helps you with managing office hours. For example, you can have an electronic appointment scheduler for students who want to visit you during office hours. A student checks the calendar, finds an open spot that matches his or her schedule, and registers for that time slot. Or you can hold "virtual office hours" by being available online at announced times. Any student who wants to "chat" can log in and ask questions from a distance. You have the advantage of being able to continue working from anywhere your computer is because it will announce that someone is online and wants to chat.

## COORDINATING MULTISECTION COURSES

In any multisection course taught by several different instructors or TAs, the problem of coordination inevitably arises. The first approach to coordination is enforced uniformity of course content, sequence of topics, testing, grading, and even examples. Such a procedure has the advantage that students who later elect more advanced courses can be presumed to have a certain uniform amount of background experience. It also is efficient in that only one final examination must be constructed, only one course outline devised, and students can transfer from section to section with no difficulty in catching up. It also circumvents problems that arise when students complain about unequal treatment.

The disadvantage of this approach is that such uniformity often makes for dull, uninteresting teaching. If the instructors or teaching assistants are unenthusiastic about the course outline, they are likely to communicate this attitude to the students. If the course can be jointly planned, this may make for greater acceptance, but may also take a great deal of time.

A second approach to this problem is to set up completely autonomous sections, with all the instructors or TAs organizing and conducting their sections as they wish. The effectiveness of giving TAs that much autonomy depends on how well you train and supervise them.

## TRAINING AND SUPERVISING TEACHING ASSISTANTS

Your responsibility begins well before the first class meetings, for your teaching assistants need to know what you are expecting in terms of attendance at lectures, participation in weekly planning and training sessions, testing and grading, office hours, and such. At my institution we have a checklist of possible TA responsibilities. At the beginning of the semester the TA and the supervising professor sit down together and work through their expectations and work assignments. Both sign and get a copy of the checklist so that there is no confusion later about what was expected and when.

Even more important than the formal requirements are the aspects of preparing the teaching assistants for meeting their first classes, establishing a good working relationship with their students, and developing the skills needed for leading discussions, answering questions, and carrying out other teaching responsibilities. Here are some suggestions for assisting teaching assistants:

1. Hold weekly meetings to discuss teaching problems and plans.

2. Collect feedback from students early in the term.

3. Observe classes and discuss your observations with the TA.

To get student feedback, you can use simple open-ended questions, such as:

"What have you liked about the class so far?"

"What suggestions do you have for improvement?"

Visiting classes or videotaping can provide useful information about nonverbal characteristics of the teacher and reactions of the students. But observation or videotaping takes time. If you have time, visit classes, but if you are short of time, there is little evidence that videotaping or observation results in significantly greater improvement in teaching than consultation on student ratings collected early in the term (and perhaps repeated a little later). So if you're short on time, invest it in consultation.

## IN CONCLUSION

Class size is important.

When taught appropriately, small classes are likely to be better than large classes for achieving long-term goals, such as retention and use of knowledge, thinking, and attitude change.

Nonetheless, when dealing with large classes, you can come closer to the outcomes of small classes by:

1. Providing discussion sections taught by trained teaching assistants

2. Using teaching methods that facilitate active, meaningful learning

The fact that in a large class you will probably spend some of the time lecturing does not mean that students can now slip into passivity. What is important in active learning is active *thinking*. The techniques discussed in this and preceding chapters can produce active thinking and learning even in large lecture halls.

## Supplementary Reading

Because almost every large university now has a program for training teaching assistants, there was a biennial meeting on training, and the papers from the meeting were typically published. The first volume is still one of the best:

▶ J. D. Nyquist, R. D. Abbott, D. H. Wulff, and J. Sprague (eds.), *Preparing the Professoriate of Tomorrow to Teach: Selected Readings in TA Training* (Dubuque, IA: Kendall/Hunt, 1991).

For teaching large classes:

▶ Jean MacGregor, James L. Cooper, Karl A. Smith, and Pamela Robinson (eds.), "Strategies for Energizing Large Classes: From Small Groups to Learning Communities," *New Directions for Learning and Teaching*, no. 81, May 2000.

▶ C. Stanly and M. E. Porter (eds.), *Engaging Large Classes: Strategies and Techniques for College Faculty* (Bolton, MA: Onker Publishing, 2002).

▶ R. J. Sternberg (ed.), *Teaching Introductory Psychology: Survival Tips from the Experts* (Washington, DC: American Psychological Association, 1997).

# Laboratory Instruction: Ensuring an Active Learning Experience

L aboratory instruction permits learners to experience phenomena directly as well as understand how new knowledge is constructed. Although laboratory instruction derives from the revered apprenticeship model for learning practical arts, it is certainly not limited to the traditional "wet laboratories" of the physical and natural sciences. From practicum experiences in psychology and education to studios in the fine and performance arts, instructors create learning environments where students can ask questions and seek answers modeled on the way in which professionals do their work. Historically, the latter performance-based disciplines do an intrinsically better job of engaging beginning students in authentic work (drawing, writing, acting) than the sciences do in getting students to do scientific inquiry and investigation.

Laboratory teaching assumes that firsthand experience is superior to other methods of developing the same skills. Laboratory instruction also presumes that the next generation of practitioners will be motivated by an opportunity to participate in practice. The prevailing rhetoric of "learning by doing" characterizes the passionate attachment that faculty have to this form of teaching.

The design of laboratory instruction reveals a historical dichotomy. The attributes of authentic research, such as hands-on, "mind's-on" work

This chapter was written by Brian P. Coppola, University of Michigan.

and individualized experimental design or decision making combined with collaborative tasks, should all theoretically contribute positively to learning about the process of constructing knowledge. However, laboratory instruction often includes validating results that are repeated year in and year out all over the world by students using rote, locked-step, or "cookbook," procedures, backed with an argument that developing careful skills can only be measured against robust, well-tested standards.

Authentic, research-based information is hard earned, emerges over extended periods of time, and would appear to be inefficiently gained in comparison with abstractions presented in more traditional instruction. Thus, one would not expect laboratory instruction to have an advantage over teaching methods whose strength is in rapidly transmitting large amounts of factual information. Rather, one might expect the difference to be revealed in retention, in ability to apply learning, or in actual skill in experimental design, observation, or manipulation of materials and equipment.

Laboratory instruction also raises an opportunity to incorporate issues that are naturally aligned with practice, such as laboratory safety, which ranges from the manipulation of concentrated chemical substances to human-subjects issues. Increasingly, formal discussion of research ethics concerning practices such as data handling, laboratory management, authorship, and peer review is being encouraged for beginning and advanced students alike (Arkright-Keeler & Stapleton, 2007; Coppola, 2000; Kovac, 1999; Sweeting, 1999).

## STYLES OF LABORATORY INSTRUCTION

In an attempt to define different instructional goals and their corresponding methodologies, Domin (1999) created a taxonomy of laboratory instruction styles that, though originally based in chemistry, holds up well across many disciplines. Explicit analogies with other areas are not provided here, for they are beyond the scope of this chapter. However, it is important to note that these methods are not simple, neutral choices. Students' early laboratory experiences, which are strongly influenced by instructional design, are often the critical gateway for the level of experience or self-confidence that influences their decisions to persist (or not) in the sciences, particularly in the cases of women and underrepresented minorities (Seymour & Hewitt, 1997; Eccles, 1994). Instructional designs that favor cooperative environments with individual accountability, opportunities for creative design and expression, and chances for reflection and analysis all contribute to positive, motivating experiences that, in turn, favor persistence and continuation.

Domin's categories are expository instruction, inquiry instruction, discovery instruction, and problem-based learning.

## Expository Instruction

The most popular and most criticized, expository instruction, features verification of pre-ordained results and an emphasis on manipulation skills, and it asks students to follow exactly prescribed directions (or "cookbook" procedures). A prelaboratory session sets out what is to be observed and how to do it. Postlaboratory sessions review and recapitulate the information. In general, the goal for this kind of instruction is for students to develop manipulative or kinesthetic skills. In a typical activity used both in high school and in college, students might all receive a block of aluminum and be asked to follow an exact procedure for determining its density, the value of which is provided. Students follow precise directions, often filling in a worksheet with numerical values according to a prescribed script. The presumption is that a student who has successfully followed the procedure and arrived at the expected answer has also learned something about measurement and how it is done.

Expository instruction can be done on a large scale with minimal engagement by the instructor, it is largely impervious to variation in who does it, and it minimizes cost, space, and equipment. Unfortunately, it also may be true that almost no meaningful learning takes place (Hofstein & Lunetta, 1982).

## Inquiry Instruction

In inquiry instruction, without a predetermined outcome, students are asked formulate their own problem from the information at hand; in doing so, they mimic the process of constructing knowledge. The density activity might begin with a question posed to the students who have been given different-sized samples of the same metal: "What is the relationship between mass and volume in this material?" Different procedures for measuring volume are provided, and the results derived from these different methods are compared. Students have more choice in design and more responsibility in making sense of their results, and they must generally face more directly the importance of reproducibility in making measurements. Follow-up questions are either posed by the teacher ("Is density an intrinsic or extrinsic property?") or elicited from the students ("Is the density of all metals the same?").

Inquiry instruction is a compromise between closed- and open-ended instruction favored by national recommendations (National Research Council, 2000). In a practical sense, it is difficult to keep inquiry laboratories vital because it is difficult to conceal the details of the solutions to these problems from one generation of students to the next without a great deal of effort. Also, the drive to make the teaching process easier can slowly turn these inquiries into exposition.

## Discovery Instruction

In discovery instruction, also called "guided inquiry," the teacher constructs an instructional setting with a prescribed outcome in mind and directs students toward that outcome. Discovery instruction seeks to make knowledge more personal for students and thereby more highly owned. Adapting the density experiment to discovery mode might begin with a prelaboratory discussion in which the exercise is introduced by a question: "What measurements can be made to determine the physical properties of materials?" The students are encouraged to make predictions, formulate hypotheses, and then design experiments. All the while, the instructor controls the discussion, steering students toward the information from prior classes, including different mass-to-volume relationships as potentially useful quantities. The instructor also uses these opportunities to evaluate the experimental designs suggested by the students, motivating them with the sense of ownership and curiosity about the undetermined result, and inevitably guides the discussion toward the preplanned experiment. Students work individually or in groups, with enough variation in their activities for the class to pool their results. Afterward, the discussion led by the instructor moves the class to the intended lesson. Discovery-based instruction can invest the student in his or her own learning and can result in deeper understanding (Horowitz, 2003).

## Problem-Based Learning

Problem-based learning (PBL) creates a context for students to generate their own questions, but it does so with strong foregrounding by the instructor (Albanese & Mitchell, 1993). PBL is popular across many disciplines. An instructor crafts and selects evidence and then presents the case study to the students, who in turn uncover what the faculty member has in mind as the root lessons.

Meta-lessons about doing research can be abstracted and returned as a PBL framework for collaborative, open-ended exercises (Coppola, 1995).

The density activity would begin with black enamel paint concealing the color of a group of differently shaped metal pieces. Wenzel's (1995, 1998) analytical chemistry program is noteworthy for its emphasis on framing a term-long investigation, often addressing a problem of high community interest (such as air quality) as the context for students to develop authentic investigative, procedural, and communications skills. The significant aspects of PBL include the following:

1. *An organizing question that students can understand is posed.* They are then expected to design experiments to solve the question. In this case, each student gets a different piece of metal; instead of asking students to identify the metal, which is far outside of their experience to design, the instructor asks them to determine who else in class has the same metal as they do.

2. *The problem cannot be answered by the work of an individual acting alone.* It requires the class to make group decisions about the experiments they carry out, how they are going to share the information, and what the standards of reasonable comparison need to be. The class might select density as the property to measure. Students will need to decide on units of measurement, how many trials must be done, and what will constitute "the same" and "different."

3. *Multiple and equally valid strategies can be used to solve the problem* (Mills et al., 2000). The students might request to do chemical tests on other samples of the metals in order to collect data. They might choose hardness, malleability, color (after scraping), or some combination of these after initial groups have been made.

4. *Experimental procedures are a means to an end.* Exposition and inquiry both have roles in carrying out an individual's work. Procedures for carrying out a known process should be able to be followed. Yet the purpose for collecting information (density) remains focused squarely on the goal (who has the same?) rather than on the measurement for its own sake.

5. *Communication and comparison are key.* Students need to decide how to share their data and how they will make their conclusions. Samples may be exchanged and tested independently if there are outlying data points or if some students have a hard time reproducing their experiments.

6. *Follow-up work is implied by the results.* Inquiry inevitably leads to new questions. Once the relative identification is made and the students have grouped themselves according to the convergence of measured properties, new questions can be posed or elicited: "What are

the identities of these metals?" "Is this information enough, or is other information needed?"

Relative identification is a widely applicable strategy for making problems. In chemistry, one might ask who has the same solid, liquid, mixture, or concentration of acid. In mathematics, one might ask who has numbers in the same type of series. In psychology, one might ask who has the same personality type; in the history of art, who has a painting from the same period; and in English, who has a paragraph with the same structure.

Some formal heuristics developed for learners in laboratory settings have demonstrated success. One of these is POE (Predict-Observe-Explain [Champagne, Klofper, & Anderson, 1980]); another is the MORE (Model-Observe-Reflect-Explain [Tien, Rickey, & Stacy, 1999]) method, which was developed for formal laboratory modules. Case studies are a kind of PBL that begins by posing questions based on a news headline ("Two would-be chemists die in explosion while attempting to make methamphetamine") and turning the case into a structured activity (Bieron & Dinan, 2000).

# STUDIO INSTRUCTION BRINGS TOGETHER THE ARTS AND SCIENCES

Many colleges have tried to work within the confines of traditional lab and lecture times, but St. Edwards University (Austin, Texas) set aside the traditional class structure and uses two four-hour lab periods so that students are able to "act as scientists and learn as a scientist learns" (Altmiller, 1973). The University of North Carolina at Charlotte's inquiry-based "intimately meshed" lecture and lab (DiBiase & Wagner, 2002) and North Carolina State University's cAcL2 (concept Advancement through chemistry Lab-Lecture) active learning environment (Oliver-Hoyo et al., 2004) are other examples. A group of four chemistry departments—at California Polytechnic Institute (Bailey et al., 2000), Rensselaer Polytechnic Institute (Apple & Cutler, 1999), California State University at Fullerton (Gonzalez et al., 1999), and the State University of West Georgia (Khan et al., 2003)—adopted the studio teaching method, inspired in part by the studio in the RPI physics department (Wilson, 1994). In general, adopting studio instruction has also involved remodeling the physical space in order to accommodate these pedagogical changes. The University of Michigan has experimented with the question of bringing this nontraditional instructional style into a traditional setting in order to lower the barrier for others who might not wish (or be able) to make the capital investment (Gottfried et al., 2003).

In a studio, learning and practice are intimately integrated and take place in the same space, so that transitions between theory and practice are unhindered (Perkins, 2005). Programs that seek to integrate the lecture and laboratory components of classes are constantly being developed (Gruenbacher, Natarajan, & Kuhn, 2006; Dunnivant et al., 2000), which speaks to the strong sense of importance for combining the theoretical with the practical, or combining the knowledge with the ways in which knowledge is constructed. In the sciences, a studio implies an environment where students have access to concepts, problem solving, and experiments in the same space and practice and theory are inseparable; interactive, hands-on experiences deliver fast results; and students use the results from one inquiry to design and carry out the next one. As in an art class, studio instruction in the sciences focuses on the artifacts created by students as the basis for discussion and further work. The studio teaching method is especially appealing because it does not limit itself to a single type of best practice. Instead, it allows mixing and matching of proven ways of teaching concepts.

The breaking of the tradition of centralized authority in teaching and learning coincides with society's demands for increasing the diversity of people who are prepared to do (or understand) science and technology. This is fortunate, because many believe that this increase can be accomplished by designing classrooms that foster success both broadly and inclusively. Seymour and Hewitt (1997) showed that "the most effective way to improve retention among women and students of color, and to build their numbers over the longer term, is to improve the quality of the learning experience for all students—including non-science majors who wish to study science and mathematics as part of their overall education." They also found that while almost all students value collaborative learning, students from underrepresented groups "appreciate it more and miss it when [it is] unavailable."

## TURNING NOVICE RESEARCHERS INTO PRACTICING SCIENTISTS

The goals for upper-level laboratories may be quite different from those for lower-level laboratories, where professional development for a specialized work force makes sense. Upper-level students who have access to better instrumentation or other resources can be asked to generate a more open-ended question derived from their entire undergraduate program. Not only can they prepare a proposal, but class members can also be asked to peer review and critique each other's work. After the work is completed (or attempted), the results can be made public via web publication or poster sessions to which other students and faculty respond (Henderson & Buising, 2000).

As illustrated previously, traditional verification laboratories can be adapted to more inquiry and open-ended activities. More than that, in recent years, there has been a strong movement to integrate more authentic research activities into the undergraduate program, not only in the form of undergraduate research projects, but also these to occur within the formal classroom structure of laboratory classes (National Science Foundation, 2003). Examples can be found throughout the sciences, including, for example, in chemistry (Center for Authentic Science Practice in Education, 2009), Geological Sciences (O'Reilly, 2002), Information Sciences (Becker, 2005), and the Biological Sciences (Eves et al., 2007).

Within the disciplines, undergraduate participation in research is probably as old as the integration of laboratory instruction into U.S. universities (Miller, 2008). Starting in the 1990s, there has been a growth of overarching institutional structures to recruit and support students in undergraduate research, which makes it easier for faculty members and students (particularly first-and second-year students) to connect with each other.

Miller (2008) points to the American Chemical Society's Committee on Professional Training, which described the following pedagogical goals for undergraduate research: a clearly communicated purpose and potential outcomes, well-defined objectives and methods (substantial in scope instead of a collection of small projects), reasonable chance of completion in the available time, contact with the professional literature, avoid repetitive work, require use of advanced concepts, require a variety of techniques, culminate in a comprehensive report, introduce students to the standards of normative practice (including research ethics) in the discipline. The Council on Undergraduate Research (CUR, 2009) provides excellent guidelines, advice, and communication on this topic.

## WHAT RESEARCH SAYS

The theoretical context for laboratory instruction is called situated learning (Lave & Wegner, 1991), which argues that the context in which learning takes place matters, so that learning about a laboratory science is more meaningful in a laboratory setting, and that research settings—because they are the most authentic context—provide the best environments for learning.

Individual studies make differential claims about the efficacy of one kind of laboratory instruction over another (Arce & Betancourt, 1997; Higginbotham, Pike, & Rice, 1998), but there is no general consensus about how one design gains advantage over another. Gains have been observed when students process information in the manner of experts in a laboratory that has an authentic design (Coppola, Ege, & Lawton , 1997). Such students are more intrinsically motivated by the course, and they develop better strategies for meaningful learning. Gains in both student learning and attitudes toward science have been reported from using the Studio format in a high school setting (Faro & Swan, 2006).

Studies on the effects of undergraduate research are helping to motivate more research-based work in standard class settings. Students who participate in research gain concrete skills (such as using the primary literature, interpreting data, and communicating results) (Bauer & Bennett, 2003; Kardash, 2000) as well as benefits to their cognitive, personal, and professional development (Hunter, Laursen, & Seymour, 2007). These students show greater persistence in science (Hathaway, Nagda, & Gregerman, 2002; Kremer & Bringle, 1990), and particularly there is a greater chance for retaining students from historically underrepresented populations (Nagda et al., 1998).

Finally, despite positive findings that support the use of inquiry to teach concepts, changing methodology alone is not a panacea. Without carefully planning to integrate the entire student population, and without serious commitment from instructors and institutions, reform-based efforts can backfire, favoring the students who are more immune to deficiencies of their instructional environment, and may actually increase achievement gaps—typically disadvantaging exactly those students whom we wish to interest and motivate (Von Secker & Lissitz, 1999; Von Secker, 2002).

## *IN CONCLUSION*

Laboratory instruction is a complex activity that needs to be examined closely and systematically. However, perhaps because expository instruction is so poor at promoting engaged and deeper learning, nearly any strategy that promotes more active learning and decision making by students is observed to produce learning gains. As is so often true, not only must the goals that one has for an instructional intervention be explicit, but their alignment with the instructional methodology must be carefully managed.

## Supplementary Reading

N. A. Glasgow's *New Curriculum for New Times: A Guide to Student-Centered, Problem-Based Learning* (Thousand Oaks, CA: Corwin Press, 1998) is an easily read and adaptable introduction.

V. L. Lechtanski's *Inquiry-Based Experiments for Chemistry* (New York: Oxford University Press, 2000) provides useful, explicit translations of standard experiments to inquiry-based methods.

L. C. McDermott and the Physics Education Group at the University of Washington, *Physics by Inquiry*, vol. 1 and vol. 2 (New York: Wiley, 1996) provide the best examples of instructional laboratory design based on disciple-centered educational research.

Student-Active Science (http://helios.hampshire.edu/~apmNS/sas_book.html) is a rich and multidisciplinary resource written by leaders in the field.

# Part 6

*Teaching for Higher-Level Goals*

# Teaching Students How to Become More Strategic and Self-Regulated Learners

F or many years, the study of student learning was divorced from the study of teaching. Good teaching practices were assumed to be universals that did not depend on individual differences among students or on teaching students how to study, learn, and think about course content. But these are exciting times for college instructors and students because findings in educational and cognitive psychology have changed our views of the teaching/learning process and provide both conceptual and practical information about the ways that students learn and how instructors can use this information to inform their teaching practices. We now know that it is the interaction of good instructional practices with students' calculated use of learning strategies and skills, motivational processes, and self-regulation that results in positive learning outcomes (Weinstein, Husman, & Dierking, 2000).

However, many college students do not know what to do to learn the content in the different domain areas they study. All instructors have some implicit or explicit conceptions or theories about what it means to

This chapter was written by Claire Ellen Weinstein of the University of Texas at Austin, Debra K. Meyer of Elmhurst College, Jenefer Husman of Arizona State University, Wilbert J. McKeachie of the University of Michigan, Cynthia A. King of Professional Research Consultants.

learn and think in their own discipline. Helping students become aware of these conceptions is an important aspect of teaching. As students learn subject matter, they also need to learn something about the skills involved in learning that subject matter. For example, students need to know how to reason through problems in engineering, how to read math texts, and how to identify important information about a particular literary work. Therefore, it is important that you use effective instructional practices for presenting content information as well as effective instructional practices for fostering the development and use of both general learning strategies (such as previewing a textbook chapter) and content-specific learning strategies (such as how to learn and understand mathematical formulas).

In the following sections, we discuss strategic learning and address several ways you can help develop students' learning-to-learn strategies and skills in the college classroom by increasing students' self-awareness, teaching domain-specific strategies, connecting new ideas with existing knowledge, modeling and teaching learning strategies, and providing feedback on students' use of learning strategies. We also highlight the instructor's role in helping students become more strategic and self-regulated in technology-rich instructional environments.

## WHAT ARE THE CHARACTERISTICS OF STRATEGIC LEARNERS?

Most college instructors can easily recall strategic learners they have seen in their own courses. These learners approach instructional activities and tasks with a high degree of confidence that they can succeed, as well as a good idea of how to try to complete them. Strategic learners are diligent and resourceful in pursuit of a learning goal and do not give up easily, even in the face of difficulty. They understand that learning and studying are active processes largely under their own control. Strategic learners know when they understand new information and, perhaps even more important, when they do not. When they do encounter problems studying or learning, they use help-seeking strategies such as getting help from the instructor or teaching assistant, their classmates, or a student learning center. They also understand that studying and learning are systematic processes, again, largely under their own control (Paris, Lipson, & Wixson, 1983; Pintrich & De Groot, 1990; Schunk & Zimmerman, 1998, 2003; Weinstein, 1994; Weinstein & Acee, 2008; Weinstein, Acee, & Jung, in press; Zimmerman, 1989, 1990, 1994, 1998, 2001; Zimmerman & Moylan, in press).

Although we are all familiar with students who are strategic learners, it is still helpful to take a systematic look at some of the characteristics of these students. Understanding these characteristics is essential for deriving instructional strategies to help students be more strategic and self-regulated in pursuing their academic goals in your course and throughout their academic careers.

## THE IMPORTANCE OF GOALS AND SELF-REFLECTION

How can you help students to become more effective learners? We know that strategic learners need to be able to set and use meaningful goals to help them learn and to help them generate and maintain their motivation for studying (Schunk & Zimmerman, 2007). We can help students become clearer about their goals by encouraging them to set useful goals for our classes. Unfortunately, many students are not clear about their educational goals in general or about their goals for specific courses. Not every course holds the same interest value for every student, but usually there are at least some aspects of the course that each person can perceive as useful. Providing your students with opportunities to identify how the material presented in your courses might be useful to them, now or in the future, as they strive to reach their own educational, personal, social, or occupational goals can enhance motivation as well as cognitive effort (Husman et al., 2004). Even a brief class discussion about upcoming topics and how these topics might relate to students' present or future interests can help. Asking students to write a brief paragraph or two about a topic and why it might be relevant to them now or in the future is another way to establish perceived relevance.

It is important to remember that we cannot give students goals—they must own their goals. However, with goal ownership comes responsibility. Students need to learn how to set, analyze, and use goals and how to respond to goal achievement and failure. Students also should learn how to implement strategies that will help them negotiate emotional responses to achieving or not achieving their goals (Boekaerts, Pintrich, & Zeidner, 2000; Schutz & Pekrun, 2007). It is also important to assist students in establishing process rather than product goals. Even simply reminding students that the goal of the exercises or projects you assign to them is to gain mastery of the content will help support effective self-evaluation. Students are more likely to evaluate their success on the pieces of a project if they have goals for each of those pieces and if they know how to create goals that are realistic, specific and measureable, and have a stated start and completion date (Schunk & Zimmerman, 2007).

# INCREASING STUDENTS' SELF-AWARENESS

Students who are aware of their learning goals tend to reflect on what it takes to learn. Thinking about thinking, or knowing about knowing, has come to be known as metacognition (Flavell, 1979; Pintrich, 2002; Zimmerman & Moylan, in press). Metacognitive processes include knowledge about oneself as a learner, knowledge about academic tasks, and knowledge about strategies to use in order to accomplish academic tasks. Awareness about oneself as a learner helps students to allocate their personal resources, or the resources that are available in their academic institution such as group study sessions, tutoring programs, and learning centers. If students do not anticipate needing help with a potentially difficult course, or if they do not monitor their own comprehension closely, it is unlikely that they will take advantage of available resources. It will also be difficult for them to judge the personal resources they will need, such as extra study time or more opportunities for review and consolidation of the material before a test (Entwistle, 1992; Winne, 1996).

Increasing student self-awareness is imperative for effective strategy instruction. If students attribute their successes or failures to luck, an easy test, or innate ability, then there is no need for effort, time management, or learning strategies. Therefore, college instructors should provide opportunities for students to reflect on the general characteristics of their approaches to, and on their specific actions toward, academic tasks. This also helps students to benefit from their mistakes and not keep repeating them. As college faculty, we should increase student self-awareness of their learning strategies and teach students when and how to use strategies (Svinicki, Hagen, & Meyer, 1995; Weinstein, Acee, & Jung, in press).

You also may want to survey students to promote self-awareness of strategies by asking them questions such as the following when they are preparing for their first major assignment or test. How many hours do you spend a week studying for this course? Are you up-to-date on course assignments and readings? How do you take notes or study while reading the textbook? How do you take notes in class? Do you review your notes? When? How? Do you stop periodically and check to see if you are understanding the material?

# USING EXISTING KNOWLEDGE TO HELP LEARN NEW THINGS

College professors have long known that teaching an introductory course is often more difficult than teaching an advanced course in the same area. Although many explanations for this finding have been offered, most of them involve the students' lack of prior knowledge. It is all but impossible to think analytically or solve problems in an area without relevant knowledge. In addition, thinking about relevant knowledge also strengthens new learning by generating meaningful relations, or bridges, to new information. For example, if students think about what they already know concerning the economic causes of World War I, this can help them understand the economic causes of the Second World War. Strategic learners understand the role of relevant prior knowledge and can use this knowledge to help themselves learn new things (Alexander & Judy, 1988; Maggioni & Alexander, in press).

We tend to use prior knowledge in one of two main ways: to create direct relations and to create analogical relations. When we create direct relations, we directly relate our prior knowledge to what we are trying to learn. For example, comparing and contrasting the causes of the two world wars involves direct relations. However, there are times when we do not have directly applicable prior knowledge but we do have knowledge in an area that is somehow similar and may help us to understand the new information, ideas, or skills we are trying to learn. For example, we use analogies to help us relate familiar and new things that share some key characteristics but are very different in other ways. Using a post office to explain aspects of computer storage, referring to social disagreements as a way to explain conflicts in organizations, and using the structure of a bird to explain design elements of an airplane are all ways we use analogies to help students build meaning for new concepts that may, at first, seem dissimilar.

# TEACHING DOMAIN-SPECIFIC AND COURSE-SPECIFIC STRATEGIES

College faculty teach students not only content but also modes of thought, and strategies for learning and thinking about the content in their courses (Donald, 1995). Different instructional means may result in students having the same amount of knowledge but not the same organization and understanding needed for different applications using this new knowledge. Comparisons of college teaching methods typically find few significant differences in tests of knowledge. There are, however, differences between teaching methods in retention, application, and transfer. (See Chapters 3–10 in this volume.)

Greeno (1991, 1997) suggests that general ways of thinking about the material need to be taught along with content because they are prerequisites to understanding content. Students who have no general modes of thinking for understanding science may be as lost in a biological science course as a student attempting to use conventional English narrative structures to understand a biology textbook. Thus, instructors have to consider ways of thinking not only as results of instruction but also as prerequisites for instruction. In addition, you must find ways of helping students transition from existing knowledge structures in their minds to more accurate or advanced knowledge structures (Pintrich, 2002; Maggioni & Alexander, in press).

Besides developing methods to provide students with instruction concerning the ways of thinking within your content domains, you should also provide direct instruction concerning strategic learning approaches for the tasks that are specific to your content area. You can impact your students' strategic learning by helping them understand the nature and requirements of academic tasks in your course. As you assign a variety of academic tasks throughout the course, you need to define clearly how each assignment relates to course learning goals so students can approach tasks strategically. There are two levels at which we should address strategies: the domain of the course (e.g., how to think and write like a psychologist) and the course-specific materials and pedagogy (e.g., how lectures and labs are organized, how collaborative problem solving is structured).

Many college students approach all their courses in the same way; therefore, we must explicitly teach learning strategies that are domain-specific to our courses. For example, different disciplines have different discourse structures, different forms of argument, and different ways of approaching and solving problems. The domain differences between our course and our students' other courses should be clearly established. To be self-regulated learners, students must learn strategies that are appropriate for the domain. College faculty have found that cognitive modeling, thinking out loud, and demonstrating the use of texts in a self-regulated manner are ways to provide opportunities for students to learn about domain-specific strategies (e.g., Coppola, 1995). Most students cannot write like a scientist unless they are taught scientific writing. Domain-specific approaches to learning are especially critical in introductory courses. Therefore, you should consider activities such as the following examples:

1. Previewing the textbook and its text structure.

2. Providing anonymous examples of student work to illustrate both DO's and DON'Ts.

3. Giving sample items from previous tests as practice.

4. Being clear about terminology that has domain-specific meaning.

In addition to learning strategies that are applicable to the domain of the course, students must learn strategies that are effective with the instructor's methodological, material, and assessment choices. When modeling the use of the course textbook as a domain-specific strategy, the instructor also can explicitly outline how the text complements or supplements the lecture or lab materials. As we introduce students to new approaches (e.g., problem-based learning or writing-across-the-curriculum techniques), it is important to also introduce them to the skills needed to successfully participate in our methods and enhance their confidence in applying these skills. Therefore, faculty should help students approach their courses strategically by outlining their individual instructional approaches and materials. For example:

1. As you deliver your first couple of lectures, take notes on the overhead to emphasize what you consider to be the important points.

2. Before you begin a specific pedagogical approach, such as the case study method, take time to explain the method and the skills necessary to use it successfully.

3. Use some simple everyday examples of the approach you will be using so students can focus on the process rather than having to focus on both the content and the process.

4. Ask questions and provide example problems at the level of under-standing that will be measured by tests or other assessments and point this out to the students.

We must remember that as faculty we can be models of self-regulated learning (Pintrich, 1995). Therefore, we should strive to model discipline-specific thinking processes and course-specific strategies for learning in our classrooms. If an instructor models self-regulation and provides feedback and guidance concerning the students' self-regulation, the instructor can have a significant affect on students' self-regulation (Schunk & Zimmerman, 2007).

We have said that strategic learners can take much of the responsibility for helping themselves study effectively and reach their learning goals. For these students, a core component of strategic learning is their repertoire of cognitive learning strategies (Weinstein & Mayer, 1986; Weinstein, Husman, & Dierking, 2000; Weinstein, Beth, Corliss, & Cho, in press). Cognitive learning strategies are goal-directed approaches and methods of thought that help students to build bridges between what they already know or have experienced and what they are trying to learn. These strategies are used to help build meaning in such a way that new information becomes part of an organized knowledge base that can be accessed in the future for recall, application, or problem solving. Research has shown that one of the hallmarks of expertise in an area is an organized knowledge base and a set of strategies for acquiring and integrating new knowledge (Chi et al., 1988).

The simplest forms of learning strategies involve repetition or review, such as reading over a difficult section of text or repeating an equation or rule. A bit more complexity is added when we try to paraphrase or summarize in our own words the material we are studying. Other strategies focus on organizing the information we are trying to learn by creating some type of scheme for the material. For example, creating an outline of the main events and characters in a story, making a timeline for historical occurrences, classifying scientific phenomena, and separating foreign vocabulary into parts of speech are all organizational strategies. Some learning strategies involve elaborating on, or analyzing, what we are trying to learn to make it more meaningful and memorable. For example, using analogies to access relevant prior knowledge, comparing and contrasting the explanations offered by two competing scientific theories, and thinking about the implications of a policy proposal are examples of elaboration strategies.

As instructors, we can all have a tremendous impact on helping students to develop a useful repertoire of learning strategies. One of the most powerful ways for teaching these strategies is through modeling. By using different types of strategies in our teaching, we can expose students to a wide variety of strategies in different content areas. However, it is not enough to simply use strategies in our teaching. It is also necessary to teach students how to do this on their own when they are studying. For example, after paraphrasing a discussion in class, point out what you did and why you did it. Briefly explain to the students what paraphrasing is and why it helps us to learn. You also could explain that it helps us to identify areas that we might not understand. If we have trouble paraphrasing something we are studying, it probably means we have not yet really learned it.

Finally, you should provide students with opportunities over time to practice and reflect on their uses of different learning strategies.

As Pintrich (1995) noted, modeling the ways in which to learn strategically in our courses is necessary but not sufficient. We must structure opportunities for students to practice using these strategies. We also need to ask students not only *what* they think, but *how* they think, and *if* this was the most effective process for them. Guided practice with feedback is a powerful way to teach students how to learn because it provides students with opportunities to practice strategies and evaluate them to see which ones are or are not useful.

Testing practices also influence students' use of learning strategies. Rote memory questions such as "According to the author the shortage of teachers depends on three factors. Which three?" produce surface-level processing, whereas deep-level processing can be induced by questions such as "Explain the meaning of the following quotation—'Too many poor teachers will drive good ones out of the market.'" According to Pressley and McCormick (1995) one of the most powerful ways to influence the degree to which students use deep rather than surface strategies is through test demands. Students are more willing to learn to use deep processing strategies when it is evident to them that these types of strategies help them to meet the demands of the test or other evaluative procedures.

## METHODS FOR CHECKING UNDERSTANDING

Strategic learners must be skillful self-regulators who periodically check on the usefulness of their learning methods by monitoring their progress toward learning goals and sub-goals (Schunk & Zimmerman, 2003). Without checking actively on their progress, many students may think that they understand when in fact they do not. Often students do not realize there are holes in their understanding until they receive their grade on a test. This is because the test is the first time they were asked to check on their new knowledge in a way that would identify gaps or misunderstandings. Strategic learners know that the time to check on understanding is before taking a test or other formal assessment measure. Checking on understanding and looking for gaps or mistakes in knowledge integration should be an ongoing activity present in every studying and learning context.

Checking our understanding can be a simple as trying to paraphrase or apply what we have been trying to learn. In fact, many homework or project assignments are designed to help students identify gaps in their knowledge or areas of misunderstanding so that they can be corrected. Getting past these problems helps students to deepen their understanding of a topic. Many of the learning strategies we discussed earlier also can be used to test understanding. For example, trying to paraphrase in our own words what we are reading in a textbook is a good way to help build meaning, but it also helps us to identify gaps or errors in our understanding. If we try to apply our knowledge and have difficulty using it, or if we try to explain it to someone else and cannot do it, we would also know that we have some comprehension problems. Monitoring our comprehension is an important part of strategic learning that fosters self-regulation. Only if we know we have a problem in our understanding or a gap in our knowledge can we do something about it.

A very useful method for checking understanding and helping to teach a variety of learning strategies is the use of cooperative learning. Cooperative learning is a method that builds on peer tutoring. We have long known that in many traditional tutoring situations the tutor, not the student receiving the tutoring, benefits the most. While processing the content for presentation, the tutor is consolidating and integrating his or her content knowledge. At the same time, the tutor is also learning a great deal about how to learn. The tutor needs to diagnose the tutee's learning problem, or knowledge gap, in order to help the tutee overcome it. Refer to Chapter 14 on group learning for a more complete discussion of the benefits of these methods.

# KNOWING HOW TO LEARN IS NOT ENOUGH— STUDENTS MUST ALSO WANT TO LEARN

Strategic learners know a lot about learning and the types of strategies that will help them meet their learning goals. However, knowing what to do is not enough. Knowing how to do it is still not enough. Students must want to learn if they are to use the knowledge, strategies, and skills we have addressed so far. It is the interaction of what Scott Paris and his colleagues have called skill and will that results in self-regulated learning (Hofer, Yu, & Pintrich, 1998; Paris, Lipson, & Wixson, 1983; Pintrich & De Groot, 1990; Schunk & Zimmerman, 2007). Many students know much more about effective study practices than they use. Just as in the case of an overweight person who is an expert in weight loss techniques, knowledge is not always sufficient for action. We all have many different potential goals and actions competing for our attention and resources at any point in time. Which goals we select and how much effort we put toward the goals we have selected are at least partially determined by our motivations. Strategic learners know how to learn, but they also want to be effective learners. It is the interaction of skill and will that gives direction to their actions and helps them to persist at tasks even in the face of obstacles.

One way to enhance students' perceptions of their competence is by giving performance feedback that focuses on strategic effort and skill development. Simply telling students that they did well does not really focus on their role in the performance. Telling a student, "This is great! I can really see the effort you put into this," says a lot more. Talking directly about students' strategic efforts and the skills they are developing helps them to focus on their role in the learning process. Remember, a key component of strategic learning is believing that you can play an active role. If students do not believe they can make a difference, they will not use many of the effective strategies we have been discussing. Many students listen to strategy instruction and believe the strategies are very useful—but not for them! Our task is to help students understand that they can take more responsibility for their own learning. Remember that motivation results from a number of interacting factors. As we discussed earlier in this chapter, establishing the potential usefulness of new learning helps to generate interest and direction for students' learning activities. See Chapter 11 for a more complete discussion of the effects of motivation on learning.

## PUTTING IT ALL TOGETHER—EXECUTIVE CONTROL PROCESSES IN STRATEGIC LEARNING

We have discussed both skill and will as important components of strategic learning. A third essential component is the use of executive control processes, or self-regulation (see Weinstein, Husman, & Dierking, 2000). These control processes are used to manage the learning process from the beginning (setting the learning goal) to the end result. Strategic learners use executive control processes to (1) organize and manage their approach to reaching a learning goal, (2) keep them on target and warn them if they are not making sufficient progress toward meeting the goal in a timely and effective manner, and (3) build up a repertoire of effective strategies that they can call on in the future to complete similar tasks, thereby increasing their learning efficiency and productivity (Paris & Paris, 2001; Weinstein & Acee, 2008). When students are facing new and unfamiliar tasks, they must do a lot of planning to help identify potentially effective methods to achieve their goals for task performance. Unfortunately, many students simply adopt a trial-and-error approach to learning, or they try to adapt other familiar strategies they have used for different tasks to the current one. Students do not realize that this approach is often neither effective nor efficient. The time invested in generating, following, monitoring, and perhaps modifying a plan is a good investment for reaching learning goals now and in the future. As we develop expertise, we do not need to dwell on developing a plan for each task we face. Generating and evaluating plans for reaching learning goals helps build up an effective repertoire that we can call on in the future when similar learning needs arise.

Several instructional approaches emphasize how college instructors can help students generate, maintain, and evaluate their learning methods—that is, self-regulate their learning within college coursework (Schunk & Zimmerman, 2007). When self-monitoring is successful, the student not only learns more but also develops better strategies. In addition, students' successes increase their self-efficacy in the course and their motivation to learn. As college instructors, we must be careful not to overemphasize one stage of learning (such as planning over implementation). Thus, another important aspect of learning is the use of volitional strategies. For example, Trawick and Corno (1995) outlined a volitional training plan that includes specific instructional activities, modeling, role playing, record keeping, and instructor and peer feedback. They emphasized that faculty need to teach volitional skills in addition to cognitive and motivational strategies. Finally, in addition to learning how to learn course content and learning how to control motivation and volition, other researchers have emphasized that students must also learn "emotion control"—the management of emotions and levels of arousal while learning (Boekaerts, 1995; Boekaerts & Niemivirta, 2000; Schutz and Pekrun, 2007).

College faculty can help facilitate self-regulated learning by encouraging students to share examples of successful approaches to learning with each other. Guided discussions about what is and is not working help students refine their own methods and get ideas for other potential approaches. Discussions of self-regulated learning should emphasize the need to change strategies in different contexts and for different purposes. Working strategically should be addressed as a challenging endeavor, cognitively, motivationally, and affectively.

We have discussed many ways to help students become more strategic, self-regulated learners in classroom learning contexts. Now we turn our attention to some of the special strategies and skills students need in online or technology-rich learning contexts.

# WHAT INSTRUCTORS CAN DO TO HELP THEIR STUDENTS SUCCEED IN ONLINE OR BLENDED INSTRUCTIONAL ENVIRONMENTS

The online revolution has begun in earnest, and we all have much to be excited about as it. However, we cannot let our euphoria over this new instructional medium and the exciting educational possibilities it offers cloud our perceptions of the challenges inherent in online instruction from a student's perspective. E-learning offers tremendous control to the learner of both the instructional resources and the technical tools provided in these learning environments. In the hands of a student prepared to take responsibility for using these tools to enhance learning, they can indeed be powerful tools. But in the hands of students who have difficulty with strategic and self-regulated learning, such as problems with managing time, meeting commitments, and maintaining motivation, online learning can offer many challenges. Although some of the problem may be attributable to poorly designed materials, or novelty, or computer phobias, it is also becoming apparent that many students simply do not know how to learn and, perhaps even more important, how to manage their learning in online instructional settings. Many studies have found that strategic and self-regulated learning variables are often the mediators between success and failure in online or blended learning contexts. (See Winters, Greene, & Costich, 2008 for an analysis of studies examining self-regulation and learning in computer-based learning environments.) With the rapid and exponentially expanding growth of online courses, it is imperative that instructors and course designers help students develop the self-regulation and skills needed to intelligently exercise learner control. The following suggestions are derived from research and applied literatures examining these issues. (See Clark & Mayer, 2008 and Mayer, 2009 for numerous guidelines for the design, instructional methods, and implementation models that can be used to enhance learning in online environments.)

1. Teach students about and how to use the special instructional features of programs, such as glossaries, self-tests, multimedia material, and supplementary information.

2. Teach students about and how to use the special technical tools available, such as chat rooms, contacting the instructor, and getting help.

3. Provide instruction in critical self-regulation areas, including:

   a. *Time management:* The flexibility of time and location is a distinguishing characteristic between most online courses and traditional classroom-based courses. This flexibility gives online learners much more choice and autonomy than traditional classroom learners. However, if they have problems with time management, they may be much more likely to put off their work more than they should and fall behind in their studies.

b. *Generating and maintaining motivation:* Online learners have a greater responsibility for generating and maintaining their motivation over time. The absence of direct instructor and peer pressure, and a study environment often full of competing tasks, such as spending more time with friends and family or at work, often make it difficult for students to commit to completing their coursework.

c. *Self-testing:* In online courses it is critical that students monitor their own understanding and progress through the material.

d. *Managing anxiety:* If learners in online courses are uncertain about what they are supposed to do in a course or experience an unexpected problem, they may feel frustrated about online learning. In addition, learners with insufficient computer skills often feel anxious about online learning. Finally, the text-based nature of online communication requires students to communicate through writing and this might be distressing for those students who do not have the ability to express themselves effectively in writing.

4. Help students create a management plan for successfully completing an online lesson or course. This plan should be checked frequently and revised when necessary. The critical steps in the plan include:

a. Setting one or more goals

b. Reflecting on the personal resources they will need to reach each goal

c. Brainstorming and creating a plan of attack to reach each goal

d. Selecting the methods they will use to accomplish their plan

e. Implementing their plan

f. Monitoring (on an ongoing basis) the success and timeliness of their plan

g. Formatively evaluating their progress

h. Modifying, if necessary, their methods or even their goals

i. Summatively evaluating the outcomes to see whether they want to use this plan again in the future or whether they need to modify or discard it

5. Teach them help-seeking techniques like e-mailing the professor, teaching assistant, or other students in the class when they are having trouble.

6. Include high-level question prompting embedded within the online course so they can check their understanding of the material as they navigate through each lesson.

7. Create online graphic organizers.

## IN CONCLUSION

Teaching strategic learning is more than an investment in your students' future learning; it also is an investment in the present. Strategic learners are better able to take advantage of your instruction and their studying activities. The time you invest will come back to you in enhanced student understanding and performance, as well as increased motivation. It is also important to remember that all of us have goals for what we hope the students in our classes will learn. In today's rapidly changing world, the ability to acquire or use knowledge and skills is more important than compiling a static knowledge base. There is an old Talmudic expression that loosely translates as: "If you feed a person a fish, you have fed them for a day, but if you teach them how to fish, you have fed them for a lifetime!" As college instructors, our task is to provide edible fish (content knowledge), but our task is also to teach our students how to fish (learning how to become strategic, self-regulated learners in our field).

### Supplementary Reading

B. K. Hofer, S. L. Yu, and P. R. Pintrich, "Teaching College Students to Be Self-Regulated Learners," in D. H. Schunk and B. J. Zimmerman (eds.), *Self-Regulated Learning: From Teaching to Self-Reflective Practice* (New York: Guilford, 1998), 57–85. This entire book is worth reading but might get a little technical for the beginner in this area. However, this chapter is focused on college students and therefore worth spending time on.

P. R. Pintrich (ed.), "Understanding Self-Regulated Learning," *New Directions for Teaching and Learning*, no. 63, June 1995, has chapters on the theories behind this important concept and the practical applications to a variety of settings, disciplines, and students.

C. E. Weinstein, J. Husman, and D. R. Dierking, "Self-Regulation Interventions with a Focus on Learning Strategies," in M. Boekaerts, P. Pintrich, and M. Zeidner (eds.), *Handbook of Self-Regulation* (San Diego: Academic Press, 2000). Another fairly complete discussion of the whole self-regulation concept.

# Teaching Thinking

istory credits Plutarch with the observation that "the mind is not a vessel to be filled but a fire to be kindled." This statement elegantly captures differing attitudes of educators about their overarching objectives in higher education. "Filling vessels" has been the dominant strategy that most college students experience. However, in the last few decades, widespread dissatisfaction with the performance of college graduates produced new pressures for higher educators to adopt Plutarch's philosophy of education. Barr and Tagg (1995) described and promoted this paradigm shift with their differentiation of *content-centered instruction* vs. *learner-centered instruction*.

Content-centered teachers share important facts and concepts with students and show limited attention to the process. Many content-centered teachers believe that merely exposing students to the ideas of the discipline will facilitate changes in students' thinking over time. Content-centered teachers often credit students' innate intelligence as responsible for their academic success. Therefore, it doesn't make much sense to invest valuable class time concentrating on process rather than using available class time to explore the important concepts, theories, or frameworks of the discipline.

---

This chapter was written by Jane S. Halonen, University of West Florida.

In contrast, learner-centered teachers embrace the responsibility for fostering changes in students' thinking skills. They believe that students grappling with ideas will lead to more meaningful and enduring learning. Factual knowledge will rapidly deteriorate unless the ideas can be meaningfully encoded or practiced with some regularity (Eriksen, 1983). Consequently, learner-centered teachers regularly turn to active learning strategies to engage students in process. Cognitive scientists report that when students think about material in more meaningful ways, underlying brain structures will change to promote more enduring learning (Leamnson, 2000). As a consequence, most colleges and universities now routinely promise the improvement of students' thinking as an explicit goal of the mission. Improving thinking is sometimes couched in terms of objectives to promote critical thinking or problem-solving skills (Halpern, 1996).

Most academic programs have responded to increased demands for accountability by crafting a thoughtful curriculum in which thoughtful sequencing of thinking and learning experiences can maximize student gains (Maki, 2004). Students can be supported as they move from simpler learning challenges, such as getting introduced to basic concepts in the discipline, through the complex performance demands that might be required in a capstone course. As such, students can move from novice to baccalaureate-level expertise and programs can capture the quality of their instruction through a well-designed assessment plan that reflects the journey.

# THREE FRAMEWORKS SUPPORTING TEACHING THINKING SKILLS

Any given course can provide a context in which students can learn to think more effectively and can make a contribution to the students' cognitive evolution, particularly when their faculty set explicit expectations for how students should think within the discipline. Many educators rely on systematic frameworks to help them design learning experiences that can be pitched to the right level of cognitive complexity. We will review three popular frameworks, including Bloom's Taxonomy (Bloom et al., 1956; Anderson & Krathwohl, 2001), Perry's Scheme (1970), and the Structure of Observed Learning Outcomes Taxonomy (Biggs & Collis, 1982; Biggs, 1999).

Bloom's Taxonomy, perhaps the most enduring "thinking" framework, differentiated categories of thinking skills and sequenced them according to their complexity. The original taxonomy distinguished *lower order skills* (e.g., knowledge, comprehension, and application) from *higher order skills* (e.g., analysis, synthesis, and evaluation). Bloom's work became widely used to promote the development of both lower order and higher order thinking skills in college classrooms by encouraging faculty to identify for students what kinds of thinking would satisfy their class objectives (cf. Shulman, Luechauer, & Shulman, 1996).

Anderson and Krathwohl (2001) revised Bloom's taxonomy to improve its pedagogical utility and accuracy. For example, Anderson's team recognized that "knowledge" was not really a process comparable to other terms in the original taxonomy. Consequently, they changed the first level of skill to "remember." Throughout the revised taxonomy, they incorporated language that worked more effectively to help educators develop workable and measurable objectives, consistent with the growing assessment demands. They changed "evaluation" to "evaluate" to stress outcomes as verbs rather than nouns. As in the original taxonomy, the new version retained a hierarchical design, but reorganized the sequence of higher order skills. As shown in Figure 21.1, Anderson and his team positioned "create" (formerly "synthesis") as the most complex cognitive skill in place of "evaluation" in the original scheme.

Whereas Bloom's taxonomy focused on explicit thinking activity, Perry's (1970) scheme provided a framework that addresses how students' thinking changes over the course of their college experience. As such, the Perry scheme is more *metacognitive*, encouraging educators to examine overarching characteristics of thinking. In Perry's model, beginning students demonstrate a strong preference for a simplistic world, a characteristic he referred to as *dualism*. As students begin to grapple with the complexities of disciplines, they will inevitably begin to accept that there are multiple perspectives that can be brought to bear on any particular problem, which Perry dubbed *multiplism*, yet the multiplistic student still shows greater comfort with simplistic viewpoints. In the next stage, called *relativism*, students experience greater comfort with multiple explanations. Finally, at the stage of *commitment*, students experience greater comfort with multiple explanations. They forge reasoned positions despite the ambiguity inherent in complex situations and problems.

An alternative taxonomy that was embraced by many Australian and European educators showed appropriate parallels to both the Bloom and Perry frameworks. Biggs and Collis (1982) developed the Structure of Observed Learning Outcomes (SOLO) taxonomy that differentiated *deep vs. shallow learning strategies* as choices that students make during their learning. The model also emphasized metacognitive changes that transpire in students as they develop more complex cognitive skills. For example, Biggs and Collis characterized unsophisticated students

The revision retains the hierarchical nature of thinking skills, but offers a new sequence in the hierarchy and emphasizes action verbs to promote more effective design of test questions and assignments.

Higher-Order
Skills

**Create**
Reorganize elements into a new pattern, structure, or purpose (*generate, plan, produce*)

**Evaluate**
Come to a conclusion about something based on standards/criteria (*checking, critiquing, judging*)

**Analyze**
Subdivide content into meaningful parts and relate the parts (*differentiating, organizing, attributing*)

**Apply**
Use procedures to solve problems or complete tasks (*execute, implement*)

**Understand**
Construct new meaning by mixing new material with existing ideas (*interpret, exemplify, classify, summarize, infer, compare, explain*)

Lower-
Order
Skills

**Remember**
Retrieve pertinent facts from long-term memory (*recognize, recall*)

Source: Anderson, L. W., & Krathwohl, D. R. (Eds.). (2001). *A taxonomy for learning, teaching, and assessing: A revision of Bloom's taxonomy of educational objectives.* New York: Longman

**FIGURE 21.1  Anderson, Krathwohl, and Colleagues' (2001) Revision of Bloom's Taxonomy**

as *prestructural* in that they collect facts in isolation, favoring shallow learning strategies. At the next stage, which the authors described as *unistructural,* students can grasp central ideas but don't tend to make independent connections between concepts. At the *multistructural phase,* students make more connections but still may not grasp larger purposes involved in their learning. At the *relational* stage, students can readily see how the component pieces of their learning fit together to produce a meaningful whole. Finally, at the *extended abstract* stage, students can generalize beyond the immediate details of learning to extract optimal meaning from their learning; in this stage, students more routinely pursue deep learning strategies.

Taken together or separately, Bloom's taxonomy, Perry's scheme, and the SOLO taxonomy provide educators with effective planning frameworks to help move students to more profound learning and more effective thinking skills. For example, educators need to expect that students will vary in their commitment to learning how to think. In some classes, students will be satisfied with shallow learning and lower-order thinking accomplishments. Large classes that promote the use of assessment strategies relying solely on memorization skills will compound student tendencies not to delve deeply in contexts where they are not required to do so. On the other hand, targeting thinking skills typically means that assessment strategies will concentrate on the development of higher order thinking skills and deep involvement in the discipline.

As students progress in their majors, they should face more complex thinking demands. Research papers, structured class discussions, and original presentations give students the appropriate opportunity to grapple when instructors frame their directions properly. Advanced courses that develop and test only lower levels of thinking simply shortchange students by limiting their conceptual development and thinking practices.

## IMPROVING THINKING QUALITY

What strategies are most useful in facilitating students learning how to think more effectively in college?

1. Be explicit in your syllabus that your goal will be to help them improve their thinking, especially learning to think "like a ___ (historian, psychologist, biologist)." Describe what constitutes successful thinking in the discipline at both lower and higher levels as explicitly as you can.

2. If you adopt a formal pedagogical framework that shapes your instructional design, explain the framework to your students in sufficient detail so they can more easily understand what you expect to see in their

work. For example, describe the Bloom model with students during the orientation to the course to clarify your goals for their cognitive development. This strategy can reduce complaints that you are trying to be "tricky" when your test items are tapping higher order skills.

3. Provide ample opportunities to practice thinking during class. The results of grappling with ideas will have a more enduring impact than mere exposure to the thinking of others. Show excitement about all aspects of thinking: good questions, odd questions, partial answers, and unsolvable problems.

4. Welcome student questions that give you an opportunity to think out loud to demonstrate a discipline in action. Don't answer every student question yourself. Turn student questions into opportunities for all of the students to think their way to a satisfying answer and experience a satisfying process.

5. Acknowledge examples of good student thinking. Students often may not appreciate what constitutes a good example until you officially label it as such. When an example is off-target or poorly developed, ask the class to collaborate to improve the response.

6. Ask students to judge the quality of their own contributions. Encouraging self-assessment can promote greater autonomy in thinking by improving self-reflection and self-regulation skills (Dunn, McEntarffer, & Halonen, 2004).

7. Design challenges that will appeal to diverse learning styles (Jarvis, 2005). Some students will require more reflection time before they can express their thinking confidently, but incorporating diverse thinking challenges will enhance student engagement.

8. Give yourself permission not to cover all of the content. Select from the relevant content to promote the thinking goals you have in mind. The trade-off involved in making this choice means a greater investment in skill development that is likely to have a more long-lasting impact than shallowly learned concepts with a fragile life-expectancy.

9. Be patient when students express greater comfort with shallower learning challenges. At the outset of a college education, it is developmentally normal to resist thinking in complex ways. The art of effective college teaching involves strategizing about ways to lower this resistance and increase the excitement of making bigger cognitive investments.

10. Regardless of your discipline, ask, "What do you think and why do you think so?" (Nessel & Graham, 2007). This strategy will work across

disciplines to develop their specific cognitive abilities and their metacognitive appreciation of how college is helping them change.

## IN CONCLUSION

Learning how to think more effectively is not easy, but students are unlikely to make systematic progress in their thinking skills without specific practice through well designed pedagogy. Along with discipline based-strategies to sharpen their thinking, students need to develop habits of reflection about their experiences, their successes and failures, their plans and purposes, and their choices and consequences.

Teaching thinking skills also is not the easiest path, but it is likely to be more gratifying than a straight lecture mode. Building thinking into course design, making expectations explicit, providing significant practice opportunities, and delivering accurate feedback facilitates the achievement of desired thinking outcomes.

### Supplementary Reading

Jeffery Howard provides helpful guidance for anyone planning a new experiential course in his *Service-Learning Course Design Workbook*, issued in Summer 2001 as a companion volume to the *Michigan Journal of Service Learning*.

A thoughtful discussion of what kinds of learning and development emerge from this form of education is found in Morris Keeton's *Experiential Learning* (San Francisco: Jossey-Bass, 1976).

A wide-ranging discussion of important pedagogical issues is found in David Kolb's *Experiential Learning* (Englewood Cliffs, NJ: Prentice Hall, 1984).

# The Ethics of Teaching and the Teaching of Ethics

magine you're teaching a course at the introductory level, one that is required of all students who want to major in your department. And let's suppose that after the first exam a student whose performance was much below standard approaches you and offers you a considerable sum of money if you'll change a grade on the exam so the student can pass. What is the ethical thing to do in this situation?

Now imagine the same situation, but instead of offering you money, the student pleads for an opportunity to retake the exam because of extenuating circumstances during the first test administration. Now what is the ethical choice?

Next, imagine the same situation, but this time you are the one who notices that a student who has been working hard in your class, and whom you expected to do very well, has instead failed the exam miserably. How does this situation compare with the others from an ethical standpoint?

The first scenario seems fairly straightforward, a definite violation of ethics if you were to accept the money to change the grade. The second example is not as straightforward. To what extent should the student be allowed an opportunity that is not available to all the other students? Does providing that opportunity constitute unethical behavior? Or is it just unfair? Or is there a difference? In the third instance, to what extent should your assessment of a student's abilities counter actual performance? Where do you draw the line in helping students?

The most difficult questions that teachers face often have nothing to do with the content of the course or the way it is presented. They focus instead on the ethical issues of teaching, how we relate to our students, to our institution, to our discipline, and to society at large. What are our responsibilities to each constituency, and what do we do when responsibilities conflict? Unfortunately, there are no easy answers to these questions. I raise them here as food for thought because you *will* face them sometime in your teaching career.

This chapter addresses the issue of ethics in teaching. What do we mean by "ethics in teaching"? In recent years, more and more has been written about the topic as the teaching mission of the university comes under increasing scrutiny (Cahn, 1994; Fisch, 1996; Lewis, 1997; Matthews, 1991; Strike, 1988). It seems only proper that those who currently teach and those who aspire to a faculty career be introduced to the concept.

What is an ethical question in teaching? Ethical questions are sometimes defined in terms of right and wrong (Strike, 1988); in terms of cultural norms such as honesty and promise keeping (Smith, 1996); or as "general guidelines, ideals, or expectations that need to be taken into account, along with other relevant conditions and circumstances, in the design and analysis of teaching" (Murray et al., 1996, p. 57).

In general, *ethical standards are intended to guide us in carrying out the responsibilities we have to the different groups with whom we interact.* Ethics violations can occur when we are tempted to act contrary to those standards. Ethical dilemmas occur when multiple responsibilities conflict or have more than one right answer (Strike, 1988). It is often surprising to consider all the different things that can cause ethical problems for instructors. They range from the obvious bribe attempt previously described, to failure to present all legitimate sides of an issue adequately, to accepting remuneration for extra tutoring for a class with which one is already connected.

In a 1991 research study of psychologists teaching at academic institutions, Tabachnick and colleagues reported reactions to various ethical questions involved in teaching at the college level. Respondents were asked to report how frequently they engaged in a wide range of various activities and the extent to which those activities were ethical or unethical. The activities included things as drastic as sexual harassment and more mundane activities such as teaching materials that the instructor had not yet fully mastered.

The behavior *most often* engaged in was teaching when not adequately prepared, although it was not a consistent pattern for most people. The authors attributed this behavior more to heavy workloads and rapid advances in the field than to the shirking of responsibilities.

The rarest of behaviors were those related to sexual harassment. Whether this study is an accurate reflection of behavior or of reluctance to report such behavior is impossible to tell. Also rare were actual sexual encounters with students.

Perhaps the most interesting sources of ethical conflicts for the Tabachnick study group were a result of the conflicting roles of mentor/sponsor and evaluator. For example, over two-thirds believed that allowing a student's likability to influence a grade was unethical, but over two-thirds reported doing it at some point anyway. The same sort of dilemma is seen when instructors interact socially with students. On the one hand, the interaction with faculty is reported as vital to student growth by Pascarella and Terenzini (1991); on the other, it raises the possibility of conflict.

In a more recent study (Braxton & Bayer, 1999), a national sample of faculty in higher education was asked to rate the acceptability of a range of violations of teaching standards, such as "The instructor insists that the student take one particular perspective on course content" or "The instructor does not introduce new teaching methods or procedures." The researchers identified 126 different behaviors that a teacher might engage in and asked the participants to rate how strong a sanction each behavior should bring. The authors then identified two levels of sanctions that they felt were present in the data. The most serious sanctions were for those norms they labeled as inviolable. These included seven clusters: condescending negativism, inattentive planning, moral turpitude, particularistic grading, personal disregard, uncommunicated course details, and uncooperative cynicism.

The second set of clusters was labeled "admonitory norms"— behaviors that, though inappropriate, didn't evoke as strong a reaction from the participants. These included advisement negligence, authoritarian classrooms, inadequate communication, inadequate course design, inconvenience avoidance, insufficient syllabus, teaching secrecy, and undermining colleagues. When these clusters were compared across institutional types and disciplines, only two were identified by all groups of faculty as inappropriate: moral turpitude and authoritarian classrooms. Demographic characteristics of the respondents did not make a difference in what they felt was inappropriate behavior. The final conclusion by the authors was that there were four values that seemed to undergird the judgments of the participants: respect for students as individuals, equal consideration for all students, an obligation to prepare for teaching, and an obligation to participate in the governance and life of the institution. If you find these results intriguing, you might want to respond to the original survey yourself and compare your responses with those of the national sample. The survey, College Teaching Behaviors

Inventory, can be found in Braxton and Bayer's 1999 book reporting their findings.

Values like these are becoming more and more common in discussions about teaching in higher education (Markie, 1994; Carr, 2000). In fact, the American Association of University Professors provided a statement of professional ethics dealing with the responsibilities of faculty members that highlights what AAUP considers to be the special responsibilities of individuals in an academic position (AAUP, 1987). A similar set of principles was developed by the Society for Teaching and Learning in Higher Education (STLHE) and distributed to faculty in Canadian institutions (Murray et al., 1996). Perhaps these standards can help highlight what a faculty member should consider when making personal choices.

## RESPONSIBILITIES TO STUDENTS

Both the AAUP guidelines and the STLHE guidelines recognize that one of a faculty member's first responsibilities is to the students. The specifics that follow illustrate the broad range of impact that faculty can have on student lives.

### To Encourage the Free Pursuit of Learning

The primary purpose of teaching is to encourage learning; therefore, the first ethical responsibility an instructor has is to that goal. All that we do to prepare and conduct well-designed instruction is part of that responsibility. The ethical instructor knows the content to be learned, the students who will do the learning, and the methods that could be used to foster the learning. The STLHE guidelines state this explicitly in their first and second principles: content competence and pedagogical competence (Murray et al., 1996). In a discussion of the ethics of teaching psychology, Matthews (1991) interprets the American Psychological Association's professional standards as they apply to teaching and cites the issues of responsibility and competence as two key contributors to encouraging learning. In her interpretation, faculty members are responsible for remaining current and presenting accurate and balanced views of the field, an idea also related to the concept of scholarly behavior discussed later in this chapter.

There are many ways an instructor might violate these standards. Here are two examples:

- Most obvious is to fail in our duties in class preparation. One can't always be in top form, but just as we expect students to come to class prepared, we must make the same effort. This is one of the most commonly occurring violations reported by the sample (Tabachnick, Keith-Spiegel, & Pope, 1991) and was identified as a key admonitory norm by Braxton and Bayer (1999).

- A second, less obvious way is failing to remain current both in the content area and in instructional methods that foster learning. Although it is unlikely that faculty would not be current in the content, it is very likely that faculty will not have kept up with research into better instructional methods.

A second part of this responsibility is to protect and encourage the autonomy of our students so that eventually they no longer need our constant guidance. The STLHE guidelines list this as the fourth of their eight principles: "to contribute to the intellectual development of the student" (Murray et al., 1996). If students are to develop into thinking individuals, we must structure our interactions with them in such a way as to both model and support independent thinking, even when this means they might end up disagreeing with us.

## To Demonstrate Respect for Students

Ethical instructors also respect the "otherness of students" (Churchill, 1982)—that is, the individual and independent nature of the students and the fact that students are at different stages of their lives than are the instructors. For example, instructors need to be aware of the special needs of their students, whether those be cultural, physical, or based on background (Matthews, 1991). This also means respecting students' goals, their choices, and their value as individuals (Strike, 1988), another key value listed by Braxton and Bayer (1999).

The most obvious venue for this particular principle is in the interactions we have with students in and out of class. During class, the way we respond to students' questions and comments should convey the idea that everyone's participation is welcome and respected. How we respond to a student's question affects more than just the student who asked it. And outside of class, the way we greet students who come to office hours or see us in the halls speaks volumes about the level of respect we have for them. We show respect by being available when we say we will be, by keeping promised appointments, by being willing to listen to students' concerns, by giving as much thought and preparation to our interactions with undergraduates as we do to those with graduate students and colleagues.

An example of a not-so-obvious need to respect students as individuals is discussed in an article by Grauerholz and Copenhaver (1994) about the use of experiential teaching methods, especially those that involve a great deal of self-disclosure by students. The choice of instructional strategies such as journaling and small-group problem sharing may violate your students' rights and be harmful as well as unethical unless done with a great deal of care and concern for the students' well-being. To guard against the possibility of harm, here are some suggestions on how to structure the experience. For example, you should carefully choose strategies and make their purpose clear to your students. It might also be appropriate to allow alternative ways of satisfying the learning requirement for those who do not feel comfortable with these methods. Use of such teaching methods raises the issue of trust because when students trust an instructor, they are more willing to engage in self-examination. Making self-examination safe for students is reason enough to be sure that your relationship with students is one of trust and respect.

Similar issues of trust arise during the discussion of sensitive topics such as race, sexual preference, and religion. When faced with a potentially sensitive situation, you can

- Provide early disclosure of the potentially sensitive nature of the topics.
- Make sure that students understand what is being presented as fact and what as opinion.
- Offer extra time outside of class to those students who need to discuss the topics and their reactions to them (Koocher & Keith-Spiegel, 1998).

I have advised faculty to draw up a set of "rules of engagement" for sensitive topics that could spark heated debate in class. These rules would specify how these debates would be conducted and would include things such as cooling-down activities, the obligation to be able to state the other person's position before attacking it, and the avoidance of personalizing arguments. If such guidelines are provided early in the course, students can feel more comfortable when sensitive topics are raised.

This does not mean that the topics will be avoided, because that would be a violation of the first of our guidelines: open inquiry. One can see how this conflict would raise ethical dilemmas for teachers, especially in disciplines where sensitive topics are the norm rather than the exception.

## To Respect Confidentiality

The issue of self-disclosure leads to another large component of respect: the belief that students have a right to privacy in their dealings with us. Not only does this principle have the weight of ethics behind it, but in many cases it also carries the weight of law. For example, it is against the law to disclose personally identifying information along with student performance information. That means no posting of grades in a way that a student can be identified. At my institution, the posting of grades in a public place in any way that would allow an individual's grade to be identified by others is prohibited. Here, however, we are speaking of less egregious violations of privacy, such as discussing a single student's situation with someone who does not have a legitimate interest in that student's case. Practices such as leaving student papers out so that they can be retrieved at the students' convenience might be a violation of this principle because that means students have access to their peers' work (Murray et al., 1996).

## To Model the Best Scholarly and Ethical Standards

A teacher, whether by accident or by design, is more to students than a content expert. The teacher is a model of all that it means to be a scholar, a thinking person. We teach not only what we know but also what we are. Part of the ethics of teaching is to realize this responsibility and to become the best models we can be, which requires some serious self-reflection on our personal standards of scholarship and living. Clark Kerr (1994), in a discussion of ethics in the academic culture, supports this struggle when he says that we are obliged to present a variety of perspectives, our own as well as others', so that the facts can be judged for themselves. This does not imply that you must always take a dispassionate stance; but even, or perhaps especially, when you feel strongly about an issue, it is necessary to demonstrate by your actions that intelligent people can disagree and still remain rational. Giving students the ability to differentiate emotion from reason is an especially important responsibility of instructors, according to Hanson (1996). As she says, "Teachers who can nimbly convey the strengths of a position they in fact oppose, who can clearly display the weaknesses in a position they in fact embrace, are *modeling* a critical engagement from which students may learn their most important lessons" (p. 35).

## To Foster Honest Academic Conduct and to Ensure Fair Evaluation

Perhaps the most obvious ethical problems arise in the area of evaluation of student learning, a point echoed in both the AAUP guidelines and those from the STLHE. Instructors are the arbiters of entrance into the profession and are therefore responsible for seeing to it that standards are upheld. However, we are also responsible for guaranteeing that all are given a fair chance of demonstrating their abilities. When we allow academic dishonesty to go unheeded, we violate the rights of all the students who are abiding by the rules. If we fail to establish an evaluation system that accurately assesses the students' progress, we are abdicating our responsibilities to both the students and the profession.

The most important type of fairness for students is interactional fairness (how individuals are treated), followed by procedural fairness (the degree to which there is impartiality in how grades are determined and performance is evaluated), and finally outcome fairness (the degree to which grades and other outcomes reflect performance) (Rodabaugh, 1996).

The conflicts most often occur when this standard of fairness is pitted against the first responsibility of respecting the individual and fostering independence. The examples that opened this chapter speak to this issue. How important is it that all students be evaluated in the same way? Are we being fairer if we maintain standards and vary conditions of evaluation or if we use individual standards according to the special situation of each student? Which factors are legitimate considerations? There is no agreement on these issues. The best we can do is to continue to discuss and deliberate, alone and in groups, because the conditions under which we operate today will not be the same as those in the future.

## To Avoid Exploitation, Harassment, or Discrimination

One of the variables that should be at the forefront of our thinking about the ethics of teaching is the great power discrepancy between teacher and students. Whether we like it or not, whether we seek it or not, by virtue of our position alone we are invested with a great deal of power over the lives of our students. To make matters worse, many students invest us with even more power than we are entitled to. For this reason, both the AAUP and the STLHE guidelines list one or more principles concerning harassment, exploitation, and discrimination.

Abuse of this power is at the base of many of the ethical traps that lie strewn across our paths as teachers. The very special nature of the relationship between teacher and student is all too easy to abuse (Smith, 1996). The most blatant examples of unethical behavior, those most frequently mentioned in written codes of ethics, deal with exploitation or harassment of various types: sexual, racial, religious, even intellectual. The most egregious of these (and possibly the most debated) is sexual harassment in the form of improper relationships between instructors and students. Braxton and Bayer (1999) list this as the one inviolable norm that retained its importance regardless of type of institution surveyed or discipline represented by the respondent. It could be held forth as the most important norm they identified. The area of the proper relationships between teachers and students is particularly difficult for graduate students, who are both teachers and students. Because of their age they occupy a place between their own students and their own professors. Thus, they can be either harasser or harassed. Intimate relationships between teachers and students are generally considered inappropriate at least. The best decision for an instructor or a student is to keep the relationship on a professional level as long as the power imbalance exists.

But there are plenty of other forms of exploitation that occur in academia. For example, requiring students to engage in class activities that are unrelated to the educational purposes of the course but that serve our personal ends is an abuse of power. Making derogatory comments about population subgroups is an obvious example of harassment.

Another area of ethical problems involves receiving special considerations or benefits as a result of being in a position of authority. For example, is it a violation of ethics to adopt a less-than-adequate book simply because of an incentive made available by the publisher? How legitimate is it to accept an invitation to a party or other event as the guest of a student in your class? Does it matter if that student is no longer in your class? Does it matter if the event is somehow connected with the student's academic program—for example, a dinner honoring that student's work? We must be aware that by our position alone we will sometimes be put in a compromised situation in all innocence on our part or the student's.

## THE TEACHING OF ETHICS

There is an aspect of this topic that seems to span all the ethical areas just discussed: the teaching of ethics and values. You can see how violation of this central question can occur in all sorts of ways. It might be violated when we fail to present all reasonable sides of an issue or fail to allow students to explore a topic in depth. It might happen when we judge students on the basis of their beliefs rather than their achievement. It might happen when we grade students' work for its conformity to our own perspective rather than for its representation of whatever position it supports. The question here is, should we teach values? Or by teaching values do we violate the ethical standards just described? I believe that we have no choice: We *will* teach our values, if not through direct instruction then through our behavior.

Valuing is as natural as thinking or breathing. We automatically make value judgments about our experiences. "This was good, that was bad; this is beautiful, that's ugly." You have already made judgments about the value of this book. Our students are continually valuing. It would be strange if their college experiences had no impact on that valuing process.

"But," you say, "isn't it a misuse of our position if we indoctrinate students with our values?" True. Probably our avoidance of explicit attention to values results from our concern about the evil of indoctrination. But there are two aspects to my answer.

The *first* is that I would have no compunction about indoctrination with respect to such values as honesty and respect for other individuals as human beings. We cannot teach our students well if they plagiarize papers, fake laboratory results, or cheat on examinations. We cannot carry out effective classroom discussions without an atmosphere of respect for others' feelings or a sense of shared humanity. In a multicultural society like ours, there is a special need for thinking seriously about values—how we differ and what we share. Certainly we want our students to value learning.

The *second* is that we can help students to become more sensitive to values issues, to recognize value implications, to understand others' values, without indoctrination. Even with respect to fundamental values (such as honesty), student discussion, exploration, and debate about their implications are more useful than simple advocacy. Open consideration of the complexity of value issues is probably less subversive than disregarding values altogether. What values should we teach?

Those who say we should be taking a neutral stance on values typically are restricting their definition of values to sociopolitical ones. Very few would dispute the fact that we are concerned about honesty, respect for others, and rationality. A major goal of education presumably is to increase students' skills in critical, rational thinking. We want students to value rational thought, but not to the exclusion of other ways of knowing and thinking. In considering problems in society or in their everyday lives, our graduates will, I hope, look for evidence rather than react on the basis of unreasoning prejudice; they will be aware of the implications of their values but not let their values close their minds. Particularly in social science courses we ask our students to ask "What is the evidence?" before jumping to conclusions. Even those who point out that "rationality" has sometimes been defined in ways that confirm power relationships present rational arguments and evidence for their positions.

Our greater sensitivity to the issues raised by feminist and other critics is itself a tribute to rationality.

The big question in teaching is what to do about controversial social and political values. Here it seems to me that we are not privileged to demand acceptance of our own values, as I think we are privileged to do with respect to requiring academic honesty. But this does not imply avoiding values issues. Too often we communicate—by the way we handle touchy material—that you don't rock the boat by taking a position. In avoiding controversial issues we communicate the notion that it may be all right to talk about these things in dormitories or in other places but not in educational settings where rational arguments and the complexities of the issue are more likely to be salient. The apple of temptation for us as teachers is that we may too easily accept affirmation of values that we share, letting students get away with simply stating a position with which we agree, without asking for rational support, as we might for a position that conflicts with our own.

On the other side, however, is the problem of dealing with those with whom we disagree. There is the danger that we will yield to the temptation of demolishing the student with the force of our logic, but arguing can also be a way of showing respect. Remember that the power you have in your role as teacher may make it difficult for the student to muster a strong defense. Take it easy until students trust you enough to argue without fear of retribution. It is all too easy to intentionally, or unintentionally, coerce students into overt agreement.

W. G. Perry Jr. (1970) and R. P. Perry and J. C. Smart (1981) described the development of Harvard students as progressing from the dualistic belief that things are either true or false, good or evil, through a stage of multiplism in which they feel all beliefs are equally valid, to a stage of relativism with commitment to values and beliefs that are recognized to be incomplete and imperfect but are open to correction and further development. We may not all reach Perry's highest stage, or we may reach it in some areas but not in others, but Perry suggests that as teachers and members of the community of learners, we have the responsibility not only to model commitment and open-mindedness but also to share our own doubts and uncertainties.

## How Can We Teach Values?

We exemplify and communicate our values in what we teach and in the way we teach. Teaching values does not mean neglecting knowledge. Knowledge is a powerful sword to protect students from biased, emotional appeals.

Probably every teacher, whether in the arts, the sciences, or the professions, tries to teach students that it is not enough simply to respond to material or performance as good or bad, but rather to be able to back up one's judgment with evidence that is reasonable in terms of the standards of that discipline. We communicate that value by our comments on papers, our reactions to student comments or performance, and ultimately by our grades. So we have a group of values that we accept and either explicitly or implicitly communicate to our students through our behavior as teachers.

Our values also affect our course planning. We begin with the goals we take for the course. Who should determine those goals? Is this something to be determined by the university, by the department, by the instructor, or should students be involved? Personally, I have faith that in a situation in which students and faculty members participate jointly, our decisions will come out with reasonable values, reasonable content, and reasonable coverage—all the things that we worry about when we're thinking about how to set up a course. A cooperative approach exemplifies the value of respect for others. Asking students to write or discuss their goals for the course involves thinking about values. Asking them at the end of the course to think about what goals they have achieved and how these are related to their long-term goals sensitizes students to values issues.

If we want students to change, they have to have a chance to express their ideas and values in words or actions and see how they work. They need reactions not only from teachers but also from peers and others who share or oppose their positions. They need to trust the teacher's good will and good sense. They need to feel that the class is a community in which each will be accepted despite differing views.

Cooperative peer learning can contribute to building community and often has a positive effect on attitudes and values. Cooperation is itself an important value in our culture, and success in learning how to work cooperatively with other students on a project or other learning experience is likely to have a positive impact on students' value for cooperation as well as on building the kinds of support and trust necessary for frank discussion of values issues.

We know that students remember the content of our courses better if they elaborate the content by relating it to other knowledge—if they question, explain, or summarize. Such elaboration is important in the values area as well. And it's important that the discussion and experiences be in places where there is mutual respect and support. Values are not likely to be changed much simply by passively listening and observing a lecturer. Change is more likely in situations in which the teacher and the students reflect, listen, and learn from one another.

## Modeling Values

We model our values and those of our discipline in almost every class. Perhaps most important is the model of ethical behavior we provide. Clearly, sarcasm, favoritism, and failure to respect the diversity of students' cultures, values, and attitudes represent a negative model. But avoiding unethical behavior is not enough. How do we handle legitimate requests for exceptions from a policy printed in our syllabus? Do we weigh individual needs or are we rule-bound? How do we handle students with handicaps or learning disabilities? When a student comment is wrong or inappropriate, do we make it clear that we are criticizing the idea and not the person?

What about the ethical decisions we face in preparing and conducting the course? Do we give proper credit to the sources we use? Are our assignments and learning assessments dictated by student learning or by our own need to save time? Are we conscientious about preparation and attendance at class? Are we ethical in our use of licensed software?

## MAKING ETHICAL CHOICES

The array of possibilities for ethical decisions seems endless. How, then, can we avoid stumbling somewhere along the line? Although there are no easy answers, there may be some ways of thinking about our actions as professionals that will maximize the possibility of acting ethically. Some very interesting strategies are suggested by several authors in a book on ethical dimensions of teaching edited by Fisch (1996), and the reader is pointed in that direction. Here, however, I draw the following principles for evaluating one's actions from two sources, the first five from Brown and Krager (1985) and the last from Schön (1983):

1. *Autonomy.* Am I acting in ways that respect freedom and treat others as autonomous?

2. *Nonmalfeasance.* Am I causing harm through either commission or omission?

3. *Beneficence.* Do my actions benefit the other person rather than myself?

4. *Justice.* Do I treat those for whom I am responsible equitably?

5. *Fidelity.* Do I uphold my part of any relationship?

6. *Acting consciously.* What are the assumptions on which I base my actions and are they valid?

## IN CONCLUSION

It is a great privilege to be a teacher. But all great privileges carry great responsibilities as well. Many of those responsibilities are subtle, thrust on us by the expectations of others rather than sought by us. Keeping those six principles in mind won't solve all the ethical dilemmas you face as a teacher, but they might give you a way to reflect on them alone and with other teachers. Teach your students to reflect both in and out of class. That reflection should never stop, because conscious reflection on values is perhaps the cornerstone of the ethics of teaching and the teaching of ethics.

### Supplementary Reading

▶ American Association of University Professors, "Statement on Professional Ethics," *Academe*, 1987, *73*(4), 49.

▶ S. M. Cahn, *Saints and Scamps: Ethics in Academia*, 2nd ed. (Totowa, NJ: Rowman & Littlefield, 1994).

▶ D. Carr, *Professionalism and Ethics in Teaching* (New York: Routledge, 2000).

▶ L. Fisch (ed.), "Ethical Dimensions of College and University Teaching: Understanding and Honoring the Special Relationship Between Teachers and Students," *New Directions for Teaching and Learning*, no. 66, 1996.

▶ W. L. Humphreys, "Values in Teaching and the Teaching of Values," *Teaching-Learning Issues*, no. 58 (Knoxville: Learning Research Center, University of Tennessee, 1986).

▶ C. Kerr, "Knowledge Ethics and the New Academic Culture," *Change*, 1994, *26*(1), 8–16.

▶ M. Lewis, *Poisoning the Ivy: The Seven Deadly Sins and Other Vices of Higher Education in America* (Armonk, NY: M. E. Sharpe, 1997).

▶ P. Markie, *A Professor's Duties: Ethical Issues in College Teaching* (Totowa, NJ: Rowman & Littlefield, 1994).

▶ D. Schön, *The Reflective Practitioner* (San Francisco: Jossey-Bass, 1983).

Self-reflective learning involves much consideration of values. See Jean MacGregor (ed.), "Student Self-Evaluation: Fostering Reflective Learning," *New Directions for Teaching and Learning*, no. 56, 1993.

Joseph Lowman has a helpful discussion of how to handle controversial issues in his book *Mastering the Techniques of Teaching* (San Francisco: Jossey-Bass, 1984).

Lawrence Kohlberg's book *Essays on Moral Development* (San Francisco: Harper & Row, 1981) is a good resource for thinking about moral issues.

Parker Palmer provides a thought-provoking resource for teaching values in *The Courage to Teach: Exploring the Inner Landscape of a Teacher's Life* (San Francisco: Jossey-Bass, 1993).

G. Collier, "Learning Moral Judgment in Higher Education," *Studies in Higher Education*, 1993, *18*(3), 287–297, provides a discussion of why and how to teach values in college classrooms, including the use of group discussion and films and literature.

L. Moore and D. Hamilton, "The Teaching of Values," *New Directions for Student Services*, no. 61, Spring 1993, 75–86. This interesting article in an interesting issue shows how academics and student affairs can work together in teaching values.

A. Colby, T. Ehrlich, E. Beaumont, and J. Stephens raise the issue of helping undergraduates become productive contributing members of the society in *Educating Citizens: Preparing America's Undergraduates for Lives of Moral and Civic Responsibility* (San Francisco: Jossey-Bass, 2003). The book is one of the many products of the Carnegie Foundation for the Advancement of Teaching dealing with the larger issues of higher education.

# Part 7

*Lifelong Learning for the Teacher*

# Chapter 23

# Vitality and Growth Throughout Your Teaching Career

**B**ill and I have both been teaching for a long time (he for 60-plus years, I for 30-plus). Neither of us is as effective as we could be because we don't know today's student culture well enough to build good bridges between the course content and what is in their heads. But both of us continue to be exhilarated going to class and to feel upbeat when we leave. And we continue to pick up new ideas to try out in next term's class. Teaching is still fun. One of Bill's students commented on the student rating form, "Dr. McKeachie comes to class everyday as if there were no place on earth he'd rather be." It is a shame that some faculty members (a minority) don't continue to develop and enjoy their teaching. What can be done to foster continued development and enjoyment?

Part of the answer lies in motivation research and theory. Human beings have survived as a species because we are learners. We enjoy learning; we become curious when we confront something more complex than we are accustomed to; we like to confront and master challenges; we take pleasure in becoming and feeling competent.

Human beings are also a social species. We are stimulated by interaction with other human beings; in times of stress, we rely on social support; we learn from one another. Recent primate research suggests that we are also naturally altruistic. We get pleasure from helping others.

Teaching is thus an ideal career. There is infinite complexity and challenge. Each class is different, each student is unique, and there is always more to learn. New developments in our discipline, new research and theory about learning and teaching, new technology, and creative new ideas for teaching continually emerge. Our roles often shift as changes in curriculum (such as an emphasis on interdisciplinary team teaching) occur or as new technology presses us to develop new skills. There are never-ending opportunities to grow in competence and understanding.

And teaching is both an intellectual and a social activity. Each term, students come up with new questions, stimulate new insights. Classes offer ever-changing interpersonal dynamics. Getting to know and like each new group provides a continuing source of satisfaction and stimulation. And it is particularly rewarding when former students speak warmly of how we have made a difference in their lives.

The human interactions also offer challenges. There are always some students who seem to be uninterested, some who are confrontational, some who seldom appear. Trying to find out more about the reasons for their behavior, getting to know them better, finding their interests and trying to relate the course material to their interests and goals, involving them in teamwork with other students, demonstrating that you are committed to their learning—all of these may fail, but when something works, what satisfaction!

From the standpoint of motivation theory, it is thus clear that teaching offers great potential for continued vitality, growth, and satisfaction. But these do not come automatically. It is easier for some than for others. Enthusiasm for one's subject matter, an outgoing personality, a commitment to teaching well—these give one a big head start. But good teaching consists of learnable skills, and all your good qualities may go for naught if you teach at a level over the students' heads, are disorganized, evaluate student performance erratically, or lack the skills to implement your good intentions.

And those who are not naturally bubbling over with enthusiasm, outgoing, or even sure that they want to teach can still become effective teachers. In fact, developing as a teacher is a recursive activity. As you develop some skills and strategies that work, they generate positive reactions; this in turn increases your confidence and liking for your students; and that in turn generates more reflection and thinking about teaching as well as interest in developing additional skills, which continues the positive cycle.

## HOW CAN YOU DEVELOP EFFECTIVE SKILLS AND STRATEGIES?

The easy answer is "Practice, practice, practice." Practice is important, but just as in sports or music, if one is practicing the wrong technique, one is not likely to improve. Psychologists would add to the "practice" maxim "Practice with feedback—knowledge of results." Moreover, there are additional complications.

1. What should one practice? If you have never heard or seen a particular method in use, such as team learning, you cannot practice it until you have read about it, heard about it, or seen it used. Thus the developing teacher needs to learn about possibly useful skills and strategies.

2. Methods of teaching differ in their difficulty. Which should you try first? As indicated in the first few chapters of this book, there are several useful techniques that are easy to implement and are likely to work well the first time you try them. Use such techniques as question posting, minute papers, and the two-column method as techniques for stimulating attention and active learning early in the term, explaining their value for learning. These are low-risk, high-payoff, easy-to-use strategies that will help both you and the students build confidence that the class will be a useful learning experience. If you are lecturing or leading discussions, they can help activate student interest and attention. And using them gives you a chance to practice your lecturing or discussion skills in smaller segments.

3. How can you continue to perfect your skills? Here is where practice with feedback comes in. How can you get good feedback on what works and what doesn't?

Let's examine in more detail how you can learn about what methods or strategies to use and how to get feedback.

## LOOKING FOR NEW IDEAS, NEW METHODS, AND ALTERNATIVE STRATEGIES FOR HANDLING PROBLEMS

There are three possibilities: reading, hearing, and seeing.

## Reading

We mention this first because you have been reading this book, which was written on the premise that most faculty members have learned how to learn from reading. At the end of each chapter are suggestions for other books or sources that can provide additional insights or suggestions. In addition to the more general resources to which we have referred, there are journals in each discipline dealing with teaching and education in that discipline. Subscribing to such a journal or to one of the newsletters or journals dealing with teaching, such as the *National Teaching and Learning Forum*, *The Teaching Professor*, *College Teaching*, *Change*, *New Directions for Teaching and Learning*, and *Innovative Higher Education*, will provide regular stimulation to think of new ideas.

Journals dealing with research on learning and teaching are also important sources. *Educational Psychologist*, *Journal of Higher Education*, *British Journal of Educational Psychology*, *Journal of Educational Research*, *Journal of Educational Psychology*, and similar journals can help you avoid falling for the latest fad as well as stimulate you to think about implications for your own teaching.

## Hearing, Discussing

Peers are among the best sources of ideas. Talking about teaching with colleagues can be an invaluable source of ideas as well as provide emotional support when a class hasn't gone well. The colleagues need not be in your own discipline. You will often get interesting ideas from teachers in other disciplines. Most professionals in teaching improvement will tell you that the typical comment on feedback sheets is: "The best thing about the workshop was getting ideas from faculty members in other fields who have similar interests and problems."

National and international conferences, such as the International Conference on Improving Learning and Teaching, as well as the disciplinary conventions, also have sessions that provide opportunities for learning.

## Seeing, Experiencing

One of the best ways to learn a new skill is to see it performed. As you talk to your colleagues about teaching, ask if they would mind if you observed a class to see how they actually use a particular method. Faculty development centers frequently sponsor workshops in which you can see and experience particular methods of teaching or uses of technology. Videotapes demonstrating various methods of teaching are also available.

## HOW CAN YOU GET AND USE FEEDBACK TO CONTINUE TO IMPROVE YOUR TEACHING?

### Feedback from Student Performance

We haven't taught well if students haven't learned; so the ultimate test of our teaching is evidence of learning. Unfortunately, just as students blame the instructor if they fail to learn, we blame the students for not learning. "The students weren't willing to work." "The class wanted to be entertained rather than taught." "These students should never have been admitted to college. They are simply not prepared for college work."

But everyone can learn. Our task is to facilitate learning, and if our students are not learning, we have not motivated them, presented material at an appropriate level, arranged activities that would promote effective learning, or taught the students how to learn more effectively.

All too often we pay attention to mistakes, poor papers, and items that were missed on examinations as the basis for assigning grades but fail to think about how we might have better taught the material that was missed. Asking a colleague to look over a few student papers will not only help determine whether your expectations were unreasonable but also result in suggestions for ways of presenting the particular area in which students are not performing well. In every discipline there are some concepts or skills that seem to be particularly difficult to teach. Often, experienced teachers have strategies for overcoming these difficulties.

### Feedback from Peers

In the preceding paragraphs we have indicated the value of peer feedback on papers and in team teaching. But probably the most common form of feedback from peers is based on classroom visitation. As Centra (1975) demonstrated, classroom observation by peers is a very unreliable source of evidence for decisions about promotion or merit pay. If you know that an observer's judgment is going to affect your career, it is likely that you will either be so anxious that you will not perform at your normal level or that you will put on an especially good performance for the observer's benefit.

Even when the observer is not there to obtain evidence for our personnel files, we are likely to be concerned about what kind of impression we will make. Consequently, the choice of the observer and the nature of the observation are important considerations. Clearly we want an observer who will be helpful and whom we can trust. Bob Wilson at Berkeley found that retired faculty members were particularly helpful, not only because of their experience in teaching the discipline, but also because they were not involved in personnel decisions. Campbell Crockett, former dean at the University of Cincinnati, formed "helping pairs" among new teachers. Here the partners are in the same boat— both learning, presumably helping and being helped by each other—a symmetrical arrangement that reduced the threat.

The usefulness of peer observation depends partly on what you want to find out. If there is a particular aspect of your teaching that you are concerned about, be sure that the observer knows what to look for. Knowing what to look for is in fact a general principle applying to observations. Meeting with the observer to tell him or her before the observation what your goals are and what you are planning to do will increase the helpfulness of the observation. Centra (1993) gives some sample forms used for colleague observations, and you may work out your own observation form using items from these forms.

But the major usefulness of colleague observation comes from your discussion after the observation. Here you have a chance to question, probe for examples, and ask for suggestions.

## Feedback from Faculty Development Specialists

Most colleges and universities now have faculty or staff members who are assigned the task of improving instruction. Often they are available to videotape or observe classes. Videotaping would seem on the face of it to be especially helpful. "To see oursels as others see us … would frae monie a blunder free us." There is certainly some truth in Robert Burns's familiar saying. Nonetheless, videotaping may not be the best feedback. Research on feedback from films half a century ago demonstrated that when we see our teaching on film (or videotape), we are so captured by our minor mannerisms and appearance that we are likely to miss the critical items of feedback. Only when the videotape is viewed with a consultant who calls our attention to the more important items is seeing the videotape likely to result in improvement.

One method used by many faculty developers is small-group instructional diagnosis (SGID), originated by D. Joseph Clark at the University of Washington. This combines observation with feedback from students.

Typically a consultant using SGID meets before the class with the instructor who desires feedback to learn about the class and the instructor's goals and needs, as well as to establish the procedures. The instructor explains the procedure to the class, assuring the class that comments will be confidential and used only to help him or her learn how the course is going. After teaching for about half the class period, the instructor turns the class over to the observer and leaves the room. The observer then asks the students to form small groups to discuss their learning experiences in the group. Often the observer asks the groups to answer such questions as "What aspects of the class have helped you learn? What aspects have been unhelpful? What suggestions do you have?"

After about 10 minutes, a member previously designated as reporter gives each group's answers to the questions. The consultant summarizes the reports and asks for student comments. After the class, the consultant discusses the reports with the teacher and offers encouragement, suggestions if the instructor is unsure about what alternatives might help, and clarification if the instructor finds some comments confusing or contradictory. At the next class meeting, the instructor discusses the feedback, indicating what changes will be made or why certain things cannot be changed.

## Feedback from Students

Probably the most familiar form of feedback from students is student ratings of teaching. Student ratings are now administered in almost all colleges and universities in the United States and are becoming common in other countries. However, their primary purpose is often to collect data for personnel evaluation, and this complicates and sometimes conflicts with their usefulness for improving teaching. One problem is that those who use student ratings for personnel purposes often feel (unjustifiably) that they need to use a standard form that can be used to compare teachers, across disciplines, in a variety of types of classes, in required as well as elective courses, in large and small classes, and in a variety of contexts. The result is that the questions on the form are so general that they may be irrelevant to a particular class and, even if relevant, are worded so generally that they offer little guidance for improvement. Moreover, they are typically given at the end of the semester, when it is too late to make much improvement for the class from which the feedback comes.

An additional barrier to the use of these forms for improvement is that faculty members are likely to be defensive about low ratings, rejecting the validity of the student responses. Among the common defenses are responses such as:

- "Students aren't competent observers or respondents."
- "Students want easy courses. I set high standards."
- "Student ratings are determined primarily by the instructor's personality rather than by competence."
- "Students may give low ratings now but will appreciate my teaching after they've been out of college a few years."

As you may suspect, each of these excuses is invalid. There has been more research on student ratings than on any other topic—something over 2,000 studies. Here's what the research says about each of the aforementioned rationalizations.[1]

1. *The validity of student ratings.* Because we've said that you can't be a good teacher unless students have learned, the question becomes: Can students judge whether or not they are learning? The answer is clearly "yes." In multisection courses, average ratings of the value of the course or of the teacher's effectiveness correlate significantly with average scores on achievement tests, both final examinations and standardized tests. Moreover, they correlate with other course outcomes, such as motivation for further learning or measures of attitude change. In addition, when an instructor is teaching more than one section or more than one course, student ratings correlate well with the instructor's own judgments of which classes were taught most successfully.

2. *Hard versus easy courses.* Large national studies reveal that, on the average, more difficult courses are given higher student ratings than easy courses. Very likely this is a curvilinear relationship. Although students prefer challenging courses, courses that are so difficult that students cannot meet the challenge will receive lower ratings (Marsh, 2001).

3. *Teacher personality.* There is little doubt that some personality characteristics affect ratings. Enthusiastic, expressive, warm, friendly teachers will in general receive higher ratings than teachers who are more reserved and distant from their students. However, these personality characteristics are also related to student learning. This doesn't mean that you need to change your personality to become effective, but if you don't have an outgoing, warm personality, you can still be effective and could become even more effective by, for example, using more gestures and learning student names.

4. *I'll be appreciated later.* I often wish this were true when I get a negative comment (and there are always a few). But both the classic studies by

---

[1] Probably the best reviews of this research may be found in Perry and Smart (1997).

Drucker and Remmers (1951) half a century ago and my more recent ones found that alumni ratings of faculty members correlate highly with those given 10 years or more before. There are very likely some cases when there is delayed appreciation of what a teacher did, but it's the exception rather than the rule.

So, how can we use student ratings for continued growth in teaching effectiveness?

## Keys to Improvement with Feedback from Students

1. *Get the feedback early enough to make a difference for the students who give it.* A good time to collect feedback from students is after the third or fourth week of the term. Others collect ratings about the middle of the term. In either case, the important thing is that you have a chance to adjust to this particular class. (Remember that each class is different. What works well in one class may not in the next.) As was mentioned with respect to SGID, you should review the feedback with the class, indicating which suggestions you intend to implement, and discussing differences of opinion among students. (Usually some students want more discussion, some want less, and all assume that everyone else feels as they do.) You can also explain why you're not adopting some suggestions and give the reasons why you believe that what you have done, and will do, is important for their learning.

2. *Don't feel that you need to use the standard form.* If you want ratings, choose items that will be useful to you. The advantage of ratings is that you can cover a number of aspects of teaching relatively quickly. But open-ended questions are often equally or more useful. Usually you can simply ask students to write on two questions:

- "What have you liked about the course so far?" or "What aspects of the course have been valuable for your learning so far?"
- "What suggestions do you have for improvement?"

Sometimes you can use questions such as:

- "What have you done that has helped you learn effectively in this course?"
- "What do you need to do to improve your learning in this course?"
- "What have you done to help other students in the course to learn?" (Helping other learners not only provides altruistic satisfaction but also aids one's own learning. And this is true for teachers as well.)

- "What has the teacher done that has helped you learn?"
- "What would you like the teacher to do that would facilitate your learning?"

If you are teaching a large multisection course, you can ask each section to choose two representatives to meet with you to provide feedback. The representatives are given a few minutes at the end of their discussion section to talk with their classmates about suggestions, and then meet with you. Because they can say, "Some students say ... ," they feel free to relay negative as well as positive reactions, and the face-to-face meeting gives you a chance to question more deeply as well as to get their suggestions about what to do.

Feedback need not be limited to midterm or end-of-term assessment. You can ask students for comments on a particular class session in the last 5 minutes of class.

3. *Supplement end-of-course ratings.* All faculty members in our college are required to collect student ratings at the end of the term. Five items are mandatory, and the rest of the items may be chosen by the department and instructor from a large list of possible items, including some open-ended items. We suggest choosing two types of items—those having to do with goals of education and those dealing with specific behaviors.

The items with respect to goals are usually something like:

- "I became more interested in the subject matter of this course."
- "My intellectual curiosity has been stimulated by this course."
- "I am learning to think more clearly about the area of this course."
  Behavioral items could include:
- "The instructor knew students' names."
- "The instructor gestures with hands and arms."
- "The instructor gives multiple examples."
- "The instructor points out practical applications."
- "The instructor encourages student questions and student comments."
- "The instructor signals transitions to a new topic."

Although faculty members often make some improvements as a result of feedback from student ratings, Murray (1983, 1997) has shown that improvement is much more likely to occur when behavioral items are used rather than more generic abstract items.

Whether or not there is a choice of items, it's helpful to ask students to rate or comment on specific aspects of the course. Some of these change from term to term, whereas some carry over if they have worked well.

These include aspects such as the syllabus, the team research project, the textbook they used, videotapes, field trips, and journals.

## Consultation

Whatever form of feedback you use, research clearly shows that you are more likely to improve if you discuss the feedback with someone. Your consultant can help you put ratings in perspective, pointing out the positives and reducing the sting of the negatives. (Most of us tend to note and remember the negative comments more than the positives.) The consultant can also suggest strategies to try that may help deal with areas that seem to need improvement. A consultant can offer support and encouragement. All too often, poor student ratings lead to defensiveness, dislike for students, and poorer teaching rather than to improvement. In such cases, hope is important, and a consultant can help promote hope.

## Classroom Assessment and Research

A little over a decade ago, Pat Cross and Tom Angelo compiled a set of 30 techniques to help faculty members monitor student learning. Five years later, they published a second edition of classroom assessment techniques, including 50 techniques (Angelo & Cross, 1993). Some of these, such as the minute paper and one-sentence summary, were described earlier in this textbook. But you cannot fail to find among the 50 several that will help you get feedback on your students' learning, including directed paraphrasing, misconception check, pro and con grid, concept maps, course-related self-confidence surveys, and "What's the principle?"

*Classroom Research* (Cross & Steadman, 1996) is an example of the *scholarship of teaching*—systematically evaluating methods, approaches, or techniques that you are using in your teaching. In fact, the Scholarship of Teaching and Learning (SOTL) has become a very important area of growth in higher education and was initiated in 1998 by the Carnegie Foundation for the Advancement of Teaching (www.carnegiefoundation. org/programs/index.asp?key=21, accessed May 2009). CASTL, as the Academy has become known, has sponsored a large number of faculty who have chosen to do research on how students learn in their classes. You might find their publications interesting and even inspirational.

In SOTL you may use some of the classroom assessment techniques to get evidence about the effectiveness of an innovation you are trying (or of something you have been doing for a long time). In addition, you may use regular classroom tests or other measures of achievement.

You may even carry out an experiment comparing two alternative methods or the method you formerly used with one you would like to try.

Both classroom assessment techniques and classroom research not only provide useful data but also are motivating. They stimulate you to think about your teaching and what you expect students to gain from it. They enrich both your conceptual thinking about education and your repertoire of skills.

## Self-evaluation

Our emphasis on gathering data and getting consultation may have implied that improvement depends on external sources of feedback and help. But self-evaluation is also a potential resource for continued growth—perhaps the most important of all. In recent years, portfolio assessment has become a major element in evaluating teaching. Although portfolios have been used primarily in evaluation for personnel decisions, preparing and maintaining a portfolio can be an important aid to improvement even if it won't be used for promotion or salary purposes. The portfolio provides a stimulus to thinking about your teaching, about your goals and the evidence that will tell you how well you've achieved your goals—all this will contribute to your continued development.[2] Preparing a portfolio takes time, but all useful activities take time. If you feel that you don't have time for a portfolio, at least keep a journal in which you write regularly about your teaching, your students, and your classes.

## *IN CONCLUSION*

The great thing about teaching is that there is always more to learn. The various sources of ideas and feedback that we have described help us to improve. As we improve, our students respond more positively, and their increased interest and enthusiasm sparks us to even more effort and enjoyment. Obviously, the course is not always onward and upward. There are moments of frustration and despair, but there are enough good times to help us through those that are not so good. And as we gain additional skill and assurance, our relations with students become more satisfying.

---

[2]As compared with some earlier editions of *Teaching Tips*, this chapter has paid much less attention to evaluation for tenure or for post-tenure review. I have deliberately focused on improvement because I believe that a teacher who uses the methods discussed here for continual development will be well equipped for personnel evaluations.

Most of this book has dealt with interactions in the classroom, but research has shown that those faculty members who have the most impact on students spend time with students outside the classroom. This is not only important for the students' development, but it also contributes to your continuing vitality as a teacher. Your interactions with students and other faculty are critical to the development of a community of learners—teachers and students, learners all.

Over the years, both Bill and I have visited hundreds of colleges and universities, both in this country and in others. What most impresses us is that, no matter how difficult the circumstances, there are always some vital, effective teachers. They come in no one personality, no one discipline, no one institution. Somehow teachers find a way to cope with adverse environments and are able to stimulate effective learning. They enjoy teaching despite unfavorable circumstances.

This chapter has discussed at length ways to grow. However much you are intrigued by new possibilities, it is important not to forget what you enjoy doing. Our final advice is, *"Have fun!"*

In Robert Bolt's *A Man for All Seasons*, Sir Thomas More assures his protégé that, if he becomes a teacher, he will be an outstanding teacher. "But if I were," demurs the ambitious young man, "who would know it?" More replies, "You, your friends, your students, God. Not a bad audience that."[3]

Not a bad audience, indeed!

## Supplementary Reading

The many books recommended as supplementary reading in previous chapters are relevant to your lifelong learning, but to save you the trouble of looking back, we will mention here once again several books that nicely cover the major areas of teaching:

▶ J. Biggs, *Teaching for Quality Learning at University* (Buckingham, UK: SRHE, and Philadelphia: Open University Press, 1999).

▶ B. G. Davis, *Tools for Teaching*, 2nd ed. (San Francisco: Jossey-Bass, 1993).

▶ J. Lowman, *Mastering the Techniques of Teaching*, 2nd ed. (San Francisco: Jossey-Bass, 1995).

---

[3] The reference to Sir Thomas More comes from Nick Skinner, who used these words in concluding his address as recipient of the Canadian Psychological Association Award for Distinguished Contribution to Psychology in Education and Training (Skinner, 2001).

▶ P. Ramsden, *Learning to Teach in Higher Education* (London and New York: Routledge, 1992).

▶ W. A. Wright and associates, *Teaching Improvement Practices: Successful Strategies for Higher Education* (Bolton, MA: Anker, 1995).

Stephen Brookfield's *Becoming a Critically Reflective Teacher* (San Francisco: Jossey-Bass, 1995) will help you with one of the most important aspects of your development—reflecting on your experience—and fits nicely with your use of classroom assessment techniques.

*Student Motivation, Cognition, and Learning: Essays in Honor of Wilbert J. McKeachie*, edited by Paul Pintrich, Donald Brown, and Claire Ellen Weinstein (Hillsdale, NJ: Erlbaum, 1994), gives you an excellent introduction to a variety of research areas relevant to teaching.

A briefer useful resource is Janet G. Donald and Arthur M. Sullivan (eds.), "Using Research to Improve Teaching," *New Directions for Teaching and Learning*, no. 23, 1985.

Three volumes are particularly helpful in the area of evaluation and assessment of teaching:

▶ J. Centra, *Reflective Faculty Evaluation: Enhancing Teaching and Determining Faculty Effectiveness* (San Francisco: Jossey-Bass, 1993).

▶ R. P. Perry and J. C. Smart (eds.), *Effective Teaching in Higher Education: Research and Practice* (New York: Agathon, 1997).

▶ P. Seldin and associates, *Changing Practices in Evaluating Teaching* (Bolton, MA: Anker, 1999).

Finally, for a thoughtful, stimulating perspective differing from American cognitivist/constructivist approaches, read Ference Marton and Shirley Booth's *Learning and Awareness* (Mahwah, NJ: Erlbaum, 1997). Marton's phenomenographic research at Gothenburg, Sweden, has been enormously influential in thinking about learning and teaching in higher education.

# REFERENCES

ABCNEWS.com. (2004, April 29). *Full-service fakery: Inside the life of a professional essay writer and test taker* [Online]. Available at: http://abcnews.go.com/Primetime/story?id=132377&page=1.

Achacoso, M., & Svinicki, M. (Eds.). (2005, Spring). New testing alternatives. *New Directions for Teaching And Learning* (no. 100). San Francisco: Jossey-Bass.

Albanese, M. A., & Mitchell, S. (1993). Problem-based learning: A review of literature on its outcomes and implementation issues. *Academic Medicine, 68*, 52–81.

Alexander, P. A., & Judy, J. E. (1988). The interaction of domain-specific and strategic knowledge in academic performance. *Review of Educational Research, 58*(4), 375–404.

Altmiller, H. (1973). Another approach to freshman chemistry. *Journal of Chemical Education, 50*, 249.

Alverno College Faculty. (1994). *Student Assessment Learning at Alverno College*. Milwaukee, WI: Alverno Productions.

American Association of University Professors (AAUP). (1987). Statement on professional ethics. *Academe, 73*(4), 49.

Ames, C. (1992). Classrooms: Goals, structures, and student motivation. *Journal of Educational Psychology, 84*, 261–271.

Anderson, L. W., & Krathwohl, D. R. (Eds.). (2001). *A taxonomy for learning, teaching, and assessing: A revision of Bloom's taxonomy of educational objectives*. New York: Longman.

Andre, T. (1987). Questions and learning from reading. *Questioning Exchange, 1*(1), 47–86.

♦ Angelo, T. A., & Cross, K. P. (1993). *Classroom assessment techniques: A handbook for college faculty* (2nd ed.). San Francisco: Jossey-Bass.

Annis, L. F. (1981). Effect of preference for assigned lecture notes on student achievement. *Journal of Educational Research, 74*, 179–181.

———. (1983a). The processes and effects of peer tutoring. *Human Learning, 2*, 39–47.

———. (1983b). *Study techniques*. Dubuque: Wm. C. Brown.

Apple, T., & Cutler, A. (1999). The Rensselaer studio General Chemistry course. *Journal of Chemical Education, 76*, 462–463.

Arce, J., & Betancourt, R. (1997). Student-designed experiments in scientific lab instruction. *Journal of College Science Teaching, 27*, 114–118.

Arkright-Keeler, D.L., & Stapleton, S. (2007). Education resources for guiding discussions on ethics in science. *Biochemistry and Molecular Biology Education*, *35*, 24–47.

Arnold, S. M., Bender, J., Cytrynbaum, S., Newman, B. M. , Ringwald, B. , Ringwald, J., & Rosenwein, R. (1970). The natural history of the classroom. In R. Mann, *The College Classroom*. New York: Wiley.

Arredondo, P. (1991). Counseling Latinas. In C. Lee & B. Richardson (Eds.), *Multicultural issues in counseling: New approaches to diversity* (pp. 143–156). Alexandria, VA: American Counseling Association.

Asante, M. K. (1987). *The Afrocentric idea*. Philadelphia: Temple University Press.

Association of American Colleges and Universities. (2000). *Americans see many benefits to diversity in higher education, finds first-ever national poll on topic* [Online]. Available at: http://www.aacu-edu.org/Initiatives/legacies.html.

Attneave, C. (1982). American Indian and Alaskan native families: Emigrants in their own homeland. In M. McGoldrick, J. Pearce, & J. Giordano (Eds.), *Ethnicity and family therapy* (pp. 55–83). New York: Guilford Press.

Avila, D., & Avila, A. (1995). Mexican Americans. In N. Vacc, S. Devaney, & J. Wittmer (Eds.), *Experiencing and counseling multicultural and diverse populations* (3rd ed., pp. 119–146). Bristol, PA: Accelerated Development.

Babb, K., & Ross, C. (2009). The timing of online lecture slide availability and its effect on attendance, participation, and exam performance. *Computers & Education*, *52*, 868–881.

Bailey, C. A., Kingsbury, K., Kulinowski, K., Paradis, J., & Schoonover, R. (2000). An integrated lecture-laboratory environment of General Chemistry. *Journal of Chemical Education*, *77*, 195–199.

Baker, L., & Lombardi, B. (1985). Students' lecture notes and their relation to test performance. *Teaching of Psychology*, *12*, 1, 28–32.

♦ Bargh, J. A., & Schul, Y. (1980). On the cognitive benefits of teaching. *Journal of Educational Psychology*, *72*(5), 593–604.

♦ Barr, R. B., & Tagg, J. (1995). From teaching to learning—A new paradigm for undergraduate education. *Change*, *27*, 12–25.

Baruth, L., & Manning, M. (1991). *Multicultural counseling and psychotherapy*. New York: Merrill.

Bauer, K. W., & Bennett, J. S. (2003). Alumni perceptions used to assess undergraduate research experience. *The Journal of Higher Education*, *74*, 210–230.

Becker, J. (2005). Cutting edge research by undergraduates on a shoestring? *Journal of Computing Sciences*, *21*, 160–168.

Benjamin, L. (1991). Personalization and active learning in the large introductory psychology class. *Teaching of Psychology, 18*(2), 68–74.

Berge, Z. (2000). Components of the online classroom. In R. E. Weiss, D. S. Knowlton, B. W. Speck (eds.). Principles of effective teaching in the online classroom (pp. 23–28). *New Directions for Teaching and Learning* (no. 84). San Francisco: Jossey-Bass.

Berlyne, D. E. (1954a). An experimental study of human curiosity. *British Journal of Psychology, 45,* 256–265.

———. (1954b). A theory of human curiosity. *British Journal of Psychology, 45,* 180–181.

♦ ———. (1960). *Conflict, arousal, and curiosity.* New York: McGraw-Hill.

Bernstein, D. & Bass, R. (2005). The scholarship of teaching and learning. *Academe, 91*(4), 37–43.

Bieron, J. F., & Dinan, F. J. (2000). Not your ordinary lab day. *Journal of College Science Teaching, 30*(1), 44–47.

Biggs, J. (1999). *Teaching for quality learning at university.* Buckingham, UK: SRHE, and Philadelphia: Open University Press.

Biggs, J. B., & Collis, K. F. (1982). *Evaluating the Quality of Learning: The SOLO Taxonomy.* New York: Academic Press.

Bligh, D. (2000). *What's the use of lectures?* San Francisco: Jossey-Bass.

Block, C. (1981). Black Americans and the cross-cultural counseling and psychotherapy experience. In A. Marsella & P. Pedersen (eds.), *Cross-cultural counseling and psychotherapy* (pp. 177–194). New York: Pergamon Press.

♦ Bloom, B. S. (Ed.). (1956). *Taxonomy of educational objectives*: The classification of educational goals. New York: Longman.

Bloxham, S., & Campbell, L. (2008). Creating a feedback dialogue: Exploring the use of interactive coversheets. Paper presented at the *Improving Student Learning Symposium*, University of Durham, Sept. 1–3.

Boekaerts, M., & Niemivirta, M. (2000). Self-regulation in learning: Finding a balance between learning- and ego-protective goals. In M. Boekaerts, P. R. Pintrich, & M. Zeidner (Eds.), *Handbook of self-regulation* (pp. 417–450). San Diego: Academic Press.

Boekaerts, M., Pintrich, P. R., & Zeidner, M. (Eds.). (2000). *Handbook of self-regulation.* San Diego: Academic Press.

Bonk, C. J., & Cunningham, D. J. (1998). Searching for learner-centered, constructivist, and sociocultural components of collaborative educational learning tools. In C. J. Bonk & S. K. King (Eds.), *Electronic collaborators: Learner-centered technologies for literacy, apprenticeship, and discourse* (pp. 25–50). Mahwah, NJ: Erlbaum.

Boud, D., Cohen, R., & Sampson, J. (2001). *Peer learning in higher education: Learning from and with each other.* Kogan Page.

◆ Boyer, E. (1990). *Scholarship reconsidered: Priorities of the professoriate*. Princeton, NJ: Carnegie Foundation for the Advancement of Teaching.

Braxton, J. M., & Bayer, A. (1999). *Faculty misconduct in collegiate teaching*. Baltimore: Johns Hopkins Press.

Brown, G. (1978). *Lecturing and explaining*. London: Methuen.

Brown, G., & Atkins, M. (1988). *Effective teaching in higher education*. London: Methuen.

Brown, J. S. (2000). Growing up digital: How the Web changes work, education, and the ways people learn. *Change, 32*(2), 11–20.

Brown, R. D., & Krager, L. (1985). Ethical issues in graduate education: Faculty and student responsibilities. *Journal of Higher Education, 56*, 403–418.

Bruff, D. (2009). *Teaching with classroom response systems: Creating active learning environments*. San Francisco: John Wiley and Sons.

Cahn, S. (1994). *Saints and scamps: Ethics in academia*. Lanham, MD: Rowan and Littlefield Publishers, Inc.

Campbell, R. (1999). Mouths, machines, and minds. *The Psychologist, 12*, 446–449.

Canada, M. and Speck, B. (2001). Developing and implementing service learning programs. *New Directions for Higher Education* (no 114). San Francisco: Jossey-Bass Publishers.

Caron, M. D., Whitbourne, S. K., & Halgin, R. P. (1992). Fraudulent excuse making among college students. *Teaching of Psychology, 19*(2), 90–93.

Carr, D. (2000). *Professionalism and ethics in teaching*. New York: Routledge.

Casteel, M. A., & Bridges, K. R. (2007) Goodbye lecture: A student-led seminar approach for teaching upper division courses. *Teaching of Psychology, 34*(2), 107–110.

Center for Authentic Science Practice in Education. (2009). [Online]. Available at: http://www.purdue.edu/dp/caspie.

Centra, J. A. (1975). Colleagues as raters of classroom instruction. *Journal of Higher Education, 46*, 327–337.

◆ ———. (1993). *Reflective faculty evaluation: Enhancing teaching and determining faculty effectiveness*. San Francisco: Jossey-Bass.

Champagne, A. B., Klofper, L. E., & Anderson, J. H. (1980). Factors influencing the learning of classical mechanics. *American Journal of Physics, 48*, 1074–1079.

Chang, T. M., Crombag, H. F., van der Drift, K. D. J. M., & Moonen, J. M. (1983). *Distance learning: On the design of an open university*. Boston: Kluwer-Nijhoff.

Chi, M. T. H., Glaser, R., & Farr, M. J. (Eds.). (1988). *The nature of expertise*. Hillsdale, NJ: Erlbaum.

Chickering, A. W. & Gamson, Z. F. (1987). Seven principles for good practice in undergraduate education, *Wingspread Journal 9*(2), special insert.

Churchill, L. R. (1982). The teaching of ethics and moral values in teaching. *Journal of Higher Education, 53*(3), 296–306.

Clark, R. & Mayer, R. E. (2008). *E-learning and the science of instruction* (2nd ed). San Francisco: Jossey-Bass.

———. (1994b). Media will never influence learning. *Educational Technology, Research and Development, 42*(2), 21–29.

Clark, R. E. (1994a). Media and method. *Educational Technology Research and Development, 42*(3), 7–10.

Coghlan, E., Futey, D., Little, J., Lomas, C., Oblinger, D., & Windham, C. (2007). *ELI Discovery Tool: Guide to Podcasting* [Online]. Retrieved February 12, 2009. Available at: http://www.educause.edu/GuideToPodcasting/12830.

Cohen, P., Kulik, J., & Kulik, C. L. (1982). Educational outcomes of tutoring: A meta-analysis of findings. *American Educational Research Journal, 19*(2), 237–248.

Collins, A. (1977). Processes in acquiring knowledge. In R. C. Anderson, R. J. Spiro, & W. E. Montague (Eds.), *Schooling and the acquisition of knowledge* (pp. 339–363). Hillsdale, NJ: Erlbaum.

Collins, A., & Stevens, A. L. (1982). Goals and strategies of inquiry teaching. In R. Glaser (Ed.), *Advances in instructional psychology* (pp. 65–119). Hillsdale, NJ: Erlbaum.

Connor-Greene, P. (2000). Making connections: Evaluating the effectiveness of journal writing in enhancing student learning. *Teaching of Psychology, 27*(1), 44–46.

Cooper, J. L., Robinson, P., & Ball, D. (Eds.). (2003). *Small group instruction in higher education: Lessons from the past, visions of the future.* Stillwater, OK: New Forums Press.

Coppola, B. P. (1995, Summer). Progress in practice: Using concepts from motivation and self-regulated learning research to improve chemistry instruction. In P. R. Pintrich (Ed.), Understanding self-regulated learning. *New directions for teaching and learning* (no. 63, pp. 87–96). San Francisco: Jossey-Bass.

———. (2000). Targeting entry points for ethics in chemistry teaching and learning. *Journal of Chemical Education, 77*, 1506–1511.

Coppola, B. P., Ege, S. N., & Lawton, R. G. (1997). The University of Michigan undergraduate chemistry curriculum: 2. Instructional strategies and assessment. *Journal of Chemical Education, 74*, 84–94.

Costin, F. (1972). Three-choice versus four-choice items: Implications for reliability and validity of objective achievement tests. *Educational and Psychological Measurement, 32*, 1035–1038.

Covington, M. V. (1999). Caring about learning: The nature and nurture of subject-matter appreciation. *Educational Psychologist, 34,* 127–136.

Creed, T. (1997). PowerPoint, No! Cyberspace, Yes. *National Teaching and Learning Forum, 6*(4), 5–7.

♦ Cronbach, L. J., & Snow, R. E. (1977). *Aptitudes and instructional methods: A handbook for research on interaction.* New York: Irvington.

♦ Cross, K. P., & Steadman, M. H. (1996). *Classroom research: Implementing the scholarship of teaching.* San Francisco: Jossey-Bass.

CUR (2009). Council on Undergraduate Research [Online]. Available at: http://www.cur.org.

Davies, P. (2000, November). Computerized peer assessment. *Innovation in Education and Training International, 37*(4), 346–355.

Day, R. S. (1980). Teaching from notes: Some cognitive consequences. *New Directions for Teaching and Learning* (no. 2, pp. 95–112). San Francisco: Jossey-Bass.

Deci, E., & Ryan, R. (2000). The "what" and "why" of goal pursuits: Human needs and the self-determination of behavior. *Psychological Inquiry, 11,* 227–268.

Dewey, R. (1995, March). Finding the right introductory psychology textbook. *APS Observer,* 32–35.

DeZure, D., Kaplan, M., & Deerman, M. (2001). Research on student notetaking: Implications for faculty and graduate student instructors. CRLT Occasional Paper, No. 16. Ann Arbor, MI: University of Michigan Center for Research on Learning and Teaching. Available at: http://www.crlt.umich.edu/publinks/CRLT_no16.pdf.

DiBiase, W. J., & Wagner, E. P. (2002). Aligning General Chemistry laboratory with lecture at a large university. *School of Science and Mathematics, 102,* 158–171.

Diederich, P. (1974). *Measuring growth in English.* Urbana: NCTE.

Dillon, J. T. (1982). The effect of questions in education and other enterprises. *Journal of Curriculum Studies, 14,* 127–152.

Domin, D. S. (1999). A review of laboratory instruction styles. *Journal of Chemical Education, 76,* 543–547.

Dunn, D. S., McEntarffer, R., & Halonen, J. S. (2004). Empowering psychology students through self-assessment. In D. S. Dunn, C. M. Mehrotra, and J. S. Halonen (Eds.), *Measuring up: Educational assessment challenges and practices for psychology.* Washington, DC: American Psychological Association.

Dunnivant, F. M., Moore, A., Alfano, M. J., Brzenk, R., Buckley, P. T., Newman, M. E. (2000). Understanding the Greenhouse Effect: Is global warming real? *Journal of Chemical Education, 77,* 1602–3.

Dweck, C. S. (1986). Motivational processes affecting learning. *American Psychologist, 41,* 1040–1048.

Dweck, C. (1999). *Self-theories: Their role in motivation, personality and development* (Philadelphia: Psychology Press).

Dweck, C. S. (2006). *Mindset: The new psychology of success*, Random House, New York.

D'Ydewalle, G., Swerts, A., & de Corte, E. (1983). Study time and test performance as a function of test expectations. *Contemporary Educational Psychology, 8*(1), 55–67.

Eccles, J. (1994). Understanding women's educational and occupational choices. *Psychology of Women Quarterly, 18*, 585–609.

The Educated Nation [Online]. Available at: http://www.educatedna-tion.com/.

The EDUCAUSE Learning Initiative. 7 things you should know about mapping mashups [Online]. Available at: http://www.educause.edu/ELI/7ThingsYouShouldKnowAboutMappi/156819.

Ehrmann, S. C. (1995, March/April). Asking the right questions: What does research tell us about technology and higher learning? *Change, 27*(2), 20–27.

Elbow, P. (2000a). Using the collage for collaborative writing. In *Everyone can write: Essays toward a hopeful theory of writing and teaching writing* (pp. 372–378). New York: Oxford University Press.

———. (2000b). Your cheatin' art: A collage. In *Everyone can write: Essays toward a hopeful theory of writing and teaching writing* (pp. 300–313). New York: Oxford University Press.

Elbow, P., & Belanoff, P. (2003). *Sharing and responding.* New York: McGraw-Hill.

El-Ghoroury, N., Salvador, D., Manning, R., & Williamson, T. (1999). *A survival guide for ethnic minority graduate students* [Online]. Available: http://www.apa.org/apags/diversity/emsg.html

Elmendorf, H., & Ottenhoff, J. (2009). The importance of conversation in learning and the value of web-based discussion tools. Academic Commons [Online]. Available at: http://www.academiccommons.org/commons/essay/importance-conversation-learning.

Elshout, J. J. (1987). Problem solving and education. In E. DeCorte, H. Lodewijks, R. Permentier, & P. Span (Eds.), *Learning and instruction: European research in an international context* (Vol. 1). Oxford: Leuven University Press/Pergamon Press.

Entwistle, N. J. (1992). Student learning and study strategies. In B. R. Clark & G. Neave (Eds.), *Encyclopedia of higher education.* Oxford: Pergamon.

Eriksen, S. C. (1983). Private measures of good teaching. *Teaching of Psychology, 10*, 133–136.

Eves, R. L.; Davis, L. E.; Brown, D. G., & Lamberts, W. L. (2007). Integration of field studies and undergraduate research into an interdisciplinary course: Natural history of tropical carbonate ecosystems. *Journal of College Science Teaching, 36,* 22–27.

Ewing, K., Richardson, T., James-Myer, L., & Russell, R. (1996). The relationship between racial identity attitudes, worldview, and African American graduate students' experience of the imposter phenomenon. *Journal of Black Psychology, 22,* 53–66.

Eyler, J., Giles, Jr., D. E., & Astin, A. (1999). *Where's the learning in service-learning?* San Francisco: Jossey-Bass.

Fallon, M. (1997). The school counselor's role in first generation students' college plans. *School Counselor, 44*(5), 384–393.

Faro, S., & Swan, K. (2006) An investigation into the efficacy of the studio model at the high school level. *Journal of Educational Computing Research, 35,* 45–59.

♦ Feldman, K. A., & Newcomb, T. M. (1969). *The impact of college on students* (Vol. 2). San Francisco: Jossey-Bass.

Feldman, S., & Rosenthal, D. (1990). The acculturation of autonomy expectations in Chinese high schoolers residing in two western nations. *International Journal of Psychology, 25,* 259–281.

Fink, L. Dee (2003) *Creating significant learning experiences.* San Francisco: Joseph Wiley & Sons, Inc.

Fisch, L. (2001). The devil's advocate strikes again. *Journal of Staff, Program, and Organizational Development, 18*(1), 49–51.

Fisch, L. (Ed.). (1996). Ethical dimensions of college and university teaching: Understanding and honoring the special relationship between teachers and students. *New Directions for Teaching and Learning* (no. 66). San Francisco: Jossey-Bass.

Flavell, J. H. (1979). Metacognition and cognitive mentoring: A new area of cognitive-developmental inquiry. *American Psychologist, 34,* 906–911.

Foos, P. W., & Fisher, R. P. (1988). Using tests as learning opportunities. *Journal of Educational Psychology, 88*(2), 179–183.

Fox, S., & Vitak, J. (2008). Degrees of access (May 2008 data). Pew Internet and American life project [Online]. Available at: http://www.pewinternet.org/Presentations/2008/Degrees-of-Access-(May-2008-data).aspx.

Fry, R. (2003). *Hispanic youth dropping out of U. S. schools: Measuring the challenge.* Washington, DC: Pew Hispanic Center.

Fryberg, S., & Markus, H. (2007). Cultural models of education in American Indian, Asian American and European American contexts. *Social Psychology of Education, 10,* 213–246.

Fuentes, M., Kiyana, A., & Rosario, E. (2003). *Keeping Latinos in high school: The role of context.* Paper presented at the annual meeting of the American Psychological Association, Toronto, Canada.

Fuligni, A., Burton, L., Marshall, S., Perez-Febles, A., Yarrington, J., Kirsch, L., & Merriwether-DeVries, C. (1999). Attitudes toward family obligations among American adolescents with Asian, Latin American, and European backgrounds. *Child Development, 70,* 1030–1044.

Furco, A. (1996). Service-learning: A balanced approach to experiential education. *Expanding Boundaries: Service and Learning.* Washington DC: Corporation for National Service, 2–6.

Gabelnick, F., MacGregor, J., Matthews, R., & Smith, R. (1990). Learning communities: Creating connections among students, faculty and disciplines. *New Directions for Teaching and Learning* (no. 11). San Francisco: Jossey-Bass Publisher.

Gamson, W. A. (1966). *SIMSOC: A manual for participants.* Ann Arbor, MI: Campus Publishers.

Garcia-Sheets, M. (2008). Perception of campus climate by university students of color: Implications for practice. Dissertation Abstracts: Section A: Humanities and Social Sciences; *69* (4A), 1231.

Garrett, J., & Garrett, M. (1994). The path of good medicine: Understanding and counseling Native American Indians. *Journal of Multicultural Counseling and Development, 22,* 134–144.

Garwick, A., & Auger, S. (2000). What do providers need to know about American Indian culture? Recommendations from urban Indian family caregivers. *Families, Systems & Health, 18,* 177–190.

Gerdeman, R. (2000). Academic dishonesty and the community college. *ERIC Digest.* ERIC Clearinghouse for Community Colleges (ED447840).

Gibbs, G. (1999). Using assessment strategically to change the way students learn. In S. Brown & A. Glassner (Eds.), *Assessment matters in higher education: Choosing and using diverse approaches* (pp. 41–54). Buckingham, UK: Society for Research in Higher Education/Open University Press.

Glaser, R., & Chi, M.T.H. (1988). Overview. In *The Nature of Expertise,* eds. M. T. H. Chi, R. Glaser, & M. Farr xv–xxviii. Hillsdale, NJ: Erlbaum.

Goldschmid, M. L. (1971). The learning cell: An instructional innovation. *Learning and Development, 2*(5), 1–6.

———. (1975, May). *When students teach students.* Paper presented at the International Conference on Improving University Teaching, Heidelberg, Germany.

♦ Goldschmid, M. L., & Shore, B. M. (1974). The learning cell: A field test of an educational innovation. In W. A. Verreck (Ed.), *Methodological problems in research and development in higher education* (pp. 218–236). Amsterdam: Swets and Zeitlinger.

Gonzalez, B. L., Wegner, P. A., Foley, B., & Thadani, V. (1999). Studio classroom and conceptual learning in chemistry. *Abstracts of Papers of the American Chemical Society*, 217th ACS National Meeting, Anaheim, CA, March 21–25, 1999; American Chemical Society: Washington, DC, 1999; CHED 071.

Gottfried, A. C., Hessler, J. A., Sweeder, R. D., Bartolin, J. M., Coppola, B. P., Banaszak Holl, M. M., Reynolds, B. P., & Stewart, I. C. (2003). Studio 130: Design, testing, and implementation. *Abstracts of Papers of the American Chemical Society*, *225*, 647.

Grauerholz, E., & Copenhaver, S. (1994). When the personal becomes problematic: The ethics of using experiential teaching methods. *Teaching Sociology*, *22*(4), 319–327.

Green, M. C. (2004). Storytelling in teaching. *APS Observer*, *17*(4), 37–39.

Greeno, J. G. (1991). Number sense as situated knowing in a conceptual domain. *Research in Mathematical Education*, *22*, 170–218.

Greeno, J. G., & the Middle-School Mathematics through Applications Project Group. (1997, November). Theories and practices of thinking and learning to think. *American Journal of Education*, *106*(1), 85–126.

Grigorenko, E., Jarvin, L., & Sternberg, R. (2002). School-based tests of the triarchic theory of intelligence: Three settings, three samples, three syllabi. *Contemporary Educational Psychology*, *27*(2), 167–208.

Gruber, H. E., & Weitman, M. (1962, April). *Self-directed study: Experiments in higher education* (Report No. 19). Boulder: University of Colorado, Behavior Research Laboratory.

Gruenbacher, D., Natarajan, B., & Kuhn, W. B. (2006). Work in progress: An integrated laboratory experience – A new environment for teaching communications. *Frontiers in Education Conference, 2006. FIE 2006.* 36th Annual, vol. 1, 28–31 Oct.; pp. 7–8.

Gudykunst, W. (2004). *Bridging differences: Effective intergroup communication* (4th ed.). Thousand Oaks, CA: Sage.

Gudykunst, W., & Matsumoto, Y. (1996). Cross-cultural variability of communication in personal relationships. In W. Gudykunst, S. Ting-Toomey, & T. Nishida (Eds.), *Communication in personal relationships across cultures* (pp. 19–56). Thousand Oaks, CA: Sage.

Gudykunst, W., Ting-Toomey, S., & Nishida, T. (Eds.). (1996). *Communication in personal relationships across cultures*. Thousand Oaks, CA: Sage.

Haines, D. B., & McKeachie, W. J. (1967). Cooperative vs. competitive discussion methods in teaching introductory psychology. *Journal of Educational Psychology*, *58*, 386–390.

Hall, Edward T. (1966). *The Hidden Dimension*. NY: Anchor Books.

Halpern, D. F. (1996). *Thought and knowledge: An introduction to critical thinking*. Mahwah, NJ: Erlbaum.

Halpern, D. F., & Hakel, M. D. (2003). Applying the science of learning to the university and beyond. *Change*, *35*(4), 36–41.

Hanson, K. (1996). Between apathy and advocacy: Teaching and modeling ethical reflection. *New Directions for Teaching and Learning* (no. 66, pp. 33–36). San Francisco: Jossey-Bass.

Harackiewicz, J., Barron, K. E., & Elliott, A. J. (1998). Rethinking achievement goals: When are they adaptive for college students and why? *Educational Psychologist, 33*, 1–21.

Harter, S. (1978). Effective motivation reconsidered: Toward a developmental model. *Human Development, 21*, 34–64.

♦ Hartley, J., & Davies, I. K. (1978). Note-taking: A critical review. *Programmed Learning and Educational Technology, 15*, 207–224.

Hartman, F. R. (1961). Recognition learning under multiple channel presentation and testing conditions. *Audio-Visual Communication Review, 9*, 24–43.

Hartman, H. J. (1990). Factors affecting the tutoring process. *Journal of Developmental Education, 14*(2), 2–6.

Hathaway, R. S., Nagda, B. A., & Gregerman, S. R. (2002). The relationship of undergraduate research participation to graduate and professional education pursuit: An empirical study. *Journal of College Student Development, 43*, 614–631.

Hattie, J., & Timperley, H. (2007). The power of feedback. *Review of Educational Research, 77*, 81–112.

Henderson, L., & Buising, C. (2000). A research-based molecular biology laboratory. *Journal of College Science Teaching, 30*(5), 322–327.

Herring, R. (1997). Counseling indigenous American youth. In C. Lee (Ed.), *Multicultural issues in counseling: New approaches to diversity* (2nd ed., pp. 53–70). Alexandria, VA: American Counseling Association.

Higginbothan, C., Pike, C. F., & Rice, J. K. (1998). Spectroscopy in sol-gel matrices: An open-ended laboratory experience for upper-level undergraduates. *Journal of Chemical Education, 75*, 461.

Hodges, E. (1994, Summer). Some realities of revision: What students don't or won't understand. *English in Texas, 25*(4), 13–16.

Hofer, B. (1997). *The development of personal epistemology: Dimensions, disciplinary differences, and instructional practices.* Unpublished doctoral thesis, University of Michigan.

Hofstein, A., & Lunetta, V. N. (1982). The role of the laboratory in science teaching: Neglected aspects of research. *Review of Educational Research, 52*(2), 201–217.

Horowitz, G. (2003). A discovery approach to three organic laboratory techniques: Extraction, recrystallization, and distillation. *Journal of Chemical Education, 80*, 1039–1043.

Houston, J. P. (1983). Alternate test forms as a means of reducing multiple-choice answer copying in the classroom. *Journal of Educational Psychology, 75*(4), 572–575.

♦ Hovland, C. I. (Ed.). (1957). *The order of presentation in persuasion.* New Haven, CT: Yale University Press.

Huang, L. (1994). An integrative approach to clinical assessment and intervention with Asian-American adolescents. *Journal of Clinical Child Psychology, 23,* 21–31.

Hunter, A. B., Laursen, S. L., & Seymour, E. (2007). Becoming a scientist: The role of undergraduate research in students' cognitive, personal, and professional development. *Science Education, 91,1,* 36-74.

Husman, J., Derryberry, W. P., Crowson, H. M., & Lomax, R. (2004). Instrumentality, task value, and intrinsic motivation: Making sense of their independent interdependence. *Contemporary Educational Psychology, 29,* 63–76.

Jarvis, M. (2005). The psychology effective learning and teaching. Cheltenham, UK: Nelson Thornes.

Jensen, J. (1985). Perspective on nonverbal intercultural communication. In L. Samovar & R. Porter (Eds.), *Intercultural communication: A reader* (pp. 256–272). Belmont, CA: Wadsworth.

Johnson, D. M. (1975). Increasing originality on essay examinations in psychology. *Teaching of Psychology, 2,* 99–102.

Johnson, D., & Johnson, R. (1995) *Creative controversy: Intellectual challenge in the classroom.* Edina, MN: Interaction Book Company.

Johnson, D., Johnson, R., & Smith, K. (2000). Constructive controversy: The educative power of intellectual conflict. *Change Magazine,* January/February, pp. 28–37.

♦ Johnson, D. W., Maruyama, G., Johnson, R., Nelson, D., & Skon, L. (1981). The effects of cooperative, competitive, and individualistic goal structures on achievement: A meta-analysis. *Psychological Bulletin, 89,* 47–62.

Jordan, A. E. (2001). College student cheating: The role of motivation, perceived norms, attitudes, and knowledge of institutional policy. *Ethics and Behavior, 11,* 233–247.

Kardash, C. M. (2000). Evaluation of an undergraduate research experience: Perceptions of undergraduate interns and their faculty mentors. *Journal of Educational Psychology, 92,* 191–201.

Katz, D. (1950). *Gestalt psychology.* New York: Ronald Press.

Keller, F. S. (1968). Goodbye teacher, ... *Journal of Applied Behavior Analysis, 10,* 165–167.

Kennedy, L. M., Smith, A., Wells, A. T., & Wellman, B. (2008). Networked families. *Pew Internet and American Life Project.* Available at: http://www.pewinternet.org/Reports/2008/Networked-Families.aspx.

Kerr, C. (1994). Knowledge ethics and the new academic culture. *Change, 26*(1), 8–16.

Khan, F. A., Leavitt, A. J., Garmon, L. B., & Harper, W. D. (2003). An integrated chemistry environment using studio, workshop, and labworks: Systematically changing the teaching of General Chemistry. *Abstracts of Papers of the American Chemical Society*, 226th ACS National Meeting, New York, September 7–11, 2003; American Chemical Society: Washington, DC, 2003; CHED 262.

Kiewra, K. A. (1989). A review of notetaking: The encoding storage paradigm and beyond. *Educational Psychology Review, 1*(2), 147–172.

Kim, S., McLeod, J. & Shantzis, C. (1992). Cultural competence for evaluators working with Asian-American communities: Some practical considerations. In M. Orlandi (Ed.). *Cultural competence for evaluators: A guide for alcohol and other drug abuse prevention practitioners working with ethnic/racial communities* (pp. 203–260). Rockville, MD: Office for Substance Abuse Prevention.

King, A. (1990). Enhancing peer interaction and learning in the classroom. *American Educational Research Journal, 27*, 664–687.

———. (1997). Ask to think—Tell why: A model of transactive peer tutoring for scaffolding higher-level complex learning. *Educational Psychologist, 32*, 221–235.

Kirschenbaum, H., Simon, S., & Napier, R. (1971). *Wad-ja-get? The grading game in American education*. New York: Hart Publishing.

Kluger, A. N., & DeNisi, A. (1996). The effects of feedback intervention on performance: A historical review, a meta-analysis, and a preliminary feedback intervention theory. *Psychological Bulletin, 119*, 254–284.

Knight, P. (2006). The local practices of assessment. *Assessment and Evaluation in Higher Education, 31*(4), 435–452.

Ko, S., & Rossen. S. (2001). *Teaching online: A practical guide*. Boston: Houghton Mifflin.

Kolb, L. (2008). *Toys to tools: Connecting student cell phones to education*. Washington D.C: International Society for Technology in Education.

Komada, N. M. (2002). First generation college students and resiliency. *Dissertation Abstracts International, 63*(6-A), 2158.

Koocher, G., & Keith-Spiegel, P. (1998). *Ethics in psychology: Professional standards and cases*. Mahwah, NJ: Erlbaum.

Kovac, J. (1999). Professional ethics in the college and university science curriculum. *Science & Education, 8*, 309–319.

Kozma, R. (1994). Will media influence learning? Reframing the debate. *Educational Technology, Research and Development, 42*(2), 7–19.

Krathwohl, D., Bloom, B. S., & Masia, B. (Eds.). (1964). *Taxonomy of educational objectives, handbook II: Affective domain*. New York: David McKay.

Kremer, J. F., & Bringle, R. G. (1990). The effects of an intensive research experience on the careers of talented undergraduates. *Journal of Research and Development in Education, 24*, 1–5.

Kulik, J. (2003). *Effects of using instructional technology in colleges and universities: What controlled evaluation studies say* [Online]. Available at: http://sri.com/policy/csted/reports/sandt/it/.

LaFromboise, T., Berman, J., & Sohi, B. (1994). American Indian women. In L. Comas-Diaz & B. Greene (Eds.), *Women of color: Integrating ethnic and gender identities in psychotherapy* (pp. 30–71). New York: Guilford Press.

LaFromboise, T., Coleman, H., & Gerton, J. (1998). Psychological impact of biculturalism. In P. Organista, K. Chun, & G. Marin (Eds.), *Readings in ethnic psychology* (pp. 123–155). New York: Routledge.

Latus, M. (2007). Stressors among first-generation college students: A retrospective inquiry. Dissertation Abstracts: Section A: Humanities and Social Sciences; *68* (1-B), 626.

Lave, J., & Wegner, E. (1991) *Situated learning: Legitimate peripheral participation*. Cambridge, UK: Cambridge University Press.

Lawrence, S. (1998). Unveiling positions of privilege: A hands-on approach to understanding racism. *Teaching of Psychology, 25*(3), 198–200.

Leamnson, R. (2000). Learning as biological brain change. *Change, 32*, 34–40.

Lee, P. (2008). Cross-cultural differences between European Americans and Chinese Americans with respect to the concepts of self and communication. Dissertation Abstracts: Section A: Humanities and Social Sciences; *69* (4-B), 2672.

Lee, W. (1999). *An introduction to multicultural counseling*. Bristol, PA: Accelerated Development.

Leith, G. O. M. (1977). Implications of cognitive psychology for the improvement of teaching and learning in universities. In B. Massey (Ed.), *Proceedings of the Third International Conference, Improving University Teaching* (pp. 111–138). College Park: University of Maryland.

Lepper, M. R., & Hodell, M. (1989). Intrinsic motivation in the classroom. In C. Ames & R. Ames (Eds.), *Research on motivation in education* (Vol. 3, pp. 73–105). San Diego: Academic Press.

Lepper, M. R., & Malone, T. W. (1985). Intrinsic motivation and instructional effectiveness in computer-based education. In R. E. Snow & M. J. Farr (Eds.), *Aptitude, learning and instruction: III. Conative and affective process analyses*. Hillsdale, NJ: Erlbaum.

Lewis, M. (1997). *Poisoning the ivy: The seven deadly sins and other vices of higher education in America*. Armonk, NY: Sharpe.

Lidren, D. M., Meier, S. E., & Brigham, T. A. (1991). The effects of minimal and maximal peer tutoring systems on the academic performance of college students. *Psychological Record*, *41*, 69–77.

Lin, Y-G., McKeachie, W. J., & Kim, Y. C. (2003). College student intrinsic and/or extrinsic motivation and learning. *Learning and Individual Differences*, *13*, 251–258.

Lone-Knapp, F. (2000). Rez talk: How reservation residents describe themselves. *American Indian Quarterly*, *24*, 635–640.

Lunsford, R. (1997). When less is more: Principles for responding in the disciplines. In M. Sorcinelli & P. Elbow (Eds.). *Writing to learn: Strategies for assigning and responding to writing across the disciplines.* San Francisco: Jossey-Bass.

MacGregor, J. (Ed.). (1993, Spring). Student self-evaluation: Fostering reflective learning. *New Directions for Teaching and Learning* (no. 56). San Francisco: Jossey-Bass.

Maehr, M., & Midgley, C. (1991, Summer–Fall). Enhancing student motivation—A schoolwide approach. *Educational Psychologist*, *26*(3–4), 399–427.

Maggioni, L., & Alexander, P. A. (in press). Knowledge domains and domain learning. In B. McGaw, P. L. Peterson, & E. Baker (Eds.), *International encyclopedia of education* (3rd ed.). Amsterdam, Netherlands: Elsevier.

Maier, N. R. F. (1952). *Principles of human relations.* New York: Wiley.

———. (1963). *Problem-solving discussions and conferences.* New York: McGraw-Hill.

♦ Maier, N. R. F., & Maier, L. A. (1957). An experimental test of the effects of "developmental" vs. "free" discussion on the quality of group decisions. *Journal of Applied Psychology*, *41*, 320–323.

Maki, P. (2004). Assessing for learning: Building a sustainable commitment across the institution. Sterling, VA: Stylus.

Maki, M., & Kitano, H. (1989). Counseling Asian Americans. In P. Pedersen, J. Draguns, W. Lonner, & J. Trimble (Eds.), *Counseling across cultures* (5th ed., pp. 109–132). Thousand Oaks, CA: Sage.

♦ Mann, R. D., et al. (1970). *The college classroom: Conflict, change, and learning.* New York: Wiley.

Marcinkiewicz, H. R., & Clariana, R. B. (1997). The performance effects of headings within multiple-choice tests. *British Journal of Educational Psychology*, *67*, 111–117.

Markie, P. (1994). *A professor's duties: Ethical issues in college teaching.* Totowa, NJ: Rowman & Littlefield.

Marsh, H. W. (2001). Distinguishing between good (useful) and bad workloads on students' evaluations of teaching. *American Educational Research Journal*, *38*, 183–212.

♦ Marton, F., & Säljö, R. (1976a). On qualitative differences in learning: I—Outcome and process. *British Journal of Educational Psychology, 46,* 4–11.

————. (1976b). On qualitative differences in learning: II—Outcome as a function of the learner's conception of the task. *British Journal of Educational Psychology, 46,* 115–127.

Maruyama, M. (1982). Yellow youth's psychological struggle. *AAPA Journal, 7*(1), 21–29.

Matthews, J. (1991). The teaching of ethics and the ethics of teaching. *Teaching of Psychology, 18*(2), 80–85.

Mayer, R. (1997). Multimedia learning: Are we asking the right questions? *Educational Psychologist, 31,* 1–19.

————. (2003). The promise of multimedia learning: Using the same instructional design methods across different media. *Learning and Instruction, 13,* 125–139.

————. (2009). *Multimedia learning.* New York: Cambridge University Press.

Mayer, R., Stull, A., DeLeeuw, K., Almeroth, K., Bimber, B., Chun, D., Bulger, M., Campbell, J., Knight, A., and Zhang, H. (2009) Clickers in college classrooms: Fostering learning with questioning methods in large lecture classes. *Contemporary Educational Psychology, 34,* 51–57.

Mazur, E. (1997). *Peer instruction: A user's manual.* Upper Saddle River, NJ: Prentice Hall.

McAdoo, H. (Ed.). (1999). *Family ethnicity: Strength in diversity* (2nd ed.). Thousand Oaks, CA: Sage.

McCabe, D. L., & Trevino, L. K. (1996). What we know about cheating in college: Longitudinal trends and recent developments. *Change, 28*(1), 29–33.

McCabe, D., & Trevino, L. (1996, January/February). What we know about cheating in college. *Change, 28*(1), 28–33.

McCabe, D., Trevino, L., & Butterfield, K. (2001, January–February). Dishonesty in academic environments: The influence of peer reporting requirements. *Journal of Higher Education, 72*(1), 29–45.

♦ McClelland, D., Atkinson, J. W., Clark, R. A., & Lowell, E. L. (1953). *The achievement motive.* New York: Appleton-Century-Crofts.

McCluskey, H. Y. (1934). An experimental comparison of two methods of correcting the outcomes of examination. *School and Society, 40,* 566–568.

McDavis, R., Parker, W., & Parker, W. (1995). Counseling African Americans. In N. Vacc, S. DeVaney, & J. Wittmer (Eds.), *Experiencing and counseling multicultural and diverse populations* (pp. 217–250). Bristol, PA: Accelerated Development.

McGregor, L. (2006). Teaching and mentoring racially and ethnically diverse students. In W. Buskist, & S. Davis (Eds.) *Handbook of the teaching of psychology*. Malden, MA: Blackwell.

♦ McKeachie, W. J., Pintrich, P. R.,& Lin, Y-G. (1985). Teaching learning strategies. *Educational Psychologist, 20*(3), 153–160.

McKeachie, W. J., Pintrich, P. R., Lin, Y-G., Smith, D. A. F., & Sharma, R. (1990). *Teaching and learning in the college classroom: A review of the research literature* (2nd ed.). Ann Arbor: NCRIPTAL, University of Michigan.

McKeachie, W. J., Pollie, D., & Speisman, J. (1955). Relieving anxiety in classroom examinations. *Journal of Abnormal and Social Psychology, 50*, 93–98.

McKinnon, M. (1999). PBL in Hong Kong. *PBL Insight, 2*(1), 1–6.

McLeod, S. H. (1992). Responding to plagiarism: The role of the WPA. *WPA: Writing Program Administration, 15*(3), 7–16.

McMurtry, K. (2001, November). E-cheating: Combating a 21st century challenge. *T. H. E. Journal Online* [Online]. Available at: http://www.thejournal.com/magazine/vault/A3724.cfm.

Mentkowski, M., et al. (2000). *Learning that lasts*. San Francisco: Jossey-Bass.

Mentkowski, M., & Loacker, G. (1985, September). Assessing and validating the outcomes of college. *New Directions for Institutional Research*, 47–64.

Metzger, R. L., Boschee, P. F., Haugen, T., & Schnobrich, B. L. (1979). The classroom as learning context: Changing rooms affects performance. *Journal of Educational Psychology, 71*(4), 440–442.

Michaelsen, L. K., Knight, A. B., & Fink, L. D. (Eds.). (2004). *Team-based learning: A transformative use of small groups*. Sterling, VA: Stylus Publications.

Miller, H. (1998). Assessment with a purpose. *Innovation Journal 1998*, 35–37.

Miller, J. E., & Groccia, J. E. (1997). Are four heads better than one? A comparison of cooperative and traditional teaching formats in an introductory biology course. *Innovative Higher Education, 21*, 253–273.

Miller, R. L. (2008). Introduction and a brief history of undergraduate research in psychology. In, R. L. Miller, R. F. Rycek, E. Balcetis, S. T. Barney, B. C. Beins, S. R. Burns, R. Smith, & M. E. Ware (Eds.), *Developing, promoting, & sustaining the undergraduate research experience in psychology* [Online]. Retrieved [06/01/09] from the *Society for the Teaching of Psychology* Website. Available at: http://teachpsych.org/resources/e-books/ur2008/ur2008.php.

Mills, P., Sweeney, W. V., Marino, R., & Clarkson, S. A. (2000). New approach to teaching introductory science: The gas module. *Journal of Chemical Education, 77*, 1161–1165.

Mindess, A. (1999). *Reading between the signs.* Yarmouth, ME: Intercultural Press.

Monaco, G. E. (1977). *Inferences as a function of test-expectancy in the classroom.* Kansas State University Psychology Series, KSU-HIPI Report 73–3.

Moran, C., (2003). What we have hoped for. *Computers and Composition, 20*(4), 343–358.

Mousavi, S., Lowe, R., & Sweller, J. (1995). Reducing cognitive load by mixing auditory and visual presentation modes. *Journal of Psychology, 87*, 319–334.

Mueller, D. J., & Wasser, V. (1977). Implications of changing answers on objective test items. *Journal of Educational Measurement, 14*(1), 9–13.

Murray, H. G. (1983). Low-inference classroom teaching behaviors and student ratings of college teaching effectiveness. *Journal of Educational Psychology, 75*, 138–149.

♦ ———. (1997). Effective teaching behaviors in the college classroom. In R. P. Perry & J. C. Smart (Eds.), *Effective teaching in higher education: Research and practice* (pp. 171–204). New York: Agathon.

Murray, H., Gillese, W., Lennon, M., Mercer, P., & Robinson, M. (1996). Ethical principles for college and university teaching. In *New directions for teaching and learning* (no. 66, pp. 57–64). San Francisco: Jossey-Bass.

Nagda, B. A., Gregerman, S. R., Jonides, J., von Hippel, W., Lerner, J. S. (1998). Undergraduate student-faculty research partnerships affect student retention. *The Review of Higher Education, 22*, 55–72.

National Research Council. (2000). *Inquiry and the national science education standards: A Guide for Teaching and Learning.* Washington, D.C.: National Academy Press.

National Science Foundation. (2003). *Exploring the concept of undergraduate research centers* [Online]. Available at: http://urc.arizona.edu.

Naveh-Benjamin, M., & Lin, Y-G. (1991). *Assessing students' organization of concepts: A manual of measuring course-specific knowledge structures.* Ann Arbor: NCRIPTAL, University of Michigan.

♦ Naveh-Benjamin, M., Lin, Y-G., & McKeachie, W. J. (1989). Development of cognitive structures in three academic disciplines and their relations to students' study skills, anxiety and motivation: Further use of the ordered-tree technique. *Journal of Higher Education Studies, 4*, 10–15.

Naveh-Benjamin, M., McKeachie, W. J., Lin, Y-G., & Tucker, D. G. (1986). Inferring students' cognitive structures and their development using the "ordered tree" technique. *Journal of Educational Psychology, 78*, 130–140.

Nessel, D. D., & Graham, J. M. (2007). *Thinking strategies for student achievement: Improving learning across the curriculum, K-12. 2nd edition.* Thousand Oaks, CA: Corwin Press.

Nevid, J. & Mahon, K. (2009) Mastery quizzing as a signaling device to cue attention to lecture material. *Teaching of Psychology*, *36*, 29–32.

Nicol, D. (2009). Assessment for learner self-regulation: Enhancing achievement in the first year using learning technologies, *Assessment and Evaluation in Higher Education*, *34*(3), 335–352.

Nicol, D. J. and Macfarlane-Dick, D. (2006). Formative assessment and self-regulated learning: A model and seven principles of good feedback practice, *Studies in Higher Education*, *31*(2), 199–218.

Nilson, L. (2007). *The graphic syllabus and outcomes map: Communicating your course*. San Francisco: Jossey-Bass.

Nishida, T. (1996). Communication in personal relationships in Japan. In W. Gudykunst, S. Ting-Toomey, & T. Nishida (Eds.), *Communication in personal relationships across cultures* (pp. 102–121). Thousand Oaks, CA: Sage.

O'Donnell, A. (2006). The role of peers and group learning. in P. Alexander and P. Winne (eds.) *Handbook of Educational Psychology*, 2nd ed. Mahwah, NJ: Lawrence Earlbaum Publisher, pp. 781–802.

Okun, B., Fried, J., & Okun, M. (1999). *Understanding diversity: A learning-as-practice primer*. Pacific Grove, CA: Brooks/Cole.

Oliver-Hoyo, M. T., Allen, D. A., Hunt, W. F., Hutson, J., & Pitts, A. (2004). Effects of an active learning environment: Teaching innovations at a Research I institution. *Journal of Chemical Education*, *81*, 441–448.

O'Reilly, R. (2002). You can lead a student to water, but can you make them think? An evaluation of a situated learning environment: An Ocean in the Classroom. *Australian Journal of Educational Technology*, *18*, 169–186.

Palomba, C., & Banta, T. (1999). *Assessment essentials: Planning, implementing, and improving assessment in higher education*. San Francisco: Jossey-Bass.

Paris, S. G., Lipson, M. Y., & Wixson, K. K. (1983). Becoming a strategic reader. *Contemporary Educational Psychology*, *8*, 293–316.

Paris, S. G., & Paris, A. H. (2001). Classroom applications of research on self-regulated learning. *Educational Psychologist*, *36*, 89–101.

Park, Y., & Kim, B. (2008). Asian and European American cultural values and communication styles among Asian American and European American college students. *Cultural Diversity and Ethnic Minority Psychology*, *13*, 47–56.

Pascarella, E. T., & Terenzini, F. (1991, 2005). *How college affects students*. Volumes 1 and 2. San Francisco: Jossey-Bass.

Patrick, H., Hicks, L., & Ryan, A. M. (1997). Relations of perceived social efficacy and social goal pursuit to self-efficacy for academic work. *Journal of Early Adolescence*, *17*(2), 109–128.

Peckham, G., & Sutherland, L. (2000). The role of self-assessment in moderating students' expectations. *South African Journal of Higher Education, 14,* 75–78.

Peper, R. J., & Mayer, R. E. (1978). Note taking as a generative activity. *Journal of Educational Psychology, 70*(4), 514–522.

Perkins, D. (2005). The case for a cooperative studio classroom: Teaching petrology in a different way. *Journal of Geoscience Education. 53,* 101–109.

Perry, R. P., & Smart, J. C. (Eds.). (1997). *Effective teaching in higher education: Research and practice.* New York: Agathon.

♦ Perry, W. G., Jr. (1970). *Forms of intellectual and ethical development in the college years: A scheme.* New York: Holt, Rinehart, and Winston.

———. (1981). Cognitive and ethical growth: The making of meaning. In A. W. Chickering (Ed.), *The modern American college* (pp. 76–116). San Francisco: Jossey-Bass.

Phillips, H. J., & Powers, R. B. (1979). The college seminar: Participation under instructor-led and student-led discussion groups. *Teaching of Psychology, 6*(2), 67–70.

Pintrich, P. R. (Ed.). (1995, Summer). Understanding self-regulated learning. In *New directions for teaching and learning* (no. 63). San Francisco: Jossey-Bass.

Pintrich, P. R. (2002). The role of metacognitive knowledge in learning, teaching and assessing. *Theory into Practice, 41*(4), 219–225.

———. (2003). Motivation and classroom learning. In W. M. Reynolds & G. E. Miller (Eds.), *Handbook of psychology: Educational psychology* (Vol. 7, pp. 103–122). New York: Wiley.

Pintrich, P. R., & De Groot, E. V. (1990). Motivational and self-regulated learning components of classroom academic performance. *Journal of Educational Psychology, 82,* 33–40.

Pintrich, P. R., & Garcia, T. (1991). Student goal orientation and self-regulation in the college classroom. In M. Maehr & P. R. Pintrich (Eds.), *Advances in motivation and achievement: Goals and self-regulatory processes* (vol. 7, pp. 371–402). Greenwich, CT: JAI Press.

Pressley, M., & McCormick, C. B. (1995). *Cognition, teaching and assessment.* New York: HarperCollins.

♦ Pressley, M., et al. (1992). Encouraging mindful use of prior knowledge: Attempting to construct explanatory answers facilitates learning. *Educational Psychologist, 27*(1), 91–109.

Prieger, J. E., & Hu, W. (2008). The broadband digital divide and the nexus of race, competition, and quality. *Information Economics and Policy 20,* 150–167.

Pulvers, K., & Diekhoff, G. (1999). The relationship between academic dishonesty and college classroom environment. *Research in Higher Education, 40*(4), 487–498.

Reyes, P., Scribner, J., & Scribner, A. (Eds.). (1999). *Lessons from high performing Hispanic schools.* New York: Teachers College Press.

Rhoads, R., & Howard, J. (1998, Winter). Academic service learning: A pedagogy of action and reflection. In *New directions for teaching and learning* (no. 73). San Francisco: Jossey-Bass.

Robinson, R. (2001, September). Calibrated peer review: An application to increase student reading and writing skills. *American Biology Teacher, 63*(7), 478–480.

Rodabaugh, R. (1996). Institutional commitment to fairness in teaching. In *New directions for teaching and learning* (no. 66, pp. 37–46). San Francisco: Jossey-Bass.

Roig, M. (2008). The relationship between learning style preference and achievement in the adult student in a multicultural college. Dissertation Abstracts: Section A: Humanities and Social Sciences; 69 (3-A), 853.

Romiszowski, A., & Mason, R. (2004). Computer-mediated communication. In D. H. Jonassen (Ed.), Handbook for research in educational communications and technology (2nd ed.), (pp. 397–432). Mahwah, NJ: Lawrence Erlbaum.

Roser, C. (2008) Encouraging students to read the texts: The jigsaw method. *Teaching history: A journal of methods, 33,* 1, 20–28.

Rovai, A. (2007) Facilitating online discussions effectively. *Internet and Higher Education, 10,* 77–88.

Royer, P. N. (1977). Effects of specificity and position of written instructional objectives on learning from a lecture. *Journal of Educational Psychology, 69,* 40–45.

Ruhl, K. L., Hughes, C. A., & Schloss, P. J. (1987). Using the pause procedure to enhance lecture recall. *Teacher Education and Special Education, 10,* 14–18.

Ruiz, P. (1995). Assessing, diagnosing and treating culturally diverse individuals: A Hispanic perspective. *Psychiatric Quarterly, 66,* 329–341.

Ruiz, R., & Padilla, A. (1977). Counseling Latinos. *Personnel and Guidance Journal, 55,* 401–408.

Russell, T. L. (1999). *No significant difference phenomenon.* North Carolina State University, Raleigh, NC.

Ryan, R., & Deci, E. (2000). When rewards compete with nature: The undermining of intrinsic motivation and self-regulation. In C. Sansone & J. Harackiewicz (Eds.), *Intrinsic and extrinsic motivation: The search for optimal motivation and performance.* San Diego: Academic Press.

Sadler, D. R. (1989). Formative assessment and the design of instructional systems, *Instructional Science, 18*, 119–144.

Sage, G. (1991). Counseling American Indian adults. In C. Lee & B. Richardson (Eds.), *Multicultural issues in counseling: New approaches to diversity* (pp. 23–35). Alexandria, VA: American Counseling Association.

Sanchez, A., & Atkinson, D. (1983). Mexican American cultural commitment, preference for counselor ethnicity, and willingness to use counseling. *Journal of Counseling Psychology, 30*, 215–220.

Schofield, T., Parke, R., Castaneda, E., & Coltrane, S. (2008). Patterns of gaze between parents and children in European American and Mexican American families. *Journal of Nonverbal Behavior, 32*, 171–186.

Schomberg, S. F. (1986, April). *Involving high ability students in learning groups.* Paper presented at AERA in San Francisco.

Schön, D. (1983). *The reflective practitioner.* San Francisco: Jossey-Bass.

Schrader-Kniffki, M. (2007). Silence and politeness in Spanish and Zapotec interactions (Oaxaca, Mexico). In M. Placencia, & C. Garcia (Eds.). *Research on politeness in the Spanish-speaking world.* Mahway, NJ: Lawrence Erlbaum.

♦ Schunk, D. H., & Zimmerman, B. J. (Eds.). (1998). *Self-regulated learning: From teaching to self-reflective practice.* New York: Guilford.

———. (2003). Self-regulation and learning. In W. M. Reynolds & G. E. Miller (Eds.). *Handbook of psychology: Educational psychology* (vol. 7, pp. 59–78). New York: John Wiley.

———. (2007). *Motivation and self-regulated learning: Theory, research and applications.* Mahwah, NJ: Erlbaum.

Schutz, P. A., & Pekrun, R. (2007). *Emotion in education.* San Diego, CA: Academic Press.

Schwarz, B. (2004). *The paradox of choice: Why more is less.* New York: ECCO.

Seymour, E., & Hewitt, N. (1997). *Talking about leaving: Why undergraduates leave the sciences.* Boulder, CO: Westview Press.

Shields, N. (2002). Anticipatory socialization, adjustment to university life, and perceived stress: Generational and sibling effects. *Social Psychology of Education, 5*(4), 365–392.

Shulman, G. M., Luechauer, D. L., & Shulman, C. (1996). Assessment for learner empowerment: The meta-cognitive map. In T. W. Banta, J. P. Lund, K. E. Black, & F. W. Oblander, Assessment in practice: Putting principles to work on colleges campuses. San Francisco. Jossey-Bass.

Shulman, L. (2002). Fostering a scholarship of teaching and learning. Louise McBee Lecture series, Institute of Higher Education, University of Georgia, Athens, GA.

Silverman, R., Welty, W. M., & Lyon, S. (1994). *Educational psychology cases for teacher problem solving*. New York: McGraw-Hill.

Skinner, N. F. (2001). A course, a course, my kingdom for a course: Reflections of an unrepentant teacher. *Canadian Psychology, 42,* 49–60.

Smith, D. (1996). The ethics of teaching. *New Directions for Teaching and Learning* (no. 66, pp. 5–14). San Francisco: Jossey-Bass.

Smith, M. K., Wood, W. B., Adams, W. K., Wieman, J. K., Knight, J. N., Guild, N., & Su, T. T. (2009). Why peer discussion improves student performance on in-class concept questions. *Science, 323* (5910), 122–124.

Smith, W. F., & Rockett, F. C. (1958). Test performance as a function of anxiety, instructor, and instructions. *Journal of Educational Research, 52,* 138–141.

Snow, R. E., & Peterson, P. L. (1980). Recognizing differences in student attitudes. *New Directions for Teaching and Learning* (no. 2). San Francisco: Jossey-Bass.

♦ Solomon, D., Rosenberg, L., & Bezdek, W. E. (1964). Teacher behavior and student learning. *Journal of Educational Psychology, 55,* 23–30.

Stanton, H. (1992). *The University Teacher, 13*(1).

Stark, J. S., & Lattuca, L. R. (1997). *Shaping the college curriculum: Academic plans in action*. Boston: Allyn & Bacon.

Sternberg, R. (2003). *The Rainbow Project: What's wrong with college admissions and how psychology can fix it*. Invited address at the annual convention of the American Psychological Association, Toronto, Canada.

Sternberg, Robert J., Grigorenko, Elena L. (2008). *Handbook of multicultural assessment: Clinical, psychological, and educational applications*. Suzuki, Lisa A. (Ed.); Ponterotto, Joseph G. (Ed.); San Francisco: Jossey-Bass, 2008.

Sterngold, A. (2004, May/June). Confronting plagiarism: How conventional teaching invites cyber-cheating. *Change, 36*(3), 16–21.

Strike, K. (1988). The ethics of teaching. *Phi Delta Kappan, 70(2),* 156–158.

Stuart, R. (2004). Twelve practical suggestions for achieving multicultural competence. *Professional Psychology, 35,* 3–9.

Sue, D. W. (2003). *Overcoming our racism: The journey to liberation*. San Francisco: Jossey-Bass.

———. (2004). *Whiteness and ethnocentric monoculturism: Making the "invisible" visible*. Invited address at the annual convention of the American Psychological Association, Honolulu, Hawaii.

Sue, D. W., & Sue, D. (2003). *Counseling the culturally diverse: Theory and practice* (4th ed.). New York: Wiley.

Suinn, R. (2007). "Welcome" spells the route to a better climate. *gradPSYCH, 5,* 40.

Suinn, R. (in press). Acculturation: Findings, measurement & directions (Why study acculturation?). In N. Trinh & Y. Rho (Eds.). *Families, Resilience and Acculturation: Implications for Mental Health in Asian Americans.* Humana Publishers.

Sutton, C., & Broken Nose, M. (1996). American Indian families: An overview. In M. McGoldrick, J. Giordano, & J. Pearce (Eds.), *Ethnicity and family therapy* (2nd ed., pp. 31–44). New York: Guilford Press.

Svinicki, M. (2004). *Learning and motivation in the postsecondary classroom.* San Francisco: Jossey-Bass.

Svinicki, M. D. (2008). The scout's motto: Be prepared. *National Teaching Learning Forum,* 17(5), 12.

♦ Svinicki, M. D., Hagen, A. S., & Meyer, D. K. (1995). Research on learning: A means to enhance instructional methods. In R. Menges & M. Weimer (Eds.), *Better teaching and learning in college: Toward more scholarly practice* (pp. 257–296). San Francisco: Jossey-Bass.

Swearingen, C. J. (1999). Originality, authenticity, imitation, and plagiarism: Augustine's Chinese cousins. In L. Buranen & A. M. Roy (Eds.), *Perspectives on plagiarism and intellectual property in a postmodern world* (pp. 5–18). Albany: State University of New York Press.

Sweeting, L. (1999). Ethics in science for undergraduate students. *Journal of Chemical Education, 76,* 369–372.

Swinomish Tribal Mental Health Project. (1991). *A gathering of wisdoms.* LaConner, WA: Swinomish Tribal Community.

Tabachnick, B., Keith-Spiegel, P., & Pope, K. (1991). Ethics of teaching: Beliefs and behaviors of psychologists as educators. *American Psychologist, 46*(5), 506–515.

Tatum, B. (1993). *Coming of age: Black youth in white communities. Focus,* 7(2), 15–16.

Tchudi, S. (Ed.). (1997). *Alternatives to grading student writing.* Urbana: NCTE.

Thompson, V., Bazile, A., & Akbar, M. (2004). African Americans' perceptions of psychotherapy and psychotherapists. *Professional Psychology: Research and Practice, 35,* 19–26.

Tien, L. T., Rickey, D., & Stacy, A. M. (1999). The MORE thinking frame: Guiding students' thinking in the laboratory. *Journal of College Science Teaching, 28*(5), 318–324.

Ting-Toomey, S. & Chung, L. (2005). *Understanding intercultural communication.* Los Angeles, CA: Roxbury.

Topping, K. (1998, Fall). Peer assessment between students in colleges and universities. *Review of Educational Research, 68*(3), 249–276.

Toppino, T. C., & Brochin, H. A. (1989). Learning from tests: The case of true-false examinations. *Journal of Educational Research, 83,* 119–124.

Travers, R. (1950). *How to make achievement tests.* New York: Odyssey Press.

Trawick, L., & Corno, L. (1995, June). Expanding the volitional resources of urban community college students (pp. 57–70). In P. Pintrich (Ed.), *Understanding self-regulated learning. New Directions for Teaching and Learning* (no. 63, pp. 57–70). San Francisco: Jossey-Bass.

Trend Data. (2009). Demographics of Internet Users. Pew Internet and American Life Project [Online]. Available at: http://www.pewinternet.org/Data-Tools/Download-Data/Trend-Data.aspx.

Trusty, J., & Harris, M. (1999). Lost talent: Predictors of the stability of educational expectations across adolescence. *Journal of Adolescent Research, 14,* 359–382.

Uchida, D., Cetron, M., & McKenzie, F. (1996). *Preparing students for the 21st century.* Arlington, VA: American Association of School Administrators.

Van Overwalle, F., Segebarth, K., & Goldchstein, M. (1989). Improving performance of freshmen through attributional testimonies from fellow students. *British Journal of Educational Psychology, 59,* 75–85.

Vasquez, M. (1982). Confronting barriers to participation of Mexican American women in higher education. *Hispanic Journal of Behavioral Sciences, 4,* 147–165.

Vea, B. (2008). The college experiences of Filipina/o Americans and other AAPI subgroups Disaggregating the data. Dissertation Abstracts: Section A: Humanities and Social Sciences; *69* (3-A0), 908.

Veenstra, M. V. J., & Elshout, J. J. (1995). Differential effects of instructional support on learning in simulation environments. *Instructional Science, 22,* 363–383.

Von Secker, C. (2002). Effects of inquiry-based teacher practices on science excellence and equity. *Journal of Educational Research, 95,* 151–160.

Von Secker, C., & Lissitz, R. W. (1999). Estimating the impact of instructional practices on student achievement in science. *Journal of Research in Science Teaching, 36,* 110–112.

Vontress, C., & Epp, L. (1997). Historical hostility in the African American client: Implications for counseling. *Journal of Multicultural Counseling and Development, 25,* 170–184.

Wales, C. E., & Nardi, A. (1982, November). *Teaching decisionmaking with guided design* (Idea paper no. 9). Kansas State University, Center for Faculty Evaluation and Development.

Walker, M. (2006). An investigation into written comments on assignments: Do students find them usable? *Assessment and Evaluation in Higher Education, 34*(1), 67–78.

Walvoord, B., & Anderson, V. (1998). *Effective grading: A tool for learning and assessment.* San Francisco: Jossey-Bass.

Weaver, M. R. (2006). Do students value feedback? Students' perceptions of tutors' written responses, *Assessment and Evaluation in Higher Education, 31*(3), 379–394.

Weaver, R. L., II, & Cotrell, H. W. (1985). Mental aerobics: The half-sheet response. *Innovative Higher Education, 10*, 23–31.

Weiner, B. (2001). Intrapersonal and interpersonal theories of motivation from an attribution perspective. In F. Salili, C. Chiu, & Y. Hong (Eds.), *Student motivation: The culture and context of learning* (pp. 17–30). New York: Kluwer.

Weinstein, C. E. (1994). Strategic learning/strategic teaching: Flip sides of a coin. In P. R. Pintrich, D. R. Brown, & C. E. Weinstein (Eds.), *Student motivation, cognition, and learning: Essays in honor of Wilbert J. McKeachie.* Hillsdale, NJ: Erlbaum.

Weinstein, C. E., & Acee, T. W. (2008). Cognitive view of learning. In N.J. Salkind (Ed.), *Encyclopedia of Educational Psychology.* Thousand Oaks, CA: Sage Publications, Inc.

Weinstein, C. E., Acee, T. W., & Jung, J. (in press). Learning Strategies. In B. McGaw, P. L. Peterson, & E. Baker (Eds.), *International Encyclopedia of Education* (3rd ed.). Oxford: Elsevier Inc.

Weinstein, C. E., Beth, A. D., Corliss, S. B., & Cho, Y. (in press). Learning how to learn for e-learning: The importance of strategic learning in technology-rich environments. In R. Nyberg (Ed.), Invited Book Chapter.

Weinstein, C. E., Husman, J., & Dierking, D. R. (2000). Self-regulation interventions with a focus on learning strategies. In M. Boekaerts, P. Pintrich, & M. Zeidner (Eds.), *Handbook of self-regulation.* San Diego: Academic Press.

♦ Weinstein, C. E., & Mayer, R. E. (1986). The teaching of learning strategies. In M. Wittrock (Ed.), *Handbook of research on teaching* (3rd ed., pp. 315–327). New York: Macmillan.

Wenzel, T. J. (1995). A new approach to undergraduate analytical chemistry. *Analytical Chemistry, 67,* 470A–475A.

Wenzel, T. J. (1998). Cooperative group learning in undergraduate analytical chemistry. *Analytical Chemistry, 70*(23), 790A–795A.

Wentzel, K., & Wigfield, A. (1998). Academic and social motivational influences on students' academic performance. *Educational Psychology Review, 10,* 155–175.

White, J., & Parham, T. (1990). *The psychology of blacks: An African-American perspective* (2nd ed.). Englewood Cliffs, NJ: Prentice Hall.

Whitley, B. (1998). Factors associated with cheating among college students: A review. *Research in Higher Education, 39*(3), 235–274.

Wigfield, A., & Eccles, J. S. (2000). Expectancy-value theory of achievement motivation. *Contemporary Educational Psychology*, 25, 68–81.

Wiggins, G., & McTighe, J. (2001). *Understanding by Design*. Columbus, OH: Merrill Education/ASCD College Textbook Series.

Wilhite, S. C. (1983). Prepassage questions: The influence of structural importance. *Journal of Educational Psychology*, 75(2), 234–244.

Williams, S. (2005) Guiding students through the jungle of research-based literature. *College Teaching*, 53, 4, 137–139.

Wilson, J. M. (1994). The CUPLE physics studio. *Physics Teacher*, 32, 518–523.

Wilson, K., & Korn, J. H. (2007). Attention during lectures: Beyond ten minutes. *Teaching of Psychology*, 34, 2, 85–89.

Wilson, M., & Sloane, K. (2000). From principles to practice: An embedded assessment system. *Applied Measurement in Education*, 12, 2, 181–208.

♦ Wilson, R. C. (1986). Improving faculty teaching: Effective use of student evaluations and consultation. *Journal of Higher Education*, 57, 196–211.

Wilson, T. D., & Linville, P. W. (1982). Improving the academic performance of college freshmen: Attribution therapy revisited. *Journal of Personality and Social Psychology*, 42, 367–376.

Wimms, H., & Maton, K. (2008). *Experiences and perceptions of doctoral graduate students: A national study*. Paper presentation at the International Counseling Psychology Conference March, 2008, Chicago, Illinois.

Winne, P. (1996). A metacognitive view of individual differences in self-regulated learning. *Learning and Individual Differences*, 8, 327–353.

Winrow, S. (2002). Factors that contribute to success in college for Native American students. Dissertation Abstracts: Section A: Humanities and Social Sciences; 62(9-A), March: 2974.

Winters, Fielding; Greene, Jeffrey; Costich, Claudine. (2008). Self-regulation of learning within computer-based learning environments: A critical analysis. Available at: http://web.ebscohost.com/ehost/viewarticle?data=dGJyMPPp44rp2%2fdV0%2bnjisfk5Ie46bZMt6exULek63nn5Kx95uXxjL6nr0evrq1Krqa3OK%2bouEiwsLFPnsbLPvLo34bx1%2bGM5%2bXsgeKzr0qxqrRPsaizT6Ti34bls%2bOGpNrgVd%2bv5j7y1%2bVVv8SkeeyzsU2urbVOsaakfu3o63nys%2bSN6uLyffbq&amp. *Educational Psychology Review*, 20 (4), December: 429–444.

Wood, D., Wood, H. and Middleton, D. (1978). An experimental evaluation of four face-to-face teaching strategies. *International Journal of Behavioural Development*, 1,131–147.

Yamauchi, L., & Tharp, R. (1995). Culturally compatible conversations in Native American classrooms. *Linguistics and Education*, 74, 349–367.

Yan, L., & Kember, D. (2004). Avoider and engager approaches by out-of-class groups: The group equivalent to individual learning approaches. *Learning and Instruction, 14,* 27–49.

Young, A. (1997, Winter). Mentoring, modeling, monitoring, motivating: Response to students' ungraded writing as academic conversation. In M. D. Sorcinelli & P. Elbow (Eds.), Writing to learn: Strategies for assigning and responding to writing across the disciplines. *New Directions for Teaching and Learning* (no. 69). San Francisco: Jossey-Bass.

Zhu, E. (2007). Teaching with Clickers. CRLT Occasional Paper, No. 22. Ann Arbor, MI: University of Michigan Center for Research on Learning and Teaching [Online]. Available at: http://www.crlt.umich.edu/publinks/CRLT_no22.pdf.

Zimmerman, B. J. (1989). Models of self-regulated learning and academic achievement. In B. J. Zimmerman & D. H. Schunk (Eds.), *Self-regulated learning and academic achievement: Theory, research, and practice* (pp. 1–25). New York: Springer-Verlag.

———. (1990). Self-regulated learning and academic achievement [Special issue]. *Educational Psychologist, 25*(1).

———. (1994). Dimensions of academic self-regulation: A conceptual framework for education. In D. H. Schunk & B. J. Zimmerman (Eds.), *Self-regulation of learning and performance: Issues and educational applications* (pp. 3–19). Hillsdale, NJ: Erlbaum.

♦ ———. (1998). Developing self-fulfilling cycles of academic regulation: An analysis of exemplary instructional models. In D. H. Schunk & B. J. Zimmerman (Eds.), *Self-regulated learning: From teaching to self-reflective practice* (pp. 1–19). New York: Guilford.

———. (2001). Theories of self-regulated learning and academic achievement: An overview and analysis. In B. J. Zimmerman & D. H. Schunk (Eds.), *Self-regulated learning and academic achievement: Theoretical perspectives* (2nd ed., pp. 1–37). Mahwah, NJ: Erlbaum.

Zimmerman, B. J., & Moylan, A. R. (in press) Self-regulation: Where metacognition and motivation intersect. In D. J. Hacker, J., Dunlosky, and A. C. Graesser (Eds.), *Handbook of Metacognition in Education.* Boca Raton, FL: Lawrence Erlbaum Associates/Taylor & Francis Group.

Note: References marked with a diamond ♦ are classic, seminal works that still offer the most reliable scholarship on their topics.

# INDEX

Note: Notes are indicated by the letter *n*.